Fields of Offerings

Fields of Offerings

Studies in Honor of Raphael Patai

Edited by
Victor D. Sanua

BOARD OF EDITORS:
Jacob M. Landau   Simon D. Messing
Dov Noy   Tuvya Preschel
          Alexander Scheiber

A Herzl Press Publication

Rutherford ● Madison ● Teaneck
Fairleigh Dickinson University Press
London and Toronto: Associated University Presses

Associated University Presses
440 Forsgate Drive
Cranbury, NJ 08512

Associated University Presses
25 Sicilian Avenue
London WC1A 2QH, England

Associated University Presses
2133 Royal Windsor Drive
Unit 1
Mississauga, Ontario L5J 1K5, Canada

Library of Congress Cataloging in Publication Data
Main entry under title:

Fields of offerings.

   "A Herzl Press publication."
   Includes bibliographical references.
    1. Jews—Folklore—Addresses, essays, lectures.
2. Zionism—History—Addresses, essays, lectures.
3. Patai, Raphael, 1910–   —Addresses, essays,
lectures.   I. Sanua, Victor D.   II. Patai, Raphael,
1910–
GR98.F53   1983   909'.04924   82-21072
ISBN 0-8386-3171-1

Printed in the United States of America

"Fields of Offerings" is taken from 2 Samuel 1:21.

Contents

Part IV: Zionism, Israel, and the Middle East

Part V: The Ancient Near East

Part VI: Hebrew Section

Contributors

JOSEPH ADLER, Ph.D., Forest Hills, N.Y.

DAN BEN-AMOS, Professor of Folklore and Folklife, University of Pennsylvania, Philadelphia, Pa.

MEIR BEN-HORIN, President and Professor of Modern Jewish Thought and Education, Cleveland College of Jewish Studies, Beachwood, Ohio

LIVIA JACKSON-BITTON, Professor of Hebrew, Lehman College of the University of the City of New York

MOSHE CARMILLY-WEINBERGER, Professor Emeritus, Yeshiva University, New York

ROBERT GORDIS, Professor of Bible and Rapaport Professor in the Philosophies of Religion, Jewish Theological Seminary of America, New York

CYRUS H. GORDON, Professor of Near Eastern Studies, Brandeis University, Waltham, Mass.

GERTRUDE HIRSCHLER, author, assistant editor of *Encyclopaedia of Zionism and Israel,* New York

SIMHA KLING, Ph.D., Rabbi of Congregation Adath Jeshurun, Louisville, Kentucky

JACOB M. LANDAU, Professor of Political Science, Hebrew University, Jerusalem

JOSEPH NEDAVA, Professor of History, University of Haifa, Mount Carmel, Haifa, Israel

GEDALIA NIGAL, Associate Professor of Hebrew literature, Bar Ilan University, Ramat Gan, Israel

DOV NOY, Max Grunwald Professor of Folklore, Hebrew University, Jerusalem

9

TUVYA PRESCHEL, Professor of Talmud, Jewish Theological Seminary of America, New York

HOWARD M. SACHAR, Professor of History, George Washington University, Washington, D.C.

VICTOR D. SANUA, Professor of Psychology, St. John's University, New York.

ALEXANDER SCHEIBER, Director of the Jewish Theological Seminary of Hungary, Budapest

HAIM SCHWARZBAUM, Director of the Institute for Jewish and Arab Folklore Research, Kiron, Israel

ALIZA SHENHAR, Chairperson, Department of Hebrew Literature and Folklore Division, University of Haifa, Mount Carmel, Haifa, Israel

AILON SHILOH, Professor and director of Graduate Studies, Department of Anthropology, University of South Florida, Tampa, Florida

SAVINA J. TEUBAL, Ph.D., Santa Monica, California

DOROTHY F. ZELIGS, Ed.D., Psychoanalyst and certified psychologist, New York

WALTER P. ZENNER, Associate Professor of Anthropology, State University of New York at Albany, N.Y.

Preface

The initiative for this volume came from Professor Alexander Scheiber, director of the Rabbinical Seminary of Budapest. Subsequently, an editorial committee was formed with the participation of Scheiber, Professor Dov Noy (Jerusalem), Professor Jacob M. Landau (Jerusalem), Professor Tuvya Preschel (New York), Professor Simon D. Messing (New Haven), and the undersigned. This committee decided at the outset to limit the articles to be included in this jubilee volume to those fields of scholarly endeavor in which Raphael Patai made his major contribution; hence the subjects covered by the section headings Folklore and Literature, Anthropology, Zionism, Israel and the Middle East, and the Ancient Near East.

Three cities were the *loci* of Raphael Patai's life story: Budapest, Jerusalem, and New York. Born in Budapest on November 22, 1910, as the eldest son of the well-known Jewish poet, author, editor, and Zionist leader Joseph Patai, he was educated there (with the exception of one year in Breslau, Germany) at the university and the rabbinical seminary. At the age of twenty-two he went to Jerusalem, enrolled as a "research student" at the Hebrew University, and in 1936 received the first Ph.D. degree to be awarded by that university. He became a teacher of Hebrew and then a research fellow in Jewish Ethnology at the Hebrew University, and in 1944 founded the Palestine Institute of Folklore and Ethnology, serving as its director of research until 1947. In that year he came to New York, where he has lived ever since. He taught at several American universities, and served as director of research of the Herzl Institute and editor of the Herzl Press from 1957 to 1971.

However, what is significant in Raphael Patai's life lies not in its external circumstances, but in the intellectual voyage on which he embarked as a teenager and which he still pursues with vigor in his seventies. While still a student in Budapest he became interested in Jewish folklore of historical and modern times. After he settled in Jerusalem his interest expanded to include Jewish and Middle Eastern ethnology and anthropology. This was followed by a shift toward Jewish mythology, and then toward the social

11

psychology of the Arabs and the Jews, with side excursions into adjacent fields. In each of these areas he made significant contributions in the form of numerous books and a profusion of articles.

I first met Raphael Patai at a lecture he gave to the Herzl Institute some twenty years ago. He spoke, I still clearly remember, about the culture of the Middle East, and as a young man born and educated in Egypt I was struck by the insights he opened up for me into that ancient culture which I had thought I knew well. I remember especially one point he made to the effect that the Middle East illustrates, as perhaps no other part of the world does, the cumulative nature of culture—the retention of old features while superimposing upon them successively new cultural layers.

Raphael Patai's life work manifests the same configuration: folklore, cultural history, anthropology, mythology, social psychology—each discipline into which he delved became superimposed upon the previous ones, resulting in an ever more comprehensive grasp of the complex phenomena of human culture and psyche, and in more and more significant studies.

I wish to express the thanks of the editorial committee to those institutions and individuals whose generosity made the publication of this volume possible: the Lucius N. Littauer Foundation and its president, Mr. Harry Starr; the Israel Matz Foundation and its president, Professor Milton Arfa; the Louis and Minna Epstein Fund of the American Academy of Jewish Research and its secretary, Professor Isaac E. Barzilay; and Dr. Ezekiel Barber of Union, N.J.

Victor Sanua

Fields of Offerings

Part I

INTRODUCTORY

Raphael Patai: An Appreciation

HOWARD M. SACHAR

Periodically, if rarely, there appear on the cultural horizon those larger-than-life figures whose scholarly achievements serve as benchmarks for entire generations of colleagues and students. Such men have been the anthropologists Malinowski and Lévy-Bruhl, the sociologists Comte and Weber, the archaeologists Breasted and Flinders Petrie, the historians von Ranke and Zunz. Such a man, surely, is Raphael Patai. For some forty years his career has been a standing inspiration to those who toil in the vineyards of anthropology, sociology, and history, and a standing reproach to those, lacking his genius, who are unwilling to accept his own heroic standards of disciplined, self-sacrificing research.

Consider, first of all, the stunning prodigality of the man. The hundreds of articles and the thirty-odd books that have flowed from his pen would challenge the absorptive powers of all but a handful of scholars—essentially those prepared to devote their most vigorous years simply to a critical evaluation of Raphael Patai's own life and work. Consider, as well, the erudition, the plain and simple cultural and linguistic virtuosity embraced in this accumulated Pataiana. The *embarras des richesses* extends from studies of Shabbatai Zvi (in Hungarian), of the history of the Jews in Hungary (in German), of Josephus (in French), of Jewish seafaring (in Hebrew), to an explosion of books and articles in Hebrew and English covering every facet of ancient and modern folk mores, from *Man and Temple in Ancient Jewish Myth and Ritual* to the seminal, widely acclaimed volumes on *The Arab Mind* and *The Jewish Mind*.

Indeed, for academic "purists," fixated by disciplinary categorizations, there is a lesson to be learned in the awesome breadth of Raphael Patai's terrain. Not for him artificial barriers between the social sciences and the humanities, between Middle Eastern and Western cultures. He has erased, devoured those barriers by force of will, stamina, and sheer intellectual muscularity. Whether applying his talents to subjects as diverse as "Hebrew

17

Installation Rites," "Indian Jews in Mexico," "Culture Contact and Its working in Modern Palestine," *Women in the Modern World, The Republic of Syria, The Republic of Lebanon,* or *The Kingdom of Jordan,* he has infused his works with identical thoroughness and exactitude of documentation, with a magisterial command of historical and regional setting, and with an intuitive balance, perspective, and toleration which, one suspects, reflects Raphael Patai's character no less than his knowledge.

It is instructive, moreover, to recall that this overpowering monographic superstructure has been erected on a career enjoying few of the luxuries normally provided by American academe. To be sure, Raphael Patai's own academic training and teaching experience have been as densely upholstered as those of any of his professional colleagues. Born in Hungary, the son of the distinguished Zionist author Joseph Patai, he earned doctorates at both the Universities of Budapest and of Jerusalem, as well as ordination at the Rabbinical Seminary of Budapest. Thereafter, he taught and acquired devoted protégés at the Hebrew University, Columbia University, New York University, Princeton University, the New School for Social Research, the University of Pennsylvania, Ohio State University, Dropsie College, and Fairleigh Dickinson University.

Yet, by contrast with those legions of academicians (alas, still the majority) who endlessly bemoan the lack of fellowships and paid leaves of absence without which, they insist, there can be no "free time" for research and publication, Raphael Patai has managed simultaneously to pursue his scholarship and to shoulder numerous challenging administrative responsibilities. During the last half-century he has served variously as research director of the Palestine Institute of Folklore and Ethnology; as director of the Syria-Jordan-Lebanon Research Project; as executive-secretary of the Israel Institute of Technology; and, most significantly, as research director of the Herzl Institute, in this latter capacity building the largest Zionist research center in the United States.

It is perhaps the confluence of these directorial achievements, no less than a vivid, unifying strand in his writings, that reveals the élan behind Raphael Patai's intellect. There is, after all, a certain particularity within the ambit of every cultural universe, and Raphael Patai is no exception to this rule. Notwithstanding his devotion to scholarship in its broadest, most universal contours, his transcending love affair unquestionably has been with Jewish civilization. Complex and resilient, modern and dynamic, cosmopolitan and nationalistic, that civilization is the corruscating penumbra of one of history's most protean peoples. Ideally, those who venture to interpret this phenomenon should embody at least some of its characteristics. In fact, Raphael Patai incarnates virtually all of them. In the most classic sense of the word, he is an authentically protean human being.

The Oeuvre of Raphael Patai

HAIM SCHWARZBAUM

The bibliography of Raphael Patai's published writings, which lists some 650 items (see below, pp. 29–53) testifies to the profusion and the variety of his scholarly output. What I intend to do in the following pages is to highlight the road of scholarly development that led him from one area of investigation to the other, always broadening his fields of interest.

In 1933, when as a young man of twenty-two he arrived in Jerusalem with a brand new doctorate in Semitic languages and literatures from the University of Budapest, Patai already had to his credit quite a few articles and studies written in Hebrew, German, and Hungarian, as well as a dissertation on an unknown eighteenth-century Italian Hebrew poet, Isreal Berekhia Fontanella, written in Hungarian and Hebrew. In Jerusalem he enrolled at the Hebrew University, which at the time was but eight years old, as one of the very few graduate students, and became a disciple of Dr. Samuel Klein, professor of Palestinian studies. As a "research student"—as graduate students were termed—Patai did not have to attend classes, since the only duty of such a student was to write a doctoral thesis under the guidance of his professor, but his thirst for knowledge motivated him to sit faithfully at the feet of such masters as Professor Klein, Dr. Joseph J. Rivlin who taught Arabic, the archaeologist Dr. Eliezer L. Sukenik, and others.

In addition to his Budapest doctorate Patai had brought along a thorough knowledge of literary Arabic (he was a student of Carl Brockelmann in Breslau in 1930–31) and a deep interest in biblical and Jewish folklore, which he had absorbed from his teacher at the Budapest Rabbinical Seminary, Professor Bernhard Heller. Professor Klein, under whom he worked in Jerusalem, was not interested in folklore; his main concern was with the historical topography of Palestine and the history of Jewish settlement in the country throughout the ages, and he suggested to Patai a thesis subject from those fields. After some discussion teacher and student reached a compromise: they settled on a subject that embraced both folklore and

19

topography, and that carried the title (when it was published three years later by the Dvir Publishing House of Tel Aviv) *Water: A Study in Palestinology and Palestinian Folklore in the Biblical and Mishnaic Periods* and was crowned with the Bialik Prize of the municipality of Tel Aviv. In the summer of 1936 Patai became the recipient of the first Ph.D. degree awarded by the Hebrew University of Jerusalem.

By that time Patai's scholarly interest was focused mainly on the folklore of the various ethnic groups that inhabited Palestine, among them, in particular, that of the Oriental Jews. His first programmatic article on folklore was published early in 1935 in the Jerusalem daily *Doar HaYom* under the title "HaFolqlor Mahu?" ("What Is Folklore?"). It was followed by several other Hebrew papers on Oriental Jewish folk custom and folk tale. His book *Jewish Seafaring in Ancient Times*, a sequel to his dissertation and published in 1938, contains an important chapter on Jewish legends of the sea. In the same year he published the first brief version of a study on water libation in the Second Temple of Jerusalem (*HaAretz*, October 9), a subject he was to discuss again in greater detail and most thoroughly a year later in the *Hebrew Union College Annual* (Cincinnati, vol. 14).

It was in these years that Patai developed what can be called his folkloristic approach to problems in the history of biblical and later Jewish religion. By adducing parallels from the folklore of the modern Middle Eastern peoples he elucidated the significance of such concepts, images, and rites as the rainbow, the purple-blue color and dye, the expiation of the polluted land, the control of rain (cf. Thompson, *Motif* D1841.4.4; D2143.1; D902), and related subjects in ancient Hebrew and Jewish folk life, while at the same time writing prolifically various articles, book reviews, and historical studies, and lecturing on the Jerusalem radio and all over the country of diverse folklore subjects.

In 1942 and 1943 were published by the Hebrew University Press two volumes of his important study *Adam vaAdama* (Man and Earth in Hebrew Custom, Belief and Legend), which was hailed by those anthropologists, folklorists, and historians of religion who could read Hebrew (among them Professor William F. Albright) as a major contribution in the study of ancient Hebrew and Jewish folk culture. In these volumes Patai opens up broad new vistas of biblical and later Jewish popular religion centering around the concept of the living earth (Thompson, *Motif* A870) and Mother Earth (*Motif* A401 and A1234.1). It is difficult to assign this book to any one particular area of scholarly study: it defies taxonomy for it straddles folklore and anthropology, history of religion and cultural history. Adopting the Frazerian comparative method, the five parts of the book discuss five major subject areas: (1) The introductory part treats of the relationship between man and the world in biblical, rabbinic, and popular Jewish view; (2) the belief that the life of the earth is similar to that of man, including chapters on the virgin earth (*Motif*, A1234.1), the marriage of the earth (*Motif* A702.5 and T126.3), the pregnancy of the earth (Motif A123.4), and the separation of the earth from her mate (*Motif* A1558); (3) the idea that the life of man is dependent on the earth. This part comprises chapters on Adam as the son of the earth (*Motif*, A1234), the parallels drawn by folk tradition between the world and man, the legend about the creation of the world from the body of a giant manlike being (*Motif* A614.1 and A831.2), the comparison between woman and field (A1234.4), the relationship between man and tree (A1236 and A1251) and man and stone (A1245), and the vast idea-complex of Mother Earth; (4) the influence of man on the earth, including the religio-magic methods of fructifying the earth, and analysis of the biblical story about Elijah on Mount Carmel, which is shown to be the account of a rain-making competition between the prophets of the Baal and the Yahwist Elijah, the water-libation celebrated in the Second Temple of Jerusalem (also a rain-making ceremony), the fascinating analysis of the role of the Jerusalem Temple as the center of the fertility of the world, and the influence of man's behavior on the world order; (5) the reverse of part 4, namely the beliefs and practices expressing the idea that the earth influences the life of man. This part was to form volume 3 of this *magnum opus*, but was never published in book form. However, major chapters from it were published in various scholarly journals, including the one on earth eating (*Motif* A1420.6), birth customs (A1560ff.), marriage ceremonies (T100), and rites of death and burial (A1335). Several of these studies were recently collected in Patai's volume of essays entitled *On Jewish Folklore* (Wayne State University Press, 1983).

Also in 1942 Patai began to publish *collectanea* from his folklore notebooks, especially on Oriental Jewish folk customs in connection with birth, marriage, and death. He maintained close contact with other Jewish folklore scholars and collectors in Palestine and the Middle East, and tried to arouse interest in folklore research in the *Yishuv* with lectures and articles such as "Let Us Erect a Monument to Jewish Customs" (*Hegeh*, Tel Aviv, May 8, 1944).

In 1944, becoming increasingly aware of, and concerned about, the missed opportunities for folklore research due to the rapid acculturation of the Oriental Jewish communities to the dominant Ashkenazi culture of the *Yishuv*, Patai founded the Palestine Institute of Folklore and Ethnology, under the patronage of Yitzhaq Ben Zvi (later President of Israel), the veteran folklorist Max Grunwald, Sephardi Chief Rabbi Ben-Zion Meir Hay Ouziel, and the folklore scholar J. L. Zlotnik (Avida). The executive committee of the Institute consisted of Joseph J. Rivlin, Abraham Elmaleh, and Raphael Patai; and the council comprised some fifty outstanding scholars and interested laymen in Palestine and abroad, all of whom were recruited by Patai. It can be said that Patai was not only the initiator and organizer, but also the moving spirit of the Institute throughout the four years of its existence.

A year later he launched and began to edit (with Dr. Rivlin as a rather passive partner) the journal *Edoth (Communities: A Quarterly for Folklore and Ethnology)*, printed first in Hebrew with English summaries, and later both in Hebrew and in English. It was Patai singlehandedly who raised the funds for this publication, solicited articles, edited them, translated into Hebrew those written in other languages, prepared the English summaries, obtained advertisements, saw the issues through the press, wrote book reviews and news items, made arrangements for the distribution of the journal, and, last but not least, contributed to it articles of major importance. While this took up much of his time, he did not allow it to interfere with his other scholarly output, and wrote several significant programmatic papers and research studies, several of which were published in England and in the United States.

In the early 1940s Patai became acquainted with Mr. Farajullah Nasrullayoff, head of the Meshhedi Jewish community in Jerusalem, and his three sons, and spent many hours sitting in the family's rug store in the Geula quarter, interviewing Mr. Nasrullayoff, who proved to be an inexhaustible fount of knowledge about the history and life of the Marrano community of Meshhed. On the basis of these and other talks with several members of the community, Patai wrote a series of studies about the folk life and folktales of the Marrano Jews of Meshhed, which were published in *Edoth* and in English folklore publications.

As he penetrated deeper into the study of Jewish folklore, Patai's interest broadened, and he felt more and more attracted to the study of other aspects of Jewish anthropology. In 1945 he published an article in the journal of the Palestinian Jewish medical association, *HaR'fu'ah*, under the title "A Call For Anthropometric Work," in which he appealed to physicians to undertake research in this field while the immigrants from various countries of the Diaspora were still alive. He wrote a number of articles in popular magazines, such as *HaGalgal* ("What Are Folklore and Ethnology?" Oct. 4, 1945), and discussed in several issues of *Edoth* the problems, tasks, achievements, and requirements of Jewish folklore and ethnology.

Although anthropological research was in its infancy in Palestine at the time, Patai used his newly established connections with the American anthropological community to inform it of what had been done in the field in Palestine during the war years (*American Anthropologist*, July–September, 1946), and conversely, kept the scholars of the *Yishuv au courant* of the international developments in anthropology (*Edoth* 1946–47).

Soon after the launching of *Edoth* Patai felt that there was a need for a separate series of publications to provide a forum for studies too bulky to be printed in that journal, and he decided to publish for the Institute a series of books under the general title *Studies in Folklore and Ethnology*. His friend Dr. Rivlin was again ready to stand by, and the series appeared under the joint editorship of Patai and Rivlin. The first volume was a scholarly edition of the medieval Jewish folktale known as *Maᶜase Yerushalmi*, by J. L. Zlotnik (*Motif* F 402.2.3 and T111; Aa-Th narrative *Type* 470* and 424). In the preface to the book Patai stated that "in this book, for the first time, a Hebrew folktale is being published in several versions, in two languages (Hebrew and Arabic), accompanied by scholarly annotations. Thus the appearance of this book has a historical significance. The study of folklore, pursued among the peoples of Europe and America for a hundred years, and considered by them a field of no less value and importance than others in the humanities, has not yet merited similar recognition from Jewish scholarship. Among all the institutions of higher learning, whether in the Diaspora or in the land of Israel, there is not one in which Jewish folklore, or its sister-science, Jewish ethnology, would have a place in the course offerings. It was in order to fill this gap that we founded the Palestine Institute of Folklore and Ethnology, and the present book—which appears as the first in our new series of publications and which shows that it is both possible and necessary to utilize methods developed in the study of world folklore for the study of the folklore of the Jews—will be a further step toward gaining recognition for the scientific study of Jewish folk life as manifested in the communities of our people next to the study of its history, literatures, and other aspects of its spiritual and material existence" (p. 8).

In 1945 and 1946 Patai worked simultaneously on several books that were published in 1947. His two-volume *The Science of Man: An Introduction to Anthropology* (Tel. Aviv: Yavne, 1947–48, constituting volumes 3 and 4 of the *Studies in Folklore and Ethnology*) was the first, and has remained to date the only, anthropology textbook in Hebrew. His small, but extremely valuable and most original book *Man and Temple in Ancient Jewish Myth and Ritual* (Edinburgh: Thomas Nelson, 1947), was an expansion and elaboration of certain ideas already adumbrated in his *Adam vaAdama*. It was critically acclaimed, and brought him the friendship of Robert Graves, which ultimately led to their collaboration on the book *Hebrew Myths*. His pamphlet *On Culture Contact and Its Working in Modern Palestine* was published as a Memoir of the American Anthropological Association, and testified to its author's interest in nonfolkloristic aspects of cultural phenomena. In the same year appeared also the first ethnological monograph in Hebrew on a Jewish community: *The Jews of Kurdistan* (volume 2 of the *Studies in Folklore and Ethnology*) written by Dr. Erich Brauer, translated into Hebrew and completed on the basis of field work among Kurdish Jews in Jerusalem by Patai. Still in the same year was published in America Patai's eighty-page study, "Hebrew Installation Rites" (in the *Hebrew Union College Annual*, 20:143–225), a unique, highly original attempt to show, with the help of African, mainly Sudanic, parallels, that certain historical accounts contained in the Bible are, in fact, references to a complex pattern of royal coronation rituals (*Motif* A 1653).

Still in 1947 Patai made arrangements for the launching of yet another book series under the auspices of the Institute, entitled *Social Studies,* to be co-edited by him and Professor Roberto Bachi, the eminent demographer. Only two volumes appeared in this series, both considered important contributions to demography and social psychology respectively.

The year 1947 was a watershed in Patai's scholarly career. He received a one-year fellowship from the Viking Fund of New York (subsequently renamed Wenner-Gren Foundation of Anthropological Research), and in September he sailed for New York, where he has made his home ever since. He did not intend to remain in America for longer than one year. But history intervened: the U.N. voted for the establishment of a Jewish state in Palestine, the *Yishuv* was attacked by the Arabs and had to fight for its life, all scholarly activity was suspended, the Palestine Institute of Folklore and Ethnology ceased to exist, and *Edoth* folded. By the Spring of 1948 Patai accepted an invitation to serve as professor of Middle Eastern Anthropology at Dropsie College (subsequently Dropsie University) in Philadelphia, and as visiting professor at Columbia University and the University of Pennsylvania. After a three-month summer field trip to Mexico, where he studied the "Jewish Indians" of Mexico City and the village of Venta Prieta, he took up his teaching duties at these institutions.

The transfer of his residence from Jerusalem to New York meant no break in the rich flow of scholarly output from Patai's pen. In 1948, while studies he had written before he left Jerusalem were being published there, in Tel Aviv, London, and New York, he worked on new subjects and produced papers that began to appear in the United States in 1949 (e.g., a study of Jewish charms to facilitate childbirth (*Motif* T580 and A 1562), another on "Musha°a Tenure and Cooperation in Palestine," etc.). In 1950 were published the first results of his Mexican studies ("The Indios Israelitas of Mexico" in *The Menorah Journal* [Winter 1950], and in 1951 appeared his first study on general Middle Eastern cultural phenomena ("Nomadism," in *Southwestern Journal of Anthropology* [Winter 1951].

Also in 1951 Patai was invited by the United Nations Economic and Social Council to prepare a report on the "Social Conditions in the Middle East," which was published in April 1952, and was the only major piece of writing of his ever to appear anonymously in conformity with the general policies of the U.N. Secretariat. While working on that study he also wrote an impressive number of book reviews, and embarked on writing his book *Israel Between East and West: A Study in Human Relations* (1953), which was widely acclaimed as the first book-length and in-depth study of the cultural relations and problems in the young State of Israel between the European and the Oriental Jews. As Patai could observe with some satisfaction in the second, enlarged edition of this book, published in 1970, practically all the predictions contained in it came true in the course of the seventeen years that had elapsed since the first edition.

From among the many papers Patai authored in these years let me mention only one, not a scholarly study, but one that shows his abiding concern for the essential cultural requirements of Israel: in 1954, long before any plan to establish a university in Tel Aviv was mooted, he published an article in the New York Hebrew weekly *HaDoar* entitled "Is There a Need for a University in Tel Aviv?" and marshaled in it cogent and convincing arguments in favor of a positive answer. Incidentally, when some years later the Tel Aviv University came into being, Patai was elected first president of the American Friends of the Tel Aviv University, in which capacity he served for twelve years.

In 1955 Patai was asked by the Human Relations Area Files of New Haven to direct a major research project with a view to producing handbook monographs on Syria, Lebanon, and Jordan. He assembled an outstanding research staff consisting of American, Lebanese, and Israeli scholars whose contributions he carefully edited, while writing a major part of the chapters himself, including those covering the general character of the society, the culture groups, the family, social values, and patterns of living, attitudes and reactions of the people, and so on. The handbooks were published in 1956 in five xeroxed volumes by the HRAF. An additional result of this work was a most useful annotated bibliography of Syria, Lebanon, and Jordan, published in 1957. The Jordan handbook was used as a basis by Patai in writing his own book, *The Kingdom of Jordan*, which was published by Princeton University Press in 1958.

In 1956 Patai accepted the position of director of research of the Herzl Institute and editor of the Herzl Press in New York. In the latter capacity he edited seven volumes of the *Herzl Year Book* (1958–71), the five volumes of *The Complete Diaries of Theodor Herzl* (1960), and the two large volumes of the *Encyclopaedia of Zionism and Israel* (1971), to mention only three of his most important publications.

While working on these projects Patai continued his private research. In 1959 was published his book *Sex and Family in the Bible and the Middle East,* which soon was to be translated and published in German and French, and in which he threw light on biblical customs and concepts relating to sexual and family life with the help of parallels culled from the folk-life of the indigenous populations and ethnic groups in the modern Middle East. In 1960 he edited, together with Francis L. Utley and Dov Noy, the volume *Studies in Biblical and Jewish Folklore,* and in 1961 was published his booklet *Cultures in Conflict,* in which he continued his investigation of the cultural clash between the Ashkenazi and the Oriental Jews in Israel with which he first dealt in his *Israel Between East and West.* The year 1962 saw the appearance of his massive volume *Golden River to Golden Road: Society, Culture and Change in the Middle East* (3d, enlarged ed., 1969), which contains the most important of Patai's writings, some of them previously published in scholarly journals, on general Middle Eastern cultural and social phenomena. In this book he introduces the concept of "culture continent," isolates the basic characteristics of the traditional Middle Eastern family and the endogamous unilineal descent group, discusses the position of women and sex mores, traces the extent and significance of cousin marriage (more precisely *ibn ʿamm - bint ʿamm* marriage) and of dual organization, treats of the noble and vassal tribes, portrays the Middle Eastern village and town, analyzes the processes of Middle Eastern nationalism and Westernization, and, in a most insightful chapter, compares the role and character of religion in Middle Eastern, Far Eastern, and Western cultures.

Also in 1962 he started his collaboration with Robert Graves on the book *Hebrew Myths: The Book of Genesis,* which was published in New York and London in 1964, and within two years also in Hebrew, Spanish, Hungarian, Croatian, and Italian translations. In 1964 he also published a seminal paper "What Is Hebrew Mythology?" (in the *Transactions of the New York Academy of Sciences*), in which he outlined the basic features that characterize Hebrew myths as against the myths of Greek and other cultures.

About this time he became interested in the feminine element in the biblical and later Jewish God concept, and published several studies dealing with this almost virgin territory in the history of biblical and Jewish folk religion (discussing the Goddess Asherah, the Shekhina, the Matronit, Lilith). In 1965 he published his important paper on "The Structure of Endogamous Unilineal Descent Groups," in which he isolated and defined for the first time the specific characteristics of the Middle Eastern endogamous kin group, which differs basically from the exogamous descent groups found in other parts of the world. In 1966 he re-edited and supplemented Angelo S. Rappoport's three-volume work *Myth and Legend of Ancient Israel.*

One of Patai's most significant and most original books appeared in 1967. It is *The Hebrew Goddess,* a wide-ranging diachronic study of the worship and legends of female deities in Hebrew and Jewish religion. In it Patai shows that down to the end of the First Temple of Jerusalem, biblical religion comprised a popular element centering on such goddesses as Asherah, Astarte, Anath, against whose worship the Yahwist prophets fought for generations, but in vain; that in the Second Temple period one of the two Cherubim in the Holy of Holies represented the female element in the sanctuary; that Talmudic and Midrashic literature testifies to the development of the *Shekhina* (the personified presence of God on earth) into a veritable feminine divine being, whose Kabbalistic form, the *Matronit,* came to occupy an important place in Medieval and later Kabbalistic thought and folk belief; and that her evil counterpart, Lilith, (cf. *Motif* G 303.12.6.1), filled an ambiguous position as a she-demon who seduced men and killed children, and as the spouse of God the King. While Orthodox Jewish critics found much of what Patai propounded in this study unpalatable, none could fault his tightly argued and meticulous perusal of a huge amount of primary source material on which he based his conclusions.

Of Patai's many publications in the 1970s only the most important can be mentioned. His *Tents of Jacob: The Diaspora Yesterday and Today* (1971) is a major study of the cultural variety of the Jewish communities all over the world. His *Myth and Modern Man* (1972) demonstrates the extent to which mythical images and concepts are present in modern thought processes. This book was also published in a Portuguese translation. His *The Arab Mind* (1973) was hailed as the most significant study of the social psychology of the Arabs and as a most penetrating objective analysis of the Arab mental characteristics. It was translated into several languages, including Japanese. In 1975 was published his book *The Myth of the Jewish Race*, written together with his daughter, the geneticist and M.D. Jennifer Patai Wing, in which the fundamental thesis is that historical and genetic data show that the Jews do not constitute a single race but show marked genetic similarities to the host peoples among whom they had dwelt for many generations. The same conclusions have since been reached independently by other scholars and human geneticists.

In 1978 was published one of Patai's most important works, *The Jewish Mind*. This massive book (624 pages) comprises three parts. The first part is short and contains Patai's answers to such questions as, What is meant by group mind? Why should the Jewish mind differ from the Gentile mind? What are the causes of Jewish cultural diversity? Why is there Jewish intracommunity variance? Which were the major cultural influences upon the Jewish mind? What is the essence of Jewishness? (Patai's answer to this last question is that it consists of two beliefs and two duties: "the belief in One God, the belief in the special relationship between God and Israel, the duty towards God, and the duty towards one's fellow man," p. 10).

Part two discusses "Six Great Historic Encounters" between the Jews and the Gentiles, which Patai considers as having had the greatest influence on the formation of the Jewish mind: the encounters with the Canaanites, with Hellenism, with the Arabs, with the Italian Renaissance, with Russian folk religion (which made its impact on Hasidism), and with the European Enlightenment (which led to the Haskala and to Assimilation, and which Patai therefore styles "Triumph and Tragedy"). But he emphasizes repeatedly that each of these encounters (with the partial exception of the sixth) "illustrates the historical law under which Jews made their way from country to country and from culture to culture, and which reads: everywhere the Jews freely admitted foreign forms into the traditional structure of their culture, while retaining its essence throughout unscathed and unaltered" (p. 221). This ability of the Jews to retain unchanged the innermost core and content of their Jewishness is, Patai suggests, the key to the secret of Jewish survival.

Part three focuses on the end-result of this long historical and cultural process, the Jewish mind as its structure and working can be observed in modern times. All the major aspects of a group psychology are discussed: Jewish intelligence, Jewish giftedness and genius, special talents, personality and character, physical and mental health, alcoholism, overeating and drug addiction, Jewish self-hate, and the fundamental Jewish values. His attitude to the subject of his study can best be epitomized by quoting the sentence with which the book concludes: "It appears that mankind would be better off if it could acquire more of the characteristics of the Jewish mind than it has done heretofore" (p. 540).

In the last three years Patai has returned to the love of his youth: Jewish folklore, and especially, the Jewish legend. In 1979 was published his book *The Messiah Texts,* which is a collection of legends from biblical to modern times on the Messiah, his life history, his wars, the Messianic banquet, the Resurrection, the Last Judgment, the new Tora, the universal blessings, and related subjects. The introduction and annotations supply the historical context and elucidate the meaning of the legends.

In 1980 followed his *Gates to the Old City: A Book of Jewish Legends,* containing a rich collection of legends culled from the Bible, the Apocrypha, the Talmud, the Midrash, Kabbalistic literature, folktales, and Hasidic writings, again with a detailed introduction and annotations. The material in both volumes (with the exception of a very few stories in *The Messiah Texts* written in English) was translated by Patai from the original Hebrew, Aramaic, Arabic, Greek, Yiddish, Ladino, German, and Hungarian sources.

In evaluating Raphael Patai's life work one can best do it by designating him a *pioneer.* He pioneered in introducing the study of Jewish folklore and ethnology into the scholarly horizon of the pre-state *Yishuv.* He organized the first institution and published the first scholarly journal in Jewish Palestine devoted to these fields. He wrote the first and to this day the only Hebrew textbook on anthropology. He was one of the first to teach Middle Eastern and Israeli anthropology in the United States. He was one of the first to utilize Middle Eastern anthropology for the elucidation of ancient Jewish cultural history and folk religion. He rehabilitated mythology in Hebrew tradition and discovered an entirely new territory in the history of Hebrew and Jewish folk religion by demonstrating the importance of the role played in it by the female divine element. He applied modern methods of social psychology to the study of the Arab and Jewish mind. He made the original form of Jewish legend available in faithful English translations to a broad readership. And he trained generations of students to follow his footsteps.

Bibliography of the Published Writings of Raphael Patai

Compiled by
GERTRUDE HIRSCHLER

(The titles of books and pamphlets are printed in CAPITALS)

1929

1. "M'shorer ʿIvri-Hungari Bilti-Nodaʿ" ("An Unknown Hebrew-Hungarian Poet"). *HaTzofe (Hazofeh) l'Ḥokhmat Yisrael* (Budapest) 13, nos. 3–4 : 353–54.

1930

2. "Ungarn" ("Hungary"). In *Jüdisches Lexikon* (Berlin) 5 : 1098–110.
3. "Kitve Yad Shel Yosef Adler" ("The Manuscripts of Joseph Adler"). *HaTzofe* (Budapest) 14 : 390–401.
4. (Book review) I. L. Landau, *Short Lectures on Modern Hebrew Literature.* Ibid. 14 : 112–13.
5. (Book review) Davidson, *Piyyutim w'Shirim* (Ginze Schechter, vol. 3). Ibid. 14 : 206–6.
6. "Anti Rosenthal." *Mult és Jövő* (Budapest) 20 (April) : 152–53.
7. "A 'Becalel' 25 Éve" ("Twenty-Five Years of the Bezalel School"). Ibid. (July-August) : 260–61.
8. "D. J. Silberbusch Jubileumára" ("The Jubilee of D. J. Silberbusch"). Ibid. (September) : 320.
9. "Bialikkal Karlsbadban és Marienbadban" ("With Bialik in Karlsbad and Marienbad"). Ibid. (September) : 326–28.
10. (Review article) "Uj héber könyvek" ("New Hebrew Books"). Ibid. (September) : 303–4.
11. (Book note) Maurice Samuel, *What Happened in Palestine.* Ibid. (January : 31.
12. (Book note) Löwinger Samuel, *Darke haNikud vehaNeginot.* Ibid. (March) : 123.

1931

13. "Sabbatai Zevi alakja a modern zsidó irodalomban" ("The Image of Shabbatai Zevi in Modern Jewish Literature"). *Az Izraelita Magyar Irodalmi Társulat Évkönyve* (Budapest). Pp. 252–86.
14. "Mária Terézia ismeretlen rendelete" ("An Unknown Decree of Maria Theresa"). *Magyar Zsidó Szemle* (Budapest) 48 (January-March) : 1–3.

15. "Haber, Samuel" (biogr. sketch). *Encyclopaedia Judaica* (Berlin) 7:768.
16. "Halász, Ignac" (biogr. sketch). Ibid. 7:855.
17. "Hatvany-Deutsch, Baron Joseph" (biogr. sketch). Ibid. 7:1023.
18. "Hauser, Karl Frank" (biogr. sketch). Ibid. 7:1024–25.
19. "Heltai, Franz" (biogr. sketch). Ibid. 7:1159.
20. "Herczel, Baron Manó, de Pusztapéteri" (biogr. sketch). Ibid. 7:1176.
21. "Hevesi, Ludwig" (biogr. sketch). Ibid. 8:23.
22. (Book review) Simon Dubnow, *Geschichte des Chassidismus*. Vol. 1. *Magyar Zsidó Szemle* (Budapest) 48 (May):201–4.
23. (Book note) Simon Dubnow, *Geschichte des Chassidismus*. Vols. 1 and 2. *Mult és Jövő* (Budapest) 21 (December):411.

1932

24. "A. fák ujéve" ("The New Year of the Trees"). *Zsidó Szemle* (Budapest) 27 (January 22):3.
25. "A messiási eszme" ("The Messianic Idea"). *Uj Kor* (Timisoara, Rumania), January 2.
26. "Hanukkat haGimnasiya haY'hudit b'Budapest" ("Dedication of the Jewish High School in Budapest"). *Doar haYom* (Jerusalem), June 23.
27. "Der Judenrichter beim Kaiser: Zum 200. Geburtstag des Hoffaktors Koppel Theben" ("The Jewish Judge Before the Emperor: On the 200th Anniversary of the 'Shtadlan' Koppel Theben"). *Die Stimme* (Vienna), September 8.
28. *Idem. Der Israelit* (Frankfort on the Main), October 13.
29. "Der Shtadlen als Kemfer far Glaykhberekhtigung" ("The Shtadlan As Fighter for Emancipation") *The Jewish World* (Cleveland, Cincinnati, Columbus) 20 (November 29):277. (Yiddish translation of no. 27.)
30. "Jesiva és Szeminárium" ("Yeshiva and Seminary"). *Zsidó Szemle* (Budapest) 27 (December 22):43–44.
31. Kaczér, Illés (biogr. sketch). *Encyclopaedia Judaica* (Berlin) 9:734.
32. "Kaufmann, Isidor" (biogr. sketch). Ibid. 9:1099–100.
33. "Kecskeméti, Armin" (biogr. sketch). Ibid. 9:1112.
34. (Book review) Simon Dubnow, *Geschichte des Chassidismus*. Vol. 2. *Magyar Zsidó Szemle* (Budapest) 49 (January-February):68–71.
35. (Book note) *Theológiai tanulmányok* (Pápa). *Mult és Jövő* (Budapest) 22 (January):23.
36. (Book note) Schalom Asch, *Von den Vätern*. Ibid., p. 24.
37. (Book note) Hajdu György, *Das kaufmännische Auskunftswesen*. Ibid.
38. (Book note) Ernst Müller, *Der Sohar*. Ibid.
39. (Book note) Karl Walter, *Hebräische Wortkunde*. Ibid. (February):57.
40. (Book note) "Norvég elbeszélök" ("Norwegian Novelists"). Ibid.
41. (Book note) Schmarja Levin, *Kindheit im Exil*. Ibid.
42. (Book note) Kner Isidor, *Félévszázad mesgyéjén*. Ibid., p. 58.
43. (Book note) Eduard König, *Hebräisches und aramäisches Wörterbuch*. Ibid.
44. (Book note) Isaac Babel, *Drei Welten*. Ibid. (March):88.
45. (Book note) Martin Buber and Franz Rosenzweig, *Die Schrift*. Ibid.
46. (Book note) Karl Dreyer, *Die religiöse Gedankenwelt des Salomo ibn Gabirol*. Ibid.
47. (Book note) Franz Feldmann, *Geschichte der Offenbarung*. Ibid., p. 89.
48. (Book note) "Lazarus Goldschmid a talmudforditó" ("Lazarus Goldschmid the Talmud-Translator"). Ibid.
49. (Book note) George Foot Moore, *Judaism*. Ibid.
50. (Book note) Stephen Wise and Jacob de Haas, *The Great Betrayal*. Ibid.
51. (Book note) "Két amerikai zsidó évkönyv" ("Two American Jewish Year Books"). Ibid. (April):116.

52. (Book note) Ludwig Lewisohn, *Scheilocks letzte Tage.* Ibid.
53. (Book note) Winkler Ernöné, *A mi életünk.* Ibid.
54. (Book note) Eckstein N. Wolf, *Zsidó mesefüzetek.* Ibid.
55. (Book note) Komlós Aladár, *A néma őrült arca.* Ibid. (May):151.
56. (Book note) Lenkei Henrik, *Isten tábora,* Ibid.
57. (Book note) Tardos-Taussig Armin, *Jelképes siremlékek.* Ibid.
58. (Book note) Schalom Asch, *Die Gefangene Gottes.* Ibid., p. 152.
59. (Book note) Heinrich Haempel, *Die Daemonen.* Ibid.
60. (Book note) Holitscher Arthur, *A viszontátott Amerika.* Ibid.
61. (Book note) Karl Lieblich, *Wir jungen Juden.* Ibid.
62. (Book note) A. R. Malachi, *Igrot Sofrim.* Ibid.
63. (Book note) Radnóti József, *Kornfeld Zsigmond.* Ibid.
64. (Book note) Jekutiel Weisz, *Dvar hamalko.* Ibid.
65. (Book note) Alfred Tolnai, *Die zwölf Titanen.* Ibid.
66. (Book note) Kecskeméti Lipót, *Jeremiás.* Ibid. (July-August):215.
67. (Book note) Fürst Ilona, *Dóczy Lajos mint német iró.* Ibid., p. 216.
68. (Book note) Hugo Gold, *Die Juden und die Judengemeinde in Pressburg.* Ibid.
69. (Book note) Tisbi Illés, *Sötét percek éneke.* Ibid.
70. (Book note) Schalom Asch, *Moszkwa.* Ibid. (September):247.
71. (Book note) Sigm. Freud, *Bevezetés.* Ibid.
72. (Book note) Abraham Hirschowitz, *Ocar kol minhage Jesurun.* Ibid.
73. (Book note) Joseph Roth, *Hiob.* Ibid.
74. (Book note) Alexander Ehrenfeld, *Der Pflichtbegriff.* Ibid. (October):279.
75. (Book note) Else Kornis, *Das wiedergefundene Lachen.* Ibid.
76. (Book note) Vidor Pál és Beneschofsky Imre, *Évkönyv.* Ibid.
77. (Book note) Az *Encyclopaedia Judaica* 9. kötete. Ibid. (November):315.
78. (Book note) N. M. Gelber, *Keresztények a zsidó fronton.* Ibid.
79. (Book note) Jabotinsky, *A zsidó légió.* Ibid.
80. (Book note) Kecskeméti Vilmos, *Zsidó évkönyv.* Ibid.
81. (Book note) Edmond Fleg, *Miért vagyok zsidó?* Ibid. (December):347.
82. (Book note) Lemberger Abraham, *Szójátékok.* Ibid.
83. (Book note) Nagy Imre, *Ötezer vicc.* Ibid.

1933

84. SHIRE R. YISRAEL BEREKHYA FONTANELLA—JISZRAEL BERECHJA FONTANELLA KÖLTEMÉNYEI (The Poems of R. Israel Berekhya Fontanella). Budapest: Hungaria Nyomda. Pp. 82 (in Hebrew) and xxi (in Hungarian). Ph.D. diss., University of Budapest.
85. "A jeruzsálemi Héber Egyetem" ("The Hebrew University of Jerusalem"). In *Izraelita Magyar Irodalmi Társulat Évkönyve* (Budapest), 14 pp.
86. "A költő: Bialik 60. születésnapjára" ("The Poet: Bialik at Sixty"). *Mult és Jövő* (Budapest) 23 (June):171.
87. "Sátoromlás—sátorépités: Szukkoth 5694" ("Collapse of Tents—Building of Tents: Sukkot 5694"). *Zsidó Szemle* (Budapest) 28 (October 3):36–37.
88. "A hőskor után" ("After the Heroic Age"). Ibid. (December 29):49.
89. (Book note) David Miller, *The Secret of the Jew. Mult és Jövő* (Budapest) 23 (January):27.
90. (Book note) Az IMIT 1932-es *Évkönyve.* Ibid.
91. (Book note) Hugo Bergmann, *HaFilosofiya shel Shlomo Maimon.* Ibid. (February:59.
92. (Book note) Martin Buber, *Das Buch Jecheskel.* Ibid.
93. (Book note) I. Weigl, *Das Judentum.* Ibid.
94. (Book note) Abraham Wolfson, *Spinoza.* Ibid.

95. (Book note) Immanuel Löw, *Tränen*. Ibid. (April):122.
96. (Book note) Drechsler Miksa, *Mekonen Avelenu*. Ibid.
97. (Book note) S. Jedidja, *Mislavoth*. Ibid.
98. (Book note) Joseph Schick, *Joseph's Harvest*. ibid.
99. (Book note) Martin Buber, *Kampf um Israel*. Ibid. (May):154.
100. (Book note) Rudolf Steiner, *Die Geheimnisse der biblischen Schöpfungsgeschichte*. Ibid. (June):185.
101. (Book note) Karl Lieblich, *Was geschieht mit den Juden?* Ibid.
102. (Book note) Ernst von der Decken, *Ein Stünder fährt in heiliges Land*. Ibid.
103. (Book note) M. A. Irwin, *The Bible, the Scholar, and the Spade*. Ibid., p. 187.
104. (Book note) *A név férfiai*. Ibid. (September):251.
105. (Book note) Nagy Imre versei. Ibid., p. 252.
106. (Book note) Leopold Greenwald, *Toldot hakohanim hag'dolim*. Ibid. (October):285.
107. (Book note) S. Spinner, *Herkunft, Entstehung und antike Umwelt des hebräischen Volkes*. Ibid.
108. (Book note) Ivar Hylander, *Der literarische Samuel-Saul-Komplex*. Ibid.
109. (Book note) Halász Sándor versei. Ibid.
110. (Book note) Keleti Jenő versei. Ibid.
111. (Book note) Thomas Mann, *Jákob*. Ibid. (November):314.
112. (Book note) Michael Goldberger hátrahagyott iràsai. Ibid.
113. Stefan Zweig, *Jeremiás*. Ibid.
114. Ilja Ehrenburg, *Lasik Roitschwanz*. Ibid.
115. (Book note) Joseph Prill, *Einführung in die hebräische Sprache*. Ibid.

1934

116. "Látogatás egy előkelő Arab házban" ("Visit in a Noble Arab House"). *Mult és Jövő* (Budapest) 24 (February):56–57.
117. "Gilgule haY'hudim b'Hungaria" ("Experiences of the Jews in Hungary"). *Doar haYom* (Jerusalem) 16 (June 24 and 25):230–31
118. "Vita a mezőn" ("Discussion in the Field"). *Mult és Jövő* (Budapest) 24 (June):173–75.
119. "HaTziyonut b'Hungaria" ("Zionism in Hungary"). *HaTziyoni haK'lali* (Jerusalem) June 30.
120. "Abrahám városában" ("In the City of Abraham"). *Mult és Jövő* (Budapest) 24 (September):245–47.
121. "Klausner, a héber ember: 60-ik születésnapjára" ("Klausner the Hebrew Man: On His 60th Birthday"). Ibid. (November):299–301.
122. "Kiss, Arnold" (biogr. sketch). *Encyclopaedia Judaica* (Berlin) 10:25.
123. "Kiss, Josef" (biogr. sketch), Ibid., pp. 25–26.
124. "Kohn, Samuel" (biogr. sketch). Ibid., pp. 192–93.
125. "Kohut, George Alexander" (biogr. sketch). Ibid., p. 196.
126. "Löw Immánuel Ünneplése a Jeruzsálemi Héber Egyetemen" ("Immanuel Löw Honored at the Hebrew University of Jerusalem"). *Mult és Jövő* (Budapest) 24 February):61.

1935

127. "HaFolqlor Mahu?" ("What is Folklore?"). *Doar haYom* (Jerusalem), 10 Adar Beth.
128. "HaMelekh Sh'lomo w'haRuhot" ("King Solomon and the Winds"). Ibid. October 25.

129. "Imitatio dei a jemeni néphitben" ("Imitation of God in Yemenite Folk Belief"). *Mult és Jövő* (Budapest) 25 (September–October):293–94.

1936

130. HAMAYIM: MEḤQAR LIDIᶜAT HA'ARETZ UL'FOLQLOR ARTZIYISR'ELI BITQUFOT HAMI-QRA W'HAMISHNA (Water: A Study in Palestinology and Palestinian Folklore in the Biblical and Mishnaic Periods). Tel Aviv: Dvir. Pp. xii, 276. Ph.D. diss., Hebrew University of Jerusalem.
131. "Vorspiel und Auswirkungen der arabischen Unruhen in Palästina" ("Prelude and Effects of the Arab Riots in Palestine"). *Pester Lloyd* (Budapest), August 2.
132. "Versäumnisse der Palästina-Regierung" ("Errors of Omission of the Government of Palestine"). Ibid., September 8.
133. "Egy vicc margójára" ("On the Margin of an Anectode"). *Zsidó Szemle* (Budapest), August 14.
134. "K'ruzim Antishemiyyim b'Budapest" ("Anti-Semitic Broadsides in Budapest"). *HaAretz* (Tel Aviv), November 27.
135. "Sokolow." *Mult és Jövő* (Budapest) 26 (June):184.
136. "Freud nyolcvan éves" ("Freud at Eighty"). Ibid., p. 188.
137. "Leon Blum képek" ("Leon Blum Pictures"). Ibid. (December):333.
138. "A Salamon-gyüjtemény menórái" ("The Menorahs of the Salomon Collection"). Ibid., 339 (illustrated).
139. (Book review) "Die Reden des Kanzlers der Hebräischen Universität" ("Addresses of the Chancellor of the Hebrew University"). *Pester Lloyd* (Budapest), June 9.
140. (Book note) H. Brody, *Moses ibn Ezra*. *Mult és Jövő* (Budapest) 26 (April):121.
141. (Book note) Szemere Samu, *A müvészet mint valóságértelmezés*. Ibid. (November):319.
142. (Book note) *Évkönyv*. Ibid.
143. (Book note) Franz Kafka, *Beschreibung eines Kampfes*. Ibid.
144. (Book note) A Chief Rabbi bibliakommentárja. Ibid. 318–19.
145. (Book note) Weisz Zoltán, *Egy emberi élet a szavak tükrében*. Ibid., 319.
146. (Book note) Ari Ibn-Zahav, *Ele maszé hazappatim*. Ibid. (December):350.
147. (Book note) I. L. Landau, *Judaism in Life and Literature*. Ibid.
148. (Book note) Marvin Lowenthal, *The Jews of Germany*. Ibid.
149. (Book note) Thomas Mann, *Joseph in Ägypten*. Ibid.
150. (Book note) *Hebrew Union College Annual 11*. Ibid.
151. (Book note) Hero és Leander héberül. Ibid.
152. (Book note) Joseph Kastein, *Jerusalem, die Geschichte eines Landes*. Ibid., pp. 350–51.
153. (Book note) Elias Auerbach, *Wüste und gelobtes Land*. Ibid., p. 351.
154. (Book note) Névai László, *Az euthanázia problémája*. Ibid.
155. (Book note) Vitéz Náray Antal és Vitéz Berló István, *Légitámadás*. Ibid.

1937

156. "Szentföldi panoráma" ("Holy Land Panorama"). In *Izraelita Magyar Irodalmi Társulat Évkönyve* (Budapest).
157. "Képek a Szentföldről" ("Pictures from the Holy Land"). *Rádióélet* (Budapest) January 8.
158. "Abel Pann, Tzayyar haT'NaKh" ("Abel Pann, Painter of the Bible"). *HaAretz* (Tel Aviv), October 14, 21:5532.

159. "HaQeshet" ("The Rainbow"). In *Sefer haYovel liProf. Sh'muel Krauss* (Jerusalem). Pp. 311–35.
160. "Some Hebrew Sea Legends." In *Dissertationes in honorem Dr. Eduardi Mahler* (Budapest). Pp. 488–93.
161. (Book note) George A. Barton, *Archaeology and the Bible. Mult és Jövő* (Budapest) 27 (October):250.

1938

162. HASAPPANUT HAʿIVRIT: MEḤQAR B'TOLDOT HATARBUT HAARTZIYISR'ELIT BIME QEDEM (Jewish Seafaring in Ancient Times: A Study in Ancient Palestinian Culture). Jerusalem: Rubin Mass for the Bialik Foundation. 244 pp. Illustrated.
163. MIVḤAR HASIPPUR HAARTZIYISR'ELI (Anthology of Palestinian Short Stories), with Zevi Wohlmuth. Jerusalem: Rubin Mass. 336 pp.
164. "A zsidó diákság és a Héber Egyetem" ("Jewish Students and the Hebrew University"). *Mult és Jövő* (Budapest) 28 June–July):173.
165. "HaMelekh Sh'lomo w'haRuḥot" ("King Solomon and the Winds"). In Yosef M'yuḥas, *Maʿasiyyot ʿAm liV'ne Qedem*, Tel Aviv: Dvir. Pp. 111–18. (Reprint of no. 128.)
166. "Yoshev Y'rushalayim Ḥatzov Borot!" ("People of Jerusalem, Dig Cisterns!"). *HaAretz* (Tel Aviv), September 4.
167. "Simḥat Bet haShoeva" ("The Joy of the House of Water-Drawing"). Ibid., October 9.
168. "Uj kezdet elé" ("Towards a New Beginning"). *A Hét = HaShavuʿa* (Jerusalem), June 3, 1:1.
169. "A tizenkettedik órában" ("In the Twelfth Hour"). Ibid., June 10, 1:2.
170. "T'khelet" ("Purple-Blue"). In *Ludwig Blau Memorial Volume* (Budapest).
171. Mavo (Introduction to the pamphlet *Ki Lo Yihye Evyon b'Eretz haY'hudim*, by Israel Friedman (Jerusalem).
172. (Book review) *Sefer Azkara* (Memorial Book for Rabbi Kook). *HaBoker*, March 25.
173. (Book review) *Toldot Eretz Yisrael*, by B. Maisler. *HaʿOlam* (Jerusalem), September 22.
174. (Book review) *HaSafa haʿAravit w'Diqduqah*, by Y. Kapliwatzki. Ibid., September 22.
175. (Book review) *Sippure Rabba bar Bar Ḥana*, by Y. D. Eisenstein. Ibid., September. 1.
176. (Book review) *Beth HaMidrash*, by A. Jellinek. Ibid., September 1.
177. (Book review) *Toldot ha'Umma ha Yisr'elit*, by Joseph Kastein. Ibid., September 1.
178. "Sod Qan haTzippor" ("The Mystery of the Bird's Nest"), by Joseph Patai. Trans. from the Hungarian into Hebrew by R. P. Ibid., April 14.

1939

179. "The ʿEgla ʿArufa, or the Expiation of the Polluted Land." *The Jewish Quarterly Review* (Philadelphia), n.s.30, no. 1:59–69.
180. "The 'Control of Rain' in Ancient Palestine." *Hebrew Union College Annual* 14:251–86.
181. "A Történetiró: Josephus Flavius születésének 1900. évfordulójára" (The Historian: The 1900th Anniversary of Josephus Flavius"). *Mult és Jövő* (March): 29:79–80.

182. "A kvúca gyermeke" ("The Child of the K'vutza"). Ibid. (April):118.
183. "Ari Ibn Zahav." *Sifrut Tz'ira,* (Jerusalem), April 27.
184. "Yosefus Flavius HaY'hudi" (Josephus Flavius the Jews"). *HaAretz,* May 26.
185. "Traitre ou Patriote: A l'occasion du 1900 anniversaire de Josephus Flavius historien juif." *La Terre Retrouvée* (Paris) 11, no. 7 (June 1):16–17.
186. "?Traidor o Patriota? En oportunidad del 1900° anniversario de Josefo Flavius, historiador judio." *La Luz* (Buenos Aires) 9, no. 17 (July 21).:371–72
187. "Traitor or Patriot? After 1900 Years This Question Is Still Asked About Josephus, Jewish Historian." *The National Jewish Monthly* (Washington) 54, no. 4 (December):116–18.
118. "A héber alef-bét fejlődése: Jakob Steinhardt fametszetsorozata" ("The Development of the Hebrew Alphabet: The Woodcuts of Jacob Steinhardt"). *Mult és Jövő* 29 (April):103.
189. (Book review) *HaMilhama 'al haG'vul,* by Ari Ibn Zahav. *Ha'Olam,* March 2.
190. (Book review) *Short Lectures on Modern Hebrew Literature,* by J. L. Landau. Ibid., May 4.
191. (Book review) *Monumenta Hungaria Judaica,* by Bernat Mandel. Ibid., September 22.
192. (Book review) *Über das Wesen der Kulturwandlungen,* by A. Fodor. Ibid., November 2.

1940

193. (Book review) "Emunat haMiqra": *Toldot haEmuna* by Y'hezq'el Kaufman. Ibid., June 20.
194. (Book review) *Mehqarim b'Miqra w'Talmud,* by A. Kaminka. Ibid., August 8.
195. (Book review) *Vilaot,* by Dov Chomsky. Ibid., August 8.

1941

196. "Jewish Seafaring in Ancient Times." *The Jewish Quarterly Review,* 32, no. 1 : 1–26.
197. "Hungary." *Universal Jewish Encyclopedia,* 5 : 483–96. (Translation of no. 2.)
198. (Book review) "Palestine's Young Immigrants," *The Palestine Post,* Sept. 5.

1942

199. ADAM WA'ADAMA: MEHQAR B'MINHAGIM, EMUNOT, W'AGADOT ETZEL YISRAEL W'UMMOT HA'OLAM (Man and Earth in Jewish Custom, Belief, and Legend). vol. 1. Jerusalem: Hebrew University Press. 283 pp.
200. "Min haFolqlor haYisr'eli: Minhage Leda Etzel Y'hude Maroqo" ("From Jewish Folklore: Birth Customs Among the Jews of Morocco"). *HaTzofe* (Jerusalem), October 9.
201. "Min haFolqlor haYisr'eli: Minhage Leda waHatuna Etzel Y'hude Mitzrayim" ("From Jewish Folklore: Birth and Marriage Customs Among the Jews of Egypt"). Ibid., October 16.
202. "Min haFolqlor haYisr'eli: Minhage Leda waHatuna Etzel Y'hude Y'rushalayim haS'faradim" ("From Jewish Folklore: Birth and Marriage Customs Among the Sephardi Jews in Jerusalem"). Ibid., October 23.
203. "Min haFolqlor haYisr'eli: Minhage Hatuna Etzel Y'hude Maroqo" ("From Jewish Folklore: Marriage Customs Among the Jews of Morocco"). Ibid., October 30.
204. "Min haFolqlor haYisr'eli: Minhage Mita uQ'vura Etzel Y'hude Mitzrayim"

("From Jewish Folklore: Death and Burial Customs Among the Jews of Egypt"); "Minhagim uS'gullot" ("Customs and Charms"). Ibid., November 20.
205. "Mr. Stewart's Omission" (letter to the editor). *The Palestine Post*, December 21.
206. (Book review) *Toldot haEmuna haYisr'elit*, by Y. Kaufman. *Ha^cOlam*, September 17.

1943

207. ADAM WA'ADAMA: MEḤQAR B'MINHAGIM, EMUNOT W'AGADOT ETZEL YISRAEL W'UMMOT HA^cOLAM (Man and Earth in Jewish Custom, Belief and Legend). vol. 2. Jerusalem: Hebrew University Press. xvi, 293 pp.

1944

208. MIVḤAR HASIPPUR HA'ARTZIYISR'ELI (Anthology of Palestinian Short Stories) with Zevi Wohlmuth. 2 vols. (2d, enlarged edition of no. 163.) Jerusalem: Rubin Mass. 240 and 262 pp.
209. "^cArisah." *The Jewish Quarterly Review*, n.s. 35, no. 1 : 165–72.
210. "Naqim Yad l'Minhage Yisrael" ("Let Us Erect a Monument to Jewish Customs"). *Hegeh* (Tel Aviv), May 8.
211. "Jewish Folk-Cures for Barrenness, I: From the Vegetable Kingdom." *Folk-Lore* (London)55 (September) : 117–24
212. "Jewish Folk-Cures for Barrenness, II: From the Animal Kingdom." Ibid., 56 (December 1944–March 1945 : 208–19.

1945

213. ^cEDOTH: RIV^cON L'FOLQLOR W'ETNOLOGIA (Communities: A Quarterly for Folklore and Ethnology). Edited by R. P. and Joseph Rivlin. vol. 1: The Palestine Institute for Folklore and Ethnoogy, 1945–46. 264 pp.
214. MASOROT HISTORIYOT UMINHAGE Q'VURA ETZEL Y'HUDE MESHHED (Historical Traditions and Mortuary Customs Among the Jews of Meshhed). Hebrew with English summary. Jerusalem: Palestine Institute of Folklore and Ethnology. 28 pp.
215. English summary of *Edoth* 1, no. 1. *Edoth* 1, no. 1 (October) : 59–64 (unsigned).
216. "Budapest's Chain Bridge." *The Palestine Post* (Jerusalem), January 4.
217. "HaFolqlor w'haEtnologia shel ^cAm Yisrael: B^cayot w'Tafqidim" ("Jewish Folklore and Ethnology: Problems and Tasks"). *Edoth* 1, no. 1 (Jerusalem) : 1–12. English summary, pp. 63–64.
218. "Naqim Yad l'Minhage Yisrael" ("Let Us Erect a Monument to Jewish Customs"). *^cAm waSefer* (Tel. Aviv), August), pp. 90–91. (Reprint of no. 210)
219. "Q'ri'a la^cAvoda Antropometrit" ("A Call for Anthropometric Work"). *HaR-'fu'a* (Tel Aviv), September 2, pp. 107–9.
220. "Folqlor w'Etnologia Mahem?" ("What Are Folklore and Ethnology?"). *HaGalgal* (Jerusalem), October 4.
221. "Two Notes: 1. The Eastertide Stoning of the Jews and Its liturgical Echoes; 2 To the Gnostic Background of the Rabbinic Adam Legends." *The Jewish Quarterly Review* 36 : 415–17
222. "M'holot b'Yom haKippurim ben Y'hude ha Kavkaz uTripolitania" ("Dancing of Maidens on the Day of Atonement among the Jews of the Caucasus and Tripolitania"). *Edoth* 1, no. 1 (October) : 55; English summary, ibid. p. 59.
223. (Book review) Two Posthumous Works by Prof. B. Malinowski. *The Palestine Post*, September 14.

224. (Book review) *'Am waSefer. Ha'Olam* (September 20).
225. (Book review) *Psikhologia shel haDat*, by M. Z. Sole. Ibid., (September 20) (unsigned).
226. (Book review) *Mortuary Customs of the Shawnee*, by Erminie Wheeler Voegelin. *Edoth* 1, no. 1 (October): 56–57.
227. (Book review) *Handbook of the Communal Villages in Palestine*, by Edwin Samuel, Ibid., p. 56.

1946

228. 'EDOTH: RIV'ON L'FOLQLOR W'ETNOLOGIA (Communities: A Quarterly for Folklore and Ethnology). Edited by R. P. and Joseph Rivlin. Vol. 2: Jerusalem: The Palestine Institute of Folklore and Ethnology, 1946–47. 314 pp.
229. "Eisenstadt." In *'Arim w'Imahot b'Yisrael* (Jerusalem)1 : 47–79.
230. "Problems and Tasks of Jewish Folklore and Ethnology." *Journal of American Folklore* 59, no. 231 (January–March): 25–39. (English version of no. 124.)
231. Haqdama w'He'arot Nosafot (Preface and Additional Notes). In J. L. Zlotnick, *Ma'ase Y'rushalmi*. Jerusalem: The Palestine Institute of Folklore and Ethnology. Pp. 7–10 (in Hebrew), and vii–xi (in English).
232. "Anthropology During the War: V. Palestine." *American Anthropologist* 48, no. 3 (July–September):477–82.
233. "Palm Leaves on Boats' Prows in Palestine." *Man* (London), (March–April). Article 46, p. 47.
234. "Three Meshhed Tales on Mulla Siman-Tobh." *Folk-Lore* (London) 57 (December): 179–84.
235. "Y'hude Meshhed" ("The Jews of Meshhed") (letter to the editor). *HaAretz*, April 7.
236. "Mumia" (comments). *Edoth* 1, no. 2 (January): 107.
237. "HaM'holot b'Yom haKippurim" ("The Dances on the Day of Atonement"). Ibid., (January): 113.
238. Unsigned news items. Ibid, pp. 113–14.
239. English summary of *Edoth* 1, no. 2. Ibid., pp. 23–28 (unsigned).
240. Comments on various articles. *Edoth* 1, no. 3 (April): 162, 165, 167, 173, 174, 176, 177, 178, 179, 180, 182.
241. HaM'holot b'Yom haKippurim" ("The Dances on the Day of Atonement"). Ibid, p. 186.
242. Unsigned news items. Ibid., pp. 186–87.
243. English summary of *Edoth* 1, No. 3. Ibid., pp. 194–98.
244. "HaHinnukh ha'Ivri b'Adat ha'Anusim b'Meshhed" ("The Hebrew Education in the Marrano Community of Meshhed"). *Edoth* 1, no. 4 (July): 213–26; English summary, ibid. pp. 261–63.
245. Comments on various articles. Ibid., pp. 234, 243.
246. "Shuv haM'holot b'Yom haKippurim" ("Again: Dances on the Day of Atonement"). Ibid., pp. 252–53.
247. Unsigned news items. Ibid., pp. 244, 255.
248. English summary of *Edoth* 1, no. 4. Ibid., pp. 260–64.
249. "Dr. M. Grunwald: l'Yovlo haShiv'im-w'Hamesh" ("Dr. M. Grunwald: On his 75th Birthday"). *Edoth* 2, nos. 1–2 (October 1946–January 1947): 5–6.
250. "LaMagga' haTarbuti b'Eretz Yisrael haHadasha" ("On Culture Contact in Modern Palestine"). Ibid., pp. 17–57.
251. Comments on various articles. Ibid., pp. 96, 127.
252. Unsigned news items. Ibid., pp. 132–36.
253. English summary of *Edoth* 2, nos. 1–2. Ibid., pp. 149–60.

254. "Minhage Leda Etzel Y'hude Kurdistan" by Erich Brauer, trans. R. P. *Edoth* 1, no. 2:65–72.
255. "Din w'Heshbon Bin-L'umi ʿAl ha'Antropolgia biShnat 1943" (International Report on Anthropology in 1943"). Translated by R. P. Ibid., pp. 116–19 (unsigned).
256. "Mila w'Yaldut Etzel Y'hude Kurdistan" ("Circumcision and Childhood Among the Jews of Kurdistan") by Erich Brauer. Translated by R. P. *Edoth* 1, no. 3:129–38 (unsigned).
257. "Din w'Heshbon Bin-L'umi ʿAl Ha'Antropologia BiShnat 1944" ("International Report on Anthropology in 1944"). Translated by R. P. Ibid., pp. 188–90 (unsigned).
258. "Noah ba'Agada haY'hudit w'haʿAravit" ("Noah in Jewish and Arab Legend"). Letter to the editor by Francis Lee Utley. Translated by R. P. *Edoth* 2, nos. 1–2:128 (unsigned).
259. "T'enat Adam—T'enat Hawa" (The Fig of Adam—the Fig of Eve"), by C. Gabriel. Translated by R. P. Ibid., pp. 128–29 (unsigned).
260. (Book review) *Studies in Divine Kingship*, by Ivan Engnell. *Edoth* 1, no. 2:120.
261. (Book review) *HaYishuv HaʿIvri b'Motza'e haMilhama*, by A. N. Polak. Ibid., pp. 120–21.
262. (Book review) *HaYadaʿta et HaAretz?*, by Joseph Braslavsky. *Edoth* 1, no. 3:191.
263. (Book review) *Twentieth Century Sociology*, by G. Gurwitch and W. E. Moore. Ibid., pp. 192–93.
264. (Book review) *Toldot haEmuna haYisr'elit*, by Y'hezq'el Kaufman. *Edoth* 1, no. 4:256–57.
265. (Book review) *The King of Ganda*, by Tor Irstam. Ibid., p. 257.
266. (Book review) *The Science of Man in the World Crisis*. *Edoth* 2, nos. 1–2:137–39.
267. (Book review) *Madrikh Eretz-Yisrael*, by Zeev Vilnay. Ibid., pp. 142–43.
268. (Book review) *HaYadaʿta et HaAretz?*, by Joseph Bratzlavsky. Ibid., pp. 143–44.

1947

269. MADAʿ HA'ADAM: MAVO L'ANTROPOLOGIA (The Science of Man: An Introduction to Anthropology), vol. 1. Tel Aviv: Yavne Publ. House. 256 pp. (illustrated).
270. MAN AND TEMPLE IN ANCIENT JEWISH MYTH AND RITUAL. Edinburgh: Thomas Nelson. ix, 227 pp.
271. ON CULTURE CONTACT AND ITS WORKING IN MODERN PALESTINE, Memoir no. 67, American Anthropological Association (October). 48 pp. English version of no. 159.
272. Y'HUDE KURDISTAN: MEHQAR ETNOLOGI (The Jews of Kurdistan: An Ethnological Study) by Erich Brauer. Completed, edited and translated into Hebrew by R. P. Jerusalem: The Palestine Institute of Folklore and Ethnology. 324 pp.
273. ʿEDOTH: RIVʿON L'FOLQLOR W'ETNOLOGIA (Communities: A Quarterly for Folklore and Ethnology). Edited by R. P. and Joseph Rivlin. Jerusalem: The Palestine Institute of Folklore and Ethnology, 1947–48. 3:116, 109, lxxii, lxi.
274. "Biblical and Rabbinical Data to the 'Culture Pattern.'" In *Semitic Studies in Memory of Immanuel Löw* (Budapest). Pp. 189–201.
275. "Hebrew Installation Rites: A Contribution to the Study of Ancient Near Eastern-African Culture Contact." *Hebrew Union College Annual*, 20:143–225.
276. "Folklore and Ethnology." *American Fund News* (New York) 3:2 (illustrated).
277. "Jewish Tree Lore." *The Jewish Advocate* (Bombay) 15:4.
278. "ʿAdat ha'Anusim b'Meshhed" ("The Marrano Community in Meshhed"). *HaDoar* (New York), January 3, pp. 243–44.

279. "HaRav Y'huda Lev Zlotnick: l'Yovlo haShishim" ("Rabbi J. L. Z.: On His Sixtieth Birthday"). *Edoth* 2, nos. 3–4:163–64.
280. "Palästina-Institut für Folklore und Ethnologie." *Jüdische Rundschau* (Berlin), October. Pp. 16–17.
281. "HaNissuim Etzel Anuse Meshhed" (Marriage Among the Marranos of Meshhed"), *Edoth* 2, nos. 3–4:163–92. English summary, pp. 311–14.
282. "Ḥatunat Shedim" (The Wedding of Demons in Gallipoli and Jerusalem") with M. ᶜAzuz. Ibid., pp. 283–85.
283. "Achievements and Requirements of Jewish Ethnology" (in Hebrew and English), *Edoth* 3, nos. 1–2:189–96 and i–x.
284. Comments on *Edoth* 2, nos. 3–4 (April–July):284, 285, 289.
285. Unsigned news items, Ibid., pp. 290–92.
286. "Din w'Ḥeshbon Bin-L'umi ᶜAl ha'Antropologia biShnat 1945" (International Report on Anthropology in 1945"), by Melville J. Herskovits. Translated by R. P. Ibid., pp. 292–96 (unsigned).
287. English summary of Ibid. *Edoth* 2, nos. 3–4:304–13.
288. "Haḥrava" ("Devastation"), by Sir John L. Myers. translated by R. P. *Edoth* 3, nos. 1–2:1–19.
289. "R'fu'a ᶜAravit Ben Y'hude Teman" ("Arab Medicine Among the Jews of Yemen"), by Max Meyerhof, translated by R. P. (unsigned). Ibid., pp. 27–32.
290. "Rishum haN'gina haMizraḥit" ("The Transcription of Oriental Music") by Edith Gerson-Kiwi. Translated by R. P. (unsigned). Ibid., pp. 73–78.
291. (Book review), *HaK'far haᶜAravi*, by Moshe Stavsky. *Edoth* 2, nos. 3–4:297–98.
292. Unsigned news items. Ibid., pp. 110–12.

1948

293. MADAᶜ HA'ADAM: MAVO L'ANTROPOLOGIA (The Science of Man: An Introduction to Anthropology). Tel Aviv: Yavne Publ. House. 2:265–532.
294. "Akhilat Adama: Pereq b'Antropologia" ("Earth-Eating: An Anthropologial Study"). In *Metsudah* (London) 5–6:330–47.
295. "A Survey of Near Eastern Anthropology." *Transactions of the New York Academy of Sciences*, series 2, 10, no. 6:200–209.
296. "A Popular 'Life of Nadir.'" *Edoth* 3, nos. 3–4:1–16 (Hebrew). *Edoth* 3, nos. 3–4: i–xx (English).
297. "Franz Boas," by Robert H. Lowie. Translated by R. P. (unsigned). Ibid., pp. 17–25.
298. Unsigned news items. Ibid., pp. 108–9.
299. (Book review) *The Nuba*, by S. F. Nadel. *American Anthropologist* 50, no. 4:675–78.

1949

300. "Massekhet S'gullot: Pereq ᶜal S'gullot la'Isha haM'qashsha Leled" ("Jewish Charms to Facilitate Childbirth"). *Sefer haShana lIhude Amerika*, (New York) 10:472–87.
301. "Mushaᶜa Tenure and Cooperation in Palestine." *American Anthropologist* 51, no. 3:436–45.
302. "Music of the Middle East—Palestine." Introduction and notes to the recordings. *Ethnic Folkways Library* (New York), EFL-1408.
303. "The Institute Rabbi Zlotnik Will Head in Israel." *S. A. Jewish Times* (Johannesburg), March 11.

304. "Adama: haAdama baMitologia" ("Earth: The Earth in Mythology"). In *HaEntziklopedia ha'Ivrit* (Jerusalem-Tel Aviv), 1:537–38.
305. "Australia: Etnologia," with Y'sha'yahu Leibowitz. Ibid., 1007–9.
306. (Book review) *A Treasury of Jewish Folklore*, by N. Ausubel. *Southern Folklore Quarterly*, 13, no. 2 (June):153–55.

1950

307. "Israel to Become Laboratory for Sociological Research." *The Jewish Weekly Times* (Brookline, Mass), October 5.
308. "The Problem of Cultural Adjustment in Israel." *The Jewish Advocate* (Boston, Mass.), October 18.
309. "The Indios Israelitas of Mexico." *The Menorah Journal* 38, no. 1 (Winter):54–67 (illustrated).
310. (Book review) *The Arab of the Desert*, by H. R. P. Dickson. *American Anthropologist* 52, no. 4 (October–December):536–38.
311. (Book review) *The Arab of the Desert*, by H. R. P. Dickson. *Middle Eastern Affairs* (New York), (November). Pp. 333–34.

1951

312. "Literature on Israel," 1948–50. *Jewish Quarterly Review* 41, no. 4 (April):425–38.
313. "Nomadism: Middle Eastern and Central Asian." *Southwestern Journal of Anthropology* 7, no. 4 (Winter):401–14.
314. "Relationship Patterns Among the Arabs." *Middle Eastern Affairs* 12, no. 5 (May):180–85.
315. "Iroqezim o Iroqwoy" ("Iroquois"). *HaEntziqlopedia ha'Ivrit*, (Jerusalem-Tel Aviv), 3:209–10 (illustrated).
316. "Comparison of Income Figures" (letter to the editor). *The New York Times*, December 14.

1952

317. "HaMi'utim haLo-Y'hudiyyim b'Yisrael" ("The Non-Jewish Minorities in Israel"), in *HaDoar Jubilee Volume*. New York: HaHistadrut ha'Ivrit b'Amerika. Pp. 89–106.
318. "Indián Zsidók Mexikóban" ("Indian Jews in Mexico"). *Mult és Jövö* (Paris) 35, no. 4 (April):88–89 (illustrated).
319. "HaY'hudim ha'Indianim b'Meqsiqo" ("The Jewish Indians in Mexico"). *Talpioth* (New York), 5:3–4, 828–44.
320. "Social Conditions in the Middle East." In *Preliminary Report on the World Social Situation*. New York: United Nations Economic and Social Council, Doc. No. E/CN.5/267, April 25, pp. 333–73; and E/CN.5/2G7/Rev. 1, September 8, pp. 148–63 (unsigned).
321. "The Cultural Challenge of Israel." *The Chicago Jewish Forum* 11, no. 1 (Fall):7–12.
322. "The Middle East As a Culture Area." *The Middle East Journal* (Washington, D.C.) 6, no. 1 (Winter):1–21.
323. "Land Reform in Iran" (letter to the editor). *The New York Times*, August 8.
324. (Book review) *Purim and Hanukkah*, by Th. H. Gaster. *HaDoar* (New York), February 29.

325. (Book review) *Tales from the Arab Tribes,* by C. G. Campbell. *Middle Eastern Affairs* 3, nos. 6–7 (June–July):190.
326. (Book review) *Life Is With People,* by M. Zborowsky and E. Herzog. *American Anthropologist* 54, no. 4 (October–December):543–45.
327. (Book review) *Falasha Anthology,* by Wolf Leslau. *Jewish Social Studies* (April), pp. 175–76.
328. (Book review), *Caravan: The Story of the Middle East,* by Carleton S. Coon. *American Anthropologist* 54, no. 3 (July–September):396–97.
329. (Book reviews) *Life Is With People,* by M. Zborowsky and E. Herzog; A Treasury of Jewish Folklore, by H. E. Goldin; *The Merry Heart,* by S. F. Mendelsohn, *Journal of American Folklore* 65, no. 258 (October–December):433–34.

1953

330. ISRAEL BETWEEN EAST AND WEST: A STUDY IN HUMAN RELATIONS. Philadelphia: The Jewish Publication Society of America, xiv, 348 p. (illustrated).
331. "HaLeda baMinhag ha ᶜAmami" (Birth in Popular Customs"). *Talpioth* 6, nos. 1–2 (New York):226–68.
332. "The Jewish 'Refugees' in the Middle East." *Journal of International Affairs* 7, no. 1:51–56.
333. "L'Va ᶜayat haGeza ᶜ haY'hudi" ("On the Problem of the Jewish Race"). *Mabua* 1, no. 2 (New York):199–206.
334. "The Phonology of 'Sabra'-Hebrew." *The Jewish Quarterly Review* 44, no. 1 (July):51–54.
335. "History of the Melkite Church" (letter to the editor). *The New York Times,* January 6.
336. "Israel and Oriental Culture" (letter to the editor). *Commentary* (November) pp. 487–88.
337. (Book review) *Arabia Reborn,* by George Kheirallah. *Jewish Social Studies* 15, no. 1 (January):69–70.
338. (Book review) *Rural Reconstruction in Action,* by H. B. Allen. *The Annals of the American Academy* (September), pp. 197–98.
339. (Book review) *The Taming of the Nations,* by F. S. C. Northrop. *American Anthropologist* 55, no. 3:438–39.
340. (Book review) *Studies in Yiddish Folklore,* by Y. L. Cahan. Ibid. 55, no. 5:744–45.
341. (Book note) *The Idea of Conflict,* by Kurt Singer. Ibid. 55, no. 3:445–46.
342. (Book note) *Anthropology Today; An Appraisal of Anthropology Today; The Nature of Culture,* by A. L. Kroeber. *Jewish Quarterly Review,* pp. 79–80.

1954

343. ACCULTURATION IN ISRAEL. The American Jewish Committee, Ad Hoc Committee on Israel, New York (November). 61 pp. (mimeographed).
344. "Religion in Middle Eastern, Far Eastern, and Western Culture." *Southwestern Journal of Anthropology* 10, no. 3 (Autumn):233–54.
345. "Age Grades and Kinship Groups," *Man* (London) 54 (May), article no. 123, p. 84.
346. "East-West Gulf and Israel." *The Chicago Jewish Forum* 12, no. 4 (Summer):213–18.
347. "Culture Change in the Muslim Town: A Challenge for Research." *United Asia* (Bombay) 6, no. 4:191–94.

348. "HaYesh Tzorekh b'Universita b'Tel Aviv?" ("Is There a Need For a University in Tel Aviv?") *HaDoar* (New York), May 7.
349. "Baganda." In *HaEntziqlopedia haKlalit* (Jerusalem-Tel Aviv), 7:611.
350. "Duda'im" ("Mandrakes"), with Michael Zohari. In *Entziqlopedia Miqrait* (Jerusalem), 2:645–46.
351. "Celestial Transport" (letter to the editor). The *New York Times Magazine*, July 4.
352. (Book review) *Song of the Arab*, by Rolla Foley. *Western Folklore* 13, no. 1 (January):70–71.
353. (Book review) *Cultural Sciences*, by Florian Znaniecki. *Jewish Social Studies*, 16, no. 2 (April):190–91.
354. (Book review) *Rebirth and Destiny of Israel*, by David Ben Gurion. *Political Science Quarterly* (New York), (June).
355. (Book review) *Israel*, by Norman Bentwich. *Jewish Social Studies* 16, no. 3 (July):282–83.
356. (Book review) *Documents Relating to the Middle East (UNESCO)*, *Middle Eastern Affairs* 5, nos. 8–9 (August–September):282–85.
357. (Book review) *Les Papis:Tribu Persane*, by C. G. Feilberg. *The Middle East Journal* 8, no. 4 (Autumn):468–69.
358. (Book review) *The Arabian Peninsula*, by R. H. Sanger. *The Chicago Jewish Forum* 13, no. 1 (Fall):67–68.
359. (Book review) *Between Past and Future*. Edited by Carl Frankenstein. *Middle Eastern Affairs* 5, no. 10 (October):318–20.

1955

360. "HaLeda baMinhag ha^cAmami" ("Birth in Popular Custom"). *Talpioth* 6, nos. 3–4 (New York):686–705. (Sequel to no. 331.)
361. "Cousin-Right in Middle Eastern Marriage." *Southwestern Journal of Anthropology* 11, no. 4 (Winter):371–90.
362. "The Dynamics of Westernization in the Middle East." *The Middle East Journal* 9, no. 1 (Winter):1–16.
363. "The Immigrant in Israel." In S. N. Fisher, ed., *Social Forces in the Middle East*. Ithaca, N.Y.:Cornell University Press. Pp. 222–36.
364. (Book review) *Interrelations of Culture (UNESCO)*, *American Anthropologist* 57, no. 1 (February):179–80.
365. (Book review) *Moslems on the March*, by F. W. Fernau. *The Chicago Jewish Forum* 13, no. 4 (Summer):261–62.
366. (Book reviews) *Between Past and Future*. Edited by C. Frankenstein; *The Absorption of Immigrants*, by S. N. Eisenstadt. *The Middle East Journal* 9, no. 4 (Autumn):453–55.
367. (Book review) *Franz Boas*, by Melville J. Herskovits. *Jewish Social Studies* 17, no. 4 (October):360–61.

1956

368. THE HASHEMITE KINGDOM OF JORDAN. Edited by R. P. Human Relations Area Files. New Haven, Conn. 605 pp. (xeroxed).
369. THE REPUBLIC OF SYRIA. Edited by R. P. Human Relations Area Files, New Haven, Conn., 2 vols. 777 pp. (xeroxed.)
370. THE REPUBLIC OF LEBANON. Edited by R. P. Human Relations Area Files, New Haven, Conn., 2 vols. 639 pp. (xeroxed.)

371. "Al-Taghayyur al-Ḥaḍari fil-Madaniyya al-Islamiyya" ("Culture Change in the Muslim Town"). In *Al-Thaqafa al-Islamiyya wal-Ḥayat al-Muʾasira*, edited by Muhammad Khalafallah. Cairo, pp. 195–202. (Arabic translation of no. 347.)
372. "HaQ'hilla bʿEdot haMizrah" ("The Community Among the Oriental Jews"). *Perakim* (New York) 1 (April): 36–42.
373. "General Character of the Society." In no. 368, pp. 1–20.
374. "Geographical Setting." In no. 368, pp. 21–31.
375. "Culture Groups." In no. 368, pp. 62–87.
376. "Social Structure." In no. 368, pp. 102–205.
377. "The Town" (with Fahim I. Qubain). In no. 368, pp. 250–91.
378. "The Family." In no. 368, pp. 292–332.
379. "Social Values and Patterns of Living." In no. 368, pp. 333–59.
380. "Health and Sanitation" (with Simon D. Messing). In no. 368, pp. 460–75.
381. "Attitudes and Reactions of the People." In no. 368, pp. 475–501.
382. "General Character of the Society." In no. 369, pp. 1–25.
383. "Geographical Setting" (with Simon D. Messing). In no. 369, pp. 26–32.
384. "Culture Groups." In no. 369, pp. 95–129.
385. "Social Structure." In no. 369, pp. 150–252.
386. "The Town" (with Fahim I. Qubain). In no. 369, pp. 323–72.
387. "The Family." In no. 369, pp. 373–414.
388. "Social Values and Patterns of Living." In no. 369, pp. 415–47.
389. "Health and Sanitation" (with Simon D. Messing). In no. 369, pp. 568–602.
390. "Public Welfare" (with Simon D. Messing). In no. 389, pp. 603–18.
391. "Attitudes and Reactions of the People." In no. 369, pp. 619–49.
392. "General Character of the Society." In no. 370, pp. 1–28.
393. "Geographical Setting" (with Simon D. Messing). In no. 370, pp. 29–34.
394. "Culture Groups." In no. 370, pp. 91–114.
395. "Social Structure: Introductory." In no. 370, pp. 131–35.
396. "The Town" (with Fahim I. Qubain). In no. 370, pp. 210–53.
397. "The Family." In no. 370, pp. 254–96.
398. "Social Values and Patterns of Living." In no. 370, pp. 297–323.
399. "Health and Sanitation" (with Simon D. Messing). In no. 370, p. 436–64.
400. "Public Welfare" (with Simon D. Messing). In no. 370, pp. 465–87.
401. "Attitudes and Reactions of the People." In no. 370, pp. 488–520.
402. (Book review) *The Origins of European Thought*, by R. B. Onians. *Jewish Social Studies* 18, no. 1 (January): 65–66.
403. (Book review) *The Clash of Cultures in Israel*, by A. Shumsky. *Judaism* (New York) 1, no. 3 (Summer): 283–84.
404. (Book review) *The Nazarene Gospel Restored*, by Robert Graves and Joshua Podro. *The Chicago Jewish Forum* 15, no. 1 (Fall): 66–67.

1957

405. JORDAN (Country Survey Series). New Haven, Conn.: Human Relations Area Files, 391 p.
406. ANNOTATED BIBLIOGRAPHY OF SYRIA, LEBANON, AND JORDAN. New Haven, Conn.: Human Relations Area Files, vii. 289 pp.
407. "Israel's Influence on American Jewry." *The Jewish Advocate* (Boston), January 31.
408. "Toynbee's Dependence on Spengler." *Judaism* (New York) 6, no. 2 (Spring): 134–41.

409. "La Influencia de Spengler sobre Toynbee." *Davar: Revista Literaria* (Buenos Aires) 73 (November–December): 31–42. (Spanish translation of no. 407.)
410. "The Danger of Levantinism in Israel." *Alliance Review* (New York) (December), pp. 17–20.
411. "Sociologists Study the Influence of Israel on American Jewry" (Summation of a conference at the Herzl Institute, 2 parts, mimeographed press release). 3 pp.; resp. 4 pp.
412. "Survey Conclusions On Israel Influence On American Jews." *The Canadian Zionist* (February).
413. (Review article) *Life in a Kibbutz*, by Murray Weingarten; *Kibbutz: Venture in Utopia*, by Melford E. Spiro; *Bridgehead: The Drama of Israel*, by Waldo Frank. *Social Problems* 5, no. 2 (Fall): 147–52.
414. (Book review) *Freedom and Control in Modern Society*, by Morroe Berger, Theodore Abel, and Charles H. Page. *The Chicago Jewish Forum* 15, no. 4 (Summer): 256.
415. (Book review) *This Is Israel*, by Theodore Heubener and Carl Hermann Voss. *American Anthropologist* 59 : 365–66.
416. (Book review) *The Bedouins: Manners and Customs*, by Touvia Ashkenazi. *The Middle East Journal* 11, no. 4 (Autumn): 451.
417. (Book review) *The Field of Yiddish*, by Uriel Weinreich. *Journal of American Folklore* 70, no. 278 (October–December): 369–70.
418. (Book review) *Cultural Assimilation and Tensions in Israel: International Social Science Bulletin 8:1*. *American Anthropologist* 59, no. 4 : 736–37.

1958

419. THE KINGDOM OF JORDAN. Princeton, N.J.: Princeton University Press, ix. 315 pp.
420. CURRENT JEWISH SOCIAL RESEARCH (An Annotated Bibliography). New York: The Theodor Herzl Foundation. 102 pp.
421. CULTURES IN CONFLICT. New York: Herzl Institute Pamphlets. 90 pp.
422. HERZL YEAR BOOK, vol. 1. Edited by R. P. New York: Herzl Press. 334 pp.
423. "Herzl's Sinai Project: A Documentary Record," in no. 422, pp. 107–44.
424. "The Changing Face of Israel: I. The People." *Congress Weekly* (New York) May 12, pp. 18–20.
425. "El Peligro del Levantinismo en Israel." *Revista de la Alliance* (New York) (October), pp. 10–13. (Spanish translation of no. 410).
426. (Book review) *An Annotated Bibliography of Books and Periodical in English Dealing with Human Relations in the Arab States of the Middle East*, by Jean T. Burke. *American Anthropologist* 60 : 184.
427. (Book review) *The Last Migration*, by Vincent Cronin. *Middle Eastern Affairs* (August–September), pp. 275–76.
428. (Book review) *The Nature of Culture*, by A. L. Kroeber. *The Chicago Jewish Forum* (Fall) p. 66.
429. (Book review) *Egypt*, by George L. Harris. *American Anthropologist* 60, no. 4 : 768–69.

1959

430. SEX AND FAMILY IN THE BIBLE AND THE MIDDLE EAST. New York: Doubleday. 282 pp.
431. HERZL YEAR BOOK: ESSAYS IN ZIONIST HISTORY AND THOUGHT. vol. 2. Edited by R. P. New York: Herzl Press. 253 pp.

432. Nationalism in Jordan." *Current History* (February), pp. 77–80.
433. "Summation" of Conference on the Impact of Israel on the American Jewish Community." *Jewish Social Studies* 21, no. 1:86.
434. (Book review) *Land Reform and Development in the Middle East*, by Doreen Warriner. *American Sociological Review*,24, no. 1 (February):119.
435. (Book review) *Iraq: Its People, Its Society, Its Culture*, by George L. Harris; *Iraq's People and Resources*, by Doris Goodrich Adams. *American Sociological Review* 24, no. 6 (December):922–23.
436. (Book review) *An Annotated Research Bibliography of Studies in Arabic, English and French of the Fellah of the Egyptian Nile*, by Lyman H. Coult. *American Anthropologist* (December), p. 1124.

1960

437. FAMILY, LOVE AND THE BIBLE. London: McGibbon & Kee. 255 pp. (British edition of no. 430.)
438. HERZL YEAR BOOK. vol. 3. Edited by R. P. New York: The Herzl Press. 280 pp.
439. THE COMPLETE DIARIES OF THEODOR HERZL. 5 vols. Translated by Harry Zohn. Edited by R. P. New York: Herzl Press and Thomas Yoseloff. 1961 pp.
440. STUDIES IN BIBLICAL AND JEWISH FOLKLORE. Edited by R. P., Francis Lee Utley, and Dov Noy. Bloomington: Indiana University Press. 374 pp.
441. "Jewish Folklore and Jewish Tradition." In no. 440, pp. 11–24.
442. "Sephardi Folklore." In Herzl Institute Pamphlets, no. 15, pp. 22–36.
443. "Jordan." In *Worldmark Encyclopedia of Nations*. New York: Worldmark and Harpers. Pp. 556–62.
444. "The Riots in Wadi Salib." *Midstream* (New York) 6, no. 1 (Winter):5–14.
445. "What the Bible Teaches About Aging." *Jewish Heritage* (Summer), pp. 17–20.
446. "Kosher." *Encyclopaedia Americana*, 16:531.
447. "Middle East: 2. The People." Ibid., 19:38e–38h.
448. (Book review) *Quelques Manifestations de l'esprit populaire dans les juiveries du Sud-Marocain*, by Pierre Flamand, *Middle Eastern Affairs* (June–July), p. 197.
449. (Book review) *The Antiquities of Jordan*, by G. Lankaster Harding. *The Muslim World* (October, pp. 326–27.
450. (Book review) *The Jewish People: A Biological History*, by Harry L. Shapiro. *Publications of the American Jewish Historical Society* 50, no. 2 (December):146–47.
451. "Herzl's Wife Julie," by Edith Patai. Translated from the Hungarian by R. P. *The American Zionist* (New York) (October–November), pp. 7–8 (December), pp. 8, 10.

1961

452. SEX AND FAMILY IN THE BIBLE AND THE MIDDLE EAST. New York: Doubleday Dolphin Books, 272 p. (Paperback edition of no. 430.)
453. CULTURES IN CONFLICT. New York: Herzl Press. 72 pp. (2d, enlarged edition of no. 421.)
454. "Education and Transculturation." In *The Quest for Creative Jewish Living*. Zionist Organization of America Pamphlet (July), pp. 45–48.
455. "A Cultural Monument for Hungarian Jewry." In *Tájékoztató* (Bulletin of the World Federation of Hungarian Jews) (New York), (July).
456. (Book review) *Middle East Diary*, by Col. Richard Meinertzhagen. *The Chicago Jewish Forum* (Spring), pp. 245–46.
457. (Book review) *Fatima and Her Sisters*, by Dorothy Van Ess. *The Chicago Jewish Forum* (Summer), p. 338.

458. (Book review) *Tribes of the Sahara,* by Lloyd Cabot Briggs. *Midstream* (Summer), pp. 101–4.
459. (Book review) *Challenge in the Middle East,* by Harry B. Ellis. *The Chicago Jewish Forum.* (Fall).
460. (Book review) *Anthropology and Folk Religion,* by Charles Leslie. Ibid. (Winter), p. 173.
461. "Scholar Cautions Wait-and-See About Significance of B.C. Synagogue Find" (letter to the editor). *The National Jewish Post and Opinion,* November 3.

1962

462. GOLDEN RIVER TO GOLDEN ROAD: SOCIETY, CULTURE AND CHANGE IN THE MIDDLE EAST. Philadelphia; University of Pennsylvania Press. 422 pp.
463. SITTE UND SIPPE IN BIBEL UND ORIENT. Frankfurt a. M.: Ner Tamid Verlag. 283 pp. (German translation of no. 430.)
464. HERZL YEAR BOOK: ESSAYS IN ZIONIST HISTORY AND THOUGHT. vol. 4. Edited by R. P. New York: Herzl Press, 1961–62. 396 pp.
465. "The Chuetas of Majorca." *Midstream* (Spring), pp. 59–68.
466. "The Ritual Approach to Hebrew-African Culture Contact." *Jewish Social Studies* (April), pp. 86–96.
467. "Myths of the Jews." *Jewish Heritage* (New York), (Summer), pp. 36–39.
468. "Bedouin." In *Encyclopaedia Britannica,* p. 368.
469. "Sephardim, Ashkenazim, and Oriental Jews." Ibid. p. 334.
470. (Book review) *Women and the New East,* by Ruth Frances Woodsmall. *The Chicago Jewish Forum* (Spring), p. 229.
471. (Book review) *Government and Politics in Israel,* by Oscar Kraines. *The Chicago Jewish Forum* (Summer), p. 328.

1963

472. HERZL YEAR BOOK: ESSAYS IN ZIONIST HISTORY AND THOUGHT. vol. 5. New York: Edited by R. P., Herzl Press. 384 pp.
473. "American Cultural Influences on Israel." In *In the Time of Harvest: Essays in Honor of Abba Hillel Silver.* New York: Macmillan. Pp. 270–83.
474. "Some Hebrew Myths and Legends" (with Robert Graves). *Encounter* (London), (February), pp. 3–18.
475. "Some Hebrew Myths and Legends II" (with Robert Graves). Ibid. (March), pp. 12–18.
476. "The Chuetas of Majorca," *Le Judaisme Sephardi* (London), (June), pp. 1125–30, 1133.
477. (Book review) *The American Bridge to the Israel Commonwealth,* by Bernard A. Rosenblatt. *Jewish Social Studies,* 25, no. 1 (January):94.
478. (Book review) *Animal and Man in Bible Lands,* by F. S. Bodenheimer. Ibid. 25 (July):207.

1964

479. HEBREW MYTHS: THE BOOK OF GENESIS (with Robert Graves). New York: Doubleday. 311 pp.
480. HEBREW MYTHS: THE BOOK OF GENESIS (with Robert Graves). London: Cassell. 311 pp. British edition of no. 479.
481. "Anusim fun Persie zurikgekert zum Yidishen Gloyben." *Unzer Wort* (Paris), January 15 and 16.

482. "Di Anusim in Persie vos hobn zikh efntlikh zurikgekert zum idishn gloybn." *El Diario Israelita*, (Buenos Aires), January 28.
483. "Indulco and Mumia." *Journal of American Folklore* (January–March), pp. 3–11.
484. "Matronit: The Goddess of the Kabbala." *History of Religions* (Summer), pp. 53–68.
485. "Lilith." *Journal of American Folklore*, 77, no. 306 (October–December): 295–314.
486. "The Shekhina." *Journal of Religion* 44, no. 4 (October): 275–88.
487. "What Is Hebrew Mythology?" *Transactions of the New York Academy of Sciences*, 2d ser., 27, no. 1 (November: 73–81.
488. "How and Why Judaism Survived in Meshhed?" *Alliance Review* (New York), (Winter), pp. 6–9.
489. News from the Herzl Press." *Herzl Institute Bulletin*. (New York), December 20, p. 6.
490. (Book review) *The Peoples of Israel*, by Howard M. Sachar. *Jewish Social Studies*, 26, no. 2 (April): 123–34.
491. (Book review) *My Friend Musa*, by Edwin Samuel. *Jewish Frontier*, (July), pp. 2425.

1965

492. HERZL YEAR BOOK: ESSAYS IN ZIONIST HISTORY AND THOUGHT. vol. 6, edited by R. P. New York: Herzl Press, 1964–65. 371 pp.
493. "The Iglesia de Dios and Zionism." In no. 492 pp. 303–10.
494. "The Goddess Asherah." *Journal of Near Eastern Studies*, (January–April), pp. 37–52.
495. "The Structure of Endogamous Unilineal Descent Groups." *Southwestern Journal of Anthropology* 21, no. 4 (Winter): 325–50.
496. "Venta Prieta Revisited." *Midstream* (March), pp. 79–92.
497. "HaLeda baMinhag haᶜAmami: Mehqar Folqloristi" ("Birth in Popular Custom: A Study in Folklore"). *Talpioth* 9, nos. 1–2 (New York, Kislev): 238–60. (Conclusion of nos. 331 and 360.)
498. "Cómo y porqué sobrevivió el Judaísmo en Meshhed?" *Revista de la Alliance* (New York), (July), pp. 21–24. (Spanish translation of no. 488.)
499. "Hoe het jodendom in Mesjed bleef bestaan." *Nieuw Israelitisch Weekblad* (Amsterdam), Jan. 14. (Dutch translation of no. 488.)
500. "Jewish Folklore and Jewish Tradition." In *A Folklore Reader*. Edited by Kenneth and Mary Clarke. Pp. 217–30. (Reprint of no. 441.)
501. "Aging—The Biblical View." *Jewish Heritage Reader*. Pp. 142–46. (Reprint of no. 445.)
502. "Zum Wesen der hebräischen Mythologie." *Paideuma: Mitteilungen zur Kulturkunde*, Wiesbaden, 11:58–67. (German translation of no. 487 by Harry Zohn.)
503. "The Dynamics of Westernization in the Middle East." In *The Contemporary Middle East: Tradition and Innovation*, edited by Benjamin Rivlin and Joseph S. Szyliowicz. Pp. 120–31. (Abridged reprint of no. 362.)

1966

504. HEBREW MYTHS: THE BOOK OF GENESIS (with Robert Graves). New York: McGraw-Hill. 311 pp. (Paperback reprint of no. 479.)
505. MYTH AND LEGEND OF ANCIENT ISRAEL, by Angelo S. Rappoport. With an Introduction and additional notes by R. P. 3 vols. New York: Ktav Publ. House. 363, 399, and 296 pp.

506. (Book review) *Muslim Death and Burial,* by Hilma Granqvist. *The Muslim World,* pp. 213–15.
507. (Book review) *Heroes and Gods,* by Moses Hadas and Morton Smith. *Jewish Frontier* (May), pp. 27–28.

1967

508. THE HEBREW GODDESS. New York: Ktav Publishing House, 349 pp.
509. WOMEN IN THE MODERN WORLD. Edited and with an introduction by R. P. New York: Free Press. 519 pp.
510. GOLDEN RIVER TO GOLDEN ROAD: SOCIETY, CULTURE AND CHANGE IN THE MIDDLE EAST. Philadelphia: University of Pennsylvania Press. 461 pp. (2d, enlarged edition of no. 462.)
511. MAN AND TEMPLE IN ANCIENT JEWISH MYTH AND RITUAL. New York: Ktav Publishing House. 247 pp. (2d, enlarged edition of no. 270.)
512. MITOSIM ʿIVRIM. Tel Aviv: Massada. 293 pp. (Hebrew translation of no. 479.)
513. L'AMOUR ET LE COUPLE AUX TEMPS BIBLIQUES. Paris: Mame. 274 pp. (French translation of no. 430.)
514. "Abba mari." In *Encyclopedia Americana* 1:8.
515. "Akiba ben Joseph." Ibid., 1:434.
516. "Anan ben David." Ibid., 1:776.
517. "Ark." Ibid., 2:311.
518. "Ashi." Ibid., 2:436.
519. "Ashkenazim." Ibid., 2:436.
520. "Asmodeus." Ibid., 2:513.
521. "Av." Ibid., 2:853.
522. "Aviv." Ibid., 2:877.
523. "Baal Shem Tov." Ibid., 3:3.
524. "Bar Kokhba." Ibid., 3:215.
525. "Bar Mitzvah." Ibid., 3:215.
526. "Bezalel." Ibid., 3:638.
527. (Book review) *The Invisibles,* by Francis Huxley; *Religion and Politics in Haiti,* by Harold Courlander and Rémy Bastien; *Parapsychology* (September), pp. 195–98.
528. (Book review) *Religion and Politics in Haiti,* by Harold Courlander, Ibid.

1968

529. "Cain." In *Encyclopedia Americana,* 5:143.
530. "Canaan." Ibid., 5:311.
531. "Cantor." Ibid., 5:577.
532. "Carmel, Mount." Ibid., 5:674.
533. "Caro, Joseph." Ibid., 5:692.
534. "Chemosh." Ibid., 6:391.
535. "Circumcision." Ibid., 6:735.
536. "Cities of Refuge." Ibid., 6:742.
537. "Letter to the Editor." *Middle East Journal* 22, no. 4 (Autumn):567–68.

1969

538. GOLDEN RIVER TO GOLDEN ROAD: SOCIETY, CULTURE AND CHANGE IN THE MIDDLE EAST. Philadelphia: University of Pennsylvania Press. 560 pp. (3d, enlarged edition of nos. 462 and 511.)
539. I MITI HEBRAICI. Milan: Longanesi. 391 pp. (Italian translation of no. 479.)

540. HEBREJSKI MITOVI. Zagreb: Maprijid. 327 pp. (Croatian translation of no. 479.)
541. HÉBER MITOSZOK. Budapest: Gondolat. 295 pp. (Hungarian translation of no. 479.)
542. LOS MITOS HEBREOS. Buenos Aires: Losada. 382 pp. (Spanish translation of no. 479.)
543. "Creation." In *Encyclopedia Americana*, 8:163–65.
544. "Haggadah." Ibid., 13:678.
545. "Israel, Ancient." Ibid., 15:538–39.
546. "Jacob." Ibid., 15:655.
547. "Jaffa." Ibid., 15:664.
548. "Jewish Calendar." Ibid., 16:59.

1970

549. ISRAEL BETWEEN EAST AND WEST: A STUDY IN HUMAN RELATIONS. Westport, Conn.: Greenwood Press. 394 pp. (2d, enlarged edition of no. 330.)
550. HERZL YEAR BOOK: ESSAYS IN ZIONIST HISTORY AND THOUGHT. vol. 5. Freeport, N.Y.: Books for Libraries Press. 384 pp. (Reprint of no. 471.)
551. "Aging." *Jewish Affairs* (November), pp. 27–29.
552. "Anthropology." In Irving A. Falk, ed., *Prophecy for the Year 2,000*. New York: Julian Messner. Pp. 49–51.
553. "Gog and Magog." *Encyclopedia Americana*, 13:6.
554. "Goliath." Ibid., 13:61.
555. "Herod the Great." Ibid., 14:146.
556. "Isaac." Ibid., 15:481.
557. "Ishmael." Ibid., 15:489.
558. "The Middle East As a Culture Area." In *Readings in Arab Middle Eastern Societies and Cultures*, edited by Abdulla M. Lutfiyya and Charles W. Churchill. The Hague: Mouton. Pp. 187–204. (Reprint of no. 322.)
559. "The Dynamics of Westernization in the Middle East." In ibid., pp. 235–51. (Reprint of no. 362.)
560. "Cousin Right in Middle Eastern Marriage." In ibid., pp. 535–53. (Reprint of no. 361.)
561. "Familism and Socialization." In ibid., pp. 578–82. (Selections from no. 462.)
562. "Seger's Review of *The Hebrew Goddess:* Was She 'Orthodox' or 'Legitimate' in Hebrew-Jewish Religion?/ A Comment." *American Anthropologist* 72:205–7.
563. (Book review) *The Sacred Mushroom and the Cross*, by John M. Allegro. *Saturday Review of Literature*, September 10, pp. 42–44.
564. (Book review) *Shabbat u-Mo^cade Yisrael*, by Haim Leshem. *Der Islam* 46:142.

1971

565. TENTS OF JACOB: THE DIASPORA YESTERDAY AND TODAY. Englewood Cliffs, N.J.: Prentice-Hall. 464 pp.
566. HERZL YEAR BOOK: ESSAYS IN ZIONIST HISTORY AND THOUGHT. vol. 7. Edited by R. P. New York: Herzl Press. 446 pp.
567. ENCYCLOPEDIA OF ZIONISM AND ISRAEL. Edited by R. P. 2 vols. New York: Herzl Press and McGraw-Hill. 1292 pp.
568. SOCIETY, CULTURE AND CHANGE IN THE MIDDLE EAST. Philadelphia: University of Pennsylvania Press. 560 pp. (Paperback reprint of no. 538.)
569. "Safed in the Sixteenth Century." *Alliance Review* (New York), (Spring), pp. 15–16.
570. "Zekher LItziat Mitzrayim." *HaDoar* (New York), April 9.

571. "Jews As a Race." In *Encyclopaedia Britannica*, pp. 1054–55.
572. "Synagogue," in *Encyclopedia Americana*, 26 : 178–79.
573. "Szold, Henrietta." Ibid., 26 : 203.
574. "Preface." In no. 567, pp. x–xii.
575. "Aliya." In no. 567, p. 21.
576. "Anglo-American Committee of Inquiry." In no. 567, pp. 4–42 (with J. Leftwich).
577. "Ashkenazim." In no. 567, pp. 85–86.
578. "Communities in Israel." In no. 567, pp. 204–5.
579. "Conquest of the Soil." In no. 567, p. 214.
580. "Diaspora." In no. 567, pp. 253–54.
581. "Ethnic Groups and Problems in Israel." In no. 567, pp. 304–7.
582. "Haskala." In no. 567, p. 466.
583. "Israel, History of: Prehistory." In no. 567, p. 555.
584. "Moshava." In no. 567, pp. 806–7.
585. "Oriental Jews." In no. 567, p. 864.
586. "Sephardim." In no. 567, pp. 1019–20.
587. "Truman, Harry S." In no. 567, pp. 1132–35.
588. "Zionism, History of." In no. 567, pp. 1262–71.
589. Various unsigned entries, mostly biographies. In no. 567.
590. (Book review) *Die Šammar-Ğerba: Beduinen im Übergang vom Nomadismus zur Sesshaftigket*, by Lothar Stein. *American Anthropologist* 73 (August) : 849–50.
591. (Book review) *Az Agrárkultusz Kutatása a Magyar és az Európai folklórban*, by Zoltán Ujváry. Ibid. 73, no. 2 : 396–98.
592. (Book review) *Social Mobility in Israel*, by Moshe Lissak. *Jewish Social Studies* 23 (April–July) : 2–3.

1972

593. MYTH AND MODERN MAN. Englewood Cliffs, N.J.: Prentice-Hall. 359 pp.
594. "Africa and Israel: Quiet Partners in the Third World," *Tuesday Magazine* (November), pp. 13–14, 37.
595. "Reply to Urrutia." *American Anthropologist* 74, no. 6 6 : 1598–99.
596. (Book review) *Sociology of the Middle East*, by C. A. O. Van Nieuwenhuijze. Ibid. 74 : 1047–50.

1973

597. THE ARAB MIND. New York: Charles Scribner's Sons. 376 pp.
598. "Western and Oriental Culture in Israel." In *Israel: Social Structure and Change*, edited by M. Curtis and M. S. Chertoff. Pp. 307–12.
599. "Judaism." In *The Americana Annual*, p. 581.
600. "The 'Sephardic' Pronunciation of Hebrew." *Alliance Review* (Fall), pp. 11–14.
601. (Book review) *Understanding the Middle East*, by Joe Pierce. *American Anthropologist* 65 no. 4 : 971.
602. (Book review) *The Spiritual Background of Early Islam: Studies in Ancient Arab Concepts*, by M. M. Bravmann. Ibid. (December), pp. 1871–72.

1974

603. ARABEN. Malmos, Sweden: Bernces. 383 pp. (Swedish Translation of no. 597.)
604. O MITO E O HOMEM MODERNO. Sao Paulo, Brazil: Cultrix. 310 pp. (Portuguese translation of no. 593.)

605. "Ius Primae Noctis." In *Folkore Research Center Studies, IV: Studies in Marriage Customs,* edited by Issachar Ben-Ami and Dov Noy (Jerusalem), pp. 177–80.
606. "History in the Bible" (letter to the editor). *Midstream* 20, no. 8 (October): 7–8.
607. (Book review) *The Middle East: A Political and Economic Survey.* 4th ed. *Midstream* (May), pp. 81–83.

1975

608. THE MYTH OF THE JEWISH RACE (with Jennifer Patai Wing). New York: Charles Scribner's Sons. 350 pp.
609. "Sephardi World View and Haskala." *Alliance Review* (Fall), pp. 16–20.
610. "Comments." In *The New World Balance and Peace in the Middle East,* edited by Seymour Maxwell Finger. Pp. 62–63.
611 "Abraham." In *Encyclopedia Americana,* 1:45.

1976

612. THE ARAB MIND. New York: Scribner's, xiii. 376 pp. (Paperback edition of no. 597, with a new introduction.)
613. "The Goddess Cult in Hebrew-Jewish Religion." In *World Anthropology: The Realm of the Extra-Human,* edited by A. Bharati. The Hague: Mouton. Pp. 197–210.
614. "Ethnohistory and Inner History." *Jewish Quarterly Review,* n.s. 47, no. 1 (July): 1–15.
615. "Pilgrimage." In *Encyclopedia Americana* 22:84–86.
616. "Western Historical Writing." Ibid. 14:229.
617. (Review article) "Marx Among the Muslims" (on *Islam and Capitalism,* by Maxime Rodinson). *Midstream* (November), pp. 74–78.
618. (Book review) *Changing Family Patterns in the Arab East,* by Edwin T. Prothro and Lutfy N. Diab. *American Anthropologist* 78, no. 3 (September): 687–88.
619. (Book review) *Legends of Judea and Samaria,* by Zev Vilnay. *Jewish Bookland* (October), p. 7.

1977

620. KOREGA ARABU: SONO MINZOKU SEI TO SHINLI NO NAZO (This Is the Arab: The Mysteries of His Character and His Philosophy). Tokyo:PHP International. 268 pp. (Japanese translation of no. 597.)
621. "Arabu Ni Okeru No Lioiki" (The Concept of Sex Among the Arabs). *PHP International Journal* 6:54–59. (Japanese translation of a chapter from no. 597.)
622. (Book review) *Mimekor Yisrael: Classical Jewish Folktales . . .* by Micha Joseph Bin Gorion. *Yiddish: A Quarterly Journal Devoted to Yiddish* 2, no. 4 (Summer): 87–90.
623. (Book review) *A History of Israel,* by Howard M. Sachar. *The American Historical Review* (Bloomington, Ind.), (June), pp. 707–8.
624. (Book review) *Folklór és tárgytörténet,* by Sándor Scheiber. *Journal of American Folklore* 90, no 357 (July–September): 362.
625. (Review article) "Israel's Zealots?" (On *Perpetual Dilemma: Jewish Religion in the Jewish State,* by S. Z. Abramov.) *Midstream* 23, no. 10 (December): 63–70.

1978

626. THE JEWISH MIND. New York: Charles Scribner's Sons. 624 pp.
627. THE HEBREW GODDESS. New York: Avon Books. 342 pp. (Enlarged, paperback edition of 509.)
628. "The Culture Areas of the Middle East." In *World Anthropology: The Nomadic Alternative*, edited by W. Weissleder. The Hague: Mouton. Pp. 3–39.
629. "Exorcism and Xenoglossia Among the Safed Kabbalists." *Journal of American Folklore*, pp. 823–33.
630. "The Breakthrough into Science." *Alliance Review* (Fall), pp. 28–31.
631. "Comments" on Paul Diener and Eugene E. Robkin, "Ecology, Evolution and the Search for Cultural Origins: The Question of Islamic Pig Prohibition." *Current Anthropology* 19, no. 3 (September):518–21.
632. (Book review) *Tradition and Politics: The Religious Parties of Israel*, by Gary S. Schiff. *The American Historical Review* (April), pp. 494–95.
633. (Book review) *Germany, Turkey and Zionism*, by Isaiah Friedman. Ibid. (December), p. 1230.

1979

634. THE MESSIAH TEXTS. Detroit: Wayne State University Press, liii. 373 pp.
635. THE MESSIAH TEXTS. New York: Avon Books. (Paperback edition of no. 634.)
636. "Islam, Arabs, Iranians. I. Unraveling the Enigma of Shiʿite Fanaticism." Released December 12 by the North American Newspaper Alliance, and published in numerous daily papers.
637. "Islam, Arabs, Iranians. II. I, My Cousins Against the World—Why the Arab People hate the West?" (Part II of the above.)
638. "Islam, Arabs, Iranians. III. Second Arab Renaissance: Which Way Will It Turn?" (Part III of the above.)
639. "HaHinnukh haʿIvri baʿAdat Anuse Meshhed." In ʿEdot Yisrael, edited by Avraham Stahl. vol. 2. Tel Aviv: ʿAm ʿOved. Pp. 251–56. (Partial reprint of no. 244.)
640. (Review essay) "The Orientalist Conspiracy" (on *Orientalism* by Edward Said). *Midstream* 29, no. 9 (November):62–66.
641. (Book review) *Magyar Néprajzi Lexikon*. Edited by Gyula Ortutay. vol. 1. *Journal of American Folklore* 92, no. 365 (July–September):352–55.
642. (Book review) *Two Rothschilds and the Land of Israel*, by Simon Schama. *The American Historical Review* (December), p. 1440.
643. (Book review) *Censorship and Freedom of Expression in Jewish History*, by Moshe Carmilly-Weinberger. *Jewish Social Studies* 41, no. 1 (Winter):89–90.

1980

644. GATES TO THE OLD CITY. New York: Avon Books, li. 807 pp. (Paperback.)
645. THE JEWISH MIND. New York: Charles Scribner's Sons. 624 pp. (Paperback reprint of no. 626.)
646. I MITI HEBRAICI (with Robert Graves). Milan: Longanesi. 391 pp. (New edition of no. 539, Italian translation of no. 479.)
647. "The Love Factor in a Hebrew-Arabic Conjuration," *The Jewish Quarterly Review* n.s. 70, no. 4:239–53.
648. "Commentary" on "Appropriating Tradition" by Jude P. Dougherty. In *The Responsibility of the Academic Community in the Search for Absolute Values, Proceed-*

ings of the Eighth International Conference on the Unity of Sciences. New York: International Cultural Foundation Press, 1:301–4.

649. "Enigma del fanatismo shi'ita." *El Comercio* (Quito, Ecuador), January 18, p. A-5. (Spanish translation of no. 636.)

650. "Odio Arabe a occidente." Ibid. January 19, p. A-5 (Spanish translation of no. 637.)

651. "Secundo renacimiento árabe." Ibid. January 20, p. A-5 (Spanish translation of no. 638.)

652. "Culture of the Middle East No Longer 'Immutable.'" *The Providence Journal*, October 19, p. B-5.

1981

653. THE VANISHED WORLDS OF JEWRY. London: Weidenfeld and Nicolson, and New York: Macmillan Publ. Co. 192 pp. (Illustrated.)

654. GATES TO THE OLD CITY. Detroit, Mich.: Wayne State University Press, li. 807 pp. Hardcover edition of no. 644.

655. "Vanished Worlds of Jewry: Yemen, Lithuania." *Jewish Chronicle* (London), January 2, pp. 18–19. (Two chapters from no. 653.)

656. "And Yet There Is a Tradition of Beauty and Nobility in Iran." Released on February 2 by the Independent News Alliance, New York, and published in numerous daily papers.

657. "Bloodshed in Islam." Released on October 15 by the Independent News Alliance, New York, and published in numerous daily papers.

658. (Book review) A. B. Yehoshua, *Between Right and Right. Judaica Book News* (New York) vol. 12, no. 1 (Fall-Winter):31.

Part II

FOLKLORE AND LITERATURE

The Idea of Folklore: An Essay

DAN BEN-AMOS

The concept of folklore emerged in Europe midway in the nineteenth century. Originally it connoted tradition, ancient customs, and surviving festivals, old ditties and dateless ballads, archaic myths, legends and fables, and timeless tales and proverbs. As these narratives rarely stood the tests of common sense and experience, folklore also implied irrationality: beliefs in ghosts and demons, fairies and goblins, sprites and spirits; it referred to credence in omens, amulets, and talismans. From the perspectives of the urbane literati, who conceived the idea of folklore, these two attributes of traditionalism and irrationality could pertain only to peasant or primitive societies. Hence they attributed to folklore a third quality: rurality. The countryside and the open space of wilderness were the proper breeding grounds for folklore. Man's close contact with nature in villages and hunting bands was considered the ultimate source of his myth and poetry. As outgrowth of human experience with nature, folklore itself was thought to be a natural expression of man, before city, commerce, civilization, and culture contaminated the purity of his life.

This triad of attributes—traditionalism, irrationality, and rurality—was to dominate the concept of folklore for many years to come; often it still does. It provided standards for inclusion or exclusion of stories, songs, and sayings in terms of the domain of folklore proper. Those which possessed at least one of these qualities were christened folktales, folksongs, riddles, and folk sayings; those which had none were reprovingly rejected.

In their turn, these three terms of meaning generated additional attributes, which together constituted the sense of the concept of folklore in common use, in print and in speech. The cloak of tradition concealed the identity of those who authored folktales, ballads, and proverbs. Compounding matters, the transmission from generation to generation obscured their origin. Thus by default and not by merit, anonymity became an earmark of folklore. Indigenous prose or poetry became part of folklore

57

only after the memory of their creator had been erased. Then the seal of anonymity sanctioned tradition as genuine. It legitimized songs and tales as integral parts of the cultural heritage of society.

Yet the anonymity of folk narratives, rhymes, and riddles hardly solved the enigma of origin. The responsibility for authorship had to be assigned to some creator, be he divine or human. So in the absence of any individual who could justifiably and willingly claim paternity of myths and legends, the entire community was held accountable for them. After all, the existing evidence appeared to support such an allegation. Narrators and singers often attribute their tales and songs not to a single individual but to the collective tradition of the community. Even in the exceptional cases in which they indeed claimed authorship, scholarship succeeded in unveiling analogues in their own and other traditions. Such parallels cast doubt upon any contention for originality and sustained the assertion of the communality of folklore.

In fact, communality has become a central attribute, rivaled only by "tradition" in the formulation of the concept of folklore. There was no room in folklore for private tales and poems. Any expression had to pass through the sieve of communal approval before it could be considered folklore. But the identification of the processes that would justify the attribution of communality to any story or song proved to be rather complex, even logically thorny. Were folktales and folksongs only in the communal domain, free to all to speak and sing? Or should these property rights have been limited to the moment of origin, thus regarding folk expressions as a communal creation, and solving along the way the question of authorship? Furthermore, how does the community foster its bond between people and their folklore, and exactly which of its aspects relate to the society at large; the themes, the language, the forms, or the particular tales, songs, and proverbs? These and other issues were the whetstones that sharpened debates that were crucial to the idea of folklore. From various viewpoints the attribute of communality implied communal creation, recreation, or, simply, expression.

Communal creation involved some anachronistic reasoning: the tales, songs, and sayings that the community shared together were also created together. Such an explanation might have solved the problem of authorship, but inferring origins from results might be valid only biologically and not logically. In the cultural and social spheres, the mode of existence could not necessarily attest to the genesis of forms. Historical processes such as diffusion of themes, dissemination of ideas, and imitation of manners do affect the state and nature of folklore. Consequently, collective knowledge of tales and songs could not be an unequivocal indicator of creation. The notion of communal recreation countered this dilemma. It prolonged the moment of origin over historical periods, and conceived of the formation of songs, for example, not in a single exhilarating burst of poetic creativity, but through repetitive recitations of singers on communal occasions. Each improvised and embellished the text, yet conformed to the communal aesthetic and ethical standards. Such an interpretation of the communality of folklore also allowed the viewing of folk prose and poetry as expressions of social fears and wishes, ideals and values. Folklore reflected the collective experience of society and was the mirror of itself that the community constantly faced.

Paradoxically, intertwined with the attribute of communality is the idea that folklore is universal. While folksongs and tales might be forged within a particular community and express its unique experience, they also transcend the boundaries that language and space impose, and emerge in diverse groups and remote countries, still maintaining sameness to a large extent. The attribute of universality appeared to be both formal and thematic. All peoples distinguish poetry from prose, pithy sayings from epic poems; all construct narratives, fictional or historical, stringing events in sequences; and all can combine music and movement with words, and sing and dance to their heart's content. These are inherent abilities of humanity.

In that sense, folklore withstood the test that language failed. While modern discoveries about animals clearly demonstrate that some master the rudiments of language communication (whales sing), so far neither monkeys nor rats have been caught telling legends to their infants. But the universality of folklore was not confined to the formal basis alone. The themes, the metaphors, and the subjects of stories, songs, and sayings of peoples who lived in countries remote from each other, and who spoke completely unrelated languages, exhibited a high degree of similarity that history could not explain. Migrations and contacts in war and peace could not account for the common features that the tales and poems of native Australians, Africans, and Americans shared. All include stories of gods, of creation, and of destruction; all tell about marvelous events, beings, and places; and all dwell upon the supernatural, the extraordinary, the absolute, and the incongruous. Their metaphors relate to nature, beliefs, and societies, and their songs celebrate victories and lament failures in the struggle for survival. Often similarities are even more striking as the same narrative episodes and verbal or visual images appear in the expressions of unrelated peoples.

The dual attributes of universality and communality were locked together and created an apparent paradox in the idea of folklore, converging the general and the particular into a single concept. Evidence supported both. The themes and forms of folklore appeared to be universal, yet no other expression was so imbued with regional, local, and cultural references, meanings, and symbols. There were two ways to resolve this contradiction. First, universality and communality could be viewed not as contradictory but as complementary attributes. The relations that govern folklore are universal; the references to culture and history are specific. The principles of distinctiveness in form and in theme—the unusual, the incongruous, and conversely, the absolutely harmonious are universal— but the languages, the social and historical experiences, the religious systems, and the moral values that make up the substance of the folklore of respective societies are communal. Second, these two attributes could be historically related, one preceding the other. If folklore was communal at first, later its properties achieved universality by historical processes, such as diffusion of themes and population contacts through migration, trade, or warfare. Such an assumption would imply a single source, or place and time of origin, from which folklore features were universally diffused. But if folklore were universal first, then its basic characteristic forms and themes should have been formulated prior to any historical and evolutionary developments. In such case, folklore embodies the original homogeneity of the culture of man before diversity, following the Tower of Babel, struck. Consequently, folklore also possesses the attribute of primariness, an attribute that made the impact of folklore on modern thought and art so powerful.

The mythology of all nations does not only tell about, but is, the dawn of humanity. It incarnates the commonality in all communities and voices the primordial expression of man. In its fundamental forms folklore emerged before human diversity developed and thus it embodies the most rudimentary forms of verbal and visual symbols. The primariness of folklore had historical and evolutionary aspects. Historically, folklore allegedly dated back to time immemorial, and hence, at its original stage, preceded any known recorded history. When man hunted and gathered his food, or even when he began to farm the land and to herd his cattle, but had not as yet quite mastered writing, he was already narrating tales and singing songs. The folklore of the world, it was hence assumed, abounds with symbols, themes, and metaphors that pertain to the beginning of human civilization, and could shed light on the dark corners of history that no other document could illuminate. The forms of folklore were regarded as the cores at the heart of artistic forms. They were the primitive, crude expressions out of which the literary, visual, and musical cultural heritage of the peoples of the world has emerged. Folklore comprised the symbolic forms at the base of the complex expressions of literate societies.

Naturally, folklore in its primary stage could not be accessible to modern man and would have been completely lost had it not been for the attempt to recapture tales and songs as they existed in nonliterate societies, that is, as they were told and sung orally without recourse to any written devices to aid in memorization and transmission of texts. No one claims that the current prose and poetry of peasants and nonliterate culture reflect human expression in its archaic, primordial form. Repeated recitations, loss of memorization, creative improvisation, and more general historical processes of cultural contacts and technical evolution contributed to alterations in both the particular themes and the general tenor of folklore. However, in spite of the recognition of such historical factors, a basic assumption in folklore is that those stories, songs, and sayings continued to exist in the same way their ancient predecessors did, that is, in oral performance, and that they were transmitted from generation to generation only orally, as they were before the advance of literacy. Hence the oral nature of folklore became one of its crucial attributes, the touchstone of authenticity and originality. As long as stories, songs, and proverbs conformed with the principle of oral circulation and transmission, they qualified as "pure" folklore, but when, alas, somewhere along the line they came in contact with written texts, they were branded contaminated. No longer could they represent the primary expression of man.

The attributes of traditionalism, irrationality, and rurality; anonymity, communality, and universality; primacy and oral circulation became consolidated in the idea of folklore. They cluster, implying one another, and suggesting the existence of intrinsic relations between them. The occurrence of one quality in a song or tale often implies most of the others. A peasant song, for example, was considered as having long-standing tradition in the community. The possibility that it might be a recent composition, or borrowed from some external source such as an urban center, would have denied the song its folkloric nature and contradicted the basic assumptions held about it. Being rural, other attributes similarly follow: the author is anonymous, and the song belongs to the cultural heritage of the entire community. Most likely, as poetry, it would express deep-seated emotions or uncontrolled desires, which in turn project universal primary human qualities, unaffected by civilization. Thus, combined in a hypothetical song, these attributes convey the meaning of the concept of folklore.

Consequently, these attributes, which are only descriptive and interpretive terms at best, acquired a normative status, setting the standards and boundaries for the substance of folklore proper. They become defining terms, bound by an a priori notion of what folklore should have been but only occasionally was, transforming the desired into necessary conditions, and injecting interpretations into alleged observations. They became terms of value with which to state the worth of songs and sayings and to rate their import in the light of ideals only implicitly understood.

In the process of research and interpretation desired goals could often turn into a priori assumptions and serve as the initial premises rather than the final results. This, in fact, had often happened with qualities attributed to stories, songs, and sayings. which became the basic premises upon which research was designed and theory constructed. Naturally, there have been sufficient examples that supported these contentions. Stories have circulated orally, existing in the traditions of rural communities for many years; their authors, if there were any, were long forgotten, and their analogues recovered in distant lands. But even if there were texts that measured up to all the criteria of folklore, these standards should not have been the defining terms for the substance of folklore.

The penalty for transferring norms into premises and ideal goals into a priori conditions is a limited range for research and theory. Past folklore scholarship paid its dues twice over. The diversity and richness that folklore is, were confined by the constraints that the notions about it imposed. The study of traditions in villages flourished, but the equivalent manifestations in cities went unnoticed. Anonymous tales and songs were avidly recorded, stored, and dissected, but equally entertaining songs and stories whose authors were alive and known were ignored as irrelevant. Other attributes became frames for interpretation. The relationship between expressions and the community was, and is, a major paradigm for analysis. The implicit irrationality of ideas found in tales and metaphors has been the only basis for their explanation, and has opened the gate to a host of psychological interpretations. Significant as they are, these notions blocked the way for alternate modes of explanation, directions of research, and construction of theories. They predefined and identified the substance and the problems of study, silencing the expressions and the people themselves. In recent years the clouds of a priori premises began to disperse. Still, with a sense of innovation and intellectual rebellion Hermann Bausinger (1961) expounded upon folk culture in a technical world, (Volkskunde in der technischen Welt), and American folklorists gathered to discuss The Urban Experience and Folk Tradition (Paredes and Stekert, 1971). Even more recently Alan Dundes and Carl R. Pagter published a collection of written materials as urban folklore in their book Urban Folklore from the Paperwork Empire (Austin, Texas: American Folklore Society, 1975), and with a similar sense of innovation Richard M. Dorson convened a conference on the subject of modern folklore, and published its papers in the volume Folklore in the Modern World, in the series World Anthropology (The Hague: Mouton, 1978). But these are recent developments when scholarly traditions yield to the demands of reality. Throughout the formative years of folklore study, and in many years that followed, the attributes of the idea of folklore dictated the conception of its substance and the limits of its research. They became unchallenged premises and assumptions that were taken for granted.

Regardless of the validity of these attributes, they contributed to the popularity of the idea of folklore. At the same time, however, these very qualities impeded the transformation of folklore from an idea into a field of scholarship. These attributes burdened folklore research with unproved assumptions, untested beliefs, and a projection of popular attitudes toward the substance that makes up the subjects of folklore inquiry. In order to progress with research in the field of folklore, it is necessary, as some have already done, to unload the attributes of the past and to observe folklore freshly, as it exists in social reality. Within this context folklore is a culturally unique mode of communication, and its distinctiveness is formal, thematic, and performative. There is a correlation between these three levels of expression, by which the speakers of folklore set it apart from any other communication in society.

As a distinct mode of communication folklore exists in any society; it is the sole property of neither peasants nor primitives. No doubt folklore could be traditional, but it is not so by definition; it could be anonymous, but it is not essentially so. Any of the qualities that were, and still are, attributed to folklore might be inherent in some forms, in some cultures; and any time they are, it is up to the folklorists to demonstrate it anew.

The Jewish Theodicy Legend

DOV NOY

The problem of evil in a world created by God and controlled by Him has always intrigued religious philosophers. In monotheistic religions, which assume the existence of Divine Providence, it has indeed been one of the main theological issues, since the concept of Providence comprises not only God's complete knowledge of the world, but also His complete control over it. Thus the problem is, How can a world planned by a good Creator and controlled by His omnipotent Presence contain the many instances of evil and injustice found in it.

The problem has been dealt with in different ways by theologians, religious writers, and moral philosophers. I shall not deal with the suggested solutions,[1] nor attempt to summarize, classify, or evaluate them. This paper is meant to be but a contribution to the study of Jewish folk religion. It is hoped that our suggested model, although arrived at on an ethnically limited basis, will be found helpful by those interested in the general study of folk religion, theoretical folkloristics, and cultural anthropology.

The study of general and Jewish folk religion has in the past focused mainly on its expression in folk literature and folk behavior, both of which substantially differ from the norms of the religious establishment. In some instances Jewish scholars have even been opposed to the term *Jewish folk-religion,* assuming that any text or ritual that deviates from the Jewish norm is pagan, and hence does not belong to the domain of Jewish religion.[2]

This study is an expanded version of the paper I presented to the Salo W. Baron Research Seminar at Columbia University on March 24, 1981. Some of my responses to comments made by Professors Baron, Theodor H. Gaster, Barbara Kirshenblatt-Gimblett, and Yosef Yerushalmi are incorporated into the notes. The method applied in this paper is especially appropriate for the Festschrift honoring Professor Raphael Patai, who since his pioneering folkloristic dissertation at the Hebrew University (for which he was awarded the first Ph.D. of this university) has shown scholars and students following in his footsteps in Palestine-Israel and abroad the way of combining field work with library research in the study of Jewish folklore.

This paper is meant to demonstrate the existence of Jewish "folk theology" or "folk philosophy." Unlike the terms *ethnopsychology, ethnobotany, ethnomusicology,* and so on, the term *ethnophilosophy* has not yet been accepted into English scholarly terminology. Folklore and theology still seem to be two contradictory realms and terms. I shall try to disprove this by using my topic as a special instance and building a general model upon it.

Usually, cultural anthropologists, folklorists, and ethnographers look for expressions of folk attitudes by interviewing or undertaking field observation. The relationship between oral literature and society has often been dealt with in folkloristics.[3] Ever since the pioneering days of Franz Boas it has been accepted that the "folktale text reflects the modal or typical mental content of the people in a society."[4] Elsewhere it has been shown, however, that a text per se cannot serve as an indicator of the folk mind, and that the cultural context of the narrating session is the dominant factor.[5] Experience based on some thirty years of field work among Jewish and non-Jewish ethnic groups in Israel and abroad has convinced me that direct statements elicited by interviewing are not adequate with regard to the study of Jewish folk thinking when it deviates from religious dogma. Questions of a philosophical-religious nature put the religiously observant informant on guard more than any other type of question. He is reluctant to admit that he is attempting to solve problems that are considered the task of the rabbinical establishment. His answers, if supplied at all, are mostly elusive. This is the case with informants who would never withhold any information on folk literature and custom, even when these deal with tabooed subjects (sex) or obscene idioms. Only in the realm of folk religion is the informant aware of a clear distinction between the normative religious tradition, mostly anchored in sacred sources, and his own folk heritage, extant mostly in oral, semi-profane tradition.

The best way to obtain information in this area proved to be the indirect approach. Hence I gave up interviewing and using questionnaires, because, as a rule, the informant was reluctant to participate in a conversation on dogmas, divine presence, and the like. Only when unaware of the interlocutor's intentions would the informant throw light on the subject, and this too in an indirect manner, mostly as a message embedded in a tale. The old Hebrew term for disclosing information in this way is *mesiaḥ l'fi tumo,* which means talking unawares, naively. The Halakha accepts as trustworthy the testimony of a witness who tells of an event in this manner, without being asked and without being aware of the possible legal implications.[6]

The message of folk theology is thus expressed in folk legends which, on the surface, seem unsophisticated and simple; yet they do convey a message of which both the narrator and the listeners are fully aware.

This method of indirectly answering philosophical or theological questions by way of narratives is deeply rooted in Jewish tradition. The Talmudic-Midrashic Agada, unlike the philosophical works of Greece, does not formulate problems in abstract terms, but the problems are evident in the story and the narrative plot. The acting characters of the story, or the sages discussing it, often manifest various philosophical attitudes.

Let me illustrate this phenomenon by a Midrashic example, found in Genesis Rabba 22:7, which is attached to the biblical verse Gen. 4:8, "And Cain said to his brother Abel, and it came to pass, when they were in the field, that Cain rose up against Abel his brother and slew him." This narrative raises the philosophical problem of the origin of evil. In Greek philosophy the issue would be formulated in abstract terms; here it is handled as an exegetical one. The verse starts by stating that "Cain said to Abel," but it does not go on to tell what it was that Cain said.[7] The passage in Genesis Rabba presents four attempts at supplementing the missing words, and at reconstructing the dispute that probably took place before Cain rose up against his brother and killed him.[8] In analyzing the four opinions and relating them to the sages who expressed them, we find that they offer four distinctive ideas on the origin of evil reminiscent of thoughts expressed elsewhere in ethical and moralistic literature.

According to the first explanation, Cain proposed to divide the world; indeed, Abel took the flocks and became a keeper of sheep, while Cain took the land and became a tiller of the soil. Following this division of property and labor, a dispute emerged between the landowner and the shepherd. What is evident here is a materialistic approach that can be paralleled with the opening of chapter three in the third book of Marx's *Das Kapital,* where the collapse of the primeval ideal commune is seen as the reason for man's fall.

The second opinion reflects an idealistic tendency. The dispute between the brothers revolved around the question: on whose territory will the Sanctuary be built? As is only too well known, differing ideals, contradictory religious dogmas, and competing holy places are sources of evil and the urge to kill. Holy wars are justified by the need to annihilate societies or segments of societies upholding doctrines opposed to what is regarded the norm by the in-group. The remaining society would be purified and exemplary in its holiness, without dissent from the imposed religious norm.

The third opinion has it that the brothers' dispute was about possessing their father's first wife, the she-demon Lilith. This would reflect the dark human instincts in the *Tiefenpsychologie* theories.

The fourth explanation is based on the narrative tradition according to which a twin sister was born with Abel, and each of the brothers claimed her for himself, using legal and logical reasoning. This would correspond to the Freudian theories of male competition over the possession of women in primitive society.

Many Agadic passages, transmitted originally by word of mouth as part of the "oral Tora," contain such folk renderings of philosophical messages and ideas dressed in narrative garb—a method prevalent in Jewish stories and sermons to this day. The raconteurs and folk preachers, addressing unsophisticated audiences, handle complex issues by telling simple stories, without even concluding them with a moral, a *musar haskel,* and without thereby changing them into parables. The audience, evidently, was expected to grasp the message without such aids.

Was the audience indeed aware of the message, or is this merely the speculative interpretation of the scholar who tries to determine the intention of the literary text? Can it be proved that the text that has reached us in writing or in print originally contained a specific message that reached the audience? Without such a proof our assumption would remain sheer speculation.

Aided by folkloristic methods of discussing the narrated text with both the narrator and the audience, an affirmative answer can be supplied. The metaliterary data collected with each story probe its ethnocultural context, the narrator's traditions and worldview, and the listeners' attitudes and reactions. In this manner the thinking of both the transmitters and the receivers about the specific text can be examined, and the past dimension of the text is transformed into a contemporary one, touching upon actual issues.

Since 1955 more than 13,500 folktales have been collected in Israel from informants representing over thirty ethnic communities; over 1,200 of the folktales have been published in Hebrew and non-Hebrew collections, often with extensive annotations. Most of the texts are fully documented in accordance with standards accepted in folkloristics and cultural anthropology. The documentation, together with the texts, is preserved in the Israel Folktale Archives (IFA) at the Ethnological Museum and Folklore Archives in Haifa, and in the Folklore Research Center at the Hebrew University in Jerusalem.[9] This large corpus is also qualitatively valuable, mainly because of the accompanying ethnocultural data, most of which is still unpublished. The following analysis is based on this folktale corpus, as well as on the informants' life stories and the documentation files.

Typologically, the theodicy legends are part of the religious folktale, which is one of the five main folktale genres according to the internationally accepted classification method of Aarne-Thompson (AT). Within the religious folktale two subgenres are distinguished: (1) The divine rewards and punishments (AT 750–79: God repays and punishes); (2) The vindication of God's justice (theodicy, in Hebrew *tzidduq hadin*).[10]

Tales belonging to subgenre 1 have been abundant in Jewish literature, myth, and legend ever since the Genesis story about Adam's transgression of God's command in the Garden of Eden. Not so theodicy tales. These are very scarce. The philosophical problem underlying theodicy is formulated several times in the Bible, mainly in its gnomic books. Here belong the questions posed by Abraham, "Wouldst Thou exterminate the righteous and the wicked alike?" (Gen. 18:23), and by Jeremiah, "Why does the way of the wicked prosper, and all that deal very treacherously are happy?"

(Jer. 12:1), and the affirmative statement in Job, "He destroys the perfect and the wicked" (Job 9:22), and "The world is given into the hand of the wicked" (Job 9:24). The problem is, however, not evident in the narratives. Formulated in postbiblical times as the double-barreled question of the suffering of the righteous and the wellbeing of the wicked *(tzaddiq w'ra^c lo, rasha^c w'tov lo)*, it remains unsolved. Even in the Book of Job, where the problem constitutes the center of the narrative frame, the body of the book gives it only a philosophical garb, and it remains without a clear solution.

The cultural context in which one would expect to find oral theodicy narratives is the type of event that can be regarded by the society witnessing it as an unjust act by Divine Providence. On such occasions an inclination may surface to question God's justice. Even though the questioning remain subconscious, as would be the case especially with deeply religious persons, one could expect that storytellers and preachers who in their messages represent the religious establishment would respond to it with narratives vindicating God's justice. Death is undoubtedly the foremost occasion calling for such vindication. In fact, the Jewish death and mourning ritual is replete with sayings such as the Tannaitic "Blessed be the Judge of truth" *(barukh Dayyan ha'emet)* (M. Berakhot 9:2, end), and with prayers of theodicy *(tzidduq hadin)*. We therefore assumed that in the "houses of mourning," during the seven days of mourning *(shiv^ca)*[11] we would be able to collect theodicy motifs and legends current among Jewish ethnic groups.

In literate and learned Jewish families, most of the mourning week is devoted to prayers and the study of specific chapters of the Mishna. Mishna and *n'shama* (soul, i.e., of the departed) are anagrams. Also halakhic treatises dealing with rules of mourning, such as the tractate S'maḥot, the relevant chapters in the codices of Maimonides, the Turim, the Shulḥan ^cArukh, and so on, are studied. However, in Jewish communities hailing from Muslim countries, in most houses of mourning neither the members of the family nor the visitors who come to comfort them would understand the halakhic points contained in these sources. Instead, the rites of the *shiv^ca* among them include the recital of stories by narrators well-known in the community or the neighborhood, or by casual visitors. These storytelling sessions are interrupted only when the time for the prayers comes, or when visitors arrive and leaves.[12]

Every occurrence of death can give rise to a questioning of Divine Providence. Only a small percentage of deaths occur at "a good old age" *(b'seva tova)*,[13] and even then the bereaved see the death as untimely. This questioning of Divine Providence on the occasion of death has a special poignancy in Israel, where so many parents have lost their young, idealistic, and religiously observant sons. Complaints against the undeserved death can easily turn into a religious protest not only in the mouth of parents deprived of their sons, but also of bereaved young sons and wives whose fathers or husbands have fallen in the wars of Israel.

We therefore expected that many of the stories narrated during the *shiv[c]a* sessions would be directly related to the mourners' overt or suppressed questions: "Why? Why he? Why we?" We expected that stories of this kind would comprise a major part of the collected corpus, and looked forward to hearing stories about the death of great rabbis, motifs connected with dying, wills, afterlife, and the like. There is a well-known Hebrew folk saying, "The distress of many is half a consolation,"[14] and accordingly we expected stories about death as the universal, common fate of all men, and the like. To our surprise, we found no such stories. Instead we found, while analyzing the more than six hundred stories collected in houses of mourning and unrelated directly to death, a common denominator in more than eighty percent of the stories, which enables us to suggest a structural model for all the variant plots and versions.

This proposed model does not mention death per se. It comprises five distinct parts ("units"), and belongs typologically to AT 759 known as "The angel of death and the hermit," in which an angel takes a hermit with him, and during their journey performs strange and seemingly unjust acts, such as killing the only cow of a poor man, or the son of a hospitable man, and the like. These acts are vindicated later on, when the angel shows the hermit why each of them was just.[15]

I propose to consider the Jewish version of this tale type[16] from a structural viewpoint, limiting myself to the narrative structure. A brief review of the five units of our model shows that we have here the model of a *legend*, conforming to its generally accepted definition: a legend is a narrative that is believed to be true, is told about a definite (real or fabulous) person, a historical figure, event, or place. All versions take place in a specified location and/or time, and most of them have a specific historical hero as one of the acting characters.[17] The five units are:

1. A pious, God-fearing person is leading a normative Jewish life full of faith, trustful devotion to the religious authority—God, the tzaddiq, the rabbi, and so on. This exposition gives the geographic-historical and biographical setting of the plot. Sometimes the mention of the pious hero's name is enough, if it is the name of a famous sage or rabbi, which does not need any additional characterization. His piety and religious fervor, which are beyond doubt, are well-known to the audience.

2. A strange deed, often an event of conspicuous injustice, is performed by the trusted authority, and is observed by the pious person. Frequently a disaster is caused by the strange behavior of the holy authority. Often the authority's followers or the listening audience act as the collective pious witness of the strange behavior, in which case the legend begins with unit 2, and presents the unjust act of an admired rabbi or saint, assuming that the audience plays the part of the pious hero.

3. The confused onlooker questions the act(s) of the venerated authority, often attacking his neutrality and silence in view of the evil that he does not prevent, although capable of doing so. The protagonist accuses the

authority, who is sometimes God himself, of not preventing the unjust deed and not punishing the evildoer(s). In case the followers or listeners are the collective protagonist, the bewilderment at the strange and unjustified deed is expressed by the narrator, who reflects the reactions and attitudes of the followers or the audience.

With this third, central part of the model the story reaches its climax. In many variants, especially in literary texts that have God himself as the character who acts strangely, the protest is played down by a self-imposed censorship, out of fear of transgression and profanation; however, in many instances strongly worded accusations against the authority are included.

4. The fourth unit contains a new dimension that explains the strange deeds and peculiar behavior of the authority in unit 2. Often it presents an independent plot, which takes place in a different spatial or temporal dimension.

5. The fifth unit closes the narrative circle of the story and is a structural return to its exposition (unit 1). The questioning protagonist admits his ignorance and mistaken judgment, asks the authority for forgiveness, and returns to his initial piety, devotion, and faith in the authority and its justice. In most theodicy legends the protagonist keeps silent at the end of the plot, and the final unit is apparently missing. (Apparently, because the silence is an intentional and meaningful one.) This unit 5 constitutes the antithesis of unit 3, in which the protagonist expresses disbelief, protest, and rebellion. It manifests the protagonist's repentance.

Let me now illustrate the first three narrative units of the model with a sample of well-known literary texts. I am using literary texts because they are available in print in English translations, and because they are always shorter than the oral versions. In using the structural approach, we are interested not in the aesthetic or linguistic analysis of the text, but in its plot, contents, and message.

The following four texts (A–D), selected to exemplify units 1–3, represent four different periods of literary composition or compilation, and different degrees of conformity with our model. All of them have oral, highly elaborated, versions in the IFA folktale corpus. Text A is found in Joshua Ibn Shuᶜaib's Tora Sermons.[18] Its protagonist is Moses, and the questioned authority is God himself.

A. At the Well

(1) It was the custom of Moses our Master to stay alone in the fields, in order to receive the Spirit of the Lord.

(2) One day he was resting under a tree, and there was a well nearby. As he looked around he saw a man coming to the well. The man drank and went his way, not noticing that he had dropped his pouch full of gold. Now

another man came, drank of the well, and found the pouch. He picked it up joyously and went his way. Then a third man came, and also drank of the well. While he was still there, the first man came hurrying back in great excitement, looking for his pouch. When he saw the second man, he exclaimed: "You found it!" The other answered him in all innocence: "I found nothing, and all I did was to drink a little water. Then I ate some food and turned aside to rest. Now I am about to go my way." But the first man began quarreling with him, and in his fury he smote and slew him.

(3) When Moses saw this act of violence, he cried unto the Lord: "O Lord, why do You show me such misdeeds, and gaze unmoved on such distress?"

The protagonist of legend B is R. Joshua ben Levi; the questioned authority, Elijah the Prophet, who is clearly God's representative. The version comes from the North African, eleventh century, collection of R. Nissim b. Jacob of Kairuwan, and has many literary and oral parallels. It is very close to AT 759.[19]

B. R. JOSHUA BEN LEVI AND ELIJAH THE PROPHET

(1) R. Joshua ben Levi fasted many a day and prayed to his Blessed Creator that he might be allowed to see Elijah. At length Elijah appeared to him and said: "What do you desire of me? I shall fulfill it." R. Joshua said: "I long to accompany you and see what you do in the world in order to benefit from it and learn wisdom." "You will be unable," Elijah told him, "to bear all that you see me doing, and it will trouble you if I should tell you the reasons for my deeds and works." R. Joshua said: "My lord, I shall not ask, and I shall not be a trial to you, nor shall I bother you with questions, for all my wish is to see your deeds and nothing more." So Elijah made it a condition that if R. Joshua should ask him to explain the reasons for his deeds and signs and wonders, he would tell him; but if he did so ask, Elijah would leave him at once.

(2a) They set out together until they reached the home of a poor man who had nothing more than a cow in his yard. The man and his wife were sitting at the entry. When they saw the wayfarers approaching, they went to meet them, wished them peace, rejoiced with them, and offered them the best in their home. They ate and drank, and spent the night there. When morning came, they rose to depart. Elijah said a prayer over the cow, and it died at once. Then they both went their way.

(3a) R. Joshua saw what had happened, and was confused, saying to himself: "What this poor man received did not befit the honor he showed us. Surely something else could have been done instead of slaying his cow when he had no other." And he said to Elijah: "My lord, why did you slay the man's cow after he had honored us so much?" But Elijah answered:

"Remember the condition we agreed to, that you would remain silent and say nothing; but if you wish us to part, I shall explain." At this R. Joshua stopped asking questions.

(2b) They both went on all day long. In the evening they came to the home of a wealthy man who disregarded them and did not honor them in any way. They stayed there without food or drink. In the house of this wealthy man there was a fallen wall that had to be rebuilt. In the morning Elijah prayed, and the wall was rebuilt by itself. They both went away from there.

(3b) R. Joshua continued to be puzzled and grieved by Elijah's deeds. But he controlled his impulse to ask him questions.

(2c) They went on all day long. In the evening they reached a synagogue with benches of gold and silver, and each man was seated according to his worth and esteem. "Who will feed these poor men tonight?" asked one. Another answered: "The bread and water and salt which will be brought here for them will be enough." They waited but were not treated with proper courtesy. They stayed there until daylight. In the morning they rose and went their way, but first Elijah said to the people in the synagogue: "May God make you all leaders!" Then they continued all day long.

(3c) R. Joshua became even more puzzled and grieved, but he said nothing.

(2d) They reached a city as the sun was declining. There the townsfolk saw them and came to welcome them with great delight. They rejoiced with them and took them to the best of their homes. There they ate and drank and lodged with much honor. In the morning Elijah prayed and then said to the townsfolk: "May the Holy and Blessed One set only one leader among you!"

(3d) Now when R. Joshua heard this, he could no longer control himself or remain silent, and he said to Elijah: "Now let me know the secret of all this!"

The protagonist of the fragmentary text C is R. Israel (Ba⁽al Shem Tov), the Besht, the "Master of the Good Name," the venerated founder of the Hasidic movement. It comes fom the first collection of legends about the Besht and his followers.[20] The devoted follower who acts as the wondering and questioning character is not mentioned explicitly in this short version, but it is clear from unit 3 that the strange behavior amazes the witnesses who play here the role of a "collective hero."

C. Action from Afar

(2) On one occasion when R. Israel[21] was sitting at a meal with his followers, he suddenly raised his hands and made many movements like one who is swimming in a river.

(3) All those who saw this wondered.

In tale D Elijah the Prophet, the folk-hero who has become timeless and deathless, is the acting character. The narrative itself has become a folktale with unspecified time and space. This version was formulated in the seventeenth century.[22]

D. The Nature of Haughtiness

(1) A pious man was once walking along the road, and Elijah, whom it is good to mention,[23] came and accompanied him.

(2) As they walked they saw at the side of the road the carcass of a horse, from which came great stench. The pious man held his nose, but Elijah did nothing whatever. They moved on, and met a handsome youth busy curling his hair. Then Elijah held his nose.

(3) Elijah's companion asked him in astonishment: "My lord, why do you hold your nose at this handsome young man, when you did not do so as we were passing the stinking carrion?"

I shall now present units 4 and 5 of our model, without, however, quoting the full texts. The methods used above for the analysis of the first three units can easily be applied to the last two ones.

In Text A, Moses is shown events that happened in the preceding generation. The protagonists of this secondary plot are the fathers of the characters who acted in unit 2: the man who loses his pouch in unit 2 is an innocent person indeed, but his father, in unit 4, is a wicked evil-doer who steals the pouch from the father of the person who later (in unit 2) finds it. Only when units 2 and 4 are intertwined is the complete plot explicable.

Similarly in text B, Elijah's answers reveal to R. Joshua facts that could not have been known to him when he asked his questions (in unit 3). The facts belong to a different spatial and cognitive dimension: (a) The slaughtered cow served as a substitute for the wife who, following a heavenly decree, should have died; (b) The miser, whose wall was rebuilt by itself, would have found a hidden treasure had he done the building; (c) The great number of leaders in the evil community will lead to disputes and cause its destruction; it is thus not a blessing, but a curse; (d) Too many captains sink the ship, and the friendly townsfolk will benefit and prosper under a single head; the apparent curse is thus, in fact, a blessing.

In text C, a man who arrives at the scene of the meal an hour later relates how, while about to drown in a river (at the time of the Besht's strange behavior) it suddenly occurred to him to "do like this" with his hands. The motions saved him from drowning.

In text D, the stench emanating from the young and handsome, but wicked, man is, in Elijah's extramundane perception, greater than that of all the carrion in the world.

Unit 4 thus clarifies the apparently strange acts described in unit 2. It proves to the individual or collective protagonists that their sense of strangeness and injustice was caused by their own lack of adequate information. Once the whole picture becomes clear, and the covert plot known, it becomes apparent that no injustice or strange behavior were involved.

As for unit 5, text A ends with God's announcement to Moses: "You have no right to cast doubt on My disposition." Moses' silence reflects his consent. In texts B and C the protagonists keep silent, and the unit is missing. Text D ends with a verse from Psalms (101:5) condemning "haughty looks and pride of heart." This condemnation is directed not only at the handsome young man (units 2, 3), but also at the onlooker, whose astonishment and lack of trust in Elijah and his acts (in unit 3) places him, too, among the "haughty and proud."[24]

Many oral versions do not contain all the units of our model, and some deviate from it. However, despite these narrative permutations, they too fit into our model.

Let me now present the English summary of an extensive story told by a Bukharian Jewish storyteller (in Hebrew), and published in 1978.[25]

E. THE STRANGE DEEDS OF THE ANGEL'S DAUGHTER

(1) A youth wishes to marry only "the daughter of an angel." The Phophet Elijah tells him in a dream that God has granted his wish, but he must not ask his future wife for an explanation of her deeds, even the strangest ones. The youth marries the girl who comes to his lodgings.

(2) She bears him three children, and after each birth she puts the newborn into a closed jar. Her husband restrains himself and does not ask her about the reasons for her acts. But when, at the funeral of his mother, the wife carries a spit in one hand and a single shoe in the other,

(3) the husband can no longer restrain himself from asking for an explanation of her behavior.

(4) She thereupon shows her husband the (symbolic) contents of the three jars, revealing to him the decreed fate of their three sons had they remained alive. The first would have been burned to death, the second drowned, and the third would have fallen from a rock to his death. The wife also reveals to her husband that his mother chased away with a spit a beggar who had come to her father for alms, and that once she had given a single shoe to a poor woman.

(5) Unit 5 is missing; it is, however, clear that the bewildered husband, left by his divine wife ("Never again did he see her" is the last sentence of the story), once he comprehends the complete plot, justifies his wife's behavior and his own punishment.

The angel's daughter, promised and presented by Elijah, plays in this

text the role of the sacred authority; the youth (later the husband), that of
the protagonist, the accuser. The single sentence in unit 3 of the above
synopsis stands for two full paragraphs in the Hebrew original, which
include strongly worded phrases and questions of protest and reprimand,
such as, "He could not stand it any more," "He angrily shouted at his wife,"
"What is this deed that you have done today?" "By your acts you put me to
shame," and so on. The connection with our model is clear, although the
story is not a legend but a folktale-conglomerate.[26]

Sometimes a story seems very remote from our model. However, if we
analyze it structurally and discuss its plot with its traditional bearers—the
transmitters and the recipients—within its cultural context, it becomes clear
that it does fit the structural model and carries the functional message.

This is evident in the beginning of a Talmudic version of a King Solomon legend that belongs to a larger cycle of "Solomon and Ashmodai"
stories.[27] Within this cycle our legend is marginal, and King Solomon is
hardly present in it. But only these marginal and fragmentary episodes
have been recited in the *shivᶜa* mourning session observed.

F. The Curious Acts of Ashmodai

(1) While Benayahu led Ashmodai in his chains,
(2) they came to a palm tree. Ashmodai rubbed against it and uprooted
it. They came to a house, and he made it collapse. They came to the hut of a
widow; she came out and begged him not to destroy it. Thereupon he
twisted his shoulder away from it, and a bone broke in his body. . . . He saw
a blind man wandering about on the road, and he set him right on his way.
He saw a drunk wandering about on the road, and he set him right on his
way. He saw people rejoicing at a wedding, and he wept. He heard a man
say to the cobbler, "Make me shoes for seven years," and he laughed. He
saw a magician make magic, and he laughed.

The number of Ashmodai's strange acts (eight) in this text exceeds the
oral-formulaic three or four (three plus one). The original strange acts
were probably increased by later additions. In fact, the first three acts
mentioned in unit 2 remain unaccounted for in the subsequent units.
Moreover, the setting of an erring blind man on his right way can hardly be
regarded as a strange or evil act.

The original strange acts that now comprise the last three in the story
(designated below as a-c), are still alive in oral folklore, and their order
follows an escalation of strangeness:

a. Weeping at a wedding. This can hardly strike the listener as a strange
act. Some people do indeed ritually weep while rejoicing at weddings, and
laments are among the ethnopoetic genres still heard at Jewish wedding
ceremonies of the East and the West.

b. Laughing while shoes are ordered. This can seem quite normal, especially in a culture in which cobblers are disdained and laughed at in stories and jokes. While laughing in the face of a cobbler and his client is indeed stranger than weeping or lamenting at a wedding, still the degree of strangeness of this act is not high.

c. Laughing at the magician is probably Ashmodai's strangest act, since magicians are revered, and their statements believed by the audience.

The above three deeds are part of the five strange acts that are questioned and explained in units 3 and 4. Each question of Benayahu is immediately answered by Ashmodai. In the original form of the legend there were probably three consecutive questions (unit 3) followed by three consecutive answers (unit 4).

(3) Upon arriving at Solomon's court, they did not bring him (Ashmodai) to Solomon for three days. . . . Finally, on the third day, he was brought before the king. Benayahu asked him: "Why, when you saw the blind man lost on the road, did you set him on his way? . . . And why, when you saw that drunk lost on the road, did you set him on his way? . . . And why did you cry when you saw that rejoicing? . . . And why did you laugh when you heard that man say to the cobbler that he should make him shoes for seven years? . . . And why did you laugh when you saw that magician make magic?"

Ashmodai's explanations of the three acts that we regard as the nucleus of the story evince a temporal gradation:

(4) a. The groom is fated to die in thirty days. b. The man ordering the shoes for seven years has only seven days left to live. c. The magician (who claims to be able to tell fortunes and to divine) is sitting on top of a royal treasure without knowing it.

The explanations move from the future to the present: Ashmodai's first two explanations can be checked only in the future, in thirty and in seven days, respectively. His third statement, however, can be probed immediately, since the royal treasure is actually buried in the very ground on which the magician flaunts his "omniscience."

Strange as it may seem, Ashmodai, the king of the demons, is the revered authority in our legend. Although our text does not mention that Benayahu believes in Ashmodai's knowledge and power, such a belief is evident in the whole Solomon and Ashmodai legend-cycle, and in the attitudes of the present-day narrators and their audiences.

While no Jewish saint figures in our legend, and the strange acts are not denounced by the protagonist Benayahu, the three acts of Ashmodai are still told in houses of mourning, and both the storytellers and the listeners are aware of the theodicy message contained in them.

The most frequently appearing protagonist in the Jewish theodicy legend is Moses. Perhaps because the biblical Moses was the only one who, when witnessing what seemed to him an unjust divine threat to his people,

found the courage, even the audacity, to cry out to God, "Blot me out of
Thy book!" (Exod. 32:32), Jewish legend sees in Moses not only the great
leader and master, but also the great rebel, the man full of passion for
social justice, who struggles for national liberation, and pleads for his people with God and the angels when they speak out against Israel. Even his
refusal to accept the decree of his own death is motivated in the legend, not
by his personal desire to live, but by the wish to complete his mission of
bringing his people into the Promised Land.[28]

The common denominator in all the stories of our model is neither the
death motif nor the theodicy message, which is never stated explicitly. The
model comprises two basic dimensions: an explicit one, describing the
strange acts that are observed by the protagonist and the listening audience
(unit 2); and an implicit one, consisting of the true meaning of these acts,
which is revealed to the wondering and protesting protagonist, and thus to
the listeners (unit 4).

In real life one usually finds only the first three units of our model. The
experience of divine injustice leads to a questioning, and even assailing, of
it by the pious in whose hearts it gives rise to doubts (unit 3). Only very
rarely is the implicit, concealed meaning of the events explained or revealed to us (unit 4).

The theodicy legends in which this covert plot is revealed and elaborated
provide the folk answer to the theodicy question. This answer is, indeed,
the message conveyed by our model: Remain silent! Keep quiet! You are a
human being, of woman born, and therefore you do not and cannot know
the hidden facts, and cannot comprehend God's acts, motivations, and
priorities. Since His deeds are beyond your understanding, follow Him—as
well as His representative on earth—with eyes closed and mouth shut.[29]
Admit that your protest was a mistake, stemming from your ignorance.

This is why in the theodicy legends God addresses Moses not as "My
servant," which is the usual form in most of the Moses legends, but as Ben
Amram, the son of Amram, a human being. Even Moses, "the father of the
prophets," is an earthly, mortal creature, whose comprehension of the
divine is limited.

The ethnophilosophical solution of the theodicy problem by not tackling
it at all ("We do not and cannot know, we do not and cannot understand")
is not a new one. It is well attested in our literary sources as one of the
solutions offered by medieval and modern Jewish philosophers.

What we did find out, however, while searching for the role the problem
plays in the life of the Jewish communities and families, is the overwhelming acceptance of this solution in contemporary Jewish folkways, and especially in the oral literature that is still alive and transmitted by folk
performers during rites of passage.

Moreover, while the written sources formulate the solution mainly in
negative terms ("Do not seek what is beyond you," etc.),[30] the legends

suggest a positive approach: keep silent, trust Him whose "deeds are perfect, for all His ways are justice" (Deut. 32:4).[31]

The conclusion reached above with reference to the solution of the theodicy problem is based on modern folkloristic field work, statistics of oral and written texts, motif analysis, and semiotic-structural considerations, which have led to the construction of our model. It may serve as a point of departure for formulating further questions about the interdependence of Jewish folklore and Jewish ethnotheological thought. Let me mention some of these questions:

What is the connection between the hidden plot (unit 4) of the Jewish theodicy legend and the Jewish concept of the thirty-six Hidden Saints?[32]

What is the connection between the covert plot (unit 4) and the components of the four methods of biblical exegesis, referred to as *Pardes,* the first of which, the *p'shat,* the literal, plain meaning, corresponds to the overt plot, while the other three methods (*remez,* allegory; *d'rush,* homiletics; *sod,* mysticism) correspond to the covert one?[33]

What is the connection between our model of the theodicy legend and the saying, "Do not look at the flask, but at what is contains" (Pirqe Avot 4:20)?[34]

What is the connection between God's hidden ways and the "seventy faces of the Tora,"[35] many of which remain concealed?[36]

Is the emergence of the Prophet Elijah as the folk hero par excellence in Jewish legends connected structurally with his strange behavior in the Bible and with his postbiblical appearance in disguise?[37]

Is there a connection between the taboo imposed on the study of mysticism, on probing into the secrets of Creation (*ma^case b'reshit*) and of the Chariot (*ma^case merkava*), and on asking questions such as "What is above you?" and the taboo imposed by the sacred authority on the pious follower in unit 1 of the theodicy legend?

Do the stories created and related during the Holocaust, and do the post-Holocaust literary works attempt to solve the theodicy problem in ways similar to our model, or in different ways?

I have no doubt that such questions, remote from our topic though they may seem, could be studied and answered by relating them to our model and combining literary scholarship with field work methods of investigating living traditions within their ethnocultural context.

NOTES

1. See, e.g., the references in Peter T. Geach, *Providence and Evil* (Cambridge: The University Press, 1977), pp. 17–19, 61–64.

2. Cf. the reviews of Joshua Trachtenberg, *Jewish Magic and Superstition* (New York, 1939), whose subtitle, "A Study in Jewish Folk Religion," was strongly questioned. Cf. also Don Yoder, "Toward a Definition of Folk Religion," *Journal of American Folklore* 33 (1974):2–15,

and my attempt to construct a practical working definition of Jewish folk religion, "Is There a Jewish Folk Religion?" in *Studies in Jewish Folklore* (Cambridge, Mass., 1980), pp. 273–85.

3. See the rich bibliography of Robert A. Georges and Michael D. Jones, *People Studying People: The Human Element in Fieldwork* (Berkeley, Calif., 1980), pp. 158 ff.

4. Ibid., p. 157, n. 9.

5. Cf. Dov Noy, "The Universe Concept of Yefet Schwili," in *Acta Ethnographica* (Budapest) 14 (1965):259–75. Similar conclusions were reached for a different Jewish ethnic group and culture area by Barbara Kirshenblatt-Gimblett, "The Concept and Varieties of Narrative Performance in East European Jewish Culture," in R. Bauman and J. Sherzer, eds., *Explorations in the Ethnography of Speaking* (New York, 1974), pp. 283–308. Cf. also TEM (1978), pp. 15–25.

6. Cf. B. Yebamot 121b.

7. In order to overcome the difficulty, some English translations substitute "spoke" for "said," thereby implying a conversation. The inconsistency of this translation is evident, e.g., in Raphael Patai, p. 288: "And Cain spoke unto Abel his brother [biblical quotation]. What did he say to him? [Midrashic question]." In the Hebrew original the same verb stands for both "spoke" and "said."

8. Cf. parallels to the passage in Ginzberg 5:138 ff., n. 17.

9. Forty-two annotated collections of folktales (750 items, ca. 5,900 pp.) were published in 1962–81 in the Israel Folktale Archives Publication Series (IFAPS), among them sixteen *Tale for Each Month* (TEM) annuals, with English summaries and indexes. For non-Hebrew representative collections of IFA folktales cf. Jason, *Märchen;* Marcus-Rush; Noy, *Folktales;* Noy, *Morocco;* Noy, *Tunisia;* Rand-Rush; Schwili; etc.

10. In the AT classification theodicy tales have been allotted one single type number (AT 759: God's justice vindicated). Later scholars agree, however, that the theodicy tales, mostly legends, belong to a specific subgroup. Cf. n. 15.

11. Shiv‘a, lit. "seven" (masc.), i.e., the seven days of mourning (cf. Gen. 50:10). Jewish folk tradition links it also with the seven close relatives (father, mother, sister, brother, wife, son, daughter), for whom full mourning rites are obligatory.

12. Cf. Haviv, pp. 11–16.

13. The Hebrew idiom *seva tova* means ripe age, good old age, etc. Cf. the trans. of Gen. 15:15; 25:8; Judges 8:32; 1 Chron. 29:28. Pirqe Avot 5:21 links *seva* with the age of 70, the normal span of life (cf. Ps. 90:10). In Jewish folk tradition *seva tova* is from 92 years upward, which number is reached by adding 22 (the "gematria" of *tova*) to 70. However, in 1 Chron. 29:28 the expression is applied to King David, who dies at the age of 70.

14. The wording in Yalqut Sim‘oni on Deut. 4:30 is "A distress which is that of many, is no distress." See Israel Davidson, *Thesaurus of Proverbs and Parables* (Jerusalem, 1957), p. 163, nn. 170, 171.

15. AT 759 and its subtypes have been studied by Heinz Wilhelm Haase, *Die Theodizeelegende vom Engel und dem Eremiten* (Göttingen, 1966). Cf. Schwarzbaum, *Studies,* p. 487.

16. Among the first 10,000 IFA folktales (collected in 1955–73) there are more than 80 versions of AT 759 (God's justice vindicated), and a dozen versions of AT 759B (Holy man has his own mass), AT 759C (The widow's meal: The widow and the wind in court; cf. AT 920 IV b), AT 759* (The hospitable widow's cow killed), and AT 759**A Hansen (The ascetic by the fountain; cf. below, n. 18). The following oicotypes have been added in the IFA type-index (Noy, TJOT): At 759*D: Three cases of generosity (5 versions); AT 759*E: Undeserved evil forestalls greater ones (3 versions). Most of the fully published IFA Hebrew texts (with annotations and English summaries) listed below belong to AT 759, and stem from Morocco (3 versions published in Baharav, Ashkelon, nos. 56a, 56b; Haviv, no. 2), Tunisia (TEM 1961, no. 6), Turkey (synopsis and analysis of IFA 30 in Schwarzbaum, *Theodicy,* pp. 168 f.), Israel (Ashkenazi version in Weinstein, no. 7), Yemen (2 versions, Schwili, no. 5, TEM 1961, no. 3 includes AT 759**A), Iraqi Kurdistan (TEM 1961, no. 1; Noy, *Iraq,* nos. 23, 71; TEM 1965, no. 2). Two Yemenite versions of AT 759C and of AT 759**A Hansen were published in Schwili, nos. 47, 52; an Afghan version of AT 759**A Hansen in Yehoshua no. 2. Two versions of the oicotype of AT 759*E were published in Noy, Iraq, no. 71, and in Noy, *Folktales,* no. 27 (from Lithuania).

17. Our definition comprises the common denominator of various definitions of the "legend" genre. Cf. Lüthi, and Dégh-Vázsonyi in Ben-Amos; chapters 2–4 in Jason, *Studies*, and the theoretical papers in Hand. On the complexity of the legend cores see Linda Dégh's note in Ben-Amos, pp. 120 f.: "The generally known main categories (of the legend)— mythological (or belief), historical, and etiological legends—are entities depending on whether the factual core of the story is a subjective belief, a visual object, or a historical fact. In reality all three are of equal quality as legend cores. Moreover, they are inseparable and might occur jointly in the legends." The corpus of Jewish legends, including the sample of the seven theodicy legends examined in this paper, fully support the last sentence of Dégh's statement. In the Jewish theodicy legends the inseparability of the historical fact and the subjective belief is particularly evident.

18. *D'rashot ʿal haTora* (Constantinople, 1522), beginning of *D'varim*. Cf. Micha Joseph Bin Gorion, *Mimekor Yisrael*, (Bloomington and London, 1976), 1. no. 38 (in the Hebrew original 1, no. 36). The English edition is the source of the following three texts (B, C, D). Text A has been studied by Ginzberg 6:56–57; ibid., 3:135–36 gives a different translation. On the basis of South American versions, the legend has been classified in Hansen as AT 759**A, which is also its standard IFA classification. Several Hebrew versions from Hasidic chapbooks and from the IFA collection (from Yemen, Iraq, and Afghanistan) have been published in Noy, *Moses*. Often Moses is replaced by another protagonist, but Ginzberg's statement (6:n. 290) linking the King Solomon legend in Gaster, *Exempla* no. 353, with Ibn Shuʿaib's Moses legend is incorrect. The Solomon legend belongs (despite the revenge motif, reminiscent of unit 2 in the Moses legend) to the cycle of "Clever acts and words in court" (AT 920–29) and to the genres of "Clever judicial stories" (AT 920: The young Solomon corrects his father David's verdict) and of the "Religious stories of truth that comes to light" (AT 780–89: Solomon revives the killed man who then reveals the truth). Gaster's Solomon story does not fit into our model and cannot be regarded as a theodicy legend.

19. *Ḥibbur Yafe Min haY'shuʿa*, as quoted in *Mimekor Yisrael*, Hebrew ed. no. 325, English ed. 2:112, reproduced here with slight changes. The legend is analyzed in Schwarzbaum, *Theodicy*. Most of the versions comprise four acts in binary units, wherein the seeming "losers" are placed opposite the seeming "gainers": The poor hospitable couple (a in our text) versus the wealthy miser (b); the rich and stingy people (c) vs. the friendly townsfolk (d). At the same time the acts are arranged according to the formula 3 + 1, which means that the fourth deed is the strangest one, causing the protagonist, who cannot restrain himself any longer, to break the silence taboo imposed on him (cf., however, Motif V. 462.1: Maintaining silence as ascetic practice). It is interesting that cursing the good townsfolk (d—the last deed) is, according to the ethnocultural values of the listening society, stranger and worse than harming property (killing the cow) or unjustly rewarding evil (b, c.).

20. *Shivḥe haBesht*, 1814, p. 31a; ed. S. A. Horodezky (Berlin, 1922), p. 104, as translated in *Mimekor Yisrael* 2:no. 361 (Hebrew ed. no. 542), reproduced here with slight changes. In text C the full name of the Besht is omitted in the English translation, and so are the strange words of the Besht, which add an audio-oral dimension to the visual one in the original: "Fool! Do so and so, and you will be saved!" The structure of the legend, and especially its unit 3 and its two plots (units 2 and 4), designate it not as a Hasidic wonder ("saints") legend (accordingly it is motif-indexed by Ben-Amos, p. 293, as Motif D 1781: Sympathetic magic, and as Motif D 1810.0.3: Magic knowledge of saints and holy men), but as a theodicy legend, fitting our model, though unit 1 is only indicated, and unit 5 is missing.

21. The revered name is enough to indicate the holiness of the acting character.

22. *Mimekor Yisrael*, Hebrew ed., no. 678, English ed. 3:no. 75, reproduced here with slight changes, from *Qav haYashar* (Frankfurt a. M., 1705), by R. Zvi Hirsh Kaydanover (d. Frankfurt a. M., 1712). This book is a reworking of the manuscript of his teacher, R. Yosef ben Yuda of Dubno, *Y'sod Yosef*, which was published much later (Shklov, 1785). *Qav haYashar* became one of the most popular eighteenth-century Hebrew ethical *(musar)* books, reprinted several times in Amsterdam, Constantinople, Venice. Its Yiddish translation by the author (Frankfurt a. M., 1709, Sulzbach, 1714 and 1795, Frankfurt a. O., 1791) became very popular with women and folk readers. E. Czerikower, "The History of a Literary Plagiarism" (in Yiddish), *Yivo-Bleter* 4 (1932):159–67, discusses the relationship between *Y'sod Yosef* and *Qav haYashar*.

23. This is I. M. Lask's translation (cf. above, n. 18) of the words *zakhur l'tov*, which follow

only the name of Elijah and differ from the customary *zikhrono liv'rakha* following the names of deceased persons. The usual English rendering of *zakhur l'tov*, "of good memory," or "who is remembered for good") sounds better than the innovated one.

24. The subsequent verse (Ps. 101:6) may have been the basis of our story: "The well-meaning (or perfect) wayfarer, he will serve me." This may be the quintessence of Elijah's attitude toward his companion. Our story begins, "*Hasid ehad haya holekh baderekh,* and the last two words of this phrase are the opening words of the Psalmist's verse. The story may have started with another word from the verse, *tamim,* which was later replaced by the present *hasid.*

25. Cf. Pinhasi, no. 4, pp. 43–46 (Hebrew text), 66–67 (English synopsis).

26. The conglomerate is classified in Noy, TJOT (cf. Pinhasi, pp. 59, 66) as AT 400–424 (Supernatural wife) + AT 759 + AT 934C (Death forestalls evil fates). For similar conglomerates see Noy, Iraq, no. 109, and Haviv, p. 54, n. 1. The motif of an evil deed (killing the newborn in our story) which prevents a larger evil (death of youngsters) or a later ("fated") disaster, is evident also in text B4a, explaining that the poor woman's cow was killed to prevent that woman's death. Cf. Motif N 121.2, where mother is shown what would have been the evil fate of her children had they not died. The motif underlies Isa. 57:1, "The righteous perishes . . . and godly men are taken away [from this world; i.e., die], none [of the living] consider that the righteous is taken away from evil to come [so as to spare him]."

27. The English translation of the Talmudic (B. Gittin 68-b) version is that of Patai, p. 188–89. For the background, literary context, sources, and parallels of the legend cf. Ginzberg 4:166–68 (text); 6:299–300, n. 86. We follow Patai's rendering "Ashmodai" rather than the conventional "Asmodeus": cf. Motif F 402.2.1.

28. The special place of Moses in the Jewish theodicy legend is discussed in Noy, Moses.

29. The eating of eggs at the funeral meal and during the mourning period is explained in many ways, cf. Gaster, Holy, p. 76, where the custom, found also in the Graeco-Roman and European tradition, is explained as symbolizing eternal life. This does not explain, however, the use of lentils and beans in the mourners' meals. The usual interpretation connects the custom of eating round food with the symbol of the "wheel of fortune." The knowledge that the wheel turns, and that "downs" in life are followed by "ups," may comfort the bereaved. The folk explanation of this custom among Oriental Jews is connected with the fact that eggs and lentils are "closed" and "have no mouth." Cf. also the East-European, Ashkenazi *Ta'ame Minhagim* by T. Sperling, Jerusalem, 1957, p. 442: "As the lentil has no mouth, so is the mourner not allowed to speak [i.e., to open his mouth]."

30. This saying of Ben Sira, 3:21, has penetrated Jewish folk tradition *via* B. Hag. 13a where it is quoted in the name of Ben Sira. The version in Y. Hag. 77:3 is closer to the Ben Sira original, cf. Theodor, Gen. Rab. p. 58. The full aphorism in Ben Sira and in the Talmudic quotation is comprised of four sentences, of which only the first has become part of Jewish proverbial lore. The other three are: Do not search what is hidden from you. Contemplate [only] things [which have been] allowed to you. Do not be concerned with concealed things.

31. This verse can be considered Moses' final statement referring to theodicy. It stresses that *all* God's ways are just, and that His deeds are perfect, without blemish. The second part of the verse states that God should be trusted and believed (*el emuna* is usually rendered in the active mode as "God of faithfulness," but a passive rendering is also possible), for (the *waw* in *w'en* is a causal connective, corresponding to *ki* in the first half of the verse) He is without iniquity (injustice), just and right. Verse 5 describes God's adversaries whose qualities are diametrically opposed to His: they are blemished, perverse, and crooked.

32. The problem of the formulistic number 36 (cf. Motif Z 71.8.7) and of its origin in the Hidden Saints tradition is a marginal one, cf. Noy, Tzaddiq. The folk explanations connect the number with the sum total of the Hanukka candles $(1 + 2 + 3 \ldots + 8 = 36)$, with numerically motivated combinations $(3 \times 13, 18 + 18,$ etc.$)$, or with various gematrias found in Biblical words and verses (*ekha,* the word *lo* in "Happy is the people that is in such a case," Ps. 144:5).

33. In mystical Biblical exegesis the correct methods are explicable only to the worthy and the initiated. Only they are blessed with grace, *hen,* meaning also, as an acronym, hidden wisdom (*hokhma nisteret*).

34. The wine concealed in the flask symbolizes the Tora. Cf. the allegorical explanations of wine in the Midrashim to Cant. 1:2, 4; 2:4; 5:1; 7:10; 8:2; 9:7. The beginning of our saying, "Do not look at the flask," is one of the most widespread saying stemming from the Pirqe Avot.

35. Otiyyot d'R. Akiva. This Midrashic saying, occurring many times in the Zohar, has

become very popular. In folk sermons it is often connected with other entities whose number in Jewish tradition is the formulistic 70 (cf. motif Z 71.5 and its sub-motifs): the nations, languages, elders, members of the Sanhedrin, names of God, Israel, Jerusalem etc.

36. The term used by the mystics, *haster panim*, concealing of the face, deviates from the original sense of the phrase in Deut. 31:17, "I will forsake them and hide my face from them," where it means God's anger, the withdrawal of God's grace.

37. Cf. Noy, *Elijah;* Schwarzbaum, *Elijah;* Schwarzbaum, *Studies* (index, s.v. Elijah), Weinreich, and bibliographical references there. *Yedaᶜ ᶜAm* 7(1961):25 is dedicated to the subject "Elijah the Prophet in the Folklore of the Various Communities in Israel," and contains rich ethnopoetic materials.

ABBREVIATIONS AND BIBLIOGRAPHY

AT. Aarne, Antti. *The Types of the Folktale.* . . . Translated and edited by Stith Thompson. Helsinki, 1961. The number following AT refers to the universal number of the tale-type. A classification number or letter added to the normative tale-type used in the IFA (cf. Noy, TJOT) is preceded by an asterisk.

Baharav, *Ashkelon.* Baharav, Z. (coll.). *Sixty Folktales Collected from Narrators in Ashkelon* (in Hebrew). Haifa, 1964.

Baharav, Dor. Baharav, Z. (coll.). *From Generation to Generation* (in Hebrew). Tel Aviv, 1968.

Ben-Amos. Ben-Amos, Dan, ed. *Folklore Genres.* Austin, Texas, 1976.

Dégh and Vázsonyi. Dégh, Linda, and Vázsonyi, Andrew. "Legend and Belief." In Ben-Amos, ed. 1976. Pp. 93–124.

Gaster, *Exempla.* Gaster, Moses. *The Exempla of the Rabbis.* London, 1924.

Gaster, *Holy.* Gaster, Theodor H. The Holy and the Profane. New York, 1955.

Ginzberg. Ginzberg, Louis. *The Legends of the Jews.* 7 vols. Philadelphia, 1909–38.

Haase. *See* n. 15.

Hand. Hand, Wayland D., ed. *American Folk Legend: A Symposium.* Berkeley, Calif., 1971.

Hansen. Hansen, Terrence L. *The Types of the Folktales in Cuba . . . and Spanish America.* Berkeley, Calif., 1957.

Haviv. Ḥaviv, Yifraḥ (coll.). *Never Despair.* Haifa, 1966.

IFA. Israel Folktale Archives, in the Haifa Municipality's Ethnological Museum and in the Folklore Research Center, Hebrew University, Jerusalem.

IFAPS. Israel Folklore Archives Publication Series (in Hebrew with English summaries).

Jason, *Märchen.* Jason, Heda, ed. *Märchen aus Israel.* Düsseldorf-Köln, 1976.

Jason, *Studies.* Jason, Heda. *Studies in Jewish Ethnopoetry.* Taipei, 1975.

Lüthi. Lüthi, Max. "Aspects of the Märchen and the Legend." in Ben-Amos, pp. 17–33.

Marcus, *Mabuᶜa.* Marcus, Eliezer, ed. *From the Fount* (in Hebrew). Haifa, 1966.

Marcus-Rush. Marcus, E., and Rush, Barbara, eds. *Jewish Folktales Around the Year.* New York, 1980.

Mizrahi. Mizrahi, Hanina (coll.). *With Elders Is Wisdom* (in Hebrew). Haifa, 1967.

Motif. Thompson, Stith. *Motif-Index of Folk Literature.*² Copenhagen and Bloomington, Ind., 1955–58.

Noy, *Elijah.* Noy, Dov. "Elijah the Prophet at the Seder Night" (in Hebrew). *Maḥanayim* 44 (1960):110–16.

Noy, *Folktales.* Noy, D. ed. *Folktales of Israel.* Chicago, 1963.

Noy, *Iraq.* Noy, D. ed. *The Beautiful Maiden and Three Princes* (in Hebrew). Tel Aviv, 1965.

Noy, *Libya.* Noy, D., ed. *Libyan Jewish Folktales* (in Hebrew). Jerusalem, 1967.

Noy, *Morocco.* Noy, D., ed. *Moroccan Jewish Folktales.* New York, 1966. Also in Hebrew (Jerusalem, 1964) and in French (Jerusalem, 1966).

Noy, *Moses.* Noy, D. "Moses our Teacher in Jewish Legends" (in Hebrew). *Mahanayim* 115 (1967):83–101.

Noy, *TJOT.* Noy, D. *The Types of the Jewish Oral Tale* (in MS.).

Noy, *Tunisia.* Noy, D. ed. *Contes populaires racontés par des Juifs de Tunisie.* Jerusalem, 1968. Also in Hebrew (Jerusalem, 1966).

Noy, *Tzaddiq.* Noy, D. "The Hidden Saint (Tzaddiq) in Theodicy Legends" (in Hebrew). *Yedaᶜ ᶜAm* 43–44 (1976):32–40. Summarized in English, p. iv.

Patai. Patai, Raphael, ed. *Gates to the Old City*. Detroit, 1980; also in paperback, New York, 1980.

Pinhasi. Pinhasi, Jacob (coll.). *Ten Folktales from Bukhara* (in Hebrew). Jerusalem, 1978.

Rand-Rush. Rand, Baruch, and Rush, Barbara, eds. *Around the World with Jewish Folktales: Jews of Kurdistan*. 2 vols. Toledo, Ohio, 1978–79.

Rush-Marcus. Rush, Barbara, and Marcus, Eliezer, eds. *Seventy and One Tales for the Jewish Year*. New York, 1980.

Schwarzbaum, Elijah. Schwarzbaum, Haim. "The Prophet Elijah and Rabbi Joshua ben Levi" (in Hebrew). *Yeda⁽ Am* 25 (1961):22–31.

Schwarzbaum, *Studies*. Schwarzbaum, H. *Studies in Jewish and World Folklore*. Berlin, 1968.

Schwarzbaum, *Theodicy*. Schwarzbaum, H. "The Jewish and Moslem Versions of Some Theodicy Legends," *Fabula* 3 (1959:119–69.

Schwili. Noy, Dov (ed.), *Jefet Schwili erzählt*, Berlin, 1963. Cf. note 5.

TEM—*A Tale for Each Month*, Haifa, 1962–76; Jerusalem, 1978. The IFA annual.

Weinreich. Weinreich, Beatrice Silverman. "Genres and Types of Yiddish Folktales about the Prophet Elijah." *The Field of Yiddish* 2 (1965):202–31.

Weinstein. Weinstein, Esther (narr.). *Grandma Esther Relates* (in Hebrew). Haifa, 1964.

Yehoshua. Yehoshua, Ben-Zion (coll.). *The Father's Will* (in Hebrew). Haifa, 196 .

Mythology, Folklore, and Tradition—Studies in Yiddish Etymology

ROBERT GORDIS

"No man is an island entire of itself. Every man is a piece of the continent, a part of the main." John Donne's[1] famous line applies not only to individuals but to all groups of men sharing our crowded little planet. However, most nations living within their own territory may have two, three, or four foreign neighbors on their borders, who will naturally exert an influence upon their life and culture.

In the case of the Jewish people, the impact, whether positive or negative, is far greater. Jews have been living in a Diaspora that began centuries before the first destruction of the national center in Palestine. The Prophet Isaiah, in the 8th century B.C.E. speaks of a future ingathering of the exiles "from Assyria and Egypt, Pathros, Nubia, Shinar, Hamat, and the coastlands of the [Mediterranean] sea."[2] When, a century later, at the time of the destruction of the First Temple (586 B.C.E.) Jeremiah was carried away to Egypt,[3] a Jewish settlement there was already in existence.

The reconstruction of the Second Jewish Commonwealth after the Babylonian Exile was accompanied by the growth of large Jewish Diasporas in Babylonia and Egypt, with smaller enclaves elsewhere along the Mediterra-

Raphael Patai has had a distinguished career marked by wide-ranging interests, extraordinary creativity, and deep involvement in the life of his times. For him, scholarship has served to illumine life, and the culture of the past has been the instrument for responding to the concerns of the present. He is an anthropologist not only in the technical sense of the term, but in its deeper and original meaning, "a student of mankind." He has contributed richly to our knowledge of general folklore, mythology, and religion, with a strong involvement in the life and thought of the Jewish people.

This paper is a small but sincere tribute to him on his seventieth birthday, reflecting *in parvo* his lifelong interest in Jewish folklore, mythology, and ritual.

I am greatly indebted to Dr. Marvin Herzog, professor of Yiddish at Columbia University, and Mr. Wolf Yunin on the staff of the YIVO Scientific Institute for the opportunity to discuss the content of this paper and profit from their expertise in Yiddish philology.

nean littoral, in southern Europe, western Asia, and North Africa. The destruction of the Second Temple by the Romans in 70 C.E., and the erosion of the Jewish position in Palestine in succeeding centuries, made the Diaspora a "normal," all-but-universal condition of Jewish life.

Today the basic pattern of homeland-*cum*-Diaspora has been reestablished. The existence and growth of the State of Israel have not led to the disappearance of the Diaspora. To be sure, most Jewish communities in Muslim lands have been evacuated because of Arab hostility. The great centers of Jewish life in Central and Eastern Europe have been destroyed by the Nazis and their allies. Undoubtedly, Jewish communities surviving in the Communist world and elsewhere, as in South America and South Africa, are in grave jeopardy, yet they continue to survive. North American Jewry, the greatest concentration of Jews in the world today, and the smaller communities of Western Europe, are still viable, their destiny being bound up with that of the free world.

In sum, Jews have been in close, day-to-day contact with practically every ethnic group in the Western world, all of whom have left their impact on the Jewish lifestyle, of which language is a prime element. Yiddish, which has accompanied Ashkenazic Jewry for nearly fifteen centuries, bears countless marks of this variegated cultural and personal influence.[4]

This external factor in the growth and development of Yiddish, fascinating as it is, is actually less significant than another, inner source that was far more pervasive. For while foreign influences upon Jewish life were intermittent and irregular, the rich and indigenous Jewish culture in which the Jew lived was both continuous and ubiquitous. The "portable fatherland" of the Diaspora Jew was the vast terrain of Torah, the highest peaks of which were the Bible, the Talmud, the Midrash, the Prayer Book, the Passover Haggadah, and the Kabbalah, towering over the hills and valleys of daily Jewish experience.

In this paper, I wish to propose etymologies for three highly interesting Yiddish usages that reflect both the external and the internal factors in Jewish history. Two of them enjoy wide currency, the third compensating by its picturesqueness for its limited use. A fourth, a Hebraism in Yiddish, paradoxically contributes to biblical exegesis! These few instances reveal interesting aspects of the impact on the Jewish psyche both of Jewish tradition and of general folklore.

I. BASHERT—"DESTINED, DETERMINED"

This term, which has always enjoyed great popularity, has entered into American colloquial speech as part of the current popularity of Yiddishisms in the United States. Its etymology, however, has remained elusive.

In many cultures, the concept exists of human life being determined by a group of supernatural figures, usually three in number and baleful in character. In Greek myth, the Moirae (called Parcae by the Romans) were Clotho, the spinning fate, Lachesis, the one who assigns or measures man's fate, and Atropos, the fate that cannot be avoided. In Greek art, Clotho is frequently represented as spinning, the thread being measured by a rod in the hand of Lachesis, and finally being snipped by Atropos's shears.[5] Homer and Virgil declare that Zeus can intervene and save men's lives if he so chooses, and that men themselves can, to some degree, control their fates by avoiding unnecessary dangers.[6] On the other hand, the more reflective writers, Aeschylus, Herodotus, Plato, and Simonides, hold that even Zeus is subject to the fates,[7] as the name Atropos, "one who cannot be turned aside," suggests.

Though the theme of the thread of life is familiar to modern readers from classical sources, it is not limited to the Greco-Roman world, but occurs in biblical sources. In Isaiah 38:12, the ailing King Hezekiah laments his imminent death:

> Like a weaver I have rolled up my life
> He cuts me off from the loom.[8]

A most beautiful and highly subtle use of this figure occurs in Job 7:6:

> My days are swifter than the weaver's shuttle;
> They end in the absence of hope.[9]

Here is a superb example of *talḥin,* a rhetorical figure that is to be distinguished from paronomasia. In paronomasia, one word suggests another of similar sound. In *talḥin,* one word conveys two levels of meaning simultaneously, one primary, the other secondary, and the readers' recognition of both is the source of aesthetic pleasure. The noun *tiqwah,* "hope," in the verse also has the meaning of "thread,"[10] so that both enter the reader's consciousness at the same time.

The theme of the thread of life being cut by shears persisted into medieval and modern times. In the English poets, the model seems to be the classical rather than the biblical prototypes. Thus in Shakespeare:

> Think you I bear the shears of destiny?
> Have I commandment on the pulse of life?[11]

Milton writes:

> Comes the blind fury with the abhorred shears,
>   and slits the thin spun life.[12]

> And sing to those who hold the vital shears
>   and turn the adamantine spindle round
>   on which the fate of gods and men is wound.[13]

I suggest that it is within this conceptual framework that the etymology of *bashert* is to be sought. Old High German had two roots, *skeran* and *seerjan*.[14] From the former are derived English *shear* and Modern German *bescheren,* "cut, clip," and the noun *Schere,* "scissors, shears, clippers." From the latter come English *share* and Modern German *bescheren,* "give as a share, make a present of." Thus the originally distinct roots have coalesced in Modern German to produce the homophone *bescheren,* a frequent phenomenon in language.[15]

With which root is the Yiddish *bashert* to be associated? In favor of relating the Yiddish *bashert* to "shear, cut off," rather than to "share," are several considerations:

(1) The meaning "share" does not occur in Yiddish, while the verb *sheren,* "cut, clip," does.

(2) The Modern German root *bescheren* is used in a favorable sense, "give as a share or present." On the other hand, the Yiddish *bashert* generally carries a negative connotation, "predestined to trouble, disaster, or sorrow."[16]

(3) The theme of "determine, decide," as these very words indicate ("determine," make an end, *de-cido,* Latin "cut off") is generally expressed by the idea of cutting off. Hebrew offers a wealth of examples in every period of the history of the language. For biblical Hebrew, we may note *haratz,*[17] *gazar,*[18] *hatakh.*[19] The two latter roots continued to be used in rabbinic Hebrew. Most common of all is the root *pasaq,* "cut," from which is derived the basic term *p'saq,* "decision," frequent in rabbinic Hebrew and Yiddish (*p'saq din*).

(4) The ubiquity of the figure of the shears of fate supports the view that the Yiddish locution means "determined, pre*destined,* fore*ordained.*"

II. MA-LE—"WHO CARES, NEVER MIND, WHAT DIFFERENCE DOES IT MAKE TO ME?"

Much of the charm of Yiddish, and its realism, wisdom, and earthiness, are imbedded in words and idioms that are untranslatable, though their meaning is unmistakable. The three renditions given above for the one Yiddish word *ma-le* are a case in point. The philologist Wolf Yunin illustrates its use by an imaginary conversation:[20]

Child: *Mame, mir vilt zikh epes nashen.*
          (Mom, I want to have something tasty.)
Mother: *Ma-le vos dir vilt zikh. Zoll zikh dir ibervellen.*
          (Who cares what you want. You had better get over it.)

Yunin comments: "*Ma-le* what, *ma-le* when, *ma-le* how much, *ma-le* where. This is a precious aid in our mother-tongue which serves us loyally whenever we need it at hand. The word comes from the Slavic *mala*, but we also use other synonyms. *Vintzik vos einer vill, nit genug vos er oder zi zogt,* "too little what one may want, not enough what he or she says." This Slavic etymology for *ma-le* has been generally accepted[21] from the Polish *mala*, "little, few," *maly*, "little, small."[22]

I believe that the proposed etymology for *ma-le* does not do justice either to its meaning or its usage. I should like to propose another etymology, the Talmudic idiom *mah li*, which has precisely the required nuance. The phrase means literally, "What (difference is it) to me, i.e., it does not matter to me, who cares whether. . . ." To cite a few examples out of many:[23]

> *B.T. Berakhot*
> What difference [*mah li*] whether it is the shorter month (i.e., of 29 days) or the longer (i.e., of 30 days)?
> *B.T. Shabbat 37a*
> Who cares [*mah li*] whether it is within it or upon it?
> *B.T. Kiddushin 65a*
> What difference [*mah li*] whether it be a case of betrothal or a case of marriage (?)
> *B.T. Baba Kamma* 103b
> What difference [*mah li*] whether he bought it or stole it?

Perhaps the most familiar instance, which became proverbial in Yiddish-speaking Torah circles in *B. Metzia* 36b:

> For the Angel of Death, what difference [*mah li*] here or there (i.e., death can strike anywhere)?

To revert to Yunin's imaginary conversation, when the child asks for some sweets the mother replies, "What is it to me, who cares what you want!"

The unique Yiddish idiom *ma-le* has its source, not in the Slavic environment, but in the Talmudic atmosphere of the Bet Hamidrash and the Yeshivah.

III. Feier Meshorsim un vasser meshorsim—"ministers of fire and ministers of water"

While the two usages discussed above were used very widely, the phrase to be considered now seems to have been restricted to some circles in Lithuanian Jewry. I have heard it only from my wife, who was born in Moghilev and came to the United States in her early childhood, and from a friend, who tells me that it was used in Vilna.

The phrase *feier meshorsim un vasser meshorsim* indicates that someone has an elaborate entourage of assistants and servants. Its ironic intent is clear—

the individual's pretensions to glory and honor are punctured by describing him as surrounded by ministers of fire and ministers of water—an epithet appropriate to God himself. There is also the implication that all the hustle and bustle is accomplishing little or nothing.

The irony is heightened by the origin of the phrase. It arises, I suggest, from combining one passage from the Psalms with another from the *Daily Siddur*. The great nature Psalm 104, which is part of the Saturday night ritual, begins by describing the creative activity of God and proceeds in verse 4 to declare "He makes the winds his messengers; his ministers [*meshartaw*], the burning fire."

In the Daily Service, the prayer *Titbarakh* contains the phrase *yotzer meshartim va'asher meshartaw kullam ^comdim,* "God creates His servants, while His servants all stand. . . ." As is well-known, many Lithuanian Jews pronounce the *Shin* as *Sin* or *Samekh*.[24] The words *va'asher meshartav* would therefore emerge in the Lithuanian Ashkenazic pronunciation as *vasser meshorsim,* "water ministers."

The combination of the two passages from Psalms and the Prayer Book therefore yield *feier meshorsim un vasser meshorsim,* "ministers of fire and ministers of water." The phrase is testimony to the intimate familiarity of the Jew with the Bible and Prayer Book. In one ironic phrase, Yiddish reveals the learning, the realism, and the scorn for pretense that are characteristic of the East-European Jewish personality.

IV. BAYLON—"AVID, EAGER, READY AND WILLING"

Special interest attaches to a Hebraism preserved in Yiddish, which, almost paradoxically, sheds light upon classical Hebrew usage and is helpful in the exegesis of several biblical passages. In the case of the Yiddish vocable *baylen*, not only the etymology but also the orthography and pronunciation are in doubt, but its meaning is clear. For example, *er iz a baylon foren aheim,* "He is eager to ride home," *er iz a baylon ihr tsu zehn,* "He is eager to see her." It occurs as a Yiddishism in some modern Hebrew writers from an East European milieu. Thus S. Y. Agnon writes: "I am avid [*ba^calan*], eager to count the money he will be returning." Hayyim Hazaz writes: "I am more than eager [*ba ^calanit*] to see this."

While the word is generally spelled *b^cln*, one suggested etymology is that it is an aural metathesis for *bl^cn*, from the Hebrew root *bala^c*, "swallow," hence, "one eager to devour, gluttonous."[25]

The final syllable *an* offers no difficulty, being an affix used to express a habitual practice or trait. While biblical Hebrew offers only one example, *rahmaniyot*, "merciful women,"[26] the form is frequent in rabbinic Hebrew, as for example, *bayshan*, "shamefaced, retiring," *arkan*, "long-winded," *watran*, "yielding, withdrawing," *qatlanit*, "murderous"[27].

However, the derivation from *bala^c*, "swallow," is doubtful semantically and difficult phonetically. As generally pronounced, the noun is iotacized, that is to say, a *Yod* is inserted after the first vowel to create a diphthong, hence *baylen*. The pronunciation corresponds exactly to that of *ka'asan*, "prone to anger, irascible," pronounced *kaysen*. This iotacization of the *'Ayin* in a closed syllasble may be illustrated by other examples. Thus, the proper noun *Ya'aqov*, "Jacob," is popularly pronounced *yaynkev* and the diminutive *Yanqel* is pronounced *yaynkele*. It therefore seems clear that the Yiddish noun *baylen* goes back to a Hebrew *ba'lan*, consisting of the noun *ba'al* with a suffixed *Nun*.

The common Hebrew noun *ba'al* is frequent in the Bible in several well-attested senses: (a) "master, owner," (b) "husband," (c) "citizen, burgher," and (d) as the name of the god *Ba'al*.

However, this constellation of meanings, "master, owner," is clearly inappropriate in Proverbs 3:27: *al timna' tov mib'alaw*. The Septuagint renders, "Do not forebear doing good to the poor *(endei)*." But none of the many Hebrew terms for "poor" bears any resemblance to *mib'alaw* graphically. Obviously, the Greek is rendering freely, according to its understanding of the passage. Nor has a plausible emendation been proposed for the noun.[28] The solution is to be sought in another direction.

The true intent of our verse is suggested by the succeeding verse, which is parallel with it: "Do not say to your friend, 'go and return and tomorrow I shall give it to you,' when you have it with you now."

The passage is not a conventional plea for the practice of charity to the poor. The reader is being urged not to postpone granting a boon to a suppliant out of a desire to indulge a sense of power.

All the modern versions recognize that the passage requires a special nuance for *b'alaw*, while trying to preserve some vestige of the meaning "owner." Thus the *Revised Standard Version* relegates to a footnote the literal translation "Do not withhold from its owners," and translates the verse, "Do not withhold good from those to whom it is due," which is the wording of the *Jewish Publication Society Version*. The same sense is transmitted more freely by the *New English Bible*, "refuse no man any favor that you owe him," and by the *New American Bible*, "refuse no one the good on which he has a claim."

However, there is nothing in the context of verse 27 or 28 to suggest that the suppliant has a claim or right to the rich man's favor. The only reason assigned is that "the benefactor" can act now, without delay.

What still remains to be established is the semantic process that yields the desired meaning. I suggest that the Yiddish and neo-Hebraic usage *ba'alan* offers the key to a solution.

The biblical noun *b'alim* has developed a special nuance from its basic meaning, "owner." Here it carries a voluntaristic nuance, "would-be owner, one who hopes to possess." The verses are, therefore, to be rendered literally:

Do not deny good to one who is avid, eager for it
   when you have it in your power to do it.
Do not say to your friend, 'Go and return,
   tomorrow I shall give it to you,'
   when you have it now.

This proposed nuance for b^calim leads to a reconsideration of at least two other biblical passages where the difficulties inherent in the usual rendering of the noun were not so obvious.

In Eccles. 7 : 12, the closing stich reads: *hahokhmah t'haye b* ^{c}*aleha.*

Like all other exegetes, I have rendered the passage in my Commentary "the advantage of knowing that wisdom preserves the lives of those who possess it."[29] However, Koheleth's frequent emphasis upon man's ignorance and his frequently reiterated skepticism as to man's capacity to attain to wisdom[30] raises the question at least as to whether he would speak of a man as possessing wisdom. A more appropriate rendering would be "Wisdom confers life upon those who desire, are avid for it."

In Eccles. 8 : 8, the closing stich reads: *Lo y'mallet resha^c et b^{c}alaw.* Here I have rendered, "Evil cannot save the wrong-doer," on the assumption that *ba^{c}al* means "master (of evil)," for which several imperfect analogies are adduced.[31] The modern versions render similarly.[32] However, if the noun is rendered "would-be possessor, avid, greedy for," the passage in Ecclesiastes would mean "even evil-doing cannot save him who is eager for it."

It is noteworthy that all three passages possess three characteristics: (a) They all use the plural of the noun *b^{c}alim;* (b) they are all examples of late biblical Hebrew, and (c) they all occur in Wisdom texts.

In sum, while this nuance for *b^{c}alim* is a distinct possibility in Ecclesiastes, it seems to be definitely called for in Proverbs. The precise nuance was preserved in the postbiblical period and survives as a Hebrism in the Yiddish *baylon.*[33]

NOTES

1. *Devotion* XVII in his *Sermons.*
2. Isa. 11 : 11. An oracle in Isa. 19 : 18 foretells that "five cities in Egypt" will be speaking Hebrew and swearing loyalty to the God of Israel. However, the Isaianic character of the section (19 : 18–25) has been doubted, a view this writer does not share.
3. Jer. 43 : 2–7.
4. A particularly striking instance is the Yiddish phrase *bobe mayseh,* popularly etymologized as "grandmother's tale." Research has demonstrated that the phrase derives from a medieval Yiddish version of a volume of Italian tales about a knight, Buovo d'Antona, itself a translation of an English collection on the exploits of Sir Bevis of Hampton.
5. Cf. E. H. Blakeney, *A Shorter Classical Dictionary* (New York: Dutton, 1926), p. 346; Robert Graves, *The Greek Myths,* 2 vols. (London: Penguin Books, 1955), 1 : 48 f.
6. Homer *Iliad* 8.69, 22.22, 29; Virgil *Aeneid* 10.814.
7. Aeschylus *Prometheus* 511–15; Herodotus *History* 1, 91; Plato *Republic* 10. 14–16; Simonides 8. 20. The Fates are also credited with the alphabet. They intervened in many other incidents in Greek mythology. Cf. Graves, *Greek Myths,* 1 : 65, 70, 131 f., 134, 183, 203, 224, 245, 264, 271, 307, 358; 2 : 9, 72.

8. So RSV. F. Perles *(Orientalische Literaturzeitung* 12 [1900]:251 f.) suggests that in Ezek. 37:11 the Masoretic text *nigzarnu lanu* should be divided differently, to yield *nigzar nawlenu,* "our thread is cut off." The change is not absolutely necessary, since the Masoretic text is satisfactory as it stands and the noun *newal, nawla,* "loom, web on the loom," does not occur in biblical Hebrew, but in Targumic and Talmudic Aramaic *(Targum* of Isa. 38:12; *Y. Baba Batra* 2, 13b; *B. Baba Batra* 13b *Yadᶜa pilkha w'nawla.* "He understands the spindle and the loom."

9. On this passage see Gordis, *The Book of Job: Commentary, New Translation and Special Studies* (New York: Jewish Theological Seminary, 1978), pp. 66, 80. For other examples of *talhin* see my paper *LiS'gullot haM'litzah b'Khitve haQodesh,* reprinted in my book, *The Word and the Book—Studies in Hebrew Language and Literature,* Hebrew section, pp. 225–60.

10. Josh. 2:18. This secondary meaning in Job is recognized by Ibn Ezra and Yellin. T. H. Gaster suggests this meaning for *tiqwah* in Ezek. 37:11 *(Myth, Legend and Custom in the Old Testament,* [New York: Harper and Row, 1969]), p. 629, where the meaning "thread" is not certain, but he does not cite the Job passage.

11. *King John,* 4. 2. 91.

12. *Lycidas,* l. 70.

13. *Arcades,* l. 65.

14. I am indebted to Professor Herzog for the O.H.G. data.

15. As an instance of this common linguistic phenomenon, biblical Hebrew has no less than four homophonic roots *ᶜanah:* I. "answer, respond" (Arabic *ᶜny, ᶜnw);* II. "sing, chant, declaim" (Num. 21:1, 7; Ps. 147:7; Job 3:1, Arabic *ghanay);* III. "be bowed down, afflicted" (Ps. 116:10; Isa. 53:7), *ᶜani,* "poor" (Akkadian *ᶜenu,* Arabic *ᶜanaw,* "be lonely"); IV. "be occupied with" (Eccles. 1:13, 3:10) *ᶜinyan,* "task" (1:12; 2:23), Syriac *'na',* Arabic *'nj, 'n',* "be concerned with."

16. This negative connotation is not absolute. The substantive *basherte* is used of one's (predestined) bride. I hesitate to suggest that this use carries an ironic nuance.

17. See Job 14:5, "his days are determined *(harūṣiṁ);* 1 Kings 20:40; Isa. 10:22; Akkadian *harâṣu,* "dig, decide," *hariṣu,* "trench."

18. See Esther 2:1 and the noun *gezērāh,* "decree"; both the verb and the noun are common in Yiddish.

19. Cf. Dan. 9:24, *Midrash Lev. Rabba,* sec. 4, *hotekhin et hahalakhah,* "they decide the law," *B. Shebuot* 30b, *'ehtekhennu,* "I will decide the case.

20. Wolf Yunin, *"Shprakhvinkl,"* in *Jewish Daily Forward,* April 17, 1979, p. 3.

21. As Professor Herzog was kind enough to inform me.

22. See J. Teslar, *New Polish Grammar* (New York, 1912), s.v.

23. The full listing of this usage in the Talmud occupies five columns in Chaim Jehoshua Kosovsky and Binyamin Kosovsky, *Otzar Leshon Hatalmud* (Jerusalem, 1970), 23:276–77.

24. The coalescence of the Two sounds *s* and *sh* is of course not limited to this community or to modern times. It can be documented in biblical Hebrew. The representation of Sin and Shin by the same symbol testifies to their phonetic similarity if not identity. It lies at the basis of the famous catchword *shibbolet,* which the Ephraimites pronounced *sibōlet* (Judg. 12:6). In Isa. 4:7, there is a striking paronomasia between *mishpat* and *mispah.* In Jer. 23:39, the prophet plays upon *massa',* "burden, vision" and the verb *nasha'.*

25. This etymology is suggested, for example, in A. Even Shoshan, *HaMillon heHadash* (Jerusalem: Kiryat Sepher, 1968), 1:259a. The suggestion was presented earlier in E. Ben Yehuda's great *Millon* (Jerusalem, Tel-Aviv, 1949), 1:578b, n. 1.

26. Lam. 4:10.

27. See M. H. Segal *Diqduq L'shon haMishnah* (Tel Aviv: Dvir, 1936), p. 83, sec. 133.

28. Thus R. Kittel, *Biblia Hebraica,* suggests *miboᶜe lo,* "from those you ask for it," from an Aramaic root, rare in Hebrew, meaning "ask." He registers his doubt by adding a question mark after the emendation.

29. See my *Koheleth, The Man and His World* (New York: Schocken, 1964), 3d augmented ed., pp. 176, 274. The various versions render similarly: RSV, "The life of him who has it, " *NEB,* "those who know her," *NAB,* "the life of its owner."

30. The crucial passages, many of which have been misunderstood, include 1:17, 18; 2:12; 3:11; 6:16; 7:23–25; 8:16, 17;l 9:12, 16, 18, 19.

31. *KMW,* pp. 182, 291.

32. *NAB* renders, "Nor are the wicked saved by their wickedness." *NEB* accepts a popular emendation of *reshaᶜ* to *ᶜosher,* and renders, "No wealth will save its possessor." *RSV* recognizes

the difficulty in the context of the usual meaning of the noun and approaches the nuance I suggest in the rendering, "Nor will wickedness deliver those who are given to it."

33. In various studies I have called attention to the valuable resources for the understanding of biblical Hebrew to be found in the later (rabbinic and medieval) stages of the language. The reader may be referred to my paper "Studies in the Relationship of Biblical and Rabbinic Hebrew," in *The Louis Ginzberg Jubilee Volumes* (New York: Jewish Theological Seminary, 1946), English vol., pp. 173–200, and *L'shon haMiqra l'Or L'shon Ḥakhamin* ("Biblical Language in the Light of Rabbinic Hebrew"), in *Sefer Tur Sinai* (Tel Aviv: *HaḤevra L'Ḥeqer HaMiqra*, 1961), pp. 149–67, among others. Both these papers are reprinted in my collected volume, *The Word and The Book, Studies in Biblical Language and Literature* (New York: Ktav, 1978).

The Moment of Desires

ALEXANDER SCHEIBER

I. JEWISH DATA

A. LITERARY SOURCES

A section of the litany *Avinu Malkenu* runs thus: "Our father, our king, let this hour be the hour of grace and the time of mercy before you."[3] "The time of mercy" *('et ratzon)* is a quotation from the Psalms (69:14). The Talmud defines this time as that "when the congregation is at prayer" (Ber. 8a). The medieval literature defines it as the time of the afternoon—to be precise, the Sabbath afternoon—prayer, since this was when the prophet Elijah was heard (1 Kings 13:36).[4]

God, however, is angry but for one moment a day (Ps. 30:6). No one but Bileam was able to work out when this moment occurred (Num. 24:16; Ber. 7a, Ab. z. 4b).[5]

The following datum is from the later Middle Ages. In the Isaiah-commentary of the Karaite Salmon b. Yeruham or Sahl, the following is found: "Stand at noon facing the Sun and then make your wish."[6] The turn of phrase appears to have come to the Karaites from the ancient *Sefer haRazim*.[7]

B. ORAL TRADITION

1. *Rosh Hashana.* According to the Jews of Tripoli it is possible to ask for wealth, wisdom, and a male child on the occasion of the *Q'dusha* at New

Men have ever sought the fulfillment of their desires from the powers above. They wanted to know the most propitious time and place for making their plea.[1] My friend Professor R. Patai studied this subject in connection with appeals for rain.[2] It will perhaps not displease him if in this Jubilee Volume dedicated to him I examine in a broad context this hitherto little-studied chapter of Jewish folklore.

This Jubilee Volume is the most appropriate place for me to wish Professor R. Patai—to whom I am bound by half a century of friendship—further years of activity and successful research for the world of scholarship.

95

Year or on the Day of Atonement, at the moment when the phrase *aye m'qom k'vodo* is reached (information from N. Munkácsi, Israel, 1956).

2. *Yom Kippur.* According to the Sephardim of Jerusalem the right moment to make one's wish is at the Neila prayer, in front of the open Holy Ark (N. Munkácsi, 1956). The Jews of Tripoli stand the children face to face with those giving the Kohenite blessing, because this is the moment when desires are fulfilled (N. Munkácsi, 1956).

Sukkot. In Subcarpathian Ruthenia it is held that a wish uttered at the time of the waving of the lulav will be fulfilled (L. Eisler, now in Israel).

4. *Hoshana Rabba.* József Patai, the father of my friend Raphael, writes as follows: On this night they waited for the moment "when the sky would split open and every desire that had been uttered would be fulfilled."[8] An illustrated Hebrew manuscript of the sixteenth century, which is erroneously regarded as being of Hungarian origin, depicts this moment when the sky opens during the night of Hoshana Rabba.[9]

5. *Shavuot.* The following quotation is from a book by D. Schön: His grandfather summoned him on the eve of the festival and told him that the sky would split open at midnight and whatever he wished for at that time would be fulfilled. He watched and waited for midnight with a trembling heart, and when his grandfather finished reading the extracts from the Bible . . . he ran out into the courtyard, lifted up his eyes to heaven, and haltingly uttered his wish aloud."[10] L. Szabolcsi writes in a similar vein: ". . . on this night every year the great gates above open up . . . On this night the sky splits open for a moment . . . and every desire we have at that time is fulfilled." "In Kálló (central north Hungary) the same belief was current;[12] in fact, this was generally believed by Jews all over the world.[13]

6. *Weekday morning prayer.* Rabbi Mendel, the Kossover Rebbe, declared: "Listen . . . tomorrow, during the morning service, whatever you will pray for will be fulfilled." They spent restless hours repeating to themselves and fixing it in their minds the desire for sustenance, *lest they forget to pray for it.* Here was a chance that might never occur again.[14]

7. *Other occasions.* As the girls at a wedding pass under the *huppa,* or grasp its supports, whatever they wish for will be fulfilled (A. Róbert, Pápa, 1950). If before burial the coffin is touched and something is desired, it will be fulfilled (G. Knöpfler. Nyíregyháza, 1962). The pilgrim places an egg in the Holy Ark of the synagogue at Djerba and writes his or her name on it, while thinking hard of something. The supplicant takes the egg out the following day and eats it. This is done chiefly by girls and women seeking husbands, children, money, or good health.[15]

II. Non-Jewish data

1. *Falling stars.* "Whatever one thinks of when one sees a star falling will come true" (Baja).[16] "It was a beautiful, mild, autumn night and stars fell

one after another, and the boys shouted out their dreams and desires over and over again."[17] "Whatever one thinks of when one sees a star falling will be fulfilled."[18] In Pushkin's *Eugene Onegin* Tatiana tries to find the right words for making a wish when she sees a star falling (5:6).

2. *Opening of the sky.* If one makes a wish the very moment that one sees the sky opening, it will come true. This is held in Gömör.[19] Someone was looking after the cattle at night on the green at Szederkény. The sky opened up in the east. He wished for a good wife, and it came true.[20] A herdsman in Taktaszada saw the sky open up three times, but he made no wish, since he did not know that was the way it would come true (L. Szabó, Taktaszada, 1968). An informant from Bodrogkeresztur also failed to make a wish when he saw the sky open. "It was so bright that you could see a needle in the grass." Yet if he had asked "It would have been granted" (L. Szabó, 1968). If one saw that the sky had opened, one had to think of something (e.g., wish for a long life) and it would be granted (Tótkomlós).[21] "The sky opened up, the angels leant out and sang; anyone seeing this must ask for something and God would grant it" (Vilmos Diószegi's collection, Aszaló, 1962, EA 7076. p. 6).

3. *Other occasions.* On New Year's Eve, a lump of sugar is broken in two; whatever is wished for at that time is fulfilled.[22] In some places in Austria a wish can be made when bells are tolled: ". . . ein Wunschglöcklein macht Hoffnung auf die Erfüllung verschiedener Herzenssachen."[23] W. Somerset Maugham writes: "A wish can be made when one sees the new moon, a cream-colored horse, when a star falls, and when the chicken's 'wishbone' is broken in two."[24]

4. *Places.* There is a window in Tihany Abbey: "Whoever first walks here and gives a sigh: whatever he sighs for shall be fulfilled."[25] Of the Rózsakő (Rose Rock) on the shores of Lake Balaton: "It was disputed whether one had to sit facing the Balaton or with one's back to it, and whether three wishes are fulfilled or just one."[26] On moving into a new house or flat, "if one has beautiful dreams, they are fulfilled."[27] In Rome, one must make a pilgrimage to St. Peter's at dawn on Good Friday: "whoever makes this pilgrimage, his desire shall be granted."[28] In Bled (Yugoslavia) there is an islet in the middle of a mountain lake: whoever pulls on the church's bell, his desire is fulfilled.[29]

The material can, of course, be multiplied.

NOTES

1. G. Róheim, *Spiegelzauber* (Leipzig-Wein, 1919), p. 6, n. 3.
2. R. Patai, "The 'Control of Rain' in Ancient Palestine," *HUCA* 14 (1939):251–86.
3. I. Davidson, *Thesaurus of Mediaeval Hebrew Poetry*, vol. 1 (New York, 1924), p. 12, n. 216.
4. I. Elbogen, *Der jüdische Gottesdienst in seiner geschichtlichen Entwicklung* (Frankfurt a/M., 1931), pp. 118, 532; Hebrew ed. (Tel-Aviv, 1972), p. 90.
5. W. Bacher, *Agada der pal. Amoräer*, vol. 1 (Strassburg, 1892), p. 148.

6. J. Mann, *Texts and Studies,* vol. 2 (Cincinnati, Ohio, 1935), p. 83.
7. Sefer HaRazim, ed. M. Margalioth (Jerusalem, 1966), pp. 72, 89, 93, 97. On the book see I. Gruenwald, *Apocalyptic and Merkavah Mysticism* (Leiden-Köln, 1980), pp. 225–34.
8. J. Patai, *A középső kapu* (Budapest, 1927), p. 74; Y.-T. Lewinsky, *Sefer haMoadim,* vol. 4 (Tel-Aviv, 1951), p. 206; J. Bergmann, *HaFolklor haYehudi* (Jerusalem, 1953), p. 82.
9. Ameisenowa, *Tarbiz* 23 (1958/59):198.
10. D. Schön, *Istenkeresők a Kárpátok alatt* (Tel-Aviv, 1964), pp. 218–19; I. Kaczér: *Ne félj, szolgám Jákób* (Tel-Aviv, n.d.), 1:27, 290.
11. L. Szabolcsi, *Délibáb* (Budapest, 1927, p. 84.
12. L. Szilágyi-Windt, *A kállói cádik* (Tel-Aviv, 1960), p. 118.
13. M. Kohen, *Mipij ha-am* (Tel-Aviv, 1979), 3:48. No. 239. Notes of H. Schwarzbaum, p. 122.
14. J. Heschel, *The Earth is the Lord's* (New York, 1950), pp. 78–79.
15. Tunézia: a "La Ghriba" zarándokai, *Magyarország,* 18, no. 25 (1980).
16. *Ethnographia* 10 (1899):311.
17. J. Székely, *Kisértés* (Budapest, 1972), p. 249.
18. F. Móra, *Négy apának egy leánya* (Budapest, 1960), p. 263; S. Sásdi, *Szabálytalan szerelem* (Budapest, 1980), p. 95.
19. L. Székely, *Ethnographia* 7 (1896):374.
20. L. Szabó, *Taktaszadai mondák* (Budapest, 1975), p. 524, no. 153.
21. A. Krupa, *Hiedelmek—varázslatok—boszorkányok* (Békéscsaba, 1974), p. 45.
22. I. Szabó and E. Szántó, *Bizalom* (film) (1980).
23. G. Gugitz, *Das Jahr und seine Feste im Volksbrauch Österreichs* (Wien, 1950), 2:62, 134.
24. W. S. Maugham, *Of Human Bondage.* In Hungarian translation: *Örök szolgaság* (Budapest, 1969), p. 57.
25. F. Karinthy, *Kentaur* (Budapest, 1947), p. 138.
26. L. Mesterházi, *Vakáció* (Budapest, 1979), p. 374.
27. A. Balázs, *Egy orvos az autóbuszon* (Budapest, 1973), p. 173.
28. Zs. Thury, *Barátok és ellenfelek* (Budapest, 1979), p. 125.
29. L. Szilvási, *Születésnap juniusban* (Budapest, 1972), p. 211.

A Jewish Moses Legend of Islamic Provenance

HAIM SCHWARZBAUM

Folktales, and particularly legends handed down orally from generation to generation, are often rooted in written, literary sources, such as biblical allusions or parables of ethical, religious significance.[1] In the following we shall examine the Arabic, Hebrew, and European versions of Aarne-Thompson narrative Type 785 ("Who ate the lamb's heart?"), and their literary sources.

The earliest, rather elaborate, Arabic version, attributed to the famous old Islamic traditional storyteller and "folklorist" Wahb Ibn Munabbih (ca. 654–728),[2] can be summarized as follows: In the course of his travels and rovings over the earth, Jesus is accompanied by a Jew who surreptitiously eats a loaf of bread out of their common provisions, and then persistently denies having eaten it. Despite various impressive miracles performed by Jesus (Thompson Motif D 1713)[3] so as to induce his companion to confess, the latter remains adamant. Later the companion makes off with the staff of Jesus, which Jesus used to resuscitate the dead (Motif E 64.1), and tries to cure a sick king by striking him with the staff. His blow kills the king, and all his efforts to imitate Jesus' acts of resuscitation with the staff fail (Motif J 2411.1.1). Accused of having slain the king, he is about to be hanged (AaTh Type 753, 753A), but Jesus arrives in time, revives the dead king, and thus saves his perfidious companion.[4] But even after being delivered by Jesus from the gallows, the mendacious fellow refuses to admit that he has eaten the loaf. Finally, in the course of their travels, they come across a treasure consisting of three gold bricks. Jesus says, "One of these gold bricks is for me, one for you, and the third for the man who ate the loaf." As soon as he hears this, the companion exclaims: "It was I who ate the loaf. . . ."[5] Jesus then advises his companion to leave the gold bricks where they lie, since they will cause the death of several greedy, avaricious men. After

99

Jesus and his companion leave, three travelers come to the place and are delighted to find the gold. One of them goes to the town to buy food for his companions and to procure a cart for the removal of the heavy gold bricks. But he harbors murderous designs against his two companions and mixes poison into the food. Meanwhile the two who guard the treasure resolve to kill the third one when he returns. They do kill him, then eat the food and die.[6] Jesus and his companion return, and when Jesus sees the three dead men he exclaims: "*La Ilāha illā Allāh!* (There is no God but Allah!) This is the result of greed!" Then Jesus raises the three men to life, they confess their guilt, repent of their evil ways, and leave the gold on the spot. Nothing, however, can make Jesus' companion overcome his greed.[7] He asks Jesus to give him the treasure. Jesus replies: "Take it! It will be your undoing in both this world and the next!" While the man tries to carry away the gold bricks, the earth opens up and swallows him. Thus far Wahb Ibn Munabbih's version, as recorded by Abū Isḥāq Ibn Muḥammad Ibn Ibrāhīm al-Thaʿlabī (d. 1036).[8]

Another early Islamic version attributed to the well-known Qur'an interpreter Ismāʿil Ibn ʿAbd al-Raḥman al-Suddī (d. 744),[9] is given by the famous historian and Qur'an commentator Abū Jaʿfar Muḥammad Ibn Jarī al-Ṭabarī (839–923).[10] Al-Suddi tries to explain, by means of our legend, the somewhat obscure passage in the Qur'an 3:45/52, in which Jesus asks: "Who will be my helpers unto Allah?"

This method of expounding a scriptural passage with the help of a tale is found frequently in the Talmudic-Midrashic Aggada.[11] In fact, the rich corpus of post-Qur'anic biblical legends owes much to this narrative method of exegesis.[12] Al-Suddi's version of our legend is similar to that of Wahb Ibn Munabbih, but he omits the miracles of curing the blind and the crippled, as well as the motif of Jesus walking on the water. He refers to only three miracles performed by Jesus: (1) the resuscitation of a sheep; (2) the bringing back to life of a slaughtered calf; and (3) the revival of the dead king. This reduction to three is in conformity with the triadic structure prevalent in narrative folklore, where three is an extremely popular formulistic number (Thompson Motif Z 71.1).

The beginning of al-Suddi's version has the following characteristic features: During the night Jesus' companion greedily swallows large mouthfuls of bread. He is sure that Jesus, being asleep, would not notice what he is doing. But suddenly Jesus asks his companion what he is doing, so that the latter has to spit out the bread so as to be able to answer Jesus that he is doing nothing. This episode is widespread in folklore,[13] and turns up in numerous aetiological legends indexed by Aarne-Thompson and J. Krzyzanowski, such as those dealing with the origin of mushrooms:[14] "St. Peter secretly eats a cake. When asked by Jesus what he is doing, he spits out chunks of cake which turn into mushrooms."[15] This subject is dealt with in a masterly fashion also by Oskar Dähnhardt,[16] who synopsizes a Flemish version as follows: "Petrus will dem Herrn (i.e., Jesus) einen frischgebacke-nen Kuchen verheimlichen und verbirgt ihn unter dem Hut; der heisse Kuchen brennt ihm die Haare weg, und so wurde St. Peter der erste Kahlkopf. . . ."[17]

A third Islamic version of Aa-Th Type 785 is found in Arabic MS.664 (599).29r-31r. in the John Rylands Library, Manchester.[18] Here Jesus' companion is named Yahuda, that is, Judas Iscariot,[19] who plots to kill Jesus. He joins him as his traveling companion, and when they reach Yahuda's dwelling place he invites Jesus to rest in his home, but then leaves him alone, ostensibly to buy some food, but actually to summon the Jews. The Jews come but are unable to find Jesus because Allah has concealed him from their eyes. Yahuda succeeds in finding Jesus. Jesus exhorts him to give up his evil design, but Yahuda claims to harbor none. Jesus tells him to go to a tree and ask it to deliver some gifts for Jesus, but instead the tree casts stones at Yahuda. Jesus sends him again to the same tree, and now the tree gives him three loaves, of which Yahuda eats one and takes only two to Jesus. Jesus, of course, knows that Yahuda has eaten one loaf (Motif V 223; D 1810.0.3; M 301.5). Next we have the miracle of the slaughtered sheep brought back to life by Jesus (Motif E 64.1), and then the episodes of the three gold bricks and of the teasure finders who murder one another (Aa-Th Type 763). Jesus strikes them with his staff and they come to life (E 64.1). Then he takes Yahuda to the sea, and as soon as he stretches out his hand two large fish appear (Motif D 2074.1.2). Jesus broils them, then tells Yahuda to consume the flesh but not to break the bones. Jesus gathers the bones and prays to Allah over them, whereupon the fish are revived and jump into the sea (Motif E 121.2; E 63; D 1652.1.10.1). Yahuda thinks that the magic power lies in Jesus' staff (Motif D 1254ff.), so he steals it and runs away. He comes to a city where he learns that the king is dangerously ill. He offers to cure him, but when he strikes the king with the staff he slays him, and is in turn killed by the people. In this version Jesus does not save his perfidious companion. In the former Islamic versions and in most versions of Aa-Th 753 and 753A Jesus is more lenient, and usually saves his com-panion from death. Our version adds that the angels seize the miraculous staff and return it to Jesus.

This version is unquestionably influenced by some features contained in the New Testament.[20] In some European versions of Aa-Th Type 785 the companion, quite naturally, is none other than Judas Iscariot.[21] In the well-known *Toldot Yeshu* we read that Jesus, St. Peter, and Judas Iscariot happen to enter an inn where they obtain one single roast goose. Because the small goose is not enough for all three, Jesus says that the one who will have the most beautiful dream should get the goose. In the middle of the night Judas secretly eats the goose. In the morning St. Peter says that he dreamed that he was sitting near the throne of the Son of *Shaddai* (God). Jesus says, "Indeed, I am the Son of *Shaddai,* and I saw you in my dream sitting near my throne. Then Judas exclaims: "And I dreamt that I swallowed the whole goose. . . ." This tale is found in numerous versions (cf. Aa-Th Type 1626) with which I have dealt elsewhere.[22] There are many other, shorter, Arabic versions of Aa-Th Type 785, some of which I discussed thirty-five years ago.[23]

Of special interest for us are those Jewish versions of Aa-Th 785 in which Moses occupies the place of Jesus as the main protagonist.[24] This substitution is in accord with the tendency prevalent in Jewish folklore of "Judaizing" foreign elements, adapting them to Jewish tradition and milieu, and stripping them of their non-Jewish trappings.[25] According to these Jewish versions, while Moses is wandering in the desert with the staff[26] he had taken from the home of Jethro,[27] he meets an old man. They decide to travel together and to combine their stock of food. Moses has three loaves of bread, the old man two. On the way each of them consumes two loaves, while the fifth is secretly eaten by the old man. After walking about half a day in the wilderness, Moses asks his companion to give him the fifth loaf. But the old man swears a mighty oath that there were never more than four loaves. Despite various miracles performed by Moses, the old man persists. His dishonest behavior is characterized as being peculiar to a member of "the tenth generation." The reference is to the tenth generation after Adam, the generation of Noah, which sinned and was punished by God with the Deluge.[28]

Moses performs three miracles: (1) He succeeds in seizing two deer with his staff; he slaughters them, without breaking any of their bones,[29] and broils them. When both men have eaten their fill, "Moses places bone to bone and puts his staff on them and prays to the Lord," whereupon the animals are brought back to life.[30] (2) Moses brings forth water from the rock with his staff so that the two travelers can quench their thirst.[31] (3) With his staff Moses resuscitates a dead elder who "was like a father to the townsfolk." Despite all these miracles the old man persists in his denial of having eaten the fifth loaf. Then Moses says: "This one must be of the tenth generation. . . ." Then, as in the Islamic versions summarized above, we have here too the episode of the old man's unsuccessful trial to imitate Moses by resuscitating a dead youngster with the help of Moses' staff. Again, it is Moses who saves his companion from death by reviving the youth. As in the Arabic versions, here too the story ends with Moses miraculously turning three mounds of earth into gold (Motif D 2102.3: "Saint magically produces treasure"). Moses says to his companion: "Let the one who ate the loaf take two mounds of gold, and the third one is for the man who did not eat it." Thereupon the old man confesses, and Moses then tells him to take the lot. Then comes the incident of the treasure finders who murder each other. The moral of the story is, "All this is told so that you should know that the tenth generation are unbelievers and wicked men. . . ."

A more recent version recorded from the lips of an old Jewish woman from Yemen[32] is entitled "Moses Our Teacher and the Last Generation."[33] Moses asks God to show him the behavior of the last generation. As in some versions of the famous theodicy legend,[34] here too Moses is told by God "to leave the Creator's work as it is," and not to interfere. Moses, however, insists on becoming familiar with a representative of "the last generation," and is told to proceed to a certain town. On his way he meets a man who asks him to be his companion. Moses agrees. Moses has six loaves of bread, while the man has no food. He asks Moses to give him a loaf, and Moses complies. This happens three times, so that only three loaves are left. Then the greedy man secretly eats the fourth loaf. They reach a river, and Moses is about to take a rest when he notices that only two loaves are left. The man denies having eaten the missing loaf. They continue on their way and come to a city, where Moses revives the dead son of the sultan with his staff. He declines to accept any reward, although the sultan wants to shower much gold upon him. The companion resents the refusal. They come to another town where the companion tries to imitate the miracle performed by Moses and resuscitate the dead king. He fails and is led to the gallows. Moses asks him: "Who ate the loaf?" In his predicament the man confesses,[35] and Moses saves him from death by reviving the dead king. Here follows the well-known legend of Moses at the well.[36] The man asks Moses to give him some money. Moses turns a lump of earth into gold (Motif D 2102.3), and gives it to him. Next we have the episode of the treasure finders who kill each other. "All this God showed to Moses for his edification."

In a Yiddish version of the tale the hero is not Moses but the Prophet Elijah.[37] It appears that this version is influenced by Slavic versions of As-Th Type 753 and 753A.[38] In other words, Type 785 is subordinated to Types 753 and 753A. In the Yiddish version an unlettered country Jew is in the habit of eating his daily meals without first washing his hands as required by Jewish ritual.[39] One day he hears a learned man interpret the biblical injunction, "Thou shalt truly tithe all the produce of they seed" (Deut. 14:22), as follows: "If one gives one rouble charity to the poor, the Lord gives him two; he who spends two, the Lord reimburses him by granting him four, etc."[40] The man is so taken by this lucrative "business" of alms-giving that he gives all his money to the poor. His conduct impresses Heaven, where it is suggested that the man should be properly rewarded. However, the accusing angels claim that the man neglects the basic rite of washing hands before meals. In order to induce the man to mend his ways Elijah is sent to him, disguised as a pauper (Motif K 1811.1). He invites the man, now totally impoverished, to join him on his begging tour.[41] The man consents, and Elijah (as do the other protagonists of Aa-Th 785 and 753a) effects a miraculous cure (Motif D 2161 and F 950), and gets six loaves of bread as a reward. His greedy companion is incensed with Elijah for having asked for bread instead of gold and silver. Elijah tells him that he has plenty of gold and is not in need of any such reward. During their travels the man secretly consumes a loaf and denies having done so. Ultimately they part company, and the man goes to a city where the governor is very sick. He pretends to be a physician and tries to imitate Elijah's miraculous cure, but fails and is about to be executed. Elijah reappears, revives the governor, and thus saves the man from death. Here too the man confesses that he has eaten the loaf without first washing his hands. When asked by the happy governor what should be his reward, Elijah asks for a spade. He does not need any money. The companion again resents this and considers Elijah's attitude extremely foolish. Elijah digs with the spade and uncovers great treasures. However, he refuses to permit the man to take them until the latter promises to wash his hands before the meals (cf. Motif D 1314.2; D 1450; N 533).

A Jewish version from Persian Kurdistan[42] exemplifies the idea that a person appearing to be saintly is in fact very greedy, and vice versa: a poor Negro proves to be a most virtuous man.[43] His virtue is manifested by providing food for a guest. Once Moses pays a visit to an ostensibly righteous man, a *tzaddiq*, who is always engrossed in Tora study and prayer. Two portions of food are sent down from Heaven to the *tzaddiq*, one for him and one for Moses. The *tzaddiq*, however, hides one portion, and divides the other into two parts, giving Moses half of it. Moses comes across a cave inhabited by a meritorious Negro who gets his daily sustenance from God.[44] Suddenly the Negro sees that God has sent him a double portion of food. He delights in putting the two portions before his dear guest, and honors Moses by waiting to taste his own food until Moses has started eating. The celestial food sent down to the Negro is of a much better quality than that granted to the *tzaddiq*. God thus shows Moses the pure heart of the Negro in contrast to that of the *tzaddiq*.

A parallel to this version, narrated by the Yemenite storyteller Yephet Shvili, is found in the Israel Folktale Archives (IFA 1146). Here too the *tzaddiq* conceals one share. Moses asks him whether God has sent one portion only. The man twice assures Moses that God has sent no portion for him. Moses, sensing the man's dishonesty, refuses to partake of the food, saying: "I will not eat of your portion. If God has not pitied me, neither should you pity me." Then Moses comes across the abode of an old woman who proves to be most hospitable and charitable. She gives Moses good food, and entertains him lavishly. Before leaving, Moses blesses her: "May God forgive all your sins!" Thereupon the woman tells Moses that she has committed the awful sin of incest. Moses sticks his finger into his throat so as to vomit out the food she has given him. But suddenly he hears a voice from Heaven: "Moses, Moses, do not spit out the woman's food! Just now she has taken the place of the *tzaddiq*, and all her sins are forgiven!" (Motif T. 412.1).[45]

As a matter of fact, Aa-Th Type 785 is of a facetious, witty character, as is the kindred Aa-Th Type 774, which is entitled "Jests About Christ and Peter." The jest (Schwank) in Aa-Th 785 consists of a holy man (Moses, Jesus, Elijah, etc.) employing a ruse or trick to induce the liar to confess. In Stith Thompson's Motif Index these tales come under the heading "Confession Obtained by a Ruse" (Motif J 1141), or "Guilty Person Deceived Into Gesture (Act) which Admits Guilt" (J 1141.1), and "Largest Part of a Prize to Go to the Guilty Man. In Order to Obtain the Prize He confesses the Earlier Crime" (J 1141.1.1 and J 1672). In the Aarne-Thompson type-index there is an extensive section entitled: "Jokes and Anecdotes" (Types 1200–1999). The question arises: why has our cycle of humorous stories not been included in this section? The answer seems to be that here the protagonists are sacred persons, and therefore they belong to the section of "Religious Tales" (Aa-Th Types 750–849), despite the facetious contents.[46]

Most important is the question of the sources or origins of Aa-Th Type 785. It seems to me that our legend is rooted in episodes and incidents related in the New Testament, and not in Christian apocryphal writings.[47] Thus we read in Matthew 8:19 f. that a doctor of the law came up to Jesus and said: "Master, I will follow you wherever you go." Jesus replied: "Foxes have their holes, the birds their roosts, but the Son of Man has nowhere to lay his head." This statement must have given rise to legends in which Jesus is portrayed as wandering from place to place together with a companion (not necessarily a doctor of the law as in Matthew, but rather a simple man, as stated in the version of Luke 9:57–62. Oral tradition has seized upon Jesus' picturesque response describing his plight. To folk imagination this statement of Jesus was clearly suggestive of an itinerant way of life.[48]

As for the motif of the mendacity and greed of Jesus' companion, who secretly eats a loaf of bread or some other food and stubbornly denies having done so, this could be related to the bread controversy or bread dialogue between Jesus and his disciples. We read in Matthew 16:5–12 that the disciples of Jesus forgot to take along bread for their crossing of Lake Gennesaret in a boat. When Jesus tells them, "Take heed and be on your guard against the leaven of the Pharisees and Sadducees," they reason, "It is because we have taken no bread." Reading their minds, Jesus says: "Why do you talk about bringing no bread? Where is your faith? How can you fail to see that I was not speaking about bread? Be on your guard, I said, against the leaven of the Pharisees and Sadducees." Only now do the disciples understand that the warning of Jesus was directed, not against the baker's leaven, but against the doctrines of the Pharisees and Sadducees. In the version of Mark 8:14 f. the disciples have with them no more than one single loaf of bread.

How this incident could have developed into our tale can be explained as follows. As already pointed out above, the impact of biblical tales on oral stories was considerable. However, folktales rooted in literary sources, and especially in the hallowed text of the Bible, usually succumb to radical changes. One can therefore speak of an oral reshaping of scriptural stories. Moreover, the storytellers not only spun the biblical narrative yarn further, in accord with popular fancy, but also tended to ignore the figurative, metaphorical interpretations of biblical episodes or legends. In the present case they adhered to the disciples' initial interpretation of Jesus' reference to "the leaven of the Pharisees," regarding it as actual baker's leaven and connecting it with the fact that they had forgotten to take bread along with them, or had brought one loaf only. It is precisely these rudimentary elements of the New Testament bread episode that have been preserved in folk memory throughout the centuries. Oral tradition seized upon the literal notion of the Pharisees' bread, or, as Mark has it, on a single loaf, as constituting the pivot of the dialogue between Jesus and his disciples. Thus the question arises: what has become of this loaf of bread? Popular imagination supplies the answer: a Pharisee, that is, a Jew, usually a hypocrite (cf. Luke's version 12:1), secretly ate it. Then the yarn is spun further: since Jesus' companion is a true Pharisee he had to deny having eaten the loaf, just as the disciples in their original dialogue with Jesus say, "We took no bread."[49]

Those versions of Aa-Th 785 in which St. Peter plays the role of Jesus' companion seem to be dependent on Peter's denial of Jesus as described in the four Gospels.[50] The fact that Peter denied Jesus no less than three times (Motif Z 71.1) undoubtedly influenced our story in which Jesus, each time after performing a miracle, urges his companion to admit that he has eaten the missing loaf. In many versions the companion refuses three times to confess. This negative image of St. Peter is not only emphasized in the several versions of our story, but he is also thus characterized in numerous other folktales in which arrogant and impudent heroes, barred from entering Heaven by the Gatekeeper, St. Peter, do not hesitate to remind him of his denial of Jesus, and Peter has no choice but to admit them (cf., e.g., Motif J 1616, "St. Peter Not Guiltless"). This also happens in some versions of As-Th 800 and 801. Oral tradition also takes account of sharp utterances of Jesus about Peter, such as those reported by Matthew 16:23 and Mark 8:33.

Also those versions which have Judas Iscariot as the perfidious protagonist[51] can be traced to popular reformulations of New Testament narratives or statements (cf. Matthew 26:14–16; Mark 14:10–11; Luke 22:3–6; John 18:25–30). The folk legend identifying Jesus' mean traveling companion with Judas Iscariot can also be traced to such utterances of Jesus as "He who eats bread with me has turned against me" John 13:18; cf. Ps. 41:10); "One who has dipped his hand into this bowl with me will betray me" (Matthew 26:23; Mark 14:18; Luke 22:21); "It is the man to whom I give this piece of bread when I have dipped it in the dish that will betray me"

(John 13:26). The betrayal of Jesus by Judas made a powerful impression on folk consciousness throughout the ages, so that it made its way easily into international folklore (cf. Motif A 2721.5).

Neither must we overlook the fact that many versions of Aa–Th 785 show the impact of a famous Aesopic fable (e.g., in Babrius's version, no. 95) about the ailing King Lion[52] who tells the fox to lure a stag out of the thicket and bring him into his presence. The sly fox tells the stag that the dying lion is anxious to appoint the stag as his successor to the throne. The stag is thus enticed to the lion's den. The lion leaps at him, but the stag manages to get away. The hungry lion then asks the fox to devise a new stratagem by which to induce the stag to visit him. The fox again succeeds in his trickery, and the lion kills the stag and has a fine banquet all by himself. The stag's heart falls aside, and the fox eats it. The lion looks for the heart, but the fox tells him that his search is in vain, for what kind of heart could the foolish stag have, since he entered the lion's den twice. This fable, popular also in Jewish folklore, has many versions.[53]

Of the numerous Slavic verions of our story let us summarize only one narrated by the famous Polish storyteller Jan Krzeptowski Sabala (1809–1894): During their travels, Jesus and Peter, disguised as beggars, are given a lamb. While preparing it for cooking, Peter secretly eats the kidneys and the heart of the lamb. When asked by Jesus, Peter replies that the lamb had neither kidneys nor a heart. Jesus makes no further inquiries, and the two continue on their way. Jesus comes across a rich treasure which he divides into three heaps: one for himself, one for Peter, and the third for the man who ate the lamb's kidneys and heart. At once Peter confesses, whereupon Jesus tells him to take two heaps out of the three. As for the third, Jesus scatters it all over the earth. Peter buries his shares in the ground, covering them with a big rock. This is the reason why to this day only one share of this vast treasure is divided among mankind, while the two other portions are still buried deep in the ground.

A similar version, found in the old Italian *Novelle Antiche,* was translated into German by Albert Wesselski.[54]

The present study of the many variants of Aa–Th 785 attempted to show that originally religious, even sacred, narratives can, in the course of time, degenerate into rather trivial folktales of a witty, humorous character,[55] and that the Jewish versions analyzed are dependent on the early Arabic patterns of Aa-Th 785.

NOTES

1. Cf. my *Studies in Jewish and World Folklore* (hereafter "*Studies*"), (1968), p. 408.
2. On the life and work of this eminent man of letters, cf. R. G. Khoury, *Wahb Ibn Munabbih* . . . (Wiesbaden: Harrassowitz, 1972), pp. 189–316.
3. This early Islamic source refers to the following miracles performed by Jesus: He cures

various ills (e.g., Matt. 12:15, 22; 14:36; 15:29–31; 17:14 ff.; Marh 3:10, 6:53–56; 7:31–37; 9:14–29; Luke 6:17–19; 9:37–43; Thompson, Motif V 221; D2161; F 950). He restores the sight of a blind man (Matt. 9:27–31; Mark 8:22–26; motif V 221.12; D1505.10; D 2161.3.1; F 952); heals a lame, crippled man (Matt. 12:9–14; Mark 3:1–6; Luke 6:6–11; 13:10–17; 14:1–6; Motif F 953). He walks on the water (Matt. 14:22–23; Mark 6:45–52; John 6:15–21; Motif D 2125.1; D2151.1; F 931; D 1841.4.3; D 1524.1). He even resuscitates a dead deer and a slaughtered calf. Motif E 121.4; E 3; E 32; E 168; E 171; and E 64.1. Cf. also D 1254 f.; D 1718.1; V 227.1; V 224.2.

4. As a matter of fact Aarne-Thompson narrative type 753, "Christ and the Smith," and Type 753A, "Unsuccessful Resuscitation," constitute salient elements of Aa–Th Type 785. Type 753 is extremely widespread in world folklore. As for Type 753A, cf. the Yiddish Elijah legend analyzed below, and Israel Folklore Archives (IFA) 560 discussed in Dov Noy, *Contes populaires racontés par les Juifs de Tunisie* (Jerusalem, 1968), pp. 112–15, "Le Médecin et son assistant," and nn., p. 316, no. 18. Cf. also IFA 2330 and 5823. J. Lompa, *Bajki i Podania* (Wroclaw and Warsaw, 1968), pp. 114–16, combines Type 753 with Type 785.

5. Cf. Motif J 1141.1.1, "Largest Part of the Prize to Go to the Guilty Man. In order to obtain the Prize, He Confesses the Earlier Crime." Cf. also Motif J 1672.

6. Cf. the famous Aa-Th Type 763, "The Treasure Finders Who Murder One Another," already extant in Chaucer's "Pardoner's Tale." Cf. my *Studies*, pp. 82, 95, and *Fabula* 7:166, Type 763, listing the Jewish versions hailing from the various "tribes" of Israel, to which the following IFA versions should be added: 5012, 5755, 7315, 7429, and 7774. Cf. also F. C. Tubach, *Index Exemplorum . . .* (Helsinki, 1969), p. 138, no. 1681.

7. Cf. Thompson, *Motif Index* W 151ff., and W 125ff.; J. Krzyzanowski's Polish type 1704, "The Greedy St. Peter Punished by Jesus."

8. Cf. His *Qiṣaṣ al-Anbiyā* (Cairo, 1324), p. 223 f. or Beirut: al-Maktaba al-Thaqāfiyya, s. a., pp. 355–57.

9. Cf. T. Nagel, *Die Qiṣaṣ al-Anbiyā . . .* (Bonn, 1967), pp. 70–74.

10. Cf. Tabari's Qur'ān Commentary, *Jāmiˁal-Bayān fi Tafsīr al-Qur'ān* (Bulaq, 1323–29), 3:198–200. In German translation, Otto Spies, "Das Grimm'sche Märchen 'Bruder Lustig' in arabischer Überlieferung," *Rheinisches Jahrbuch für Volkskunde* (1951, 2:48–60, which sheds much fresh light on Aa-Th 785. Of much interest is also Mirkhond's *Rauzat al-ṣafā*, trans. into English by E. Rehatsek (London, 1892), part 1, 2:173 ff.

11. For this exegetical method cf. my *The Mishle Shu ˁalim (Fox Fables) of Rabbi Berechiah Ha-Nakdan . . .* Kiron: Inst. for Jewish and Arab Folklore Research, 1979), pp. xiv-vii, introduction, and pp. xlv-vii, nn. 69–80.

12. Cf. Nagel, *Die Qiṣaṣ*, pp. 26–79, and my forthcoming *Biblical and Extra-Biblical Legends in Islamic Folk-Literature.*

13. Cf. Aa-Th 774 N., "St. Peter's Gluttony. Jesus Keeps Asking Him Questions So that He Must Continually Spit Out Mouthfuls."

14. Cf. Aa-Th 774 L, "Mushrooms from St. Peter's Spittle," and J. Krzyzanowski, Polish Type 1704, no. 2636, Cf. also Dähnhardt, *Natursagen*, 2:107 ff., "Entstehung der Pilze."

15. Cf. also Aa-Th 774 J, "Why Peter Became Bald: He Did Not Divide Cakes With Jesus."

16. Cf. Dähnhardt, *Natursagen*, 2:172 ff., "Der Ursprung von Petrus' Glatze."

17. Ibid., p. 173. Cf. also E. Rona-Sklarek, *Ungarische Volksmärchen* (Neue Folge (Leipzig. 1909), pp. 279–80, no. 31, and nn., p. 301.

18. Cf. J. Robson, "Stories of Jesus and Mary," *The Muslim World* 40 (1950):240.

19. On Judas Iscariot cf. P. Dinzelbacher, *Judastraditionen* (Vienna: Oesterr. Museum f. Volkskunde, 1977); B. Heller, MGWJ, 1932, 76:33-,421; 1933, 77:198–210.

20. Cf. Matt. 26:14–16; Marh 14:10–11; Luke 22:3–6.

21. Cf., e.g., Bolte and Polivka, *Anmerkugen*, 2:150.

22. Cf. my essay in *Sefarad* (Madrid, 1962), 22:37–46, and my *Studies*, pp. 188–89, 358–59; *Fabula* 7:213–14, type 1626, to which add IFA 5550, 5593, 8706, 8768, 8847..

23. Cf. my essay in *Edoth* (Jerusalem, 1946–47), 2:101 f., to which add the version of Ghazzālī (1058–1111), *Ihyā ˁUlūm al-Dīn*, 3:188f; Damīrī (1344–1405, *Ḥayāt al-Hayawān*, 1:266. Cf. also Michael Asin, in *Patrologia Orientalis* (Paris, 1915), 13:335 ff., no. 54 ff.; René Basset, *Mille et un contes recits et legendes Arabes* (Paris, 1927), 3:180–83, no. 112, with important comparative notes; H. Honti, in *HWB des deutschen Märchens*, 2:612–14; Tubach, *Index Exemplorum*, p. 256, no 3295 should be added to Bolte and Polivka, *Anmerkungen*, 2:149–63.

24. Cf. Samuel Krauss, *Jewish Quarterly Review 2* n.s. (1911–12):339–64; M. J. Bin Gorion, *Mimekor Yisrael* . . . (Bloomington an London, 1976), 1:82–85, 3:1494, no. 35; and my *Mimekor Yisrael w'Yishma ᶜel* . . . (Tel Aviv, 1975), pp. 249–59.

25. Cf. my *Studies*, p. 548, Index, s.v. "Judaizing non-Jewish Folktales."

26. Many linguistic features in the Hebrew version show the impact of the Arabic language, e.g., Hebrew *Matte* (staff), is usually masculine, but in our version it is feminine, as is its Arabic equivalent, ᶜaṣā.

27. Motif D 1254, often attested in the Bible, cf. Exod. 4:2 ff.

28. Cf. Mishna Avot 5:2.

29. Cf. Exod. 12:46, and Num. 9:12. Cf. S. Krauss, *JQR* 2 (1911–12): 348 f.

30. Cf. Motif E 174, "Bones Wrapped in Sheepskin Inscribed with Holy Name Revive," and E 32, "Resuscitated Eaten Animal."

31. Cf. Ex. 17:5–6, and Motif D 1567.6, "Stroke of Staff Brings Water from Rock," and Motif A 941. 5.1, "Springs Break Forth Where Saint Smites Rock."

32. Cf. IFA, no. 2995.

33. Dov Noy, *A Tale For Each Month—1961* (Haifa, 1962), pp. 20–25, Hebrew section, and ms. p. 89.

34. Aa-Th Type 759, examined by me in a special study, "The Jewish and Moslem Versions of Some Theodicy Legends," *Fabula* 3:119–69, and esp. pp. 141–42, n. 141, to which add *Fabula* 7:165, Type 759** A (Hansen). Cf. also Ziporah Kagan, *A Tale For Each Month—1963* (Haifa, 1964) pp. 35–36, and n. p. 87, no. 7.

35. In many versions the perfidious man does not confess even when he is about to be hanged. He confesses only when he learns that he can obtain riches by confessing.

36. Cf. Terrence L. Hansen, *The Types of the Folktale in Cuba, Puerto Rico* . . . (Berkeley and Los Angeles, 1957), p. 88 (type 759**). Cf. also H. W. Haase, "Die Theodizeelegende . . .," Göttingen diss., 1966, pp. 203–35. For a Falasha version cf. M. Wurmbrand, *Yedaᶜ ᶜAm* (1965), 11:30:48f. Cf also n. 34 above.

37. Cf. Samuel Lehmann, "Eliyahu Hanavi in der Folks-Fantazi," *Arkhiv far Yidisher Sprakhvisnshaft* . . ., ed. N. Prilutzki and S. Lehmann (Warsaw, 1926–33). pp. 115–22; and my *Studies*, pp. 7–8. Elijah is the protagonist also in IFA 560, 2330, 5823, and many other legends where he acts as the miraculous healer, just as Medea does.

38. Cf. e.g. J. Krzyżanowski, *Polska bajka ludova* (1962), 2:233–34, 247, Type 753, esp. no. 4, starting with Type 753 and ending with Type 785, and 2:247, bearing on Type 785. Cf. also the numerous variants in Bolte and Polivka, *Anmerkungen*, 2:156, esp. those Polish versions emphasizing ten or hundredfold rewards of almsgiving, which are similar to our Yiddish version. That the principal motif of Type 785 is included in Type 753 has already been stressed by W. R. S. Ralston, *Russian Folktales* (London, 1873), p. 355.

39. This is reminiscent of the New Testament story of Jesus being approached by a group of Pharisees with the question: "Why do your disciples break the ancient tradition? They do not wash their hands before meals," Matt. 15:1 ff.; Mark 7:1–23. Our Yiddish version seems to be a reflection on this issue.

40. Cf. n. 38 above.

41. It is quite clear here why Elijah is anxious to have precisely this man as his companion: he wants to teach him a lesson.

42. Eliezer Marcus, *Min haMabu'a, Forty Four Folktales* . . . (Haifa, 1966), pp. 81–83, 168–69, no. 17.

43. Cf. my *Studies*, pp. 128–32, 465.

44. This is a very common motif in both Arab and Jewish folklore, cf., e.g., my essay in *Yeda' 'Am* 18 (1976):20–28; Joseph Campbell, *The Portable Arabian Nights* (New York, 1952), pp. 395–97.

45. Dov Noy, ed., *Jefet Schwili erzählt* . . . (Berlin, 1963), p. 147.

46. Curiously enough, a facetious story such as Aarne-Thompson 1348, basically akin to Aa-Th 785, sometimes has both Jesus and Peter as its protagonists. Peter says that he saw a gigantic hare. Jesus resorts to a ruse to induse him to confess that the size of the hare was quite ordinary. Aa-Th 1348 is very popular also in Jewish folklore, cf., e.g., Imm. Olsvanger, *L'Chayim*, no. 142; Z. Ariel, *Hakhamim wTipshim* (Tel Aviv, 1950), pp. 173, 294; M. Schnitzer, *Rabbi Lach* (Hamburg, 1922), pp. 121 f.; M. Präger and S. Schmitz, *Jüdische Schwänke* (Vienna and Leipzig, 1928), no. 227. Cf. also Motif X 904.1; X 904.2; Q 263; D. 1318.17; B. E. Perry,

Aesopica (Urbana, Ill., 1952), pp. 703–4, no. 707; B. Holbek, *Aesops levned og fabler* (Copenhagen, 1961–62), 2:185, no. 136; L. Uffer, *Rätoromanische Märchen* . . . (Basel, 1945), p. 50, no. 1; E. K. Blümmel, *Schnurren und Schwänke des franz. Bauernvolkes* (Leipzig, 1906), pp. 192 f., no. 70, and K. Ranke, *Die Welt der einfachen Formen* (Berlin and New York, 1978), pp. 261 ff.

47. Cf., e.g., Ernst Kuhn, *Barlaam und Josaphat* (Munich, 1893), p. 82; Otto Spies, *Rheinisches Jb. f. Volkskunde* 2 (1951):59.

48. Cf. F. X. Told, *Die Wanderungen Jesu* . . . (Memel, 1864); Stith Thompson, *Motif Index*, (1966), 6:138–39; A. Aarne and S. Thompson, *The Types of the Folktale* (Helsinki, 1961), p. 552 (Index), s.v. "Christ and Peter."

49. Another example of this folk tendency to take figurative expressions in their literal sense is supplied by the folkloristic treatment of John the Baptist's reference to the mission of Jesus. John says: "I indeed baptize you with water unto repentance, but he that cometh after me . . . shall baptize you with the Holy Ghost and with fire. Whose fan is in his hand, and he will thoroughly purge his [threshing] floor, and gather his wheat into the garner, but he will burn up the chaff with unquenchable fire" (Matt. 3:11–12; cf. Mark 1:7–8; Luke 3:16–17; John 2:26–28; and cf. Isa. 41:15 f.; Hosea 13:3; Obadiah 1:18). This episode has become literalized in the widespread Aarne-Thompson narrative type 752 A: "Christ and Peter in the Barn. Threshing with Fire. The peasant forces them to rise early and thresh in payment for lodging. They separate the grain by means of fire. When the peasant tries to do the same thing the barn burns down." Thus are figurative statements turned by folk tradition into tangible, real, and concrete events. By the way, the unsuccessful attempt to imitate miracles is well-known in folklore (Motif J 2411).

50. Cf. Matt. 26:69–75; Mark 14:66–72; Luke 22:56–62; John 18:25–27.

51. E. g., the Arab version discussed above, and many European versions referred to by Bolte and Polivka, *Anmerkungen*, 2:150 and Dähnhardt, *Natursagen*, 2:239–40; etc.

52. Cf. my *Mishle Shuᶜalim*, pp. 509, 510, n. 29, 511, n. 32.

53. Ibid., pp. 504ff.

54. Cf. A. Wesselski, *Märchen des Mittelalters* (Berlin, 1925), pp. 88–89, 218, no. 30. Cf. Also Bolte and Polivka, *Anmerkungen*, 2:151 ff.

55. E. g., Story no. 81, "Bruder Lustig," in the collection of the Grimm brothers, studied by Bolte and Polivka, and by Spies; cf. above, n. 10.

The Woman with the Animal Face:
The Emergence of a Jewish Fairy Tale

ALIZA SHENHAR

The comparative study of folk literature has dealt primarily with the problem of themes and motifs circulating in various cultural traditions. As a result of this approach, and within its framework, genre is conceived of as a thematic category. The criterion for the classification of story texts into genres has, therefore, come to devolve upon the question, "What is the story about?"[1] Thus legends tell of saints, heroes, miracles, and other supernatural occurrences; *Märchen* revolve upon "unpretentious heroes who kill their opponents, become kings and marry princesses";[2] fables depict the doings of plants and animals; and proverbs express traditional wisdom. This approach is founded on the presupposition that thematic similarity implies universal identity of genre. For this reason, the formalistic character of the folkloristic expression is thought of as being impressed upon its contents; stories on a single theme belong to a single genre.

The thematic categorization of folk literature no doubt has a pragmatic value for the development of comparative research. Nevertheless, the basic principle of a direct relationship between theme and folkloristic genre, on which this method is based, does not always stand the test of empirical investigation. Those researchers who employed the historical method did not, as a matter of fact, intend to deal with the classification of material into genres. Their research had three aims: the reconstruction of the primary form from the existing versions; the identification of the place and period in which the work was created; and the tracing of the geographical dispersion of the work, focusing on the shape it took in various areas.[3]

Indeed, Thompson explicitly declared that the effort invested in coining precise terminology for the various types of folk stories was unproductive. He went as far as to describe the lack of terminological clarity as an advantage, since it often obviated lengthy discussion of the precise genre to which a particular story belonged.[4]

Nevertheless, the indexing of tale types led to their classification into genres, even though this term was not employed. Thus, for example, the term *novella* designates love stories that make up the fourth section of the *Index of Tale Types*.[5] The focal point of such stories is the confrontation of man and woman; one or both of the lovers encounter obstacles but succeed in overcoming them, achieving their desire at the conclusion of the story. In order to heighten the polarization inherent in the confrontation, the two lovers represent two different nations, religions, social classes, and the like. In this way, "natural" obstacles existing from birth and even before, such as ancestry, are thrown up in the path of the heroes.

Hedda Jason has suggested a different set of distinctions to be used in classifying stories into genres. Her method takes into account the entire complex of elements that make up the story: character, object, spatial and temporal dimension. Jason's principal distinction is the "mode" in which the story is set; this is defined as: "The existential medium relationship between man and the world, as manifested in ethnopoetry. Mode is one of the most important formative elements of ethnopoetic genre and each genre is 'set' in a particular mode."[6]

Jason further distinguishes between three types of modes:[7]

(a) Realistic Mode. The mode of genre in which man confronts his fellows on the human level, involving essentially no extra-natural (fabulous, according to modern scientific standards) elements; some nonnatural elements may appear on a secondary level. Genres set in this mode are the novella, the epic, the lyric, and the ballad.

(b) Fabulous Mode. Mode in which man confronts extra-natural forces. The fabulous mode is divided into the numinous and the marvelous modes.

(1) Numinous Mode. A mode in which man confronts an extra-natural world, which is part of the society's belief systems. The numinous mode has three subdivisions: *the creative* (myth and trickster tale); *the miraculous:* the sacred (sacred legend, ritual texts, and the etiological legend), the satanic (legend of the satanic) and the magic (legend of the magic); and *the demonic modes* (demonic legend, the animal legend, robber legend, and the legend about early populations).

(2) Marvelous Mode. Mode in which man confronts a world that is irrelevant to the belief system or moral codes of the narrating community, and is a system in its own right. The marvelous is composed of majestas and fascinosum. Genre set in this mode is the fairy tale.

(c) Symbolic Mode. Mode in which the character and the requisites fulfill a role that has no relation to their natural or fabulous qualities, and thus either symbolize other entities or expose a structural aspect of the ethnopoetic work. Genres set in this mode are the formula tale, the tall tale, the numskull tale, the parable, the proverb, the riddle, and the joke.

In this system of classification, the novella is set in the realistic mode. The confrontation, which is central to the story, involves human beings. The resolution of the complications developed in the plot comes about through the agency of one of the protagonists who represents a particular human trait.

According to the systems of both Jason and Thompson,[8] the universal tale type AT 873 can be classified as a novella. Its subject is a king who discovers his unknown son. The lover, in this case the king in disguise, leaves personal objects (usually a ring) with his beloved to give to their son whom she is to bear.[9] The son, provoked by his fellows for being a bastard,[10] sets out in search of his unknown father. On the way, he becomes romantically involved with a girl. Their affair is discovered, and the son is sentenced to death by the king, his father. Just before the execution is carried out, the son and the king become aware of their relationship through the discovery of the recognition token.[11] The king acknowledges his son and marries the mother, who is generally of a different and inferior class.[12].

This tale type has its Jewish oicotype,[13] that is, a special development of the international tale type, unique to ethnic Jewish society. The oicotype emerges from the international tale type but differs from it in many important details.

The first version of this oicotype to appear in written form is included in the story anthology of Y. S. Farhi, ʿOse Fele ("The Wonder-Worker").[14] It has been reworked several times in later collections.[15] The Israel Folktale Archives (IFA)[16] preserves ten versions of this tale type related by narrators originally from Morocco(3),[17] Syria,[18] Yemen(3),[19] Iraq,[20] Persia,[21] and Poland.[22] The plot elements of all these folktales are similar:

A. A famous rabbi has a daughter who is renowned for her learning but has the face of an animal. She lives in seclusion, hidden from view. However, she resolves talmudic difficulties that scholars have found insoluble, both the questions and her answers being exchanged in writing, on pieces of paper.

B. One of the rabbi's students, who comes from a distant town, is so impressed by the wisdon of her answers that he decides to marry her despite the warnings of her parents.

C. The bride arrives at the wedding with her face veiled. When her veil is removed the bridegroom is shocked. The morning following their wedding night he abandons her, leaving several tokens behind for her: a prayer shawl, a ring, and phylacteries.

D. The abandoned wife bears a son, who, provoked by his fellows for being fatherless, sets out in search of his father. The son meets his grandfather in a synagogue, and makes himself known to his father by means of the recognition tokens.

E. The devoted son prays to God to help him reunite his father and mother. The father agrees to return home, for in the meanwhile the mother has magically (through the mediation of the Prophet Elijah) turned into a beautiful woman. In the end, the family is united.

The analysis of these oral versions raises several fundamental questions.[23] What are the main changes and deviations occurring in the Jewish versions still narrated by Jewish raconteurs, which differentiate them from the standard tale-type? What are the narrative traits and trends, common among Jewish narrators originating from various culture areas, but at the same time different from the narrative traits and trends current among their non-Jewish neighbors?

Two kinds of change can be noted:[24] (a) Minor ethnic and local substitutions; (b) Major deviations and reworkings of the narrative structures and plots:

(a) The minor changes cluster mainly around "Judaized" realia which replace the original, universal ones. thus the synagogue instead of the magic palace serves as *locus actionis;* a Hebrew (mostly biblical) verse or the Ineffable Name substitutes for the universal magic formula; the hero is a Jew, and so on. These minor changes do not justify the exclusion of a newly collected tale from the standard classification frame. This tale is simply another version of the AT tale-type, and should be classified under the same universal tale-number.

(b) However, the standard classification could not fit tales in which major changes occurred. Then a new number, or a new letter following an unchanged AT number, should be allotted. This addition is designated by an asterisk preceding it, signifying a local oicotype, fitting the general AT pattern, but being at the same time culturally so far removed from the universal story that the standard AT classification is unsuitable for it.

In trying to establish the common denominator of the Jewish oicotypes added to the IFA type-index, three main laws emerge—"Jewish oicotype laws" that influence and even direct the process of differentiation and oicotype-formation ("oicotypification"):

1. The narrative deviation and the main structural changes are made at the beginning and at the end of the tale; the main body of the tale-type is left intact.

2. The main plot is linked with a biblical verse and its traditional homiletic interpretations. In accordance with the first oicotype law, the link occurs at the beginning and end of the tale, and is calculated to stress a culturally Jewish pattern.

3. The associative element that connects the creative storyteller with the cultural heritage of his audience is mainly external, linguistic, and based on

wordplay; it is generally not connected with the plot and the narrative content.

In order to understand the way in which the international tale-type has been "Judaized," it is necessary to examine each of the components of the Jewish oicotype and the sources upon which they drew. The first and most fundamental difference between the international tale-type and the Jewish oicotype is that in the former the contact between the two lovers is fortuitous, while this is not the case in the Jewish oicotype. In the Jewish versions the husband abandons his wife, whom he has married "according to the law of Moses and Israel."[25] While the international tale-type centers on the efforts of the son to find a father whose identity and place of origin are unknown to him, the Jewish son seeks to find a father (his mother's husband) whose identity, and even place of origin, are a matter of official record.

It should be noted that in Jewish *Märchen* the family serves as a kind of permanent, natural framework within which the events described take place and in which the protagonists of the stories live; the story begins and ends within this framework. The *locus actionis* of the *Märchen* is not, however, confined to the boundaries of the original family; rather, the events of the plot usually transpire at some remove from it.[26]

It is clear that the basic interrelationships depicted in the Jewish story are deeply colored by the characteristic features of Jewish life. These elements are deemed essential by the storyteller and his Jewish audience, who have been brought up to observe the Halakha that regulates such human interrelationships. For example, "It is a positive commandment to give a woman in mariage, for it is written, 'For when a man shall take a wife . . .'" (Maimonides, *The Book of the Commandments,* positive commandment no. 213). Maimonides states in the introduction to his codification of the Laws of Personal Status that before the Tora was given it was the practise for a man to meet a woman in the marketplace; if the two wished to marry, the man would bring the woman into his home, have intercourse with her in seclusion, and by this act she would become his wife. When the Tora was given, Israel was commanded that if a man wished to marry a woman, he first must purchase her in the presence of witnesses and after that she would be his wife. Similarly, the sages of the Talmud prohibited marriage to be concluded by means of intercourse alone because of the licentiousness resulting from the necessity of having witnesses to the fact that the man and woman were together in private (Qiddushin 12b). For this reason, "Rav decreed that the punishment of flogging be inflicted upon those who concluded marriage through intercourse, or in the marketplace, or without the proper preliminary negotiations."

It can be seen that in the Jewish story, the nature of the married couple's relationship undergoes a considerable change. But this does not detract

from the story; on the contrary, it serves to heighten the confrontation
between the two central protagonists. Since they have become man and
wife, the husband's desertion leaves her an *ʿaguna* (abandoned wife) who
cannot divorce her husband and remarry according to Jewish law. In contrast, the international folk story is based upon a difference in class status
between the man and woman; this fact lies at the root of the tale-type and
determines its narrative framework: A sexual encounter at the beginning
of the story, and marriage at its conclusion. This difference in class status is
not preserved in the Jewish stories. The husband is generally a scholar or a
Yeshiva student, while the girl is the daughter of a rabbi and is herself
learned. However, in contrast to the audience's expectations and the conventions of Jewish society, the girl turns out not only to know the Bible,
Talmud, and Midrash, but to be remarkably acute in their interpretation;
she succeeds in resolving a difficulty that the hero and his fellow students
were unable to resolve despite arduous study. The difference in class status
characteristic of the international folk story is replaced in the Jewish story
by a different contrast: The bridegroom is a human being who discovers on
his wedding night that his bride is an unnatural being—a woman with an
animal face.

Together with the hero of the story, the audience, by this time caught up
in the narrative, discovers the secret of the girl. The surprise therefore is
twofold: That of the hero who is part of the story and that of the audience
listening to it. It is possible that there is an implicit connection between the
girl's extraordinary wisdom[27] and her extraordinarly external appearance.[28]

It should be noted that the bridegroom does not see his bride's face,
which remains veiled, until after the wedding—this despite the rule that "it
is forbidden for a man to wed a woman until he has seen her" (B. Qiddushin 41a).[29] Indeed, it is customary for the bride to wear a veil over her
face, the precedent for this practice being Rebecca, who covered her face
when she saw Isaac (Gen. 24:65). However, it may be assumed that covering, concealment, or hiding of the bride, a well-known and common practise in various folk societies,[30] is connected with the folk belief that the
bride must be guarded from demons who are envious of her and liable to
do her injury. For marriage is conceived of by folk mentality as a central
event in the human life-cycle, that is, as one of the critical "rites de passage"
(birth, puberty, and death).[31] Indeed, marriage is the sole event in the
human life-cycle that directly affects two persons (the couple entering into
marriage) in equal measure.

Such contact between two individuals who are unknown to each other (in
this case the bride and bridegroom) or between two social units (the
families of the married couple) creates a multi-faceted kind of tension. On
the one hand there is the socioeconomic tension between the two families;

on the other, the emotional, psychological tension between members of different sexes. Though the young man and woman still hardly know each other, the eyes of society are focused on them as a couple throughout the marriage ceremony and on the wedding night. The wedding serves to alleviate the threat of the envious demons. This release from tensions, and the accompanying increase in self-confidence, are achieved, by and large, through customs based on sympathetic magic: Changing the bride and bridegroom's physical appearance by shaving off their hair, dressing them in special costumes, concealing them, applying "henna," and so forth.

Similarly, the tension between the two families must be relieved. For the two sides cannot simply give up their two opposed collective egos and ignore the solidarity and identity of interests within each family. The need arises, therefore, for a kind of competition between the two opposing sides, a kind of battle without casualties. One of the most pronounced forms of play that serves as a surrogate for such combat is the riddle, which has played and still continues to play a clear and defined role in the wedding ceremonies of various societies.[32]

Traces of marriage ceremony riddles are to be found in ancient Hebrew sources, such as the riddles of Samson in the Bible and those posed by the queen of Sheba to Solomon recorded in the Aggadic literature. It is possible that the story of the animal-faced woman also contains some traces of this custom. In many novelistic folk stories the narrative plot is linked to a riddle, and its solution is a precondition for marriage (AT 851). However, folktales from Jewish communities employ a particular sort of riddle, which lacks the usual erotic allusions and images relating to the occasion and characteristic of riddles from all over the world.

Moreover, it is natural that the critical event of marriage should attract folk stories like a magnet. These stories are the product of creative popular imagination that reflects primal memories, instincts, fears, and desires. A most graphic illustration of this tendency is to be found in the story of the woman with the animal face. In several of its versions the animal she resembles is specified: the face of a donkey (in the Iraqi and Syrian versions); the face of a cow (in the Persian version); the horns of a bull rising from her head (in one of the Yemenite versions), and so on.

It would seem, then, that these stories reflect the tensions and fears of the bridegroom, who on his wedding night makes his first real acquaintance with his wife and is liable to be surprised and even disappointed by her facial appearance. She is liable to be shockingly ugly—as ugly "as an animal." Needless to say, the distance between the simile "a woman as ugly as an animal" and the literary motif "a woman with an animal face" is not great. This tallies with the well-known fact that the world of fairy tales has no room for intermediate states of compromise, but is populated only by extreme or even polarized absolutes.

Nevertheless the motif of "the girl with the animal face" is rather curious, and we are led to ask, How did this motif find its way into our story? It should first be noted that this motif falls into the category of "wonders," that is to say, abnormal phenomena that are manifest as facts in the story. This is to be distinguished from the category of "magic," in which some change takes place before the eyes of the listener who is able to actually witness the transformation from a normal to an abnormal state.

It should be further noted that Talmudic-Midrashic literature contains several traditions about two-headed men (see Menahot, 37a);[33] in Aggadic literature this "abnormality" is said to be the sign with which the descendants of Cain are marked.[34] D. Noy[35] has pointed out that this motif is given a philosophical meaning in the Zohar (I, 9b, 157a; II, 80a; III, 10a), where it symbolizes confusion, doubt, a sense of misgiving, and the lack of independent wholeness; this is, however, a totally different conception of the motif from that which we find in folk stories, where the motif of "two-headedness" is solely an indication of monstrosity. This is almost certainly the meaning attached to the motif of the woman-animal hybrid in the story under discussion here.

Such hybrids are quite common in international folk literature, principally in Egyptian and Greek mythology. These include centaur (man-horse),[36] satyr (man-goat),[37] sphinx (man-bird),[38] mermaid (woman-fish),[39] merman (man-fish),[40] and others.[41] References to hybrid creatures can also be found in Jewish legend: "It was asked of Abba Kohen bar Dala: '[Why does Scripture speak of] Adam, Seth, Enosh (lit. "human") and then stop?' He answered, 'Up to this point [men were created] in the likeness and image [of Adam, i.e., Man; see Gen. 5:3]; but from this point on [men are as] centaurs'" (Gen. Rb. 23:6). It is also related in the Aggada that the Holy One, blessed be He, punished Nebuchadnezzar by turning him into a hybrid. From his head to his navel he had the appearance of an ox, and from his navel down he looked like a lion; he would eat grass like an ox, and mangle and eat many criminal and sinful men like a lion (Tanhuma, ed Buber, Shemot 23; Yerahmiel XL, 205–6).[42]

The great frequency with which such hybrid creatures figure in folk literature[43] indicates that this was a subject of great interest to folk imagination. Since such hybrids have no basis in reality, we must seek an explanation for their existence in folk literature and belief in other realms. From a psychological point of view, such monstrosities are a reflection of fears and suppressed desires related to man's ambivalent relation to the animal world of both dependence and fear. From an etiological perspective, the belief in such partially human beings grows out of the fact that in primitive societies, particularly those based on a pastoral ecology, men often have sexual relations with domesticated animals. This practice is explicitly prohibited in the Bible, which indicates that there was a definite need to legislate against it. Moreover, in rabbinic literature it is stated, "R. El'azar said, What is the meaning of the verse, 'And Adam said, This is now bone of my bones, and flesh of my flesh (Gen. 2 : 23)'? This implies that Adam had intercourse with every animal and beast but his lust was not cooled until he had intercourse with Eve" (B. Yevamot, 63a). Similarly, the Epic of Gilgamesh tells that Enkidu lived with the does until he was civilized by the priestess Aruru.[44] According to folk imagination, it is inconceivable that a man should have sexual relations with an animal without suffering some terrible consequences. Therefore a man who lies with a sheep will, according to folk belief, cause it to bear a creature that is half man and half sheep.[45]

There is yet another explanation for the existence of such hybrids in folk literature. From the literary-aesthetic perspective, such a supernatural motif, the product of creative imagination, grips the listener's imagination and thus prevents him from remaining passively apathetic to what is being related. Folk society loves to hear and tell of matters beyond the grasp of reason. This is why precisely those stories which contain supernatural motifs are most readily accepted by society and thus remain alive, while realistic parallels are rejected and fail to be transmitted.

However, the existence of such motifs in folk literature does not supply an answer to the question, Why does the good and wise daughter of the rabbi, the heroine of our story, have the face of an animal? For neither she nor her parents are said to have committed any transgression; on the contrary, they are portrayed as righteous Jews. It is possible that this story expresses the fears and longings of a young woman, a prospective bride, who sees herself as ugly and dreads the inevitable disappointment of her groom. His disappointment is given extreme expression in the story: The bridegroom abandons his bride on their wedding night. It is clear that the story presents the confrontation, in this case with ugliness and apprehension, in a most extreme and narratively graphic manner. This leads us to suspect that the story actually gives expression to a prospective bride's hope that she will be appreciated by her husband for her inner rather than for her external virtues. Such a deeper view of feminine virtue is expressed in the biblical verse, "Charm is deceitful, and beauty is vain; but a woman that feareth the Lord, she shall be praised" (Proverbs 31 : 30).

On the other hand, Jewish sources do attach much iportance to feminine beauty. For example: "Happy is the man who has a beautiful wife; the number of his days is double" (B. Yevamot 63b); "Woman is only for beauty" (B. Ketubot, 59b); "Three things make a man feel expansive: a lovely home, a lovely wife, and lovely clothes" (B. Berakhot 57b). In the same vein one can sense a great deal of irony in the Talmudic story of the man who swore to his wife: "By the sacrificial service, you shall have no benefit of me unless you are able to show R. Ishmael ben R. Yose that you have one beautiful feature. He [R. Ishmael] said to them, Perhaps her head is beautiful? They replied, It is perfectly round. Perhaps her hair is beautiful? It looks like flax stalks. Perhaps she has beautiful eyes? They are bleary. Perhaps she has beautiful ears? They are creased. Perhaps she has a beautiful nose? It is swollen. Perhaps her name is beautiful? Her name is 'Filthy.' He said to them, Well, her name does fit her beautifully: she is called 'Filthy' for she is filthy with defects. With that he released the man from his vow" (B. Nedarim 66b).

It should be noted that many stories are of a humoristic or sarcastic nature recounting the incredible ugliness of a woman.[46] Similarly, various versions have been recorded of a Jewish tradition from eastern Europe,[47] in which the jokester hero of the story informs a woman that her husband who has fled the house will never return. Though the rabbi has said otherwise, this is the case, says the jokester; for her husband has seen what an ugly face she has, while the rabbi has not.[48] Such jokes about the importance of physical beauty stand in total contradiction to the maxim recorded in *Pirqe Avot* (4:20): "Pay no heed to the container, but rather to what it contains." It would seem that the forces of life are more powerful than rabbinic dicta.

The hero of the story of the woman with the animal face discovers his bride's physical defect only at the actual marriage ceremony, though he had previously been forewarned to expect something horrid. According to the version of the story in *ʿOse Fele*, for example, the young man nevertheless entreats the rabbi, who is the girl's father, to let him marry her.

According to the other versions as well, the bridegroom is forewarned. However, he does not find out what physical defect mars the girl until, at the very climax of the story, he actually sees his bride and is shocked. In this version, the biblical association with the story of Jacob and Leah is quite pronounced. The bridegroom is shocked and repelled by his bride's ugliness, as presumably, Jacob was by the "weak" eyes of Leah. This element is emphasized in most of the versions: For example, according to the Syrian version, the bridegroom is so shocked that his soul almost abandons his body and he seeks to flee; according to one of the versions from Yemen, he is stunned, sits in a corner of the room, and begins to weep; while in the Polish version, he falls down in a faint.

Incidentally, the Polish version has many details that are quite different from those found in the versions recorded from Jews originally from Islamic countries. The Polish version may be classified as a legend, the hero of the story being "the Seer of Lublin." This element gives the story a definite historical and geographical background; the names of the father and the daughter and the place where the events took place are all made explicit. In this version only, the father shows his daughter to the bridegroom before the wedding. Nevertheless, the young man marries the woman in order to keep a vow he made to her father, who is also his teacher. This version is also unique in that the husband disappears after having lived with his new wife for half a year.

The bridegroom's shock upon seeing his wife's face is, of course, completely understandable to the audience and does not cause them to take a critical attitude toward him. However, the bride also is a figure with whom they can identify and for whom they feel sympathy.

In most of the versions, the bride's efforts ("I entreat you to show pity for me and fulfill your commandment") are ultimately crowned with success. It is possible that the tendency of the storytellers to pass over this part of the story quite tersely reflects their fear of censorship of erotic themes. They merely note that the bridegroom departs in the morning and disappears.

The motif of the hero's abandonment of his family is thus repeated in the plot. For in the beginning of the story the framework of the family is broken by the young hero's leaving home to journey abroad. D. Noy has pointed out[49] that such breaking of the family framework attests to conflicts of interests in the family. When the confrontation between the sides is explicit, it takes the form of an argument; but often, indeed most of the time, the conflict is implicit. In both cases, certain members of the family leave home. By this act they reveal the disguised breakdown, call the family framework into question, and ultimately destroy it. Generally, the reasons for the hero's separation from his home and family and the reasons for his moving away are not made explicit in the story. But the act itself demonstrates that the one who leaves home is either not capable, or does not want, to continue to live within the framework into which he was born and in which he grew up.

However, in our story the motif of "leaving home" is both explicit and Jewish in nature. In most of the versions, the hero leaves his parental home in order to study Tora in some distant place. Yet we can read between the lines that his real motivation is to see the world, to experience the unknown, and thus to break out of the mold into which fate has cast him.

In most folk novellas, the hero, after experiencing various adventures such as solving riddles and performing tasks, wins the girl of his desires. Thus the marriage of the hero and the heroine serves as the resolution of the plot. However, in the story of the girl with the animal face, the bride's physical appearance causes the bridegroom to run off. This act is, in effect, a second "leaving home" in the plot of the story.

At his wife's request, the husband leaves her three tokens: a seal or ring, a prayer shawl (*tallit*) or one fringe of it, and a set of phylacteries or a prayer book (it is possible that "phylacteries" (*tefillin*] has changed to "prayer book" [*sefer tefillot*] because of the similarity in the sound of the words). These are clearly specifically Jewish symbols. One can hardly help noticing the relationship between these tokens and the tokens that Judah leaves with Tamar after having had sexual liaison with her (Gen. 38:18): a seal, a cord, and a staff. It is interesting to note that in the biblical story, as in the universal tale-type, the sexual contact between the man and the woman occurs only once and does not constitute a formal union. However, as in the Jewish oicotype, Tamar covers herself with a veil, hiding her face so that Judah thinks her a prostitute; as a result of this encounter, she bears twins. In this way, Tamar gets Judah to do unknowingly what the Law commands (the Levirate marriage, which her own brother-in-law should have performed).

The story of Judah and Tamar suggests that among the early Hebrews no opprobrium was attached to men who visited prostitutes.[50] In some of the versions of our story the hero, after having traveled far from his first wife, takes a second wife—an act completely acceptable in Jewish communities in Muslim countries in which Rabbenu Gershom's ban on polygamy was not in force. Thus the Iraqi Jewish version of the story provides an elaborate description of the harmonious relations in the extended family when the husband returns with his second wife and their eight children. In the version in ʿOse Fele, on the other hand, the second wife is barren—perhaps as a punishment for the husband's abandonment of his first wife—and what becomes of this second wife is not mentioned in the conclusion of the story. In the other versions, this motif has apparently been deleted; it would seem that storytellers and their audiences living in the modern state of Israel felt that such a reference to polygamy was in bad taste.

In all versions of the story, however, the return of the husband to his animal-faced wife is a result of the efforts of their son. The boy has grown up in the home of his grandparents without knowing that they are not his real parents; only after being taunted by his friends for having no mother and father (and, according to one of the Yemenite versions, for being "the son of a whore") does he set out to find his father. However, the epithet "bastard" (mamzer) does not occur in the Jewish stories, despite its frequent occurrence in the international folktales in which the king violates established custom and his child is therefore considered a bastard.

Indeed, according to Jewish law, a child simply born out of wedlock is not considered a "bastard" (mamzer), this term being reserved for children of adulterous and incestuous unions (see Mishna Yevamot 4:13). "Who is considered a "bastard" (mamzer) as mentioned in the Tora? One born of one of the forbidden sexual unions, except for a child conceived by a menstruant woman; . . ." (Maimonides, Mishne Tora, Laws of Forbidden Unions, 15:1).

A motif similar to that in our story is found in the Oedipus legend. Oedipus learns that he is not the son of the prince of Corinth and sets out to inquire of the oracle as to his birth.[51]

In some of the versions of the Jewish oicotype, the efforts of the son to reunite his father and mother take on the character of a threat. However, in most of the Jewish versions the father is influenced to return by both the son's just demands and the magical change that has taken place in his wife's appearance after she drank a therapeutic potion.[52] Now that she is rid of her animal face, the husband, who was willing to grant his abandoned wife a divorce but not to return to her, has no reason to stay away. The place of meeting between the grandfather and grandson, a synagogue, and the tokens by which the grandfather recognizes his grandson, his own son's prayer shawl and phylacteries, are of course a clearly Jewish element in the plot of the story.

Moreover, the drinking of the magical potion creates an explicit taboo: nobody must see the "cured" woman, except for her son, who was involved in the cure and now must prevent her from being seen. This type of taboo, against looking at certain things,[53] is a familiar motif in international folk literature. The examples that come most readily to mind are the taboo on looking into a certain container, "Pandora's box," and the taboo on looking backward, Orpheus in Hades and Lot's wife.[54] This taboo against looking is, for the most part, attached to sacred phenomena, such as the "priestly blessing" by the Kohanim. It may be assumed that the taboo against looking in our story originates in the belief that it is best to avoid speaking, having physical contact with, or seeing sacred phenomena such as a magical process taking place. This is reflected in the Aggadic story of Lot's wife:

Do not look back, for the Divine Presence of the Holy One, blessed be He, has descended, so that He could rain fire and brimstone on Sodom and Gomorrah . . . but she looked back . . . and saw behind her the Divine Presence. *(Pirqe R. Eliezer,* chap. 25)

The motif of the change in the heroine's physical appearance represents a change in the novelistic character of the story. As mentioned above, the novella is characterized by realism, according to both Thompson and Jason. It is difficult to designate the Jewish oicotype a "novella" according to Thompson's classification, primarily because the marriage quest does not take pride of place in the story plot, while the common denominator of the stories classified as novellae in the type index is the sometimes fatally dangerous efforts of the hero to win the hand of his beloved; the "happy ending" is thus the wedding that takes place at the end of the story. The marriage quest and its successful conclusion in marriage does not, therefore, reflect deep emotion and the desire for true love, but rather the competition for social status, that is, the struggle for prestige and social advancement. According to this view, the novella constitutes a link between two different and distant social classes: it expresses the ambition of the lower-class hero to win the hand of the princess and thus to rise in the social scale. This ambition, which has the approval of society, is not confined to members of the strong sex alone. Stories of fate,[55] which as a rule begin with some supernatural announcement (dream, heavenly voice, prophecy) of a decree concerning the hero, generally in some matter of romance, belong to this category.[56]

It is also of primary importance that in the novelistic story the hero (or heroine) wins the hand of his (her) beloved principally by realistic means and not with the help of magical assistance. The determining factor in such stories is often some deception, affectation or cleverness, and not necessarily magic, as in our story. The potion, which brings about the magical transformation of the animal-faced woman into a beautiful woman, expresses a suppressed desire of women of all time.

Also, according to Jason's classification our story cannot be considered a novella story, for supernatural forces are involved in the plot. The supernatural force in the Jewish oicotype is Elijah the prophet, the most popular hero in the folk literature of all Jewish communities; it is he who characteristically grants magical powers, cures, and even life itself. It is thus Elijah who gives the son the magic potion for his mother's transformation. This sacred, magical figure is anchored in the living, religious belief of the society and in its moral system. This stands in contradiction to the *Märchen* whose *Weltanschauung* is secular and utopian; its supernatural heroes who help the hero to resolve the conflict are not related to any religious being and have no relationship to the moral system of the society.

The mode in which the story is set is therefore the mode of the miraculous, as defined by Jason: "In this mode man confronts the miraculous aspect of his society's official belief system. The special property of the miraculous is the ability to perform miracles, as opposed to creative change. The manifestation of the miraculous is the mode of sacred in which the extra-natural entity confronting man is the sacred power of the official religion, friendly to man and to his society. The sacred is composed of all three components of the fabulous."[57]

Thus the emergence of the Jewish oicotype from the international tale-type involves a transformation in the genre of the story. What was a realistic novella becomes a sacred legend: "Legend (man confronts the various numinous worlds), in which the sacred power of the official religion solves the conflicts in the narrative. The sacred is set in the sacred mode and in the historical and eschatologic epochs."

More specifically: "Saints legend—A sacred legend recounting miracles performed by a holy man or for his sake by the sacred power."[58]

However, elements of the fairy tale are worked into the Jewish archetype. The fairy tale, according to Jason's definition, is a "narrative in which man confronts the marvellous world. In the fairy tale weak man is helped by marvellous forces to win a royal spouse, kingdom, and/or a treasure; thereby he "demarvelizes" the marvellous world. The fairy tale is set in the marvellous mode, in human and marvellous time."[59]

The heroine of the Jewish oicotype, the woman with the animal face, overcomes the miraculous world of the epic fairy tale. This world strives to be redeemed from its miraculous characteristics and to become human. To this purpose our story employs, as the hero, a human figure who has entered the realm of the miraculous. The transformation of the wondrously desirable princess in the epic fairy tale to a human figure exemplifies this process of redemption.

However, the redemption of the girl is made possible through the legendary intervention of Elijah the prophet, whose action may clearly be considered a miracle: "An isolated act of change of the order of nature brought about by the sacred power; though its results may be permanent, this act has no consequences for the order of nature and society in the future."[60]

After the intervention of Elijah and the resolution of the conflict, the plot reaches its harmonious and idealistic conclusion, the reunification of the couple—a feature common to both the international folk tale and its Jewish version. In ʿOse Fele it is explicitly stated that "They set up the bridal canopy fresh to the sound of gladness and joy"; this has clearly been added to the story by the editor of the anthology, for it is definitely superfluous since a completely binding marriage had already been performed, obviating the necessity for a second ceremony. The other versions merely note that the family lived happily ever after; this note, of course, also expresses a suppressed desire on the part of the storytellers and their audiences.

It should be noted that the harmonious conclusions play a strictly formal role; from the perspective of content, they do not reflect the actual relations between the woman and her husband. To the audience it is certainly clear that what the father did can never be forgiven. But the plot of the fairy tale necessarily concludes with artificial forgiveness. It is also clear that, in a legend, the reward of the righteous hero and the punishment of the evil villain would have been emphasized.

The final reunification of the family demonstrates that in Jewish folklore the family is the primary legitimate framework in life;[61] from it all proceed and unto it all return. All plots that deal with human lives develop "from it and unto it." This framework awakens a sense of wholeness, harmony, and security in the society represented by both the storytellers and their audience. Family life is depicted, in the conclusion of the story, as a life of happiness and satisfaction.

There are a few non-Jewish parallels that differ from the international tale-type in ways that make them similar to the Jewish oicotype. There is a certain similarity between the Jewish oicotype and the Tibetan story of ugly Durjiyah, the daughter of King Saljal and Queen Barli.[62] Like the Jewish woman with the animal face, Durjiyah is miraculously made beautiful with the aid of supernatural force, and this story too concludes on a note of harmonious happiness. However, the Tibetan story differs from its Jewish counterpart in many details. The marriage of the monstrously ugly girl is instigated by her father, and the motivations of the bridegroom are made explicit: he has made a promise to her father and is attracted by her elevated social position rather than by her wisdom. Moreover, the motif of the husband's abandonment of his wife and his son's search for him are missing in the Tibetan story. The place of Elijah the prophet in the Jewish story is filled by Buddha, and the turning point in the Tibetan story comes as the result of a spiritual, ecstatic experience. This contrasts with the

Jewish story which emphasizes that the miracle occurred because of the son's love, care, perseverance, and prayers.

We may conclude that what remains the same is the essential folk imagination, which seems common to different cultural groupings. What changes is the way in which the essential story is presented; it is this that conveys the tenor of the story and reveals the underlying beliefs, way of life, and particular customs of each culture.

NOTES

1. Dan Ben-Amos, "Analytical Categories and Ethnic Genres," *Genre* 2, no. 3 (1969):275–301.

2. Stith Thompson, *The Folktale* (New York, 1946), p. 8.

3. Ibid; Richard U. Dorson, "Current Folklore Theories; *Current Anthropology* 4 (1963):93–112; Kaarle Krohn, *Folklore Methodology*...(Austin, Texas, 1971); Archer Taylor, "Precursors of the Finnish Method of Folklore Study," *Modern Philology* 25 (1927–28):481–91.

4. Thompson, *Folktale*, p. 7.

5. Antti Aarne, *The Types of the Folktale*...2d rev. ed. trans. and enl. by Stith Thompson. (Helsinki, 1962), Types 850–999.

6. Hedda Jason, *Ethnopoetics—A Multilingual Terminology* (Jerusalem, 1975), p. 36.

7. Ibid., pp. 36–40.

8. Stith Thompson, *Motif Index of Folk Literature*, 6 vols. (Copenhagen and Bloomington, Ill., 1955, 1958), pp. 71, 94.

9. Motif H81.8; T645.

10. Motif H1381.2.2.1.1; T646.

11. Motif N731.

12. Motif L161.

13. Carl von Sydow, "Geography and Folktale Oicotypes," *Selected Papers on Folklore*, ed. Laurits Bodker, (Copenhagen, 1948), pp. 44–53. See also Laurits Bodker, *Folk-Literature, Germanic*, (Copenhagen, 1965), p. 220; Alan Dundes, ed., *The Study of Folklore* (New York, 1965), pp. 219–20.

14. Yosef S. Farhi, ʿOse-Fele (Livorno, 1902), pp. 152–60. See M. J. Bin Gorion, *Mimekor Yisrael—Classical Jewish folktales*, (Bloomington-London, 1976), 3:1056–67.

15. *Hashgahat Ha-Bore* (Limberg, 1912), p. 2.

16. Recent information on the Israel Folktale Archives (IFA) is included in *A Tale for Each Month 1973* ed. Aliza Shenhar (Haifa, 1974), pp. 8–13. The Archives were established (1956) in the Haifa Ethnological Museum and Folklore Archives by Prof. Dov Noy.

17.a. IFA 4510; Dov Noy, A Tale of Each Month 1962 (Haifa, 1963), n. 2; Eliezer Marcus, ed., *Min Ha-Mabuʿa* (from the Fountainhead) (Haifa, 1966), n. 3; Dov Noy, ed., *Moroccan Jewish Folktales* (New York, 1960), n. 26.

b. IFA 8148.

c. IFA 9480; Edna Cheichel, ed., *A Tale for Each Month 1972* (Haifa, 1973), n. 7.

18. IFA 1014.

19.a. IFA 3811; Zalman Baharav, *Shishim Sipure ʿAm miPi M'saprim b'Ashqelon* (Sixty Folktales from Narrators in Ashkelon), ed. Dov Noy (Haifa, 1955), n. 52.

b. IFA 7591.

c. IFA 7959.

20. IFA 640; Dov Noy, ed., *HaNaʿara haYefefiya uShloshet B'ne haMelekh* (The Beautiful Maiden and the Three Princes): 120 Jewish Iraqi Folktales (Tel Aviv, 1965), n. 62.

21. IFA 5800.

22. IFA 1338.

23. Dov Noy, "The Jewish Versions of the 'Animal Languages' Folktale (AT 670)—A Typological-Structural Study," *Scripta Hierosolymitana* (Publications of The Hebrew University, Jerusalem) 22 (1971):173–74.

24. Type 873A. The tales deviate so much from the collective general tale-type as formulated in the AT Index that new classification numbers (or subnumbers) had to be allotted to them. Cf. Dov Noy, "The First Thousand Folktales in the Israel Folktale Archives," *Internationaler Kongress der Volkserzählungs . . . in Kiel und Kopenhagen* (Berlin, 1961), 236–46; Hedda Jason, "Types of Jewish Oriental Oral Tales," *Fabula* 7 (1964): MS-224; Dov Noy and Otto Schnitzler, "Type-Index of IFA 7000–7599," *A Tale for Each Month (TEM) 1966* (Haifa, 1967), pp. 142–64; idem, "Type-Index of IFA 7600–7999," *TEM 1967* (Haifa, 1967), pp. 131–52; idem, "Type-Index of IFA 8000–8799, *TEM 1968–69* (Haifa, 1970), pp. 243–81; idem, "Type-Index of IFA 8800–8999," *TEM 1970* (Haifa, 1971), pp. 166–89; idem, "Type-Index of IFA 9000–9299," *TEM-1971* (Haifa, 1972), pp. 97–125.

25. Motif T165.4.

26. Dov Noy, "Family Confrontation and Conflict in Jewish Magic Folk Tales," *Folklore Research Centre Studies* (Jerusalem, 1970), 1: 201–28.

27. Motif F645.

28. Motif F510.

29. See *Mimekor Yisrael,* p. 1058, IFA 4510, and the Syrian version.

30. Theodor Gaster, *The Holy and the Profane* (New York, 1955), pp. 103–4.

31. Issachar Ben-Ami and Dov Noy, eds., *Studies in Marriage Customs,* Folklore Research Centre Studies, vol. 4 (Jerusalem, 1974).

32. Max Hippe, "Hochzeitsraetsel des Jahrhunderts," *Festschrift Theodor Siebs* (Breslau, 1953).

33. Motif F 511.0.2.1.

34. Louis Ginzberg, *The Legends of the Jews,* 7 vols. (Philadelphia, 1909–46), 6: 286, n. 29.

35. Dov Noy, *Forms and Themes in Folk Literature* (in Hebrew) (Jerusalem, 1970), p. 176.

36. Motif B21.

37. Motif B24.

38. Motif B25.

39. Motif B29.4.

40. Motif B29.7.

41. Motif B26 (Man-Tiger); B27 (Man-Lion); B28 (Man-Elephant); B.29.5 (Man-Wolf); B22 (Man-Ass); B28.9 (Man-Ape).

42. See Dov Noy, *Forms,* pp. 102–3.

43. Motif B20 (Man-Beast).

44. Robert Graves and Raphael Patai, *Hebrew Myths* (London, 1964), p. 10, n. 1.

45. Motif B29.3.

46. Motif X 137.

47. Salcia Landman, *Jüdische Witze* (Munich, 1964), p. 90.

48. IFA 8181, Malka Gutter, *Honour Your Mother—Twelve Folktales from Buczacz,* ed. Aliza Shenhar (Haifa, 1969), n. 6.

49. See Noy, "Family Confrontation . . ." (above, n. 26), p. 208–9.

50. See Graves and Patai, *Hebrew-Myths,* p. 246, n. 4.

51. Sophocles, *Oedipus the King,* trans. K. McLeish (London, 1967), p. 31.

52. Motif D1864; D1500.1.18.

53. Motif C300.

54. Motif C331.

55. AT 930–49.

56. Motifs T 0–99.

57. Jason, *Ethnopoetics,* n. 6, p. 38.

58. Ibid, p. 42.

59. Ibid, p. 45.

60. Ibid, n. 38.

61. See Noy, "Family Confrontation" (n. 26 above), pp. 202–3.

62. Micha J. Bin-Gorion, *Der Born Judas* (Leipzig, 1918), 1: 349–53.

The Magic Bird

MOSHE CARMILLY-WEINBERGER

Animals and inanimate objects become divine in the thinking of primitive man. Animism attributes spirits to inanimate objects.[1] The soul, it is believed, enters the bodies of animals, reptiles, and plants. This spirit can be that of an ancestor or of a deceased warrior, which in its transformation will protect man from his enemies. Animals with their superior physical power had a tremendous impact upon human beings. Animal headed figures were therefore endowed with magic powers; they became symbols, mediators between man and the astral powers. The cave paintings found in France and dating from 15,000 to 10,000 B.C.E.[2] had a magical purpose: to assure the survival of the living animals. One famous figure, that of the "Sorcerer," has the paws of a bear, the tail of a wolf, the beard of a man, and the body of a lion; its purpose was to evoke a strange, magical feeling of awe in the onlooker—the feeling that Rudolf Otto defined as "numinous": ". . . the magical is nothing but a suppressed and dimmed form of the numinous, a crude form of it, which great art purifies and ennobles."[3] Thus animal-headed beings were depicted in sculptures, paintings, and amulets. Strange combinations, hybrid forms, had their awesome, magic, mysterious impact upon human beings.[4]

I shall concentrate here only on the magic birds in different cultures. The bird—eagle, hawk, falcon, phoenix—had a very important place in human fantasy: it became a magic power due to its ability to fly. The flight of birds exerted a fascination on man's imagination, as shown by the myth of Daedalus and Icarus, who fashioned wings to escape into the air. Man saw himself soaring on the wings of magic birds. Many people throughout the world imagined and believed that the soul departed from the body in the form of a bird.

The ancient Egyptians believed that the soul escaped from the tomb as a bird and flew toward the sun, where it found its eternal resting place.[5] The symbol of Ra, the sun-god, is a falcon. Among the mythical animals described in the bestiaries or in Physiologus mention is made of the Charadrius bird, which flew up to the sun taking with it the disease of a man who was destined to stay alive. The disease was burned by the heat of the sun. The color of the Charadrius bird changed due to the sickness it absorbed. Returning from its mission, it resumed its original coloration. Royal families were anxious to have such a bird in their homes. This concept had its origin in Hittite civilization, and it can be found also in Persia and India.[6] The flying bird became the symbol of a cured person in the Bible (Lev. 14:7). If the leper was healed, the priest cleansed him with two birds, one of which was killed and the other set free. The priest pronounced the man clean, and let go the live bird into the open field as a sign that the man was free of leprosy.

The idea of the flying bird as a symbol of the soul is well-known among the peoples of ancient Assyria, Babylonia, Egypt, and of Japan, Brazil, British Columbia, Melanesia, and Sumatra.[7] In Germany, in case of death, a window was opened so that the soul of the deceased should be able to fly away.

BIRDS AS GODS

In ancient Mesopotamia the birds, among them the eagle, were elevated to an exalted position. They were symbols of living creatures or of gods. The head of an eagle was identified with the god Ninurta, and the lion-headed eagle with outspread wings became the emblem of the god Ningirsu. These symbols appear on stelae and seals. The lion-headed eagle was carried into the battlefield. It was followed by the god Ninurta and his worshipers. The eagle became a symbol of succor and victory. Birds in general symbolized triumph, good luck, and justice, as well as the soul. The eagle was sacred to Zeus in Greece and Jupiter in Rome as a sign of victory. The Roman emperors, who identified themselves with Jupiter, chose the eagle as their emblem.[8]

The Assyrians and Babylonians were influenced by the mythical concepts of the Hittites, the rulers of the Near East in the seventeenth–twelfth centuries B.C.E. They believed in the transmigration of the souls of the dead. Inanimate objects, such as trees or stones, were "spiritualized," and the souls of the deceased were believed to find resting places in them. No wonder that the art of these ancient peoples reflects this mythical belief. It is mirrored in the winged animals with human heads, or figures with human bodies and animal heads. It is thought that wings were adopted later under Egyptian influence. Sphinxes with lions' bodies and human heads guard the road to the temple of Luxor and the doors of the kings' tombs. In China, not far from Peking, the "Avenue of the Animals" leading to the Ming tombs is lined with twelve standing or kneeling statutes on each side.

Human- and eagle-headed winged beings worshipping the sacred tree. The Metropolitan Museum of Art, Gift of John D. Rockefeller, 1932.

Huge statues of lions, elephants, and mythical beasts guard the route, which once was forbidden to people.

The excavations of Nimrud, which became the capital of Assyria replacing Nineveh by the decision of Assurnasirpal II (883–859 B.C.E.), unearthed winged deities and animals.[9] Some of the finds are in the Metropolitan Museum of Art in New York. On the wall reliefs of the northwest section of the palace are displayed winged, eagle-headed divinities standing on both sides of the "sacred tree," a well-known motif in Assyrian art. They carry a purifier in their right hands, and a cup in their left. This sacred tree is not identical with the tree of life popular in Persian, Hindu, Jewish, and Christian art and literature, and is not a symbol of immortality. The Assyrian sacred tree, and especially the palm tree and the cypress, symbolized the goddess, the divine bride. It was the allegory of life given by the goddess. It appeared as a cult-object in Assyria and Babylonia. Women attended it, and in a later period it became the symbol of fertility.[10]

On the wall reliefs of Assurnasirpal's palace the sacred tree is attended by two winged, eagle-headed or human-headed divinities, but only the bird-headed figures have in their hands the fertilizer (perhaps a cluster of palms) and the cup. These winged, bird-headed figures stood at the gates to protect the palace from enemies, evil spirits. Among the excavated clay sculptures are bird-faced or winged human figures. They appear also on the garment worn by the king. The bird-headed figures were the protectors of the king's life.[11]

It is interesting to note that in a Hebrew manuscript in the Paris Bibliothèque Nationale (dated 1298, Germany) there is an illustration that resembles the sacred tree found in Nimrud.[12] On the right side of a Menorah-shaped tree with seven branches stands a man with a Jewish hat, holding a pot in his left hand, and picking olives with his right. On the left side of the tree are two persons (one with a Jewish hat) pressing oil from the olives.

In Persian literature the bird is a symbol of the god Simurgh, the defender of the race.[13] The tree of life, with a bird on each side, is characteristic of the Sassanian period (242–651). In a Persian silk fabric, dated from the eighth to the tenth century, two birds are attending the tree of life. The tree of life motif with the two birds is a well-known design in Europe's home industry connected with wedding presents. It is shown on a sixth to seventh-century ceramic, now in Vienna.[14] It can be found in a Hebrew manuscript dated from the fourteenth century, West Germany. On a vignette under the Hebrew word w'ele a winged animal (dragon?) is shown guarding the tree of life. Above it two birds (eagles?) face each other.[15]

THE POWER OF THE MAGIC BIRD

In Egyptian mythology the falcon is the symbol of might. On a palette of Narmer, (ca. 3000 B.C.E.) there is an indication that an Egyptian ruler defeated his enemies with the help of the magic power of a bird (falcon?). On that palette four small figures are visible, carrying the flag of the four corners of the world. Birds are seated on the top of two flags. In the right corner of the palette ten beheaded enemies are lying, their severed heads between their legs. Over them is a bird, indicating its invincible power.[16]

The power of the bird is clearly evident in a manuscript of the Book of the Dead, dated from the early Ptolemaic period (350–250 B.C.E.), found in the Metropolitan Museum of Art.[17] Falcons are depicted on many vignettes of this papyrus as a clear indication that the deceased could enter the hereafter only with the help of the magic power of the birds. The Egyp-

tians had a strong belief in afterlife, as expressed in their prayers, incantations, hymns, and especially in the Book of the Dead. They wrote their
prayers and incantations on the flanks of wooden coffins, and on papyri
placed in the coffins alongside the deceased. They obtained spells from
special scribes, who inserted the name of the deceased into the text. These
spells assumed a definite, fixed form in the fifth century B.C.E. and became
known as the Book of the Dead, which had magic powers to help the
deceased enter into the hereafter.[18]

The MS of the Book of the Dead in the Metropolitan Museum is divided
into 175 columns and 164 chapters. It belonged to a priest. It is possible
that the MS originated in the city of Meir (Tjehne). It is well illustrated. I
shall indicate only those columns and chapters in which animals and birds
are found.

Column 5, chapter 16 shows baboons praying to Ra, the god of the sun,
whose symbol is the falcon. The jackal-headed Anubis, the falcon-headed
Horus, and other falcon-headed birds decorate column 24. In the top
vignette (center) of chapter 24–25 the deceased himself is depicted praying
to a bird to provide him with the magic power and enable him to enter the
hereafter. In column 26–31, chapters 29–30 various animals (four
crocodiles, a serpent, insect, etc.) appear. The text reads: "Back, retreat!
Back up, O Crocodile! Do not come after me, for I live on magic!" The
deceased is confident that he received magic strength from the falcon, and
the animals therefore can neither harm him nor prevent his entry through
the gates of the hereafter. The deceased also goes through a transformation; he changes into a bird. Man's belief was that if he could be
transformed into an animal or a bird, he could escape from his enemies.
The Egyptians believed that the deceased came back to visit his home, the
places where he lived; he therefore had to be a bird that could fly freely
between the two worlds.[19] It is thus not surprising that in the illustrations
of the MS we see innumerable bird-headed animals (column 77, chapter
111–16). At the end of the MS of the Book of the Dead the goddess of
righteousness appears. Her head is represented by one feather only. The
top row (col. 87) of that illustration is composed of bird-headed figures.
Their meaning is clear: the deceased succeeded in his voyage and he is now
near the goddess of justice, Maat. The magic birds helped him. Maat
placed his heart on a scale to weigh his merits. The fate of the deceased
depends on Maat's decision. In the next scene the Ibis-headed Thoth presents the record of the deceased to Osiris.[20]

Ram-headed animals stand guard at the gates of the hereafter (col. 105–
6, chap. 144–47). Seven cows, which provided food to the deceased in his
long voyage, a bull and four falcon-headed rudders appear in the MS,
which ends with winged figures. One of them has three heads, an erect
phallus, and lion's claws.[21]

The magic birds succeeded in defeating the wild animals and the evil

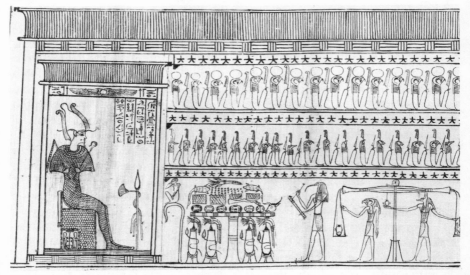

The Ibis-headed Thoth prepares the record of the deceased for Maat. The Metropolitan Museum of Art, Gift of Edward S. Harkness, 1935.

spirits, and the deceased Egyptian entered the hereafter. He was found worthy after standing trial before Maat with one feather (the symbol of the magic bird) on her head. One feather is enough to possess invincible power. The supreme god of Egypt, Amon (Amun), who is identified with Ra, the sun-god, whence he is called Amon-Ra, is represented by a sacred animal with the head of a ram and sometimes by two long feathers.[22]

The Iranian god Huarenah, the "source of water and light," also has a bird symbol: the Varegan bird. Its feathers protect against the black magic of enemies. A single feather or a bone of the Varegan bird is enough to prevent a man from suffering defeat in his struggles and to protect him from being killed.[23]

The Magic Bird in Jewish Literature and Art

In the Talmud and Midrash the soul is viewed as a bird,[24] and is often described as a flying bird. For example, the soul circles three days around the body of the deceased, trying to return into it.[25] While asleep, a man's soul wanders about in the world and returns at the time of his awakening. The Zohar speaks of two birds, one at each side of the departing soul, guiding it to its destination, to the "World to Come" (ʿOlam haBa).[26] The pious will take part in the "Feast of the Righteous in Paradise" (The Messianic Banquet). They will be served the meat of Leviathan, the king of the fishes, and of Ziz, the ruler over the birds.[27]

One of the finest illustrations of this feast can be found in the Ambrosian

Bible (Milan, Ambrosian Library, MS B.32, vol. iii, fol. 136). In the closing illustration the artist (of the South German school, Ulm (?), 1236–38) divided the page into two sections; in the upper half three mythical animals appear, the winged Ziz, Leviathan, and the wild ox, *Shor haBar*. In the lower half, five animal-headed humans can be seen, standing or sitting near a table laden with mythical food. In the center, a bird-headed man drinks from a cup; on his right a deer (ass?) and a lion (dog?)-headed man, on his left a bear (lion?) and a donkey (bull?)-shaped man, each with a crown on its head, take part in the banquet. In the corner, two musicians, having the form of lion cubs with a cat's head, entertain the participants with their musical instruments.

The three mythical animals of the Feast of the Righteous in Paradise correspond—perhaps—to the three monsters known in Persian mythology as Hadhayosh, Khar, and Caena-maergha. Some would indentify the Leviathan and the wild ox with Tiamat and Kingu of the Babylonian myth.[28] Bezalel Narkiss suggests that the reason for depicting the animal figures must be sought in the iconoclastic attitude of the rabbinical authorities of twelfth-century Germany, and in the influence of Christian and Muslim art, in which saints and evangelists were depicted with animal heads. Christian influence in Muslim art is due to the Christian artists who were employed by rich Muslims to illustrate MSS of secular content.[29] The difficulty with this explanation is that occasionally one and the same illustration contains both bird-headed and human-headed figures. If the biblical Second Commandment were the reason for introducing animal-headed figures in the Jewish illustrations then, of course, no human face would be found in them at all.

The "Bird's Head Haggadah" (Bezalel National Museum, Jerusalem, MS 180/57)[30] dates from thirteenth-century Germany. As its name indicates, it contains mainly bird-headed figures, but also human faces. This Haggadah was written and illustrated at the same time as the above-mentioned Ambrosian Bible MS in Germany, and still it also contains pictures of human beings. It would therefore seem that the bird heads are based not on iconoclastic considerations, but on some other, possibly magic, motivation. For example, in the Bird's Head Haggadah, card no. 26, the Egyptians and Pharaoh have human faces, but the Jews are shown with birds' heads, which could be an indication of magic power. The same idea is projected in card no. 42, in the bird-headed figures of Abraham, Isaac, and Jacob, shown walking toward Paradise. The Hebrew words *ze hagan Eden* (This is Paradise) are visible at the top of the illustration. An angel waits to lead them into Paradise at whose gate two pairs of winged angels with human heads face each other. In the Midrash it is the angel Michael who greets the souls of the righteous at the gates of Heavenly Jerusalem and guides them toward the throne of God (Mid. haNeᶜelam, Zohar 1:125b).

The Hebrew text, which covers two thirds of one page, is a quotation from the Psalms, which ends with the verse, "Open to me the gates of righteousness; I will enter into them, I will give thanks unto the Lord; the righteous shall enter into it" (Ps. 118:19–20). This is a clear reference to paradise, toward which the bird-headed Jews with their pointed hats are walking. There are also women, but they have human faces; this may express the idea that only the bird-headed male figures have the right to go forward, lifting their right arms toward Heavenly Jerusalem as a gesture of adoration.[31]

In another Mahzor MS (British Museum MS 22413) there is an illustration showing Moses receiving the Ten Commandments on Mount Sinai. Moses, Aaron, and seven other figures have human heads, but Sarah, Rebekah, Rachel, and Leah, who were not alive at the time of the revelation at Mount Sinai, have animal heads, which in this case seems to be symbolic of their "astral" position.[32]

Winged angels appear in illustrated Hebrew works. They are either faceless (as in the Sarajevo Haggadah[33]), or have human faces (Golden Haggadah).[34] In the Regensburg Bible only the angel has a bird's face; all the other figures have human faces to indicate the angel's heavenly status.[35] This is the case also in the illustrated Siddur MS 1300, from Austria.[36] In the scene showing the Sacrifice of Isaac, Abraham and Isaac are depicted with human faces (Abraham wearing a Jewish hat), but the winged angel appears in the shape of a black eagle with a crown on its head. In a Hebrew Bible illustration from the first half of the fourteenth century, found in a Cracow synagogue subsequently destroyed in World War II, an eagle-headed angel restrains Abraham from sacrificing his son.[37]

On amulets used against Lilith the child killer, birds have magic power. The three angels Senoy, Sansenoy, and Semangelof appear in bird form on an amulet prepared to protect the life of the newborn and the mother in childbed.[38] A magic bird is visible on a German Jewish amulet from the seventeenth to eighteenth century, used for the protection of the child against the Evil Eye.[39]

In Hebrew literature, sources as far apart in time as the Apocalypse of Baruch (first cent. C.E.) and Yalqut Reubeni (seventeenth cent.) describe heavens inhabited by animal-headed human beings and by hybrid creatures with bodies of humans and heads of lions, serpents, or oxen.[40] Such imaginary figures appear also in illustrated MSS.[41]

The Midrash refers to magic birds that helped Moses to conquer a city, to Balak, the Moabite king who wanted to destroy the Children of Israel and to King Solomon, who tried to prevent his daughter from marrying a poor youth. Interesting is the legend that describes Moses as the ruler of Ethiopia who ordered the people to catch young storks, raise them, and teach them to fly. After the storks grew up, they were starved for three days, and on the third day Moses said to the people: "Let every man put on his armor and gird his sword upon him. Each one shall mount his horse,

Kay Kavus ascends to the sky. The Metropolitan Museum of Art, Gift of Arthur A. Houghton, Jr., 1970.

Kay Kavus's unsuccessful flight. The Metropolitan Museum of Art, Bequest of Monroe C. Gutman, 1974.

and each shall set his stork upon his hand, and we will rise up and fight against the city. . . ." Upon reaching the enemy-held city, each man let his stork fly, and the storks ate the snakes that had surrounded the city and had made it impossible to approach.[42] In a Persian illustrated MS in the New York Metropolitan Museum of Art depicting Kay Kaus ascending to the sky, the hero tries to fly up to heaven with the help of four starved eagles lured upward by the bait of meat placed on the four corners of a wooden carriage. The people watching Kay Kaus's efforts laughed at him.[43] In another MS, called "Small Shah-Name" (from the early fourteenth century, Iran), the same theme is illustrated, but here Kay Kaus falls from the sky. His head, as well as the heads of the four eagles, is shown upside down. The hero failed in his efforts to escape with the help of the magic birds.[44]

"Nostro Pelicano"

The story of the pelican who opens his chest and with his own blood brings the dead birds back to life inspired Dante to call Jesus "Nostro Pelicano." There is a vast literature dealing with animal symbolism in Christianity.[45] Animal-headed evangelists can be seen on the first page of the Book of Kells and on Byzantine reliefs.[46] The basis of these representations is the Book of Revelation 4:7, in which three of four creatures are depicted with animal faces: those of a lion, an ox, and an eagle. The fourth has a human face. In a prayer book from the thirteenth century in the possession of the Basle diocese, three evangelists have faces of a dog, a cow, and a bird.[47] St. Christopher appears in the East and in the West with a dog's head.

In conclusion a word about the dove which in Christianity became the symbol of the soul and of the Holy Spirit. The soul of a true, baptized Christian flies like a dove up to God. The dove appears in the catacombs as the symbol of the souls of Christians. It is symbolic of simplicity, purity of heart, and love.[48] Christian art and architecture mirror the animal and bird symbolism in abundance.[49]

The magic bird flew all over the world. It found its way to, and became reflected in, many different religions and cultures.

Notes

1. E. B. Tylor, *Primitive Culture* (London, 1871); R. R. Marett, *The Threshold of Religion* (London, 1914); Rudolf Wittkover, "Eagle and Serpent: A Study in the Migration of Symbols," *Journal of the Warburg and Courtauld Institutes* 2, no. 4:293–325.
2. Gardners, *Art Through the Ages*, 6th ed. (New York, 1975), pp. 31–32.
3. Rudolf Otto, *The Idea of the Holy* (New York, 1958), p. 67.

4. Ibid. 121–31.

5. M. Lurker, *Symbol, Mythos und Legende in der Kunst* (Baden-Baden, 1978), p. 30; Luise Klebs, "Der aegyptische Seelenvogel," *Zeitschrift für Aegyptische Sprache und Altertumskunde* 61 (1926):104–8; A. Piankoff, *The Wandering of the Soul*, Bollingen Series 40, Princeton, N.J., 1974.

6. Arthur H. Collins, *Symbolism of Animals and Birds* (London, 1913), p. 114.

7. M. Lurker, *Symbol, Mythos*, pp. 30–31; Alfred Bertholet, *Wörterbuch der Religionen* (Stuttgart, 1952), p. 435.

8. J. G. Frazer, *The New Golden Bough*. Ed. with notes and foreword by Theodor Gaster (New York, 1959); M. Lurker, *Bibliographie zur Symbolkunde* 3 vols. (Baden-Baden, 1964–68).

9. Vaughn E. Crawford; Prudence O. Harper; Holly Pittman, *Assyrian Reliefs and Ivories in the Metropolitan Museum of Art. Palace Reliefs of Assurnasirpal II and Ivory Carvings from Nimrud.* (New York: The Metropolitan Museum of Art, 1980); Samuel M. Paley, *King of the World: Ashur-nasir-pal II of Assyria, 883–859* B.C. (New York, 1976).

10. E. Douglas Van Buren, *Symbols of the Gods in Mesopotamian Art*, Analecta Orientalia Commentationes Scientificae de Rebus Orientis Antiqui. No. 23. Pontificum Institutum Biblicum (Rome, 1945), p. 22.

11. *Assyrian Reliefs and Ivories in the Metropolitan Museum of Art*, pp. 28, 31.

12. Z. Ameisenowa, "The Tree of Life in Jewish Iconography," *Journal of the Warburg and Courtauld Institutes* 2, no. 4:326–45; Johanna Fleming, *Der Lebensbaum in der altchristlichen, byzantischen und byzantinisch beeinflussten Kunst* (Jena, 1963).

13. Karl Spiess, *Der Vogel: Bedeutung und Gestalt in sagtuemlicher und bildlicher Ueberlieferung* (Klagenfurt, 1969), p. 109.

14. Ibid., p. 151.

15. Ameisenowa, "Tree of Life," p. 399.

16. Karl Spiess, *Der Vogel*, pp. 161–62.

17. Edward S. Harkness MSS. 1933. 35. 9. 20.

18. *The Book of the Dead . . .*, The Oriental Institute of the University of Chicago: Studies in Ancient Oriental Civilization no. 37, 10 vols. (1974), 1:306; *Ancient Egyptian Magical Texts*, trans. J. F. Borghouts (Leiden, 1978).

19. *The Book of the Dead*, p. 192; Dagni Carter, *The Symbol of the Beast* (New York, 1957), pp. 12–13.

20. The weighing of the soul was a popular theme in Medieval art. In a MS. of a prayer book (Bodleian MS. Laud. Or. 321 f.166) the animal-headed, winged angel Michael holds the scales, and Gabriel the quill to record the merits of the soul.

21. Edward S. Harkness MS. col. 175; chap. 150–64.

22. *New Catholic Encyclopedia*, 1:451.

23. Josef Strzygowsky, *Origin of Christian Church Art: New Facts and Principles of Research*. Trans. from the German by O. M. Dalton, M. A., and H. J. Braunholz, M.A. (Oxford, 1923), p. 121.

24. V. Aptowitzer, "Die Seele als Vogel:Ein Beitrag zu den Anschauungen der Agada," *Monatsschrift fuer Geschichte und Wissenschaft des Judentums* (MGWJ) 69 (1925):150–69; Erwin R. Goodenough, *Jewish Symbols in the Greco-Roman Period*, vol. 8: *Pagan Symbols in Judaism* (New York: Bollingen Series, 1958), pp. 22–166.

25. V. Aptowitzer, "Die Seele als Vogel," p. 159; Gershom Scholem, "Seelenwanderung und Sympathie der Seelen in der juedischen Mystik," *Eranos Jahrbuch* 24 (1955): 55–118.

26. Zohar I, 12b.

27. Louis Ginzberg, *The Legends of the Jews* (Philadelphia: The Jewish Publication Society of America, 1909), 1:28–30; 5:45–47; Z. Ameisenowa, "Das messianische Gastmahl der Gerechten in einer hebraeischen Bibel aus dem XIII.Jahrhundert." *MGWJ* 79 (1935):409–22. Raphael Patai, *The Messiah Texts* (New York: Avon Books, 1979), pp. 235–46.

28. Z. Ameisenowa, "Animal-Headed Gods, Evangelists, Saints and Righteous Men," *Journal of the Warburg and Courtauld Institutes*, 12 (1949):28; Ginzberg, *Legends of the Jews*, 5:46, n. 127.

29. Bezalel Narkiss, *Hebrew Illuminated Manuscripts* (Jerusalem, 1969), p. 90, plate 25.

30. Bezalel Narkiss and Gabriella Sed-Rajna, *Bird's Head Haggadah: Iconographical Index of Hebrew Illuminated Manuscripts* (Jerusalem-Paris, 1976).

31. Ibid., card no. 26, 42.

32. Narkiss, *Hebrew Illuminated Manuscripts* (Jerusalem, 1969) p. 108, plate 34; Tripartite Mahzor, vol. 2. The first volume of the Mahzor is in the Hungarian Academy of Science, Budapest (Kaufmann Collection. MS. A384); vol. 3 is in the Bodleian Library (Oxford. MS. Mich. 619). Concerning J. Gutmann's view on animal-headed and bird-headed human beings see his *Hebrew Manuscript Painting* (New York, 1978), pp. 25, 94–95.

33. *The Sarajevo Haggadah,* text by Cecil Roth (Belgrade n.d.), plate 10.

34. London, British Museum. ADD. MS. 27210. Narkiss, *Hebrew Illuminated Manuscripts,* plate 8.

35. Jerusalem, Israel Museum.MS.180/52. *Hebrew Illuminated Manuscripts,* p. 98.

36. In the Jewish Theological Seminary of America.

37. Ameisenowa, "Animal-Headed Gods," p. 27.

38. Raphael Patai, *The Hebrew Goddess* (New York: Avon Books, 1978), p. 205.

39. *Encyclopaedia Judaica,* 2:910, fig. 5; E. A. W. Budge, *Amulets and Superstitions* (London, 1930).

40. Apoc. of Baruch, trans. E. Kautzsch (1900), 2:44; Yalqut Reubeni, fol. 2. col. 4.

41. Hamilton Siddur (Berlin, Preussische Staatsbibliothek) MS. Ham. 288; Kennicott Bible (Oxford, Bodleian Library) MS. Kennicott I; Dragon Haggadah (Hamburg, Staats and Universitaetsbibliothek) Cod. Heb. 155.

42. Ginzberg, *Legends* 2:286-87; 3:353; 4:175–76.

43. Arthur A. Houghton, Jr., MS. 1970. 301.21. Folio 134 recto.

44. Metropolitan Museum of Art. Monroe C. Gutman MS. 1974, 290, 9; Sir Thomas W. Arnold, *Painting in Islam: A Study of the Place of Pictorial Art in Muslim Culture.* With a new Introduction by B. W. Robinson (New York, 1965), p. 64.

45. Elizabeth E. Goldsmith, *Sacred Symbols in Art* (New York-London, 1911); James Hall, *Dictionary of Subjects and Symbols in Art* (London, 1974); Wera von Blakenburg, *Heilige und daemonische Tiere* (Leipzig, 1943); Karl Kuenstle, *Ikonographie der Christlichen Kunst* (Freiburg, 1926–28); Manfred Lurker, *Bibliographie zur Symbolkunde,* 3 vols. (Baden-Baden, 1964–68); Engelbert Kirschbaum, et al. *Lexicon der Christlichen Ikonographie* (Freiburg im Bresgau, 1968–1972).

46. Ameisenowa, *Animal-Headed Gods,* p. 39; J. Strzygowsky, "Das byzantinische Relief aus Tusla im Berliner Museum." *Jahrbuch der Preuss. Kunstsammlung,* (1898), pp. 58–66.

47. Ameisenowa, "Animal-Headed Gods," p. 40.

48. Erwin R. Goodenough, *Jewish Symbols,* 8:37–40 (The Dove in Christianity) 8:41–46 (The Dove in Judaism); Paula Seethaler, "Die Taube des Heiligen Geistes," *Bibel und Leben* 4 (1963):115–30; George Ferguson, *Signs and Symbols in Christian Art* (New York, 1954).

49. E. P. Evans, *Animal Symbolism in Ecclesiastical Architecture* (London, 1896); Louis Réau, *Iconographie de l'art chrétien,* 6 vols. (Paris, 1955–59).

The Jew as Literary Hero

LIVIA BITTON JACKSON

At first glance, it appears as if there were two distinct currents in fictional portrayal of the Jew from the mid-eighteenth century on: the Jew-hero appears on the stage of the Enlightenment, and seems to rival his antithesis, the Jew-villain. In fact, however, there are no rival parallel tendencies in the portrayal of the Jew in literature: the mainstream of Jew-villains is only sporadically trailed by a string of Jew-heroes.

While the Jew-villain image is a centuries-old expression of deep-seated Gentile feelings about the Jew, the Jew-hero image is an artificially created literary commodity attractively designed for popular consumption. Fashioned by well-meaning sympathizers with the Jews for the express purpose of helping the Jew, of breaking the Jew-villain image, the Jew-hero remained a synthetic and alien phenomenon in the face of the authenticity and proliferation of the Jew-villain.

Lessing's play, *Die Juden,* the first such pro-Jewish effort, was presented on the Berlin stage in 1749. It had considerable popular acclaim, and has been hailed by Jewish historians as a milestone in the history of the Jew in literature. It was the first play in which the Jew is not a villain but a hero: he is honest and eager to serve justice; he helps to track down and unmask the thief, a Gentile of noble birth.

Die Juden was soon followed by C. F. Gellert's novel, *Briefe der Schwedischen Gräfin von Guilderstern* (1752), in which a Polish Jew, a kind, honest, pious man, befriends the count of Guilderstern and performs loyal services to him, sometimes at risk of his own life.

These two literary works, pioneers in their presentation of the positive Jew image, served as an introduction to a new concept. The creation of the Jew-hero, a figure deliberately designed as an antithesis to the stereotypical Jew-villain, fell to Lessing's *Nathan der Weise,* in 1779. Nathan the Jew became the undisputed superhero of Enlightenment drama and literature, exercising great influence on the creation of a host of Jew-heroes beyond the geographic boundaries of Germany and the chronological ones of the Enlightenment.

Nathan was modeled after Moses Mendelssohn, the great Jewish philosopher of Berlin and the friend of Lessing. He is the positive counter-image of Shakespeare's Shylock: he is noble where Shylock is knavish, generous where Shylock is miserly, loving where Shylock is hating, wise where Shylock is foolishly egocentric. Nathan is as unrealistically superhuman as Shylock is subhuman. Intended as an antistereotype, Nathan soon became a stereotype himself: on the German, French, English, and Russian stage, and in prose fiction, Nathan-type Jew-heroes began to appear concurrently with their more familiar Jew-villain counterparts.

Even though Lessing's Nathan became the prototype of the literary Jew-hero, Tobias Smollett's "honest Hebrew" character preceded him chronologically. He was Joshua Manasseh, who made his appearance on the English stage in *The Adventures of Count Fathom* (1753) more than twenty-five years prior to the spectacular entry of Nathan into literary fame as a revolutionary Jewish character. Yet Smollett's Jew-hero, a kind, unselfish moneylender, has not been credited with setting a new trend, even though the second Jew-hero of English letters, Richard B. Sheridan's Moses ("honest Israelite") is his direct descendant.

Why such neglect? In part, it may be due to Smollett's earlier negative treatment of the Jewish character, which had established the author's reputation as none too friendly to Jews. The prominence of Lessing, on the other hand, as the leading German humanist in the forefront of the struggle for civil rights for Jews added luster to the figure of Nathan and helped assure the popularity of the play itself. Nathan, in addition to his role as Jew-hero, served also as a larger-than-life symbol composed of the ideals and values of the Enlightenment. Smollett's Manasseh, although likewise unrealistically benign and generous (he refused to take interest on money advanced to poor Gentiles), does not reach Nathan's exaggerated stature in any respect. He is a rich, kind-hearted, sentimental moneylender, unbelievable in the extreme magnanimity he exhibits, yet he remains a "typical" Jew with repulsive looks and an offensive voice. Retaining some of the trappings of the Jew-villain, Manasseh exudes an aura of objectionability. thus his heroic quality, which would otherwise distinguish him, is greatly minimized. Nathan, on the other hand, handsome, dignified, elegant, and well educated, is the very summit of noblemindedness. He is kind and solicitous to Gentile, Muslim, and Jew alike, and serves as a towering example of virtues rarely found in perfect harmony within one human being.

Nathan, as the model and the product of the Enlightenment, was a guaranteed box office hit, a fact that bode well for the fate of the Jew. The changing emotional climate of the age allowed for a positive place for the Jew in drama and literature, and encouraged imitation. The combination

Enlightenment-Jew-superhero became a popular literary feature as the century progressed, and gradually prepared the ground for Jewish emancipation.

Nonetheless, the Jew-hero still had to contend with the ever-present figure of the veteran Jew-villain. It is to the credit of the Age of Reason that the Jew-hero managed to become a more or less fixed literary commodity, at times challenging the tradition-sanctioned figure of the Jew-villain. It is hardly surprising that the Jew-hero was unable to modify the portrayal of the Jew-villain or reduce the frequency of its presentation. Although the Jew-hero himself survived beyond the period in which he was fashioned, he was forced to play second fiddle to a more vigorous and prolific step-brother.

The new trend of portraying Jews as heroes brought about an amazing change of heart in the approach of some prominent English authors. In their early works, several distinguished playwrights and writers presented the most despicable Jew-villains; then, in a sudden change of attitude, they produced strikingly antithetical, idealized Jew-heroes in later works.

The first example of this dramatic change is Smollett himself, the creator of the first English Jew-hero. His gracious Manasseh was preceded five years earlier by one of the most deplorable specimens of the Jew-villain, Isaac Rapine, the "old cent-per-cent fornicator" in his *The Adventures of Roderick Random* (1748). Similarly, Sheridan's Moses, in *The School for Scandal* (1777), a friendly and honest usurer, is the second Jew-character of the brilliant Irish playwright. Two years earlier, in his comic opera *The Duenna* (1775), he presented Isaac Mendoza, a disagreeable Jew-villain, a target of scorn and ridicule.

Richard Cumberland also presented two extreme portraits of the Jew. His Jew-villain, the greedy, unscrupulous Naphtali, appeared in his popular play *The Fashionable Lover* in 1772. Twenty-two years later Cumberland dedicated a comedy, *The Jew* (1794), to the noble figure of Sheva, a kind-hearted money-lender, "the widow's friend, the orphan's father, the poor man's protector"—the Jew as universal philanthropist.

Two prominent nineteenth-century authors displayed a similar change of attitude toward Jewish characterization. One was Maria Edgeworth and the other Charles Dickens. Maria Edgeworth introduced a long string of Jew-villains in her novels and short stories until, in 1817, with the publication of *Harrington,* the series came to an abrupt halt. Jewish characters in this late novel are superheroes, each a conglomeration of virtue in his own right. Jacob and Simon, a young and an old peddler, are wise and honest. Mr. Montenero is a cultured, elegant, generous, and tolerant gentleman-merchant. Professor Israel Lyons is a worldly, brilliant, sophisticated, kind-hearted, and gentle Hebrew scholar.

In the preface to the novel, Richard Lovell Edgeworth, the father of the novelist, reveals that *Harrington* was written in response to an American Jewish lady's letter of protest against Miss Edgeworth's earlier misrepresentations of the Jewish character. The complaint of Miss Rachel Mordecai of Richmond, Virginia, apparently caused the novelist to examine her motives in selecting Jews as villains. Her self-analysis yielded an explanation in the first chapter of *Harrington*, one that may be applied to literary characterization of Jews in general. Maria Edgeworth admits to having simply adopted stereotypical representations of Jews as "allegorical personifications of the devil," without much inquiry as to the reality or honesty of such presentation. The total reversal of her attitude in *Harrington* became more than a simple atonement for past sins. It was, in effect, a reappraisal of a literary process, an effort at thoughtful selection of characters rather than the automatic and random recourse to stereotypes.

She did not succeed in this objective. In her effort to compensate, as so often happens, she overcompensated. Trying to avoid stereotypical Jew-villains, she created their converse, stereotypical Jew-heroes.

Charles Dickens, prompted by a like experience, fell into a similar trap of literary maneuvering. The arch-thief Fagin of *Oliver Twist* (1838), possessing all the conventional characteristics of the Jew-villain, both in appearance and in manner, stirred wide criticism of Dickens. In defense of his choice of character, Dickens claimed that Fagin's Jewishness was incidental and had no bearing on the author's views of Jews. There was no association or similarity whatever between Jews living in London at the time and the figure of Fagin, the writer insisted.

The critical exchange, however, resulted in an eventual reevaluation of Dickens's literary practices. Twenty-six years after Fagin, he presented a Jew as a protagonist in *Our Mutual Friend* (1864). Mr. Riah, the benevolent, generous moneylender thus joined the glittering gallery of Jew-heroes with virtues exaggerated ad absurdum.

The two facets of Jew-portrayal continued: the Jew-villains proliferated in their unmitigated wickedness, and the Jew-heroes, in their unadulterated purity, made rarer and rather isolated appearances. The literature of following decades witnessed a host of vicious, miserly usurers, as against some kindly, generous moneylenders, an array of fraudulent peddlers opposite one or two honest ones, a whole class of offensive, boorish, parvenu bankers opposite an occasional refined, well-bred financier. The token appearance of a "good Jew" in a sea of demonic wickedness represented by Jews on the stage and in literature was of course ineffective as a social or political weapon.

It is significant that Smollett's Joshua Manasseh, the first Jew-hero of English literature, made an appearance in the year when the first Jew Bill was introduced in the British Parliament (1753). While this attempt at securing civil rights for the Jews of England was defeated, several other such bills were introduced and debated during the second half of the eighteenth century. Each renewed effort at the emancipation of Jews was accompanied by the appearance of Jew-heroes on the stage and in the novel.

Discussion of Jewish rights was especially lively from the 1820s till mid-century when, in 1858, the Jews of England finally achieved full emancipation. During these decades several celebrated Jew-heroes became popular in England. From George Walker's Shechem Bensadi, the benevolent and charitable moneylender in *Theodore Cyphon, or the Benevolent Jew* (1823), and Horace Smith's pious Rav (1828), to Disraeli's (1831–47), Reede's (1856), Bulwer-Lytton's (1853), and Mrs. Scott's (1857) Jew-heroes, the political orientation of their portrayals seems obvious. Thomas Wade, in the introduction to his drama *The Jew of Arragon; or the Hebrew Queen*, performed in Covent Garden in 1830, discloses his intention in presenting the figure of Xavier, the "good Jew," as a modest effort to alleviate the burdens of his fellow residents of Jewish faith, and to promote their cause to gain full citizenship rights.

The Jew-heroes of this period have one common denominator: their chief virtue lies in their usefulness to Christians. The kindly moneylender lends to poor Christians without interest. The honest peddler sells below cost. Other Jews do invaluable services to Christians, such as saving their lives at the risk of their own, delivering money and goods amid perilous circumstances, and converting to Christianity out of love. The most popular service rendered by heroic Jews, however, is the adoption of abandoned Christian children, almost exclusively girls, and their loving upbringing till adulthood, when they are returned to the folds of Christianity.

Since the ultimate measure of the Jew is his value to Christians, the extent of his heroism depends on the degree of his devotion to them. The finest quality displayed by a Jew, therefore, is that which yields the most benefit. Becoming a foster parent to a Christian infant unwanted by Christians, and returning her to Christianity in full-grown maidenhood, seem to have been the most desirable service a Jew could render. Thus, the Jew-foster father pattern became popular.

The ingredients of the pattern were invariable. The kindly Jew embraces the Gentile infant rejected by her kin and brings her up as his own. The young Gentile girl grows in the Jewish home, having received a Jewish name and Jewish education, Jewish love and indulgence, and becomes a beautiful Jewess. Her true identity is unknown to all except the wise and loving foster father-Jew. A Christian lover appears on the scene and falls in love with the maiden. At the dramatic moment, when her happiness with the Christian hangs in precarious balance (the Christian youth faces parental prejudice against her as a Jewess and objection to their marriage), the self-sacrificing, devoted Jew-hero-father reveals the secret of her birth, thus bringing happiness to a great number of Christians. The marriage between the two young people can take place, the parents of the groom are spared embarrassment, and the Christian Church regains a soul.

Lessing's famous Nathan was the first of this noble breed of Jew-foster fathers. His foster daughter was the abandoned child of a Muslim father and a Christian mother, rejected by both faiths but received warmly by the Jew. In German literature Nathan was soon imitated by Johann K. Lotich, whose Jew Wolf becomes the adoptive father of a Christian waif in *Wer war wohl mehr Jude?* (1783), and by Karl Steinberg, whose kindly Isaac Mendel adopts and tends a Christian girl in *Menschen und Menschensituationen* (1787). In Kotzebue's *Kind der Liebe* (1791) the compassionate Jew comes to the aid of a Gentile woman who, in her hour of dire need after bearing a "child of love," was heartlessly abandoned by members of her own faith and family. In Hensler's *Judenmädchen von Prag* the Jew Isaac offers to pay the bill of a poor Gentile neighbor whose plight was ignored by his Christian kin and friends.

The most celebrated foster father-Jew in English fiction is Mr. Montenero, Maria Edgeworth's superb gentleman-merchant of *Harrington*. He brings up the charming Berenice and places at her disposal culture and wealth; yet his greatest gift to her is his selfless yielding of her person to the Gentile Harrington and to Christianity at the romantic climax of the story.

The selection of girls and the exclusion of boys from the adoptive role in the Jew-foster father pattern is not accidental. The choice of a girl as the object of a Jew's fatherly care implied the distinct possibility, if not certainty, of her eventual return to Christianity through marriage to a Christian. A boy brought up and educated in the Jewish faith, would be, the Gentile authors believed, less likely to return to the fold, even if he were to meet a Gentile maiden. It is the woman who is expected to follow her man into his faith.

The pattern is reversed in George Eliot's monumental *Daniel Deronda* (1876). Daniel is brought up by an English aristocrat unaware of his Jewish origins. Yet, instinctively, he matures into a Jew with all the positive characteristics of a Jew in the super-Jew tradition. The disclosure of his Jewish birth opens the door not only to total identification with Jewishness, but also to marriage with a beautiful Jewess who would have refused his hand had he remained a Christian.

Daniel Deronda is the first, truly genuine, effort at emancipating the Jewish character. The Jew-heroes are still unrealistically idealized; they are still merely attractive vessels for beautiful ideals. Their nobility and compassion, their generosity and loving-kindness, however, are not created solely for the purpose of serving the Christian world that would otherwise reject them. George Eliot allowed her Jewish heroes the luxury of having values of their own, of employing their superior virtues for the betterment of their own people. She went even a step farther: she granted the privilege of pride to her hero at the discovery of his Jewishness, and permitted the happy ending of his romance to hinge on it.

Measured against Daniel Deronda, Nathan seems an anemic figure indeed. The one-dimensional Jew-hero of the previous century, reflecting the humanistic values of that age, was now replaced by a Jewish character who combined those universal virtues with Jewish nationalist aspirations. Mordochai, another Jew-hero of George Eliot's *Daniel Deronda,* is a neo-prophet, an exponent of modern Zionism. The passage of a hundred years between Nathan and Daniel Deronda, the changing conditions and expectations of the Jews, are vividly reflected in the difference between these two Jew-heroes.

The nineteenth century presented a dilemma to the Jew—the choice between assimilation and Jewish nationalism. Assimilation held the promise of total emancipation in the countries of their residence; Jewish nationalism nurtured the dream of a return to Zion. This critical issue is echoed in the portrayal of nineteenth-century Jew-heroes. Some, like George Eliot's Mordochai, espouse Zionist ideals; most of them, however, are representatives of assimilation, for it is this objective that inspired Gentile authors to create them.

Benjamin Disraeli, himself a converted Jew, chose to present the case for Jewish identification. He has his heroes extol Judaism as a superior culture. The cause of Jewish nationalism is represented by the prophetic Hebrew leader David Alrui in his *Alroy* (1831) and by the arguments of Sidonia in *Coningsby* (1844). Sidonia, an idealized portrait of Lionel de Rothschild, is a man of superior intelligence, wit, and insight; a financier and diplomat who eloquently offers irrefutable proof of Jewish intellectual and artistic superiority. In Mr. Besso of *Tancred* (1847) Disraeli combines an expression of Jewish pride with humanitarian kindness.

The desirability of assimilation, preferably to the extent of conversion, fashioned numerous Jew-heroes. Mrs. Scott's Jewish philosopher, Mr. Mendelssohn, and young Joseph in *Joseph the Jew* (1857) love Christians and Christianity with great devotion, and Joseph adopts the latter as his own faith. Mr. Levy, the handsome, wealthy, generous, and cultured Jew of Bulwer-Lytton's *My Novel* (1853), achieves recognition in Gentile society: he is raised to the rank of nobility. Two generations confront each other in the struggle for emancipation in Chester B. Fernald's *The Ghetto* (1889). The son of Sachel, Rafael, defies his father and leaves the ghetto with its Jewish values: in his search for social recognition he submerges in English culture. The father, in his stubborn resistence to assimilation, remains in the ghetto.

Acceptance by the Gentiles continued to be the theme of Jew-hero portrayal also in twentieth-century English literature. Social recognition as a desirable goal, and the efforts through assimilation to achieve it, the responses of an often antagonistic Gentile environment, and the resultant sense of alienation of the Jew continued to be facets of the Jewish reality in England, and subject to literary treatment. Gilbert Canaan's Mendel Kühler (*Mendel*, 1916) and Sembal (*Sembal*, 1923) epitomize the problem of the English Jew in his struggle for assimilation. Mendel, the son of Polish Jewish immigrants in London, is a talented young artist. Although he is the only creative talent among them, or perhaps partly because of it, his Gentile colleagues display open resentment toward him. They are irritated by the intense young Jew's uncouth manners and primitive vitality, and exclude him from their select "English" circle. Sembal dedicates his talents to the Socialist idea. He is an idealist who devotes his time and energy to the welfare of his fellow men, yet he is rejected even by his Socialist associates as an alien. Sembal, the optimist Jew that he is, does not give up. He attempts to overcome the anti-Semitism of his environment by severing completely his ties with the Jewish world he had belonged to, and offering even more unstintingly his love to the Gentile English world that rejected him. W. S. Maugham's Jewish family in "The Alien Corn" (from his collection of short stories *First Person Singular*, 1931) are proud of their "non-Jewish" looks and manners, and make every effort to conceal their Jewishness. Arnold Lunn's Daniel Martiñez attains social recognition by marrying a Gentile woman of social rank (*Family Name*, 1931).

Despite these efforts to be embraced by Gentile English society, the Jew remained an alien. His acceptance as a man among men continued to depend on his ability to dissociate himself from his Jewish background and its identifying features. Often, the only distinction of a literary Jew-hero was that he was unlike a Jew. S. G. Millin's Mr. Nathan, for instance, was a kindly old "untypical Jew." The mayor of the village in *The Coming of the Lord* (1927), in describing Mr. Nathan's character, says, ". . . it was only to wonder that so decent a fellow should belong to this impossible race." An American visitor in London exclaims incredulously, after the Jew-hero of the novel *Caste* (1927) by Cosmo Hamilton was spoken of in terms of high praise: "Haven't you heard that this man is a Jew? He may be a gentleman, he may be a genius, but the fact that he is a Jew, makes him, with us in America, a pariah-dog." The same sentiment is expressed by the friends of Mr. Garstein, the gentlemanly Jewish businessman, in Richard Blaker's *Here Lies a Most Beautiful Lady* (1935). In discussing the Jew-hero, one of his Gentile acquaintances remarks, "and you'll forget that he's a Jew as soon as you've met him. . . ."

In attempting to find a dignified solution to the Jew's dilemma of identification, Amy Baker introduces Mr. Mosenheimer in her *Dear Yesterday* (1917). Because of his German sounding name, Mosenheimer is taken for a German. But he proudly sets the record straight, claiming that he is an English Jew and not a German Gentile. Even though the opportunity afforded it, Baker's Jew did not conceal his Jewish identity. Anthony Thorne dealt with this Jewish dilemma in like manner. In his *Delay of the Sun* (1935), the Jew Grunbaum, like so many of his literary counterparts, is an aggressive social climber until he meets and marries a Jewess who makes him aware of his Jewish identity. Thereafter he ceases to ape the Gentiles' manners, asserts himself as a Jew, and finds true contentment.

The Jew as a pragmatist—a capable industrialist, an intellectual, a clever attorney—figures quite prominently in English prose of the period. H. G. Wells's Jew, the rich businessman Sir Rupert Solomonson (*Marriage*, 1912), seems to prove the converse of the rule established by Millin, Hamilton, and Baker with regard to the "race" of their Jewish heroes: Sir Rupert is "full of that practical loyalty and honesty that distinguishes his race." Storm Jameson's Marcel Cohen (*Love in Winter*, 1935) is also a rich, clever man of commerce whose Jewishness did not detract from his human merit. Sir Rupert and Marcel Cohen belong to the string of the unsentimental, over-intellectualized professionals representing the Jewish personality in those works of fiction which seek to find a modus vivendi for the Jew on the precarious marginal line between Jewishness and Gentile recognition. It is their disciplined intellect devoid of excessive idealism that establishes a nook of recognition for these Jews, not irrespective of their Jewishness, but because of it. Rose Macaulay, who dedicates her novel *Potterism* (1921) "to the unsentimental precisians in thought, who have, on this confused, inaccurate, and emotional planet, no fit habitation," chose a Jewish journalist, Arthur Gideon, to epitomize intellectual clarity and precision. Also Emil Stern, Compton Mackenzie's Jew in *South Wind of Love* (1937) is a fanatic of intellectualism. Although Mackenzie, unlike Miss Macaulay, is not an admirer of pure, cold brain power, he does not make the Jew appear unattractive because the latter measures everything against thinking ability; neither does the author ascribe the Jew's intellectual snobbishness to his being a Jew.

Yet Emil Stern's Jewishness is not incidental. Whether a humanist, a Zionist, a Socialist, or a pragmatist, the Jew-hero is delineated in extreme contours. He stands out against either a background of contemporary ideals that he is called upon to represent, or as the embodiment of the authors' objectives. Literary Jew-heroes ever since the prototypal Nathan of Lessing can at random be selected as key figures in tracing the development and change of ideas, so neatly do they conform to the role of models. Anatole Leroy-Beaulieu, in his *Israël chez les nations* (1893), for instance, draws a line from Lessing's Nathan to Daniel, the Zionist visionary in *La Femme de Claude* (1873) of Dumas fils, to Eliot's Mordochai. Following that line of comparison, one perceives the expansion of the humanist ideal into a combination of Zionism and humanism.

The Zionist Daniel is a unique figure among French Jew-heroes. In France, the idealized image of the Jew was either that of a supreme French patriot, or that of a cosmopolitan par excellence. As elsewhere, the French Jew-hero was made to portray that which was the optimal desirability of the age. During the second half of the nineteenth century, a period of extreme nationalism, the first Jew-heroes to represent the virtues of passionate devotion to France appeared in French literature. Within the context of total dedication to the French *patrie* and an absolute commitment to its service, the Jew-hero of French letters, like his German or English counterpart, was also an idealized model of positive human qualities. While nationalism was the dominant mood of the age, the values of the Revolution still prevailed, and the Jew as a cosmopolitan lover of all mankind made for a desirable image. Thus, French literature yielded both types of Jew-characters, albeit in small numbers.

The first of the perfect patriots, Reb David of Erckmann-Chatrian in the novel *L'Ami Fritz* (1864), is a noble patriarch who appears to have the welfare of France as his sole ambition in life. His concern for the needs of the French fatherland prompts him to arrange a match for his Gentile friend so that the latter produces numerous offspring, an essential contribution to the survival of France. Reb David thus translates his Jewish survival instinct into efforts for the benefit of his beloved country. After the popularity of the character Reb David on the stage in a play *(L'Ami Fritz)* adapted from the novel in 1876, he became the prototype of patriotic Jew-heroes in French literature and drama.

Ponson du Terrail patterned his Samuel in *La Juive du Chateau-Trompotte* (1879) after the English style of kindly usurer who is good to poor Christians. Samuel is first and foremost a loyal French citizen, as is Albert Compain's Gustav Ledermann in *L'Opprobre* (1905), in addition to being a rich and honest merchant. Anatole France's Clavelin in *L'Orme du Mail* (1897) is a progressive liberal government employee, who on occasion is willing to sacrifice his liberalism for the sake of his government. He is trustworthy and trusting, an idealistic, honest official with an absolute loyalty to the republican regime.

Vandèrem's Schleifmann (*Les deux Rives,* 1898) belongs to the cosmopolitan school of French heroes. His love extends beyond the borders of France to all men, interpreting the ideals of Liberté, Fraternité, Egalité in terms of Marxist Socialism. Fired by prophetic zeal, Schleifmann does more than preach universal love and equality. At the risk of a long prison term, he commits large sums to promote the realization of his ideals. Vogue's Elzear Bayonne (*Les Morts qui parlent,* 1900) and Paul Bourget's Cremieux-Dax (*L'Etape,* 1902) are Schleifmann's spiritual offspring. Both espouse universal brotherhood while denigrating Judaism as outdated and provincial. Elzear Bayonne strives to achieve his goal of helping mankind by becoming a member of Parliament, and Cremieux-Dax founds the Tolstoy Union to win adherents for the Socialist cause. Although both fail to attain their noble objectives, they do succeed in leaving a heroic impression on the public during the period of the Dreyfus affair—a sympathetic effort at Jewish apologetics.

L'Affaire Dreyfus pitted royalists against republicans, dividing the country into Dreyfusard and anti-Dreyfusard camps, and stirring up lively literary campaigns. Liberal writers, such as Emile Zola, Charles Péguy, and Anatole France, took an unpopular and courageous stand with their support of the Dreyfusards in literary pronunciamentos, while Teramond and Vogue lent their support by means of apologetic novels. Zola's fictional characterization of Jews also changed in the wake of the Dreyfus case: in his novel *Vérité* (1902), the Jews appear in a radically transformed role, markedly more sympathetic than in his earlier novels. Anatole France's apologetic novels, *L'Anneau d'Améthyste* (1899) and *Le Procurateur de Judée* (1902), were followed by Edmond Gautier Teramond's *La Maitresse Juive* (1903), each devised to stem the swelling tide of anti-Semitism.

This role fell to German writers of pro-Jewish fiction as well. As the aims of the Enlightenment gradually degenerated into the desperate struggle of the nineteenth century, the noble ideal that Nathan the Wise was fashioned to serve gradually became an immediate and urgent need. As nineteenth-century rabid nationalism gave rise to fierce anti-Semitism, the immediate objective of Jew-hero characterization was to counter it by enhancing the positive Jew image.

Jew-heroes in direct line of descent from Nathan the Wise of Lessing bore close resemblance to their progenitor, even to the extent of imitating the name. Reinicke's Nathan in *Nathan der Deutsche* (1784) was followed by Jacob Bischoff's Nathan in *Dina, das Judenmädchen aus Franken* (1802); and then there were the noble Baruch fashioned after Nathan in Iffland's *Dienstpflicht* (1795), and the kind-hearted Jewish characters in Ziegelhäuser's *Juden* (1807). These were characters whose impeccable nobility recommended them as spokesmen for Jewish rights; their monolithic perfection served as a plea for Jewish emancipation. But when Jewish rights were finally granted during the first decades of the nineteenth century and were soon threatened by the growing wave of anti-Jewish sentiment, the image of the Jew had to be adjusted to these changed conditions in order to combat them. No longer was perfection of human virtue sufficient as heroic trait. Devotion to the German fatherland was now the foremost ideal: the Jew-hero of the age was redesigned to accommodate the current need. He became a German patriot.

Bernard Ehrenthal of Gustav Freytag's *Soll und Haben* (1855) was fashioned to fit the new mold of the Jew-hero. His loyalty to Germany and to the superior German culture is so intense that he virtually dies of shame when he fails to convert his father, a despicable Jew-villain type, to decency. Isaac of Felix Dahn's *Ein Kampf um Rom* (1904) goes even farther. His assimilation to Germanism is so complete that he himself is a fierce anti-Semite. He despises the puny, cowardly, traitorous, "typically" Jewish Jochem. Then, to give final and ultimate proof of his dedication to the *Vaterland,* he sacrifices his life for the Germanic cause after having demonstrated his renunciation of Judaism by murdering the Jew Jochem.

There was only limited space for Jew-heroes in the Volk novel of the pre-

Nazi era. Racist ideology came to dominate German life and literature, and
no virtues could be ascribed to the Jew-hero. His racial affiliation canceled
out every possibility of virtue, and there was no way to exonerate the stigma
of Jewish "blood." While the Enlightenment Jew figure became the summit
of all values and expectations of the eighteenth century in order to qualify
for the heroic role, and the Jew figure of the nineteenth century stood for
patriotism at its peak in order to prove the Jew's elemental worth, twentieth-century racist literature could produce no Jew-heroes. A Jew-hero
would have been anomalous to the very concept of Aryanism. Thus, much
before it became a political movement and gained power to cause the
destruction of European Jewry, Aryan racism proved unassailable on the
literary plane. This fact alone accounted for a substantial share of the
Hitlerian genocide. While literary propaganda in every form promoted
that mass hatred and fear of the Jew that eventually moved the Third
Reich to commit the gravest crime in history, no counter propaganda in the
form of literary images could be devised, because the nature of the racial
theory made such efforts futile. No Jew-hero existed as antithesis to the
Jew-villains mass-produced by the Nazi regime.

Thus German literature, which launched the prototype of the glorified
Jew-hero, provided the shortest span for his career. In no other literature
did the like of Nathan capture such an exalted place during the Enlightenment, and in no other literature did the Jew-hero vanish so abruptly. From
the height of idealization during the last decades of the eighteenth century
to his total disappearance during the first decades of the twentieth, the
German Jew-hero demonstrates a most spectacular, steep curve of decline.
In English literature, where the Jew-hero made his appearance a quarter of
a century earlier, and in a less glorified, less idealized form, he did not
disappear with the advent of the twentieth century but gradually faded into
the realistic portrayal of our day. In French literature the birth of the Jew-
hero trailed his German counterpart (1779) by a century with Dumas's
Daniel (1873). The latter, however, was more of a Jew and less of an ideal
in comparison to the German Nathan. The image of Daniel was much
closer to a realistic portrayal of a Jew, and just as much farther from the
idealized hero image. In French, just as in English literature, the Jew-hero
continued into twentieth-century realism.

Russian literature followed Western models in the initial stages of Jew-
hero portrayal but soon produced its own antithesis to its own Jew-villain.
Nor can the career of the Jew-hero in Russian literature be compared to
the German pattern. The history of the Russian Jew-hero is unique: it is the
exception that proves the theory about the artificiality of Jew-hero portrayal.

Perhaps Lazhechnikov's Zkharia, a learned, romantic, utterly selfless,
and self-sacrificing Jew in his *Basurman* (1850), and Salomon, a paragon of
Christian virtues to the extent of eventual baptism in his *Doch Yevreya*

(1855), are the only characters in Russian fiction reminiscent of Nathan. The Russian Jew-hero to emerge in later works is a small-time hero with unheroic measurements. No great humanitarians or Zionist visionaries of prophetic proportions appear in pro-Jewish Russian fiction. The Jew-heroes presented by Russian pro-Semitic authors are sympathetic figures with positive human characteristics outweighing inevitable flaws. A host of pleasant Jewish characters populate the Russian novel, short story, and drama of the late nineteenth and early twentieth century, from Chekhov's Moisei Moiseyevich, the ludicrous but kindly inn-keeper in *The Steppe*, and Kuprin's pitiful Khazkel in *The Jewess*, to Sologub's good-natured tailor, Teitelbaum, in *Evening Glow*, Dobronranov's gifted violinist, Fikhmann, in *Life Creating*, and Machtet's sensitive young student, David, in *The Jew*. Real-life, lovable, often comic characters appear in the works of Potapenko and Uspensky—Jews as tailors, jewelers, fruit-peddlers. The World War I novel often includes Jews as soldiers, often anachronistic figures but treated with sympathy, good humor, or outright admiration. Stanin-kovich's Isaika, a timid intellectual, is an incongruous figure in the Russian navy, but he is a kind fellow, loyal to Mother Russia ("Isaika"). Gusev-Orenburgsky's unnamed heroic little Jew vies with Artsibashev's Sol-oveitchik *(Sanin)* in distinguishing himself on the battlefield, while Hershel Mak's Jewish sympathies are observed with understanding when "the little Jew" meets another Jew in the Austrian enemy he was about to shoot, and the two embrace in the midst of battle (Artsibashev, *The Jew*). There are also some Jewish revolutionaries drawn with an objective pen. Savinkov's David Cohn and others (*What Never Happened,* 1912) appear with flaws and weaknesses but are deeply committed to the Revolution. Nikifirov's Gur-vich is an outright hero playing an admirable role in the first post-Revolution decade (*Grey Days*, 1926).

The Jew-hero in Russian writing is indeed an antithesis to the Russian Jew-villain: inasmuch as the Russian Jew-villain was not a monstrous, all-powerful symbol of evil but a ludicrous, contemptible creature scorned rather than feared, the figure fashioned to counter him did not have to be a super hero. The Russian Jew-hero's mild heroism was tailored to fit the Russian Jew-villain's low-grade villainy.

While in Lermontov's Moisei (*Ispanci* 1830) we meet the only Russian "benevolent money-lender," in Chirikov's Nakhman, in the play *The Jews* (1904), we meet the only Russian Zionist. Aside from these characters, the Russian literary Jew figures, whether hero or villain, do not conform to Western patterns.

Solzhenitsin's Jews of the post-World War II era are truly heroic charac-ters within the context of human dimensions and the particular limitations of their world. It is the world of political prison, the elite circle of scientists and intellectuals caught up in the nihilistic machinery of the state during the Stalin era. It is the portrait of a mammoth uncomprehending and incomprehensible system crushing with impartial indifference dedicated, discriminating servants and opportunistic, ruthless informers. The Jewish characters, however, manage to distinguish themselves with a particular humanity, each in his own subtle yet impressive manner.

Lev Grigorich Rubin, "a great hulk of a man with the thick black beard of a Biblical prophet," is an intellectual totally devoted to the Communist cause. Entrusted with a top-secret, top-priority mission during the war— that of training German prisoners of war in espionage against their own country—Lev Grigorich is credited with valor for his success. At the end of the war, though, he expresses disapproval of destruction for its own sake, "blood for blood and death for death," and is sentenced to a long prison term. In prison, his expansive kindness embraces even the German prisoners of war, now sharing his fate. The bitterness of that fate precipitates a quiet resignation in Lev Rubin but does not break his humanity.

Isaac Moiseyevich Kagan, the "short, dark, shaggy director of the battery room," is arrested for refusing to inform against his fellow workers. He considers informing vile, but to say so to State Security is dangerous, and so Isaac stalls, until he finds himself under a long-term prison sentence for not cooperating with the impersonal state machine. Isaac is no heroic martyr whose nobility of deed is displayed for emulation; secret informing is simply "repulsive" to him. "It was not that he was incapable of informing. Without a tremor he would have informed on anyone who had harmed or humiliated him. But it would have nauseated him to inform on people who had been good or even indifferent to him." So Isaac's natural inclination to integrity makes him a victim of an inhuman system, yet not its heroic martyr.

Adam Veniaminovich Roitmann is the third Jew of *The First Circle*. He is not a prisoner but belongs to those who constitute the hierarchy of control over the lives of prisoners. An MGB major and Stalin Medal awardee, Roitmann nevertheless remains unaffected by his position, so that the prisoners are "never resentful of Roitmann. On the contrary, they liked him because he didn't act like a jailer but like a decent human being." In time, Roitmann also becomes a victim of the Stalin regime. The myth of "cosmopolitanism" creeps into the system's propaganda machinery and threatens the position, liberty, and life of every Jew. For "cosmopolitan" is but another word for Jew, as is "kike," and it has a connotation synonymous with treason. Roitmann's dilemma is the timeless dilemma of the Jew:

> But in Roitmann's case, the real hurt lay in the fact that at bottom one wants to belong, wants to be the same as everyone else. But they don't want you, they reject you, they say you are an alien. You have no roots. You're a "kike."

The Jews of Solzhenitsin, sincerely dedicated to the Communist cause, become victims of the Communist machinery solely because in essence they are not identified with it. They remain individuals and retain the basic values of humanity inalienable to Jewish morality. And this, according to Solzhenitsin, renders them heroes.

Perhaps Solzhenitsin's Jew-heroes are the classic literary response of a writer who is sympathetic to Jews to present-day anti-Semitism in the USSR. They were created with the intent of combating the contemporary negative Jew image in the Soviet Union. Like Solzhenitsin, Anatoly Kuznetsov undertook the recording and documentation of the Babi Yar massacre after that mass murder of more than a hundred thousand Kiev Jews by the Nazis was officially suppressed by the anti-Semitic Soviet governmental policy.

Solzhenitsin claims that his disclosures are notivated by love and concern for his country. Likewise, the Jewish sympathizers of other times and other places were the staunchest patriots to whom the freedom and equality of the Jew were analogous to the dignity of their fatherland. In final analysis, Solzhenitsin in essence joins the ranks of the great patriots of history who in fighting for freedom and equality created positive images in order to combat the prejudicial negative stereotypes that buttress prevailing injustice.

In a way, the history of the Jew-hero in American literature resembles that of the Russian Jew-hero. The good Jew in the literature of the United States is at first also an import, and later grows into a character adapted to the American scene.

The first Jew-heroes appearing in the mid-nineteenth century are clearly transplants from English Romanticism into the fledgling literature of the New World. Otto Rupius's old Jewish peddler who saves the life and later the property and honor of the young Gentile protagonist in *The Peddler* (1857) is followed by John Richter Jones's Solomon Isaacki, the benevolent Jewish pawnbroker who unselfishly dedicates his financial resources to the cause of the American Revolution in *The Quaker Soldier, or the British in Philadelphia* (1858). The romanticized figure of the Jew-hero differs little from his English counterpart of this period. His first appearance on the scene is obviously designed to dispel stereotypical prejudices:

> The face and forehead were grand, full of intellect and benevolence with a slight seasoning of something like cunning, though not enough to impair the general effect; you could not but wonder what these features were doing on the shoulders of a pawnbroker. . . . In support of the cause of the Revolution none was more ready to sacrifice what men hold more precious; few were more meritorious.

Grand features full of intellect and benevolence were incongruous with the figure of a pawnbroker, that is to say, a Jew. Yet Solomon Isaacki possessed them because he was not a typical Jew as Gentiles portrayed him, but a token Jew created as a symbol, and an abstract symbol at that.

Romantic reverence for the Bible created another type of Jew-hero in American literature, that of the biblical sage enshrined in poetry. English models may have played a role in the creation of this poetic Jew-hero, for Milton, Wordsworth, Shelley, Browning, and especially Byron, exercised great influence abroad with their biblical themes. Just as Lermontov imitated Byron's *Hebrew Melodies* in composing several *Hebrew Melodies* of his own, so the Wandering Jew theme of Wordsworth and Shelley had impact on works with this subject matter. However, the New England poets writing about the biblical Jew—Longfellow, Whittier, and Holmes—were themselves sufficiently steeped in biblical tradition to produce biblical Jew-heroes independently of European models. Yet the predominance of English literary patterns in nineteenth-century American literature suggests the likelihood of such a connection.

Henry Wadsworth Longfellow's handsome Spanish Jew in his prelude to *Tales of a Wayside Inn* is a patriarchal personality of wisdom, wealth, and dignity, while John Greenleaf Whittier's figure of Ezekiel ("Ezekiel," 1844), and of Samson ("The Wife of Manoah to Her Husband" 1847) are contemporary portrayals of Hebrew prophetic figures. In "The Two Rabbins" (1868), the biblical image of the Jew evolved into the image of a Talmudic sage or that of the compassionate Hasidic rebbe. In his "Rabbi Ishmael" (1881), the saintly rabbi, as the embodiment of compassion, begs God for a blessing of mercy to prevail in the universe. Oliver Wendell Holmes makes an attempt to reconcile the image of the biblical Jew with that of contemporary Jews in his poem "At the Pantomime" (1874), identifying the Jews he personally encountered as direct descendants of Jesus.

Later Jew-figures gradually departed from the idealized model and assumed a semblance of reality. Hamlin Garland's Mr. Somins, for instance, is a good-natured, gay, chubby German-Jewish salesman in *Rose of Dutcher's Cooly* (1895), the type the author may have often met peddling wares around town during the last decades of the nineteenth century. Even this nonvillainous peddler is still referred to as "not too much of a Jew" in an embarrassed attempt to justify his positive traits instead of the conventional Jew-villain type of peddler. The first Jew-hero of the stage likewise appeared during this period. In a role reminiscent of Lessing's Jewish protagonist in *Die Juden*, Sam'l of G. H. Jessup's *Sam'l of Posen, or the Commercial Drummer* (1881), the honest German-Jewish salesman, unmasks the Gentile jewel thief, and then adds kindness to honesty by generously helping an Irish mother of fourteen in her hour of need.

Sam'l of Posen became the Nathan the Wise of American literature. He was followed by a colorful array of heroic Jews in all sizes, until their valor became modified by the conventions of twentieth-century literary realism. Henry Harland's saintly Mr. Nathan in *Mrs. Peixada* (1886), and the misunderstood young artist, Elias Bacharach, in his *The Yoke of the Torah* (1887) were replaced by kindly ghetto and immigrant types in Hapgood's *The*

Spirit of the Ghetto (1902) and *Types from the City Streets* (1910), and in Myra Kelly's *A Soul Above Buttons* (1907).

To combat popular resentment against mass immigration of East-European Jews during the pre-World War I period, and the growing anti-Semitic sentiment during the decades following the war that were blighted by the Depression and the rise of Hitler, Dorothy Canfield Fisher created several magnificent Jew-heroes. As if to counteract the mob-approach of anti-Semitism in addition to attacking prejudice itself, Mrs. Fisher's Jew-heroes are highly individualistic types, their heroism inherent in their poignant humanity.

A Jewish art dealer, sensitive, warm, possessing a fine understanding of art, is the Jew-hero of her short story "The Artist" (*Hillsboro People*, 1915), while a celebrated Jewish actor from Russia, who becomes an unassuming gardener in a small American town, is the hero of her "The City of Refuge" (*The Real Motive*, 1916). Contrary to the stereotypical Jew, this actor prefers the life of the small town, and honest, simple physical labor in contact with the soil, to the limelight of the entertainment world and its financial rewards. He refuses to return to New York even after his impresario assures him a lucrative role. A scholarly philologist, a humble and dignified professional who, as a handwriting expert, fearlessly testifies in favor of Dreyfus, is the hero of a third short story by Mrs. Fisher, "Professor Paul Meyer, Master of the Word" (*Raw Material*, 1923). Meyer is attacked by jeering anti-Semites because of his testimony, but emerges victorious from the encounter, having vanquished the abusive assailants by his sheer dignity.

Sinclair Lewis's Dr. Max Gottlieb, the brilliant but dry and stubborn scientist in *Arrowsmith* (1925), is of the same subtle fiber of herosim as Fisher's Professor Meyer. The Jew as a dedicated man of science and an incorruptible idealist, a man of uncompromising integrity and professional honesty, a man of touching simplicity and warmth, was the image to fill the need of the hour in the United States of the 1920s. It was the decade that followed the lynching of a young Jew in Atlanta, Georgia, the decade in which the *Protocols of the Elders of Zion* were publicized in the press and in novel form, the decade that saw the rapid rise of Ku Klux Klan terror and institutionalized discrimination against Jews in education, employment, housing, and membership in professional societies. The figures of Paul Meyer and Max Gottlieb, and, to some extent even the figure of Poldy Bloom in James Joyce's *Ulysses* (1922), which reached the American reading public in this period, served as admirable antitheses to the growing anti-Semitic myth of the Jew as both aggressive money-man and hungry Socialist.

The literary response of the 1930s to the American Jewish reality was most visible in the theater. It was the figure of the successful Jewish lawyer and of the prominent Jewish doctor that became translated into dramatic characters on the stage. Elmer Rice's *Counsellor-at-Law* (1931) and John

Wexley's *They Shall Not Die* (1932) present, among others, outstanding legal personalities as their Jew-heroes, Mr. Simon and Mr. Rubin respectively. The latter is a man of high ideals, a crusader for justice. In the field of medicine, Sidney Kingsley's Dr. Hochberg, a man of scientific integrity in *Men in White* (1933), and Sidney Howard's young Jewish soldier Bush from Chicago, a courageous volunteer for science in *Yellow Jack* (1934), are distinguished as heroes. In a contemporary treatment of the Jewish problem, Clifford Odets's Dr. Benjamin, a fine physician, is dropped from his hospital appointment because he is a Jew (*Waiting for Lefty*, 1934).

In the genre of the novel, with the exception of Dos Passos's Compton, a heroic Jew in his *1919* (1932), it was only during the 1940s that Gentile writers returned to challenging American attitudes with the portrayal of Jew-heroes. Richard Wright's Jewish lawyer, the staunch fighter for Negro rights in *Native Son* (1940), who braves an unsympathetic press and the threat of mob violence in defending a Negro murderer, is one such bona fide Jew-hero. Another, of a quite different stripe, is Monroe Stahr, the paternalistic Hollywood tycoon of F. Scott Fitzgerald's unfinished last novel, *The Last Tycoon* (1940). His Jew-heroism lies in his warm humanity amid the cold realism of post-Depression Hollywood. Manny Schwartz, another Jewish character in the novel, is portrayed as being racially indifferent, a member of one of the many national minorities to be integrated into the American scene.

World War II awakened some Jewish sensibilities and produced a string of Jew-heroes fashioned specifically to disprove one aspect of the negative Jew-image: cowardice as defined by Gentiles. Norman Mailer's Roth in *The Naked and the Dead* (1948), Irwin Shaw's Noah Ackerman in *The Young Lions* (1948), and Herman Wouk's Greenwald in *The Caine Mutiny* (1951) encounter anti-Semitism in the U.S. armed forces and cope with it by adapting themselves to the Gentiles' code of honor. Recreating themselves in the Gentile image of virtue, they outdo their Gentile buddies in acts of heroism and in an expansive display of patriotism.

The impact of the State of Israel changed all that. Two thousand years of ghetto history have been negated by the Israeli farmer and the Israeli soldier. The formerly rootless cosmopolitan has done wonders with the arid soil, and the perennial coward has defeated, repeatedly, overwhelming armed numbers and equipment. The Jew in Israel is a clerk, a storekeeper, a bus driver, a policeman, a fireman, a diplomat, a street-cleaner, a scientist, a garage mechanic, in addition to being a banker and a businessman. The Jew in Israel is a capitalist, a Socialist; he is clerical and anticlerical, a cosmopolitan, a patriot, a Communist, and an extreme Conservative. He lives on the kibbutz or in the urban centers. He is tall and brawny, or short and fat and aggressive, or small and thin and intellectual and aggressive; he is blond and long-haired, or black-bearded and ear-locked; he speaks Hebrew with a foreign accent, or Oxford English without. He is a celebrated musician, an artist, a scientist-president; an archaeologist-general; a scholar-prime minister, a farmer-scholar, a farmer-prime minister. There is nothing left to prove. And nothing to disprove.

How will this display of Jewish reality affect the Jew's image? Having been totally detached from reality, will it continue to thrive unhampered by its challenging presence, or will it vanish into obsolescence for lack of expediency and resources of illusion?

Part III

ANTHROPOLOGY

Anthropology: A Case Study in Holocaust Blindness?

AILON SHILOH

In Mexico City, in November 1974, at the 73d Annual Meeting of the American Anthropological Association, I read a paper on "Psychological Anthropology: A Case Study in Culture Blindness?"

In that paper I postulated that the Nazi Holocaust against the Jews was an anthropological phenomenon unique in the history of our species, incredible in its conception, terrible in its execution. Even by extrapolation back down our hominid evolution, no such horrifying event had ever been planned, let alone so monstrously consummated.

I went on to state that, since anthropology was concerned with describing and analyzing human behavior through time and space, it was logical to expect that the Holocaust, as a widespread, long-term, and mass-scale human behavioral phenomenon, should be subjected to intensive psychological-anthropological study.

In an analysis of the anthropological material, I documented that the Holocaust was a nonevent. As far as psychological anthropology specifically, and anthropology in general, were concerned, the Nazi war against the Jews either never happened or is of little anthropological significance.

My paper dealing with this phenomenon was published in December 1975 in *Current Anthropology* (16, no. 4:618–20).

Current Anthropology subsequently received and published exactly four letters responding to my paper. The editor gave me the opportunity to reply to these four letters (Sept. 1976, 17, no. 3:554–55). In closing, I noted that this response came perilously close to a thunderous silence. The purpose of the present paper is to update and amplify my presentation of 1975.[1]

Recently, there seems to have been an increasing volume of Holocaust

165

oral histories, documented records, novels, films, television productions, public commemorations, observances, conferences. Interest in, and concern with, the Nazi slaughter of the Jews seems to be growing in international awareness and intensity. The Congress of the United States designated April 22–29, 1979, as "Days of Remembrance of Victims of the Holocaust."

Helen Epstein recently published her *Children of the Holocaust: Conversations with Sons and Daughters of Survivors* (New York: G. P. Putnam's Sons, 1979), in which she has documented, through case studies, that certain of the effects, the trauma, the scars, are being manifested by the children of the survivors. The cultural shock is being transmitted to the next generation.

How is anthropology, the so-called science of man, responding? Has there been any change, awareness, sensitivity, or recognition of the possible implications, for anthropology, of the Nazi Holocaust?

Let us consider the most recent anthropological textbooks.

In 1979 Joseph B. Aceves and H. Gill King published their *Introduction to Anthropology* (Morristown, N. J.: General Learning Press, Scott, Foresman) and Elmer S. Miller and Charles A. Weitz their *Introduction to Anthropology* (Englewood Cliffs, N. J.: Prentice-Hall). Both of these massive introductory texts cover the broad field of anthropology from biological evolution to the archaeological record, from the sociobiology of human behavior to the stages of cultural development. Social control, religion, war, aggression, political organizations—all are covered in a detailed manner, from the *Australopithecines* to *Homo sapiens*, from the Yanomamo to the United Nations. However, none of these authors found it necessary to comment, even in a cursory manner, on the activities of the Nazis.

Also in 1979 David W. McCurdy and James P. Spradley published their volume on *Issues in Cultural Anthropology: Selected Readings* (Boston: Little, Brown). In this volume, containing a total of twenty-seven articles, three deal with the sacred cattle of India; three with the Northwest Coast Indian potlatch, particularly among the Kwakiutl and the Salish; warfare is studied among the Maring of New Guinea, religion in India. The incest taboo and mating habits among humans and animals are studied. Yet in this collection of papers on the most diverse issues in cultural anthropology, no paper is devoted to the significance of the murder, in our lifetime, of six million Jews.

The Cultural Dimension of the Human Adventure by Gretel H. Pelto and Pertti J. Pelto, both of the University of Connecticut (New York: Macmillan 1979) does include a whole chapter analyzing "Aggression, Suicide and War: Our Most Dangerous Achievements." But the authors found nothing to analyze about the Nazis—their aggression, war, and genocide.

In 1978 Oriol Pi-Sunyer and Zdenek Salzmann, both of the University of Massachusetts, published their *Humanity and Culture: An Introduction to An-*

thropology (Boston: Houghton Mifflin). After careful analyses of the Ik of Uganda, the Nayar of India, the Arapesh of New Guinea, the Pygmies of Zaire, the American Apache, Arapaho, Cherokee, Cheyenne, Haida, Hopi, Hupa, Kiowa, Kwakiutl, Micmac, Natchez, Navajo, Nootka, Northern Paiute, Ojibwa, Penobscot, Sioux, Yaqui, and Zuni, to mention only a few, on p. 223 the authors note in passing that during World War II and shortly thereafter, a number of anthropologists studied, and published, "psychocultural analyses of such diverse groups as the Japanese, Germans, Russians, Chinese, and Americans."

In her *Psychological Anthropology: An Introduction to Human Nature and Cultural Differences,* (New York: Holt, Rinehart and Winston, 1979) Erika Bourguignon claims that she is covering a "broader field" than usual, and that she has "come home" to study aspects of modern societies as well as traditional peasant and primitive cultures, in her cross-cultural, historical, and interdisciplinary analysis. She claims that she has "cast a wide net"— wider "than has been customary so far." But nowhere does she find anything of significance to analyze in connection with the Nazis, genocide, and the Holocaust.

The 1977 *Annual Review of Anthropology,* edited by Bernard J. Siegal, Alan R. Beals, and Stephen A. Tyler (Palo Alto, Calif.: Annual Reviews, Inc., vol. 6), nowhere considers the implications for anthropology of the Nazis and their genocidal program.

The second edition of *An Introduction to Cultural and Social Anthropology* by Peter B. Hammond (New York: Macmillan, 1978) says nothing about the Nazis, genocide, the Holocaust. Similarly, the second edition of *Cultural Anthropology* by William A. Haviland (New York: Holt, Rinehart and Winston, 1978); the second edition of *Anthropology: Contemporary Perspectives,* edited by David E. Hunter and Phillip Whitten (Boston: Little, Brown, 1979); the third edition of *Modern Cultural Anthropology* by Philip K. Bock (New York: Alfred A. Knopf, 1979), maintains complete silence on the Holocaust.

In 1976 John H. Bodley published his book *Anthropology and Contemporary Human Problems* (Menlo Park, Calif.: Cummings). In it Bodley declares that he was targeting, specifically, on the large-scale complex problems of the contemporary world. But he found nothing to say about the Nazis, the Holocaust, the genocide.

Occasionally, when the terms *genocide* or *ghetto* are mentioned, they are carefully stripped of any Jewish connotation, content, tragedy.

For example, in his *Culture in Process* (New York: Holt, Rinehart and Winston, 1979, 3d ed.), Professor Alan R. Beals defines the term *genocide* as "the killing of all of the members of a cultural system" (p. 359), and the example of genocide he cites is that of the Sioux Indians by the American government (p. 335).

Frontiers of Anthropology: An Introduction to Anthropological Thinking, edited by Murray J. Leaf (New York: D. Van Nostrand, 1974), has despite its title, nothing to say about the Nazis, genocide, the Holocaust. The word *ghetto*, when used, is stripped of any Jewish reference and defined "loosely" as "any culturally distinct residential area" (p. 172).

The third edition of *Anthropology: An Introduction* (New York: John Wiley, 1981) by Lowell D. Holmes and Wayne Parris has nothing to say about the Holocaust or genocide, and their only mention "German culture" refers to that noted by Tacitus—in A.D. 98.

Now there are a few isolated anthropological acknowledgments of the Holocaust. The second edition of *Anthropology* by Carol R. Ember and Melvin Ember (Englewood Cliffs, N.J.: Prentice-Hall, 1977), is a closely reasoned textbook of over 500 pages. On page 133 the authors note that Hitler tried to destroy members of the "Jewish race," and, on page 374, they note, referring to the Nazis, that many of the German officials, regarded as normal by their neighbors, committed acts of such inhumanity and viciousness as to be considered criminally insane by observers in other Western societies.

The preliminary edition of *Anthropology: The Biocultural View*, by Francis E. Johnston and Henry Selby (Dubuque, Iowa: William C. Brown Company, 1978) is a carefully written textbook of over 600 pages. On pages 311–12, in a discussion of cultural relativism, the authors note in four sentences that Hitler's Nazi Germany was an evil society trying to subvert the German culture, impose the Nazi way on all of Europe, and destroy other peoples and nations.

On page 18 of the fifth edition of *An Introduction to Anthropology* by Ralph Beals, Harry Hoijer, and Alan R. Beals (New York: Macmillan, 1977) the authors mention that there were German anthropologists who were killed or forced into exile by Adolf Hitler.

This dreary litany could go on and on. As far as virtually all of modern anthropology is concerned—the Holocaust never happened. The long-term, wide spread mass torture, and the slow, agonizing murder of millions of men, women, and children, apparently continues to be of absolutely no human significance. Anthropology is a case study in Holocaust blindness.

What is the explanation of this incredible fact?

I postulate that there could be at least three significant factors operating:

1. Apparently, despite all the lip service to the contrary, many anthropologists are still not comfortable with contemporary Western events. Anthropologists, apparently, still seem to be most comfortable with non-Western exotica, and preferably with past periods of time. When contemporary Western material is considered, the tendency too often is to discuss it relatively briefly, simplistically, and with a variety of generalizations. Such material, when included, for example, in introductory anthropological textbooks, is too often found at the end of the book, in the last chapter, or in the epilogue.

Furthermore, applied research or action publications, when dealing with contemporary Western problems, still seem to be primarily oriented to studying, servicing, helping, the "underdogs" in the Western society—the weak, the poor, the dispossessed, the victims of bias, prejudice, economic distress.

Under such terms of reference, the Jews, like many other populations of whatever cultural circumstances, just do not seem to be considered subjects for anthropology.

Whether or not one agrees with this reasoning, apparently this is an anthropological given, and one that might be dealt with at the level of study of the criteria for the parameters of the science.[2]

(Perhaps this is another example of what Spicer referred to as the "strange cocoon" of academic anthropology in his "Beyond Analysis and Explanation? Notes on the Life and Times of the Society for Applied Anthropology," in *Human Organization* 35, no. 4 (Winter 1976):335–43).

2. Many of our contemporary anthropologists are Jews. In my opinion, many of these Jews seem to have deliberately alienated themselves from their Jewishness. They seem to have consciously cut themselves off from their religion, their heritage, their identification. With full awareness, they seem to have made their decision against identifying with anything Jewish, or even smacking of Jewishness.

This observation is being presented as one avenue of approach to the understanding of the fact that anthropology is indeed suffering from being a case of Holocaust blindness. It illustrates again, if necessary, the powerful influence that unconscious subjectivity can exert in defining the parameters and priorities of science.[3]

3. The few anthropologists, Jews and non-Jews, who recognize the significance of the Holocaust and its implications for anthropology, may be simply overwhelmed by the enormity of the horror, the magnitude of the tragedy. We cannot yet cope in a scientific manner with the shock of its evil. It is just too much. We seem to be unable, as scientists, to separate our emotions, to detach ourselves, to achieve the degree of distance and objectivity necessary for the scientific study of any phenomenon, let alone large-scale, long-term torture and slaughter of fellow human beings. This interpretation points not so much to anthropological blindness as to anthropological shock. It may be regrettable, but it is something that we as scientists must recognize and confront.

These interpretations are put forward as three possible hypotheses for the demonstrated fact that contemporary anthropology has almost completely ignored the Holocaust and its implications. In my opinion, a full-scale study of these interpretations is itself a highly worthwhile anthropological research project.[4]

In order to create an awareness of the significance of the Holocaust for anthropology, and an involvement in research into its human behavior aspect and its anthropological implications, I suggest that we initiate, now, at the very least, the teaching of the Holocaust as a behavioral phenomenon of great relevance to all introductory courses in anthropology. We should supplement class lectures with documentary films. Students should be assigned readings from the growing number of publications of personal accounts and oral histories of some of the survivors, as well as from the preserved official records of the Nazis. Courses in biological anthropology, cultural anthropology, and psychological anthropology should include the study of the Holocaust. The Holocaust, as an anthropological phenomenon, should be made a special course in which issues of the theoretical, evolutionary, sociobiological, cultural, and other value systems and culture norms could be raised, explored, studied. Graduate students should be encouraged to recognize the Holocaust as a behavioral event significant, indeed even crucial, to anthropological research. Professional anthropologists—faculty, scientists, others—should begin to study aspects of the Nazi politics, the genocide program, the Holocaust process, the cultural circumstances prevalent at the time of its origin, growth, and florescence, and the cultural norms operative in the reaction of the world to it, at the time it was carried out and subsequently. Such research should be initiated now, while some of the perpetrators and survivors are still alive.

In this manner, perhaps the events and significance of the Holocaust will begin to be recognized by anthropology and integrated into the corpus of "the science of man"; and never again will an anthropologist have to write a paper asking Is anthropology a case study in holocaust blindness?

Notes

1. Even though I tried to cover the relevant anthropological material in as representative and legitimate a manner as possible, I may have inadvertently missed certain anthropological publications that have studied the Holocaust. Worse, perhaps in this broad summary I may have misinterpreted or misrepresented some anthropologists. I shall sincerely appreciate it if any such omissions or errors are called to my attention.

2. The issue is not entirely academic. According to the *New York Times* (reprinted in the *Tampa Tribune* on May 10, 1979), a public opinion survey measuring the effect of the TV production *Holocaust* on West Germans revealed that 30 percent of the Germans replied that "Nazism was a basically good idea that was only carried out badly."

Others may be struck with the Nazi implications of the New Sociobiology as delineated in, for example, *Biology as a Social Weapon* (Minneapolis, Minn.: The Ann Arbor Science for the People Editorial Collective, Burgess Pub. Co., 1977) and *From Genesis to Genocide* by Stephen L. Chorover (Cambridge, Mass.: The MIT Press, 1979).

One volume that anthropologists should find theoretically and substantively very sound is the third edition of *Genocide and State Power* by Irving Louis Horowitz (New Brunswick, N.J.: Transaction Books, 1979).

3. Incidentally, lest this be considered a purely parochial concern, I should note that while six million Jewish men, women, and children perished in the Holocaust, more than one million Jews, many of them children, did survive in the very crucible of Nazi-occupied Europe. This could not have been accomplished, emphasizes Holocaust historian Philip Friedman, "without the active assistance of the Christian population." Even this isolated and frag-

mented bravery, in the face of massive terror, is ignored by the scientists concerned with the study of man. For an extensive analysis of this subject see Helen Fein, *Accounting for Genocide* (New York: The Free Press, 1979).

4. Alexander Alland, Jr., of Columbia University has recently published his *To Be Human: An Introduction to Anthropology* (New York: John Wiley, 1981). Neither genocide nor holocaust figures in his glossary or index. In chapter 27, "The Nature of Human Nature," however, Alland writes about the Ik of Uganda and the victims of the Nazi death camps. Alland does not comment about the legitimacy of comparing the Ik (some hundreds) to the Nazi victims (over ten million), and he provides an interestingly antiseptic version of the Nazi Holocaust— Jews are nowhere mentioned, genocide is nowhere considered, the medical experiments and torture chambers are nowhere acknowledged. What Alland does is to cite material that seems to imply that somehow the fate of the victims was actually, to a large degree, in their own hands: "Those who lost the will to survive died" (p. 363).

Syrian Jews in New York Twenty Years Ago

WALTER P. ZENNER

Background

In the summer of 1958, I received a small grant from Columbia University to do research on Syrian Jews in New York City. My initial desire had been to compare a group of Syrian Jews with a group of Syrian Christians, but this proved too formidable a task for a fledgling field worker. I continued this field work into 1959. Later I did library research on the Jews in Syria and field work among Syrian Jews in Jerusalem. The latter resulted in my doctoral dissertation, *Syrian Jewish Identification in Israel* (Zenner, 1966). I incorporated the results of my work in New York into my dissertation and other publications, because Syrian Jewish adjustment in the American metropolis was in sharp contrast to what had happened in Israel (Zenner 1965, 1968, 1970). Because my research in New York was of an exploratory nature, I have published a full account outside of my dissertation.

Prior to 1960, there were few anthropologists who taught courses on the Middle East in the United States. One of that small number was Raphael Patai. I had read his works on Israel while I was still an undergraduate. My first graduate courses at Columbia were with Patai. He introduced us to the classics of Middle Eastern ethnography like Lane and Musil, which continue to be of use. If our models today differ from his, it is because he gave us a foundation of theories and hypotheses that could be tested.

My research on Syrian Jews was supported by a summer grant from Columbia University in 1959 and a National Institute of Mental Health grant, 1961–63. I benefited greatly from criticisms of this work during my period of doctoral study by Conrad Arensberg, the late Margaret Mead, and Raphael Patai. This research would have been impossible without the cooperation of Syrian Jews in Brooklyn and elsewhere and by Ashkenazic residents of Brooklyn and Bradley Beach. Their comments and later their letters have been of immense help. I also want to thank Victor Sanua for his encouragement over the years.

Since writing my initial draft, I have read Joseph Sutton's book on this community. While I have modified my paper and referred to his book, my account should be viewed as a separate document from his.

173

In the past twenty years, interest in Sephardi Jews in the United States had increased (Sanua 1977). New studies of these groups have been published (Sutton 1979; Ginsburg 1981). Victor Sanua and others have indicated to me that I should make my work available. I now feel that despite the preliminary and fragmentary nature of the study, it still can constitute a portrait of the Syrian Sephardi community of Brooklyn as it was in the late 1950s and early 1960s, as well as an attempt to fit them into a broader framework for the study of American Jews. This paper will include some materials collected after my last visits in the community in the 1960s.

My own field work was based on a number of methods. I visited the neighborhood where the majority of Syrian Jews lived at that time, Bensonhurst. I interviewed key informants, such as rabbis and old men whose names had been given to me. I also interviewed individuals who had been identified by my fellow graduate students as "Syrian Jews," whether or not they lived and participated in the Syrian Jewish community. There also were others with whom I spoke, such as workers at luncheonette counters in Bensonhurst and the director of a Jewish community center in the area. I spent several days in Bradley Beach, New Jersey, which was at the time the principal Syrian Jewish summer resort area. Most of the field work was completed in 1958–59. In 1962–63, after I had returned from a year of field work in Israel, I followed some Israeli-born Syrian Jews to Brooklyn, where they were now living or where they had relatives.

While I have not done any field work in New York since 1963, I have maintained an open file on the Syrians. Occasionally I have received inquiries from Syrians and from others who would like information on the community. On a few occasions, people who have read my dissertation have sent me their reactions to my work.

Jews in the Syrian Emigration

Most Jews in Syria during the nineteenth century lived in the cities of Aleppo and Damascus, with a small but increasing number in the newer entrepot of Beirut. The Jewish communities of the two main Syrian cities were quite old. Both contained people whose ancestors had lived in the Fertile Crescent from Roman and Arab times, while others were descended from the Spanish exiles of the fifteenth century. There were small Jewish communities in southeastern Turkey, northern Syria near Aleppo, and Lebanon. Most of the Jews in Syria were merchants, peddlers, or craftsmen. The Jews in Syria in this period were orthopraxic and their rituals were close to the Sephardi rites of Livorno, with some local modifications (Zenner 1966; 1968; 1971; 1979; 1980).

A great emigration from Syria and surrounding Arab provinces of the Ottoman Empire began in the last decade of the nineteenth century. First, some Syrians, especially Jews and Christians, sought opportunities in

Egypt. Then Syrians emigrated to various parts of the Americas and West Africa. In the first instance, the search for increased economic opportunities was the prime motivation. After 1909, when Jews and Christians became subject to conscription in the embattled Ottoman Empire (during that period of Balkan wars and World War I), many Jewish young men sought refuge in the New World, arriving between 1908 and 1915 (Herling 1929). The main period of immigration lasted until the immigration law that imposed quotas was passed in the 1920s. Under this law, Syria (including Lebanon until 1944) was restricted to a hundred immigrants a year. This included Muslims, Christians, and Jews.

Almost from the beginning, the Syrian Jews separated themselves from their Christian compatriots. Such distance was kept against the background of tension in Syria between Christians and Jews who were commercial competitors (Miller 1903). Many of the Syrian Christians had deep-seated anti-Jewish sentiments (Felton 1912). The Jews reciprocated. Despite this, there were and continue to be some contacts between the Syrian Jews and the Christians. The two groups of Syrian immigrants were in similar businesses, particularly textile imports, and they must have maintained commercial ties (Kayal & Kayal 1975:84–90; 94–105). Some Syrian Jews have continued to purchase Middle Eastern foods on Atlantic Avenue, while in 1958 a Syrian Jew acted as the agent for a belly dancer in an advertisement in a Christian Arabic-language newspaper.

The separation of Syrian Jews from other Arabic-speaking immigrants was marked by their respective residence patterns. While the Christians first moved to the Lower West Side, near Wall Street, and downtown Brooklyn, Syrian Jews first lived on the Lower East Side in predominantly Jewish areas. Many of the Christians moved to Bay Ridge at a later date, while Bensonhurst-Mapleton Park in Brooklyn was the main center of Syrian Jewry in the 1920s until the 1960s. More recently, the main area of residence has been along Ocean Parkway. All of the areas where the Syrian Jews have lived are Jewish neighborhoods (Miller 1903; Herling 1929; Seruya 1952; Zenner 1965; Koppman 1979; Sutton 1979).

The Jewish neighborhoods into which the Syrian Jews moved have generally been East European Ashkenazi, which is natural considering the composition of New York Jewry. It is noteworthy that Syrian Jews live apart from the main concentrations of other non-Ashkenazi Jews in Brooklyn, such as Ladino-speaking Sephardim, Yemenites, and Bukharians. In the late 1950s, however, many Egyptian Jewish immigrants, many of a more distant Syrian origin, did move into Bensonhurst and the part of Flatbush where the Syrians lived (cf. Sanua 1967; Sutton 1979:46; Ibrahim 1977). More recently the descendants of Syrians, who had immigrated to Lebanon and Israel, have also moved to Flatbush.

The Syrian Jews maintain a relatively high profile as a homogeneous and cohesive minority. There are several Syrian synagogues in Bensonhurst

and on Ocean Parkway, as well as a day school, a community center, and a
ritual bath. The relative cohesiveness of this community was noted by me
when I compared this group with Sephardim in Israel, while Sanua perceived this relative to the United States.

The Economic Base

The occupational structure of Syrian Jewry in New York has been
marked by a tendency toward specialization on an ethnic basis. Both Christians and Jews from Syria often began their American careers as peddlers
(Hitti 1924; Kayal and Kayal 1975:84–90; Herling 1929). While some of
the Damascus Jews became textile workers, Aleppo Jews generally started
as peddlers or merchants. Sale of lingerie, lace, and linen were Syrian
specialties. The progression was from immigration as unskilled workers to
peddling. Usually the Syrians started with household linen and moved on
to lingerie and linen stores. Many of the peddlers peddled at resorts (Herling 1929). Despite religious antagonism between Syrian Christians and
Syrian Jews, some Syrian Jews were aided in obtaining or received their
first consignment of goods by Christian merchants (Sutton 1979:63–64;
also, a Christian informant). As late as 1960, many of the wholesalers of
both groups had offices on lower Fifth Avenue.

The Depression affected most of the Syrian Jewish shopkeepers, peddlers, and wholesalers adversely. During World War II, however, many
began to prosper. Few, even of the American born, entered the professions
in the postwar period, because there was little stress on higher education.
Many entered the infant-ware line or imported cheap tourist trade items.
In addition to these specialties, there were Syrians who had other occupations, including some in the electrical trades, candy stores, groceries, as well
as a butcher and a masseuse. By the end of the 1950s, several Syrians had
become academically trained professionals including a lawyer, a certified
public accountant, a chemist, a psychologist, and specialists in Middle Eastern studies. While the lawyer and C.P.A. worked for firms that dealt with
the Syrian business community, many of the more academic professionals
no longer interacted with Syrians outside of occasional visits to kin.

The main form of economic organization has continued to be the family
firm supported by a kin and ethnic network. Most New York Syrians were
self-employed or worked in shops owned by other Syrians or in Syrian-
owned wholesale houses. A young man, after completing high school,
would work in a store owned by another Syrian, usually a relative, until he
could afford to go into business for himself. Wholesalers or other wealthy
members of the community would give loans to the younger men. Sometimes a dowry given at marriage would be used to set the groom up in
business.[1] In the late 1950s Syrians only hired members of their own group
as shopclerks or for the more important jobs in the business. Partnerships

were formed by relatives. Sometimes men would "import" relatives to be their employees and/or junior partners, sending for kinsmen in Syria, Israel, or Latin America.

Where the family firm predominates, branching often consists of sending forth kinsmen to do business elsewhere. Such was the case with the Syrian Jews. Different members of a family followed the same line of business in different cities, such as Washington or Chicago and even different countries, such as Panama and Hong Kong. In some cases, Syrian Jewish entrepreneurs invested money in building factories in those countries, especially after World War II (Zenner 1970).

The concentration in export-import trade has led to a number of Syrian Jewish lines of specialization. The so-called tourist bazaars, which are located in old central business districts of major cities were, for a time, such a specialty. These are shops that sell imported cameras, electronic equipment, rugs, and a variety of bric-a-brac. Another line is that of "bargain-discount stores," which sell standard merchandise at a low overhead in self-service stores, usually in working-class neighborhoods (Miller 1903; Catlin 1915; Brady 1970; Horsley 1975; Zenner 1979b, 1980b; Sutton 1979:10–19; 62–73).

Familial Ties

As in many other ethnic groups, the family lies at the core of the Syrian Jewish community. Relatives have been favored as business partners. People prefer to marry cousins or other members of their origin group. Men "imported" brides and partners from among their relatives in Israel, Syria, or Latin America. The connection between marriage and business arrangements was recognized. Some informants claimed that the reason why men preferred Syrian brides was that a man expected a dowry from a Syrian bride's parents. Men often deferred their marriages until they were established in business, which often meant that they were in their late 20s, while they wanted as wives young women—between 18 and 20. Beauty, youth, and wealth were what they valued in the women.

The importance of beauty, youth and wealth for marriage was emphasized in conversations with women or about sisters and other female relatives. One woman said that she had lied about her age for as long as she could, so that people would think she was younger. Another woman said that despite her family's relative poverty, she had been sought as a bride because of her fair hair, a quality admired in the Levant. In several instances, the reason given for women marrying Ashkenazi Jews was the fact that they were "old maids" from poor families, that is, women in their twenties.

Syrian Jews in Brooklyn were caught between their traditional view of guarding the virtue of their daughters and the dating pattern prevalent in

American society. Preferring to keep marriages within the group, they at the same time allowed their sons to date outside the group. The young men might hang around with others as on a corner or in a luncheonette (Kaufman 1972). It was said among the young men that if a Syrian boy went out with a Syrian girl more than two or three times, it was assumed that he would marry her. Consequently, he might often turn to girls outside the group for premarital dating. Affairs with Ashkenazi girls sometimes led to marriages. Thus, in spite of strong negative attitudes toward outgroup marriage, certain pressures from within the group were leading both men and women to Ashkenazi mates. One Ashkenazi rabbi serving a Syrian congregation estimated that as many as 25 percent of weddings in the late 1950s were with Ashkenazim. This pattern continues, despite the reputation of the Syrians as a cohesive group. Cohen (1971) in his survey of American Sephardim found that one-third of the daughters-in-law and 80 percent of the sons-in-law of his U.S.-born Syrian respondents were Ashkenazim, while nearly 16 percent acknowledged that some (possibly distant) relatives had Gentile spouses.

After marriage, those young couples who continued to live in Brooklyn, lived in neighborhoods close to where their parents lived. In the 1950s, many Syrians had moved from Bensonhurst down Avenue P to the Ocean Parkway area of Flatbush (see map). This was still a short ride from the older neighborhood. Most Syrians lived in one- and two-family houses, even those who were relatively poor, unlike Ashkenazim who often lived in apartments (Herling 1929; Steinhardt 1960). This is, in part, due to the large families of the Syrians.

Family ties continued to be close. There were frequent telephone conversations and mutual visiting among the women. While during the 1920s women helped out in the stores and while some unmarried women worked in offices or shops prior to marriage, married women generally did not seek employment outside the home. Women are responsible for housework and child care.

In the past, Syrian families were quite large, with as many as ten children. By the late 1950s, according to one rabbi, the number of children had declined but many women still gave birth to more than two children. In some very large families the older children might occupy one apartment in a two-family house, while the parents and younger children lived in the other apartment.

A double standard of morality was accepted by Syrians in the 1950s. Young men sometimes had affairs outside the group, and there was much gossip about the extramarital relationships of the men. When a women's group in 1963 produced a play, they chose Claire Boothe Luce's *The Women*, a melodrama from the 1930s that addressed itself to this problem.

While women were concerned with housework, some women did voluntary work for the community during the late 1950s. For instance, there was an active Parents-Teachers Organization connected to the Syrian day school. During the 1960s, some women continued their education after marriage. In general, however, the Syrian Jewish family in New York City in the late 1950s was one in which women took care of the house and the children while men worked and even played away from home.

Communal Organization and Voluntary Associations

In New York City, despite constant complaints about general indifference and monopolistic control by certain cliques, voluntary organizations of Syrian Jews have been active. The richness of such voluntary activity in the United States, especially among the Ashkenazi Jews who are an important group with whom the Syrian Jews compare themselves, is a factor in this, as is the relative leisure of many Syrian Jewish women in the United States. Many of the forms utilized by the Syrians in New York have been adopted from the local Ashkenazi Jews, including the forms and functions of contemporary synagogues.

The Syrian synagogues in Bensonhurst, Flatbush, and Bradley Beach were multifunctional and included facilities for recreation as well as for sacred learning and prayer. As noted above, a women's group had a theatrical performance in a synagogue. At Bradley Beach, the New Jersey coastal resort frequented by the Brooklyn Syrians, there is a synagogue building used several times a week for social purposes. Men and women would go there to meet their friends, drink Turkish coffee, and play cards or backgammon. While the propriety of using a synagogue for gambling was debated by the Syrians as it has been by American religious groups generally, the practice was allowed.

Since most of the Syrian Jews in Brooklyn are of Aleppan origin, most synagogues are "Halabi." In Bensonhurst, there was one Damascus or Shaami congregation, Ahi-Ezer, only four blocks away from the then largest Halabi synagogue, Magen David. Each had its own rabbi and cantor. By the late 1950s, there was also a congregation on Ocean Parkway called Shaare Zion, which was led by an Ashkenazi rabbi who still serves that congregation. In addition to these three synagogues, there were services held in other communal buildings, such as the Magen David Community Center as well as a number of private prayer quorums and the Syrian synagogue in Bradley Beach. While in the late 1950s Bensonhurst was still the center, it had moved to Flatbush by the 1970s. By then, a permanent community had settled in Deal, near Bradley Beach (Frank 1968; 1971; 1972; Koppman 1979; Eisenherg 1979; Sutton 1979:44–45).

In the late 1950s, there were other voluntary associations, including a B'nai B'rith Lodge, a religious day school (*yeshiva*), a Parent-Teachers organization associated with the yeshiva, and a burial society, as well as a number of social clubs. The Magen David Yeshiva PTA Community Bulletins of October and November 1959 give us a picture of the degree to which these organizations, at least in their public presentations, were like those of comparable Gentile and Jewish organizations elsewhere in North America. They also show the importance of Ashkenazim as a reference group and as professional aids to the Syrians in Brooklyn.

The PTA Bulletin was a standard four-page bulletin, much like that issued by synagogues and similar groups. It had news of what was going on the school, PTA events, religious and educational columns by the school principal and/or a teacher, columns for the Magen David Community Center sisterhood (the Community Center shared a building with the school), other Syrian community announcements, B'nai B'rith announcements, Milestones (announcements of births, bar mitzvahs, engagements, marriages, etc.), and advertisements. Analysis of each feature indicates the degree to which the Syrian community was integrated, at the same time that it maintained a separate identity through often parallel institutions.

For instance, both the English and the Hebrew principals of the yeshiva were Ashkenazi Jews. The advice that the Hebrew principal gives parents in each bulletin is noteworthy. In the October issue he stressed regular home observance of Jewish ritual, especially the Sabbath, to reinforce the teaching of the day school. In the November issue, he suggested where to take children during school holidays, particularly the attractions of Manhattan. PTA and Sisterhood activities are what one would expect of an American women's auxiliary during this period: cake sales, card parties, membership teas, and raffle drawings, fashion shows, and gala dances. The same is true of the B'nai B'rith chapter. In the October issue there was an announcement of the formation of a Girl Scout troop at the new congregation—it was termed the first "S.Y. Girl Scout troop" (S.Y. is a Syrian term for Syrian as opposed to J.—dub, for Jew or Ashkenazi). Most of the teachers in the school mentioned in Bulletin had non-Syrian names, like Masters and Golubshik, while only one PTA officer listed had a distinctly Ashkenazi name. The neighborhood businessmen who advertised in the Bulletin were both Syrian and non-Syrian.

Syrian Jews participated in activities at the Jewish Community House of Bensonhurst. During the 1930s, this center was used by Syrians for religious services before they built their own synagogues. A community center was organized after World War II by younger Syrians in Bensonhurst. Such an organization was, however, opposed by the older leaders and its own members became indifferent. By 1958 the Center building had become the day school building and the Center was simply another Syrian synagogue, as noted above. With the movement of Syrian Jews to Flatbush, new efforts were made to build a separate Syrian Jewish Community Center. The building for the Sephardi Syrian Community Center was dedicated in 1979 (Koppman 1979).[2] The tendency toward parallel organization was also present with regard to B'nai B'rith. Some sources indicated that there had been all-Syrian Jewish Masonic and Odd Fellow lodges. In the B'nai B'rith lodge, members were generally second-generation Americans. In addition to these organizations, which have Jewish aims, there were several social clubs that had card playing and parties as their main activities. Membership in these clubs was reputed to be on the basis of wealth and was considered to be an exclusive privilege.

The "umbrella" organization of the Syrian Jews was headed, I was told, by self-appointed leaders. This was similar to the situation in Jerusalem in the 1940s, 1950s, and 1960s (Zenner 1967). There was fund-raising on behalf of new synagogues, the day school, the Sephardi Porat Yosef Yeshiva in Jerusalem (a rabbinical seminary), general Jewish philanthropies, and special funds set up by New York Syrian Jews. These include Otsar HaTorah, which established Jewish religious schools in a number of Muslim countries after the Second World War.[3] The leaders were said to be the main contributors. They were wealthy religious men, generally of the immigrant generation. One rabbi was called the Haham Bashi (the old Ottoman term for chief rabbi), but he was considered to be only *primus inter pares* by the other rabbis. At various times he had presided over a rabbinic court, which handled cases involving Syrian and other Sephardi Jews in New York and elsewhere (Frank 1968; De Sola Pool 1935).

Unlike the American Jewish community, in which private morticians play an important role, the Syrian Jews in Brooklyn have maintained a Burial Society. If the individual is a member of the Society and the community, the Society will bury him without extra cost. In this they continue the medieval tradition that was common to most Jewish communities. Most Syrian Jews are members and the society does not give preference to rich or poor. There was also a *mikveh*. Recently, in fact, a new *mikveh* was built in the Ocean Parkway area. (Ginsberg 1981).

Religion

Syrian Jews in Brooklyn and in Bradley Beach were considered "very religious" or traditional by their Ashkenazi neighbors. In both places, there was good attendance by men, including those in their 20s and 30s. The attendance was better than one would find in equivalent Ashkenazi Conservative and Orthodox congregations. On the other hand, many Syrians kept their shops open and worked in them on the Sabbath. Many younger men did go out to dances and parties on the Sabbath. In Bradley Beach most of them went to the beach on Saturday afternoon, even some who were conscientiously Orthodox.

Observance of the dietary laws in the home was prevalent among Syrian Jews, although some ate nonkosher meat away from home. The ritual bath was maintained in one synagogue, although the degree to which women went there after their menstrual period was not ascertained.

Daily prayer quorums, sacred study sessions, and the singing of *pizmonim* (sacred Hebrew songs) continued in Brooklyn. The main participants were older men and a group of younger "ultra-orthodox" individuals. After-school classes for girls who attended public school and needed instruction in Judaism were given in addition to Hebrew classes for boys.

The impact of outside influences on the Syrian Jews in Brooklyn can be seen during their transitional rites. In one wedding that I observed in 1963, the wedding ritual itself followed the Sephardi rite. In the reception, how-ever, the American and Ashkenazi influences were quite evident. The wed-ding was held in a New York-style wedding hall, and the caterer served Ashkenazi-style hors-d'oeuvres and food at the dinner.

Religious observance in Brooklyn ranged from rebels who identified as atheists through those who were indifferent or casual, to those who were conscientiously Orthodox, or even ultra-Orthodox. All of the Syrian con-gregations were and are Orthodox in affiliation. Movements of rebellion among Syrian Jews have expressed themselves in religious terms. During the 1930s, I was told that there were a number of young men who identified themselves as Communists. They are said to have read left-wing pamphlets in the synagogue, hidden in their prayerbooks. They were jok-ingly called "*lahimajin* Communists." *Lahimajin* is a Syrian and Armenian equivalent to pizza, consisting of flat Syrian bread with some meat and tomato sauce on top. The young men in that group remained in the com-munity and became businessmen, although some other Syrians who be-came leftists left the community.

In the late 1950s, a group of young men became "ultra-Orthodox." This group gathered around a young rabbi who was the assistant in one of the congregations, had come from Latin America, and had studied in an Ash-kenazi yeshiva. As a result of his activities, he was forced to leave the congregation. He was young and enthusiastic, wanting to revive the "greatness of Sephardi greatness." His message contained religious, ethical, and ethnic themes. His followers were men in their teens and twenties, although there were also a few middle-aged men. He encouraged his fol-lowers to study both traditional texts, such as the Talmud, and secular subjects, particularly philosophy. The group was critical of the business and recreational practices of Syrian Jews, including the celebration of the secular New Year's Eve as pagan. The older leaders of both the Halabi and Damascan communities opposed this young rabbi and eventually he left the community.

Certain realms of folk religion persisted for a time in America. The Halabis and Shaamis brought their traditions of magic and medicine to America. About forty years ago, rabbis still said prayers over boys who were diagnosed as having become ill on account of "frights." As recently as twenty years ago, a wealthy Halabi in Los Angeles requested an amulet from a saintly rabbi in Jerusalem for the cure of a neighbor's son (Zenner 1965). Younger Syrians view these traditions as superstitions.

Syrian Jewish religious life was greatly influenced by the American Ashkenazi environment. Still religious Syrians from Jerusalem expressed surprise that their American counterparts still believed that "the Torah came out of Aram Sobah" (Aram Sobah-Aleppo). The opinions of Syrian rabbis were still preferred over those of Ashkenazim and many would rather send their children to the Syrian day school than to Ashkenazi yeshivot. But this was only a superficial impression. Several Syrian synagogues and the Syrian yeshiva had Ashkenazi rabbis, principals, and teachers. Many sent their chilidren to Ashkenazi day schools. Most of the younger Syrians who received higher religious education did so at Yeshiva University and other Ashkenazi-controlled institutions. As indicated above, the synagogues in Brooklyn acquired the traits of American synagogues.

"Secular" Tastes and Leisure

The New York Syrian Jews are subject to several influences in their tastes. Middle Eastern music in both its Arabic and Hebrew forms was extant in New York City. Around 1960 there were several Greek and Armenian cabarets where one could see belly-dancing. Some of the tourist bazaars sold records of Arabic music. At one time one of the Bensonhurst movie houses exhibited Arabic films. In the late 1950s, some Jews went to the Brooklyn Academy of Music to see Egyptian films. The Academy of Music is near Atlantic Avenue, which was a center of the Syrian Christians and has continued to be an area of Arab restaurants. Arab music is an ethnic symbol for the Syrians. At a party some women would perform belly dances. In the PTA Bulletin (cited above), one Halabi offered "Music of Distinction Orchestras Large and Small Custom Made to Your Affair." Syrian Jews, however, appreciated popular American music as well as that of the Middle East.

The Brooklyn Syrians were familiar with the films, nightclubs, and social dancing as they existed in New York City. Some attended "legitimate" theatrical performances. A few even attended the opera regularly. Card playing was a popular activity. Certain card games, one informant said, were known to him only in a Syrian context. Backgammon was played in the 1960s primarily by older men before its American revival. Card playing was as popular among women as among men, in both home and clubs.

Israeli Halabim in New York said that Syrian foods were better in New York than in Jerusalem. The Syrians in New York were richer than those in Israel. Ingredients such as pistachios were easier to get here than in Israel. One Syrian woman published a cookbook of Syrian Jewish dishes. More recently, C. Roden, an Egyptian woman of Syrian Jewish descent, published the popular *Book of Middle Eastern Food* (1972), which contains some distinctly Halabi recipes (Sokolov 1973). There were some general American and Ashkenazi influences that were illustrated by the Deal Sisterhood's cookbook, containing many international recipes (Sisterhood of Deal 1980). Some Barton's Confectionary branches in Brooklyn were owned by Syrian Jews. One Syrian Jew owned a typically American Jewish kosher delicatessen in a Syrian neighborhood and he had many Syrian customers. The menu included corned beef and pastrami on rye bread, chicken soup with noodles, and salami, but no Middle Eastern dish appeared on the menu. A recent Egyptian Jewish immigrant owned a pastry shop that also served food, all in Middle Eastern style. Syrian bread (pita) was available; some was packaged by Syrian (Christian) firms on Atlantic Avenue.

School Performance and "Intellectualism"

In the late 1950s, relatively few Syrian Jews graduated from colleges and universities. Those who did were often among the alienated. While this is derived from both Syrian and Ashkenazi informants, there was general agreement about the fact. By that time, the Brooklyn Syrians were sufficiently prosperous to be able to afford to send their children to college.[4] It appeared that Syrian Jews had not chosen the "educational" route of social mobility.

In 1929 the educational performance of Syrian Jews was also lower than that of their Ashkenazi neighbors. At that time there was a high rate of school "retardation" among the Syrians. Their rate for being held back or flunking was 44.0 percent, that of the American-born was 17.8 percent, and the Italian rate was 59.3 percent. Ashkenazi origin groups, such as "Poles," had retardation rates that were far lower than even the Americans (Herling 1929). Boris M. Levinson (1956) reports that in a study of intelligence quotients of children in Jewish day schools in New York City, the average in Syrian school was 102.43 while the mean I.Q. for children in other (Ashkenazi) schools was 114.88. He attributes the relatively low performance to "unknown cultural factors." Gross's findings are similarly attributed to the "commercial" orientation of the Syrians and the high value set on educational performance among Ashkenazim (1967; 1969).

The Syrian case has some interesting implications. First, these findings of Herling, Levinson and Gross fit certain stereotypes of Middle Easterners. Catlin (1915) claimed that Syrians (= Christians) are imaginative and practical, but "have little capacity for abstract thought." Studies of Oriental Jewish children in Israel in the 1950s made the same claim about that population (Ortar in Frankenstein 1953:290). At the same time, the research among Syrian Jews contradicts the association often made between poor school performance and such factors as lack of economic success and poverty. The Syrian Jews could not be characterized as an impoverished group in any meaningful economic sense, nor did they lack achievement. It is also noteworthy that by the 1960s one finds that Syro-Lebanese Christians in America, who as immigrants had a similar background to the Syrian Jews, were using the educational, as well as economic, route (Kayal and Kayal 1975:105–111). Among Syrian Jews who had left the community, or had never been part of it, one also finds some academic success stories. By the late 1970s, I have indications from my students and others that the number of Syrian Jews going to college had been steadily increasing (e.g., Sutton 1979:101–3).

The Alienated and the Assimilating

While there was an ethnic entity in which any Syrian Jew could participate, there were those who for a variety of reasons had left the Syrian community and lived outside it. Even in Brooklyn, in the neighborhoods where the Syrian Jews resided, some Syrians kept their participation at a minimum.

Some of those who were assimilating had never been part of the Brooklyn Syrian Jewish group. Many Syrians opened businesses in such far-off places as Chicago; Laredo, Texas; and St. Petersburg, Florida. While some of these later moved to Brooklyn, so that their children would be reared in a Sephardi Jewish environment, some did not. Their children married Jews of other origins or even non-Jews. Similarly, the paths of immigration for some Syrian Jews were idiosyncratic.

Albert Harari was born in Istanbul of Halabi parents. After his emigration to the United States, he joined the Marines. Later he married a Jewish woman from Poland. He now lives in New York. While he is Syrian, he never settled among the Syrian Jews in Brooklyn and has little to do with them. His daughter, Joan, knows that her father is Syrian or part Syrian, but she has never lived in a Syrian Jewish context. She has some identification with the Syrians and will speak about the "Syrian personality." Other paths of immigration would have been by way of Great Britain, Israel, Egypt, or South America, rather than directly from Aleppo. While in many cases these led to settlement among the Syrians in Brooklyn, others followed paths quite different.

Among the Syrian Jews in Brooklyn, there were those who were alienated from the dominant ways of the community and from its leadership. The "*lahimajin* Communists" and the ultra-Orthodox group were examples of young men of this variety, although most of them remained within the community and continued to participate in it. Some remained on the periphery. One man in his twenties, for instance, went to college and to graduate school. While he continued to live in Brooklyn, he went generally to Ashkenazi synagogues.

There were some who left the Syrian Jewish group entirely, although they maintained ties with their kin. Ralph Abbady grew up in Brooklyn. In his teens he rebelled strongly against Syrian attitudes toward intellectual activity and commerce. In fact, he developed a strong aversion to commercial activity. After he served in the army in World War II, he went to university and worked for a doctoral degree. Since then he has lived away from the Syrian Jews in New York. His wife was of European Jewish background. He sees his siblings mainly on the occasion of rites of passage, such as weddings. While Ralph was assimilating into a general American intellectual group and while he had broken with the Syrian group, he did not try to "pass." He remembered and identified with his Middle Eastern background. For instance, he bought records of Arabic music. He gave his son a name that he occasionally Arabized. Nevertheless, he does not participate in Syrian activities.

Gladys Mizrahi Jacobs was born to a relatively poor family in Panama. After her family moved to Brooklyn, she suffered from their poverty. Because she was considered beautiful, she did receive a proposal to marry a wealthy, but older, Syrian Jew. She rejected this offer and, instead, broke with her family and married an Ashkenazi Jew. She moved away from Brooklyn and has few ties to her family.

"A Minority within a Minority"

The Syrian Jews of Brooklyn were connected to other Jews in the United States; yet they were (and are) identifiably separate. M. Steinhardt (1960 ms) termed them "a minority within a minority." They had a separate set of names for themselves: *Halabiye,* Syrians, S.Y.'s, Sephardim. They called the Ashkenazim: Jews, Yiddish, Itchies, and Jay-dubs (J-w). The simple term *Syrian* referred to the dominant Halabi group. If you talked to a Halabi, he would refer to the Damascans as Shaamis or *Shawam.* Plotnick (1958) noted that the Spaniole Sephardim of New Lots similarly differentiated themselves from the dominant Ashkenazi group, although his report aroused indignant censure by Sephardim. The Syrians were recognized as a separate ethnic group in the Brooklyn neighborhoods, as well as in the New Jersey resort, which was also an Ashkenazi resort. If one asked people what "nationalities" lived in the neighborhood, they answered: Jews, Italians, and Syrians. However, if one asked about the religion of the Syrians: are they Christian? one would be told that they were Jews, in fact, Orthodox Jews.

It is difficult to explain the reasons for the disengagement of the Syrians and other Separdim from East European Jews. A number of factors may account for this. Ashkenazi Jews did not give Ladino-speaking and Arabic-speaking Jews full recognition as Jews because of their exotic ways. One Lebanese Jew was praying one weekday morning in a Chicago synagogue around 1914, I was told. He was wearing, as an Orthodox Jew would, his prayer shawl and phylacteries, when a fellow worshiper started speaking to him in Yiddish. He replied that he did not understand that language and the man then asked him if he was a Jew. The Ashkenazim had preempted the term *Jew* for themselves. Jewish as a language means Yiddish and "Jewish food" is East European in origin. The Syrian Jews were probably soon aware of the negative, anti-Semitic stereotypes that Christian Americans held of the East European Jews and they may have preferred to identify as other than Jewish for public purposes. Syrians were a less important target as scapegoats than were Jews.

The local Jews of East European descent were the most significant ethnic group for Syrian Jews. Other Sephardi groups were separated from them by neighborhood and language of origin. Most other Sephardim were Ladino speakers, as well as some Persians. In Bensonhurst there were some other Sephardim. By 1960 the latter included a number of recent Egyptian refugees, some of whom were Halabis, but they were "more French" than the American Syrians (Sanua 1967; Ibrahim 1977; Sutton 1979). Relations with Arabic-speaking Christians were very distant. They were similar to what they were in Syria, except that there was less interaction in Brooklyn. The attitudes of Syrian-American Christians toward Jews was complicated. While some were very sympathetic to the Arab cause, others, particularly the Maronites, viewed pan-Arabism as a threat to Middle Eastern Christians. Syrian-American Christians were sometimes mistaken for Jews and even called themselves "Christian Jews."

The main Gentile group in the neighborhoods where Syrian Jews lived was the Italians. Otherwise the two neighborhoods were predominantly Jewish. Many of the teachers in the public and religious day schools were Ashkenazi Jews, as were the professionals (doctors, lawyers, accountants) and the politicians. In the U.S. Army, a Brooklyn Syrian had an opportunity to meet members of other groups, but that was an experience separated from civilian life.

The integration of Syrian Jews into American life showed some distinctive features. All went to schools that taught American values. They paid taxes and served in the armed forces when conscripted. The second generation spoke English as its mother tongue. Some said that they could tell a Syrian Jew in Brooklyn from an Ashkenazi, but both spoke with New York accents.

One major difference between the New York Ashkenazi and the New York Syrian Jew was the apolitical attitudes of most Syrian Jews. According to one Halabi who was active in local politics, few Syrians, even among the American-born, bothered to vote, whereas, he said, 90 percent of the Ashkenazim did vote. There were, however, some exceptions to this nonparticipation in politics, such as the leftists of the 1930s. In the 1950s one rabbi's son was a member of a Zionist youth group and a lawyer was active in local Democratic politics. Some older leaders in the community were active in Jewish fund-raising, including campaigns on behalf of Israel and of non-Zionist *yeshivot (New York Times,* 1979).

The Ashkenazi stereotype of the Syrian Jews in Brooklyn, as elicited by Steinhardt (1960 ms.) and me, is that the Syrians are considered "thieves and swindlers," big spenders, and big gamblers. The Syrians were seen as foreign and as having a false sense of superiority. Steinhardt's interviews with middle-aged Syrian women in Bensonhurst brought out responses of indifference toward the Ashkenazim. They felt that the latter were jealous of their (Syrian) success in America. The Syrian Sephardim had a stronger identification as Sephardim and Syrians, while the Ashkenazi women felt more American. The Ashkenazim identify simply as Jewish, rather than as Ashkenazi. They used the word *Turk* for the Syrians in a derogatory manner. They believed that Syrian marriages were prearranged by the parents. On the whole, the Ashkenazi occupational structure in Bensonhurst was more diversified than the Syrian. It included postal workers, jewelers, and furriers as well as retailers and wholesalers. On the other hand, Steinhardt found that richer Ashkenazim moved to the suburbs more readily than the equivalent Syrian group.

The Syrian stereotype of Ashkenazim was more difficult to elicit. The fact that the interviewers (Steinhardt and I) were Ashkenazim may have been part of the difficulty. Some younger Syrians were concerned over the fact that there were more Ashkenazi professionals and college graduates. On the other hand, Steinhardt found that the goal of wealth was pursued with more openness among the Syrians than among other Americans. Syrians tended to underestimate their wealth in response to questions more than Ashkenazim did. I found that Syrians felt that Ashkenazi women were too independent. One informant said that one reason more Syrian women married Ashkenazi men than vice versa was that Ashkenazi men were better around the house while, the women were too free. Steinhardt found that while Ashkenazim said that Syrians had four, five, or six children, above the average, Syrian women claimed that they had no more than average. This finding may have been a respondent's reaction to the interviewer rather than their belief. Steinhardt found that Syrians and Italians in Bensonhurst tend to live more in homes or two-family houses, whereas Ashkenazim were apartment-house dwellers. Herling (1929) suggests this too.

Steinhardt's main finding was that the Ashkenazim were the main reference group in American society with which the Syrians had contact. On the other hand, they had a feeling of indifference and self-confidence toward the Ashkenazim, in their own way. To the Ashkenazim, the Syrians were of little concern. From the discussion of Syrian Jewish institutions in Brooklyn, it is clear that the indifference to the local Ashkenazim was only partial.

Conclusion

In most of this paper, I have not attempted to draw any explicit conclusions about the theoretical position of Syrian Jews in New York City. Elsewhere I have written about this group as an example of a "sojourning" middleman minority. The association of a disproportionate number of Syrians in a number of related lines of trade, their strong family and kinship system, their family firms, their worldwide familial and commercial connections, and their maintenance of distinctive synagogues were part of a single picture. Their cohesiveness and their occupational specialization were connected, as I showed in contrasting them with Israeli Halabim where this linkage was broken (Zenner 1968; 1979a; 1980b).

The Syrian Jewish community of Brooklyn, however, can no more be contained by a single portrayal than any other entity. While Syrian Jews have maintained a high degree of ethnic solidarity, their culture has been affected by the surrounding society, and there is considerable intermarriage with other Jews. A new occupational structure is, no doubt, arising out of the old. The Syrian Jewish community in Brooklyn has changed considerably in the past twenty years, but a portrait of its past will help in understanding its present.

NOTES

1. More recently dowries were also used to further the professional education of the groom, instead of for investment in a business.

2. Koppman wrote a version of the history that omitted mention of the abortive Magen David Community Center.

3. See Loeb (1977:137–147) for a critical account of these schools in Iran.

4. One should keep in mind, however, that Syrian Jews still had a fairly high birth rate, which would make higher education, even in the then tuition-free New York City college system, expensive.

5. In Zenner (1966:351–52) I did speculate about these "cultural factors" as follows:

> This "nonintellectual trend" may be associated with other traits in the culture. For instance, Syrians prefer to play card-games such as rummy and poker and the board game of backgammon, rather than games like chess and bridge. These latter require more strategic thought. In Talmud, the Halebi method of study is less casuistic than the East European. One might conclude from this that Middle Easterners "have little capacity for abstract thought." One does, however, find certain groups in Middle Eastern and North African society who play chess very well. According to one American academician, who has traveled extensively in the Middle East, some Arab students are good in theoretical physics and theoretical economics.
>
> Both in Brooklyn and in Israel, Syrian Jews compete in school with Ashkenazic children. Both in Brooklyn and in Israel, Jews of East European origin have positions of importance in the school system. The Ashkenazic group is one group which places great emphasis and value on intellectual endeavor. The school is oriented towards students with what Patai (1953:114) called "reading habit." "Reading habit" is the frequent and habitual reading of both books and periodicals. It is distinct from "literacy," which is the ability to read and write, but does not indicate how often it is used. Patai feels that Europeans, especially European Jews, read voraciously, but that Middle Easterners by and large do not.

All these names are pseudonyms. Cf. also Sutton's chapter, "Six Families" (1979:109–135) for a picture of assimilatory trends.

BIBLIOGRAPHY

The bibliography includes a number of items not cited in the text, because this article is viewed as one to stimulate further research into the Syrian Sephardim of Brooklyn.

Apple, R. W., Jr.
    1964   Haddad-Farbstein Campaign Draws Attention to Syrian Jews. *The New York Times,* June 1, 1964, p. 21.
Berger, Morroe
    1958   Americans from the Arab World. *Commentary* 25, no. 4:314–23.
Berman, Susan
    1978   *Seven Grooms for Seven Brides. New York Magazine* 11:31 (July 31):34–38.
Brady, Thomas F.
    1970   Gunman and Policeman Die in Times Square Area Battle. *New York Times,* March 1, pp. 1 and 24.
Catlin, Louise E.
    1915   The Americanizing of the Syrian South Ferry Colony. Master's thesis, Columbia University, 1915.
Cohen, Hayyim J.
    1971   Sephardic Jews in the United States: Marriages with Ashkenazim and Non-Jews. *Dispersion and Unity* 13/14:151–60.

Da Sola Pool, D.
1935   Annual Report, Union of Sephardic Congregations, New York.
Eisenberg, Howard
1979   Those Splendid Syrians Weekend in Deal. *Jewish Living* (September–October), pp. 36–40.
Felton, Ralph A.
1912   A Sociological Study of the Syrians in Greater New York. Master's thesis, Columbia University, 1912.
Fredman, Ruth Gruber
1981   Cosmopolitans at Home: the Sephardic Jews of Washington, D.C. *Anthropological Quarterly* 54, no. 2:61–67.
Frank, Ben G.
1968   Our Syrian Jewish Community. *American Examiner,* September 14. pp. 29–30. (J.T.A.—Jewish Telegraphic Agency).
1971   Homogeneity of Syrian Jews Here Noted in Summer Synagogue. (Schenectady) *Jewish World,* September 16, p. 4 (J.T.A.)
1972   Where Mideast Meets in West. *Sentinel,* December 14.
Frankenstein, Carl ed.
1953   *Between Past and Present.* Jerusalem, Henrietta Szold Foundation.
Ginsberg, Fay
1981   Power, Purity and Pollution: Menstrual Rituals in Judaism. Paper presented at the 21st Annual Meeting of the Northeastern Anthropological Association. Saratoga, N.Y., March 28.
Gross, Morris
1967   Learning Readiness in Two Jewish Settings. New York: Center for Urban Education.
Gupte, Pranay
1977   Brooklyn Synagogue Celebrates Coming Arrival of Syrian Brides. *The New York Times,* July 31, p. 34.
Gwertzman Bernard
1977   Syrian Proxy-Marraige Plan Lets Jewish Women Emigrate to U.S. *The New York Times,* July 31, pp. 1 and 34.
Harari, Joseph
1972   Letter to the Editor. *New York Times,* April 11.
Herling, Lillian
1929   Study in Retardation with Special Regard to the Status of Syrians. Master's thesis. Columbia University, 1929.
Hitti, Philip
1924   *Syrians in America.* New York: George Doran.
Horsley, Carter B.
1975   Inroads by Tourist Trade Shops Troubling Fifth Avenue. *New York Times,* Real Estate Section, April 20, Section 8:pp. 1 and 12.
Ibrahim, Youssef M.
1977   Egyptian Jews in Brooklyn Take Hope in Sadat's Peace Initiatives. *New York Times,* December 12, p. 35.
Kaufman, Michael T.
1972   Candy Store Alumni Honor the "Boss." *New York Times,* January 24, p. 36.
Kayal, Philip M. and Kayal, Joseph M.
1975   *The Syrian-Lebanese in America.* Boston: Twayne.
Koppman, Lionel
        A Dream Grows in Brooklyn: 1st Syrian JCC is Born of Joint Jewish Community Efforts. *J.W.B. Circle,* 36, no. 5:9–11.

Lavender, Abraham, ed.
    1977   *A Coat of Many Colors: Jewish Sub-Communities in the United States.* Westport,
          Conn.: Greenwood.

Levinson, B. M.
    1956   Note on the Davis-Eells Test of General Intelligence. *Psychological Reports*
          6:242.

Loeb, Laurence
    1977   *Outcaste: Jewish Life in Southern Iran.* London and New York: Gordon &
          Breach.

Magen David Yeshiva
    1959   *Community Bulletin.* Brooklyn, N. Y. 3, nos. 3–9.

Miller, L. C.
    1971   *A Study of the Syrian Population of Greater New York. New York* (n.p., avail-
          able at Columbia University Library).

New York Times
    1971   Youths Protest at the UN on Behalf of Syrian Jews. December 16, p. 60.
    1979   Joseph Ashear, 82, Manufacturer and an Activist in Jewish Affairs. Jan-
          uary 4, pp. 8–19.

Patai, Raphael
    1953   *Israel Between East and West.* Philadelphia: Jewish Publication Society.

Plotnik, L.
    1958   The Sephardim of New Lots. *Commentary* 25:28–35.

Polakoff, Joseph
    1976   Critic Churba Finds Gen. Brown Only Can 'Dish' It Out. Schenectady.
          Jewish World (J.T.A.), November 25.

Roden, Claudia
    1972   *A Book of Middle Eastern Food.* New York: Knopf.

Sanua, Victor D.
    1967   A Study of the Adjustment of Sephardi Jews in the New York Metropoli-
          tan Area. *Jewish Journal of Sociology* 9:25–33.
    1977   Contemporary Studies of Sephardi Jews in the United States. *In* A. La-
          vender, ed. *Coat of Many Colors.* Westport, Conn.: Greenwood, pp.
          281–288.

Schumach, Murray
          Three 'Proxy' Brides from Syria Wed New Suitors in Brooklyn Jewish
          Rites. *New York Times,* Jan. 3, pp. 27 and 49.

Seruya, B.
    1952   History of the Syrian-Sephardic Community in America. *NIR* (Annual,
          Teachers Institute), New York: Yeshiva University, pp. 89–92. (He-
          brew)

Sisterhood of Deal
    1980   *Deal Delights.* Deal, N. J.: Synagogue of Deal.

Sitton, D.
    1962   Groups of Sephardic Jews in New York, *BaMaᶜarakha.* (Jerusalem) 2,
          no. 1:3–4. (Hebrew)

Sokolov, Raymond A.
    1973   Jews Whose Tradition Includes Stuffed Grape Leaves at the Seder. *New
          York Times,* April 12, p. 54.

Steinhardt, Michael
    1960   A Minority Within a Minority. Bachelor's honors thesis, University of
          Pennsylvania, 1960.

Sutton, Joseph A. D.
    1979   *Magic Carpet: Aleppo in Flatbush.* Brooklyn: Thayer-Jacoby.

Zenner, Walter P.
    1965   Saints and Piecemeal Supernaturalism among the Jerusalem Sephardim. *Anthropological Quarterly* 38, 4:201–17.
    1966   Syrian Jewish Identification in Israel. Ph.D. dissertation, Columbia University. Ann Arbor: Univ. Microfilms, Order No. 66–8536.
    1967   Sephardic voluntary Organizations in Israel. *Middle East Journal* 21:173–186.
    1968   Syrian Jews in Three Social Settings. *Jewish Journal of Sociology* 10:101–20.
    1970   International Networks of a Migrant Ethnic Group. In *Migration and Anthropology*, edited by R. F. Spencer. Proceedings of Annual Spring Meeting of American Ethnological Association, Seattle: University of Washington Press, 36–48.
    1979a   Arabic-Speaking Immigrants in North America as Middleman Minorities. Paper presented at the American Anthropological Association Meeting. Cincinnati, Dec. 1.
    1979b   The Inner Life of Syrian Jews in the Late Ottoman Period. *Paᶜamim* 3:45–58 (Hebrew).
    1980a   Censorship and Syncretism: Social Anthropological Approaches to the Study of Middle Eastern Jews. In *Studies in Jewish Folklore*, edited by F. Talmage, D. Noy, coordinator. New York: Ktav for the Association for Jewish Studies (Cambridge, Mass):377–94.
    1980b   American Jewry in the Light of Middleman Minority Theories. *Contemporary Jewry* 5, 1:11–30.

Part IV

ZIONISM, ISRAEL AND THE MIDDLE EAST

The "Young Turks" and Zionism: Some Comments

JACOB M. LANDAU

History has not yet provided us with any clear definition of the attitudes toward Zionism adopted by the "Young Turks" or, more precisely, by the Committee of Union and Progress (C.U.P.), which—as a semi-clandestine organization and then as a political party—ruled the Ottoman Empire (first *de facto* and later *de jure* as well) during the years 1908–19.[1] This article does not claim to offer any definitive answers regarding these attitudes but rather attempts to describe and analyze their more salient features. This appears particulaly necessary because both eyewitness observers and subsequent analysts have differed considerably in their interpretations. Many of the stands adopted are in fact diametrically opposed to one another.

One school of thought maintains that the Young Turks were essentially ardent Pro-Zionists, overtly or covertly. This approach has been largely characteristic of some C.U.P. opponents during the decade in which the party occupied a central place in Ottoman political life. The contention voiced by proponents of this view may be summed up in the unproved argument that Zionists continued the plot against Sultan Abdul Hamid II in order to penalize him for his refusal to grant Herzl a charter on Palestine. In order to bolster this claim, its proponents considerably exaggerated Jewish involvement in the preparatory stages of the Young Turk revolution, an argument set in its proper historical perspective in a recent article by the late David Farhi.[2] They also overstated Jewish participation in C.U.P. activities, a claim refuted twenty years ago by Bernard Lewis[3] and by Elie Kedourie ten years later.[4]

During and following World War I, these views were common not only among Turkish and Arab politicians and journalists, as demonstrated by Neville Mandel,[5] but also in British Government circles, as we are informed by Isaiah Friedman.[6] It found support among several Turkish historians

and journalists (although not the best ones) as well in the generation following Mustafa Kemal's death, when it became fashionable to yearn for the
days of Abdul Hamid II and to denigrate the Young Turks. Among its
exponents were Cevat Rifat Atilhan,[7] a military officer turned anti-Semitic
journalist,[8] and others.[9]

A second school commences with opposite premises, claiming that the
Young Turks—and especially the C.U.P. leadership—adopted an uncom-
promisingly anti-Zionist stand. The arguments proferred by this school are
somewhat better substantiated, based as they are on more verifiable proof,
that is, on actions and decisions taken by Ottoman leaders. This school tells
us of the suspicions harbored by several C.U.P. leaders concerning the
intentions of the Zionist movement to establish a large Jewish center in
Palestine (or in the Middle East) and their apprehension lest it turn into a
political unit that would secede from the Ottoman Empire. The existence
of such suspicions and apprehensions is mentioned, time and again, in the
reports of Victor Jacobsohn, Istanbul representative of the Zionist Organization, and others now on file in Jerusalem's Central Zionist Archives.[10]
The various anti-Zionist measures taken, including forbidding Jews from
acquiring land in Palestine, anti-Zionist speeches delivered in the Ottoman
Parliament during March and May 1911,[11] and the disbanding of Zionist
groups in Istanbul in April 1914[12] are all indications of the failure of
organized Zionism to dispel the fears of the Ottoman authorities.

Similarly, certain official steps and pronouncements against Zionism
have also been variously explained as the result of Arab propaganda activities, most especially those of Palestinian and Syrian Arabs. Mandel, for
example, discusses only briefly the suspicions of the Ottoman leadership
toward Zionism's political aims, but writes at some length on Arab contributions toward intensification of these suspicions through their violent pro-
panda against Jews' buying land in Palestine.[13] Obviously, Mandel's
approach is conditioned by the topic of his research, Arabs and Zionism,
which did not initially intend to branch into investigating Ottoman policies
toward Zionism. His interpretation has recently received support in new
materials uncovered and published by scholars researching the Arab national movement.[14] Nevertheless, even though this second school has based
its studies upon better documentation than the first, and even though its
selection of facts appears to have been more carefully researched, its conclusions are still too extreme: it has hardly considered the moderation in
Ottoman policy toward Zionism just before World War I, when the Government was hoping for Jewish financial aid from abroad,[15] nor the events
of December 1917 and January 1918, when Talat Pasha, one of C.U.P.'s
leaders and then Grand Vizier, briefly[16] indicated some readiness for accommodation with Zionism, thus aiming to react to the Balfour Declaration.[17]

From all the above and additional sources, one may deduce that the second approach appears closer to historical truth. Nevertheless, as already indicated, the opposition of the C.U.P. leadership to Zionism was not continuously uncompromising, having been affected by tactical considerations, although it did display a fair degree of consistency. In attempting to explain the reasons for official attitudes to Zionism, it is not sufficient to refer merely to Zionist failures or Arab successes in presenting their respective positions. These explanations are valid, but it is doubtful whether they really strike the core of the matter. A fuller understanding is provided by an examination of the pragmatic-ideological aspect of C.U.P.'s general policies, on the one hand, and attitudes toward Zionism held by influential Ottoman Jews, on the other.

The key issue concerning the Ottoman Empire during the first twenty years of this century was survival in the face of its decline in military power, economic situation, and international relations. One frequently posed question was "How can we save the Ottoman state?" The vital necessity for reply was a cardinal concern of C.U.P. leaders, with the problem becoming even more urgent following uprisings within the empire and armed aggression from without. Under such conditions, official circles' suspicion of nationalist movements among the empire's minorities became a prime mover in shaping internal and external policies alike.

Few of the leading figures in the C.U.P.—especially among the decision-makers—had had any well-formulated *Weltanschauung*. Rather, the ideologies they proferred were pragmatic—adapted to the empire's advantage and to their own. Pragmatism had never been uncommon within Ottoman political leadership and was obviously to be found elsewhere as well. Within our own context it is significant to note that the various ideologies of ruling elites in the late Ottoman Empire were all liable to exert adverse influence upon official attitudes to Zionism.

When the C.U.P. seized power in 1908–9, they found Pan-Islam to be the ideology fostered—not unsuccessfully—by Abdul Hamid II. The basic concept of Pan-Islam was encouragement of rapprochement among all Muslims, under the guidance of the sultan, with the general objective of increasing power in both internal and external affairs. The Young Turks, however, hesitated to direct their main efforts within the scope of an ideology propounded by their arch-enemy, Abdul Hamid II, especially since they knew they lacked the sultan's authority and prestige; in addition, there is good reason to doubt their religious piety. However, they carefully refrained from publicly abjuring Islam, in order not to alienate unnecessarily the numerous Muslims within and without the Ottoman Empire. Also, they correctly estimated that Islam, and Pan-Islam in particular, afforded them a means of exerting pressure on various powers, in the first place on Great Britain, whose dominion included many Muslims.[18] Consequently, the C.U.P.'s leaders continued to employ the services of the former sultan's agents, even though some of the Pan-Islam activity was then intended chiefly to serve as a cover for other objectives.[19] However, they gradually evolved two alternative ideologies, Ottomanism and Pan-Turkism.

Ottomanism consisted of an all-out effort, directed from above, to unite the empire against the dangers facing it by attempting to convince all its inhabitants that they were citizens with equal rights and duties, thus mobilizing their loyalty to a common fatherland. This was to be achieved through fusion of all peoples within the empire into one single unit, headed by a centralized Turkish leadership.[20] Application of this ideology pleased neither the Turks nor other elements, however; the former feared loss of their special privileges within a context of parity, while the latter disapproved of and vehemently protested imposed Turkification.[21] During the early years of C.U.P. rule, Turkification did indeed encompass culture no less than commerce and business; this meant imposition of the Turkish language upon others in education and economic life as an officially sponsored state policy. Although Ottomanism was intended for the whole of the empire's population, much of it was directed toward the Muslim population in particular, as a sort of combined Ottomanism and Islam (or Pan-Islam).[22] After all, the ruling elite had more in common with the empire's Muslims (i.e., religion, evidently) than with the non-Muslims.

Some C.U.P. leaders began to reconsider their positions, owing to nationalist fermentation among various peoples within the Ottoman Empire, the nonidentification of these peoples with the empire, and their obvious reservations regarding the policy of Ottomanization. This led to adoption of a new policy, Pan-Turkism, as the central state ideology, along with a downgrading of both Pan-Islam and Ottomanism. Pan-Turkism's main objective was to strive for rapprochement among Turks within the Ottoman Empire and those of Turkish origin living outside it (in the czarist empire, China, Iran, Greece, Cyprus, and elsewhere). This rapprochement, which envisaged a possible union in the future, was mainly intended to strengthen the Turks as the rulers of the Ottoman Empire and to recruit support for them in both internal and external matters.[23] With this in view, guided Turkification was intensified,[24] essentially meaning that the policy was applied beyond the cultural and linguistic level and increasingly related to the economic one, as in the systematic campaign favoring business relations with Turks, for example. In foreign affairs it was translated into a significant change in orientation, namely a trend to compensate the empire for its losses in Africa (chiefly in Libya) and Europe (mostly in the Balkans) by mobilizing support in Asia and southern Russia.[25] The military objectives of the Ottoman Empire during World War I well exemplified this volte-face in orientation, as expressed in a concentration of military effort toward thrusts into southern Russia.[26] Enver Pasha, then minister of war, was the most outspoken advocate of Pan-Turkist ideology and its prime mover in decision-making circles in the Ottoman Empire.

In practice, Pan-Turkist ideology did not wholly supplant the Ottomanist and Pan-Islamist approaches, but rather downgraded them, coexisting with them on both the strategic and tactical level in a manifestly pragmatic manner. Each of the three ideologies dictated a specific policy: Pan-Islam fostered relations with Arabs and other Muslims inside the empire and a multitude of Muslims outside it; Ottomanism continued to guide internal policies toward minorities within the empire; while Pan-Turkism became the basis for connections with groups of kindred Turkic origins, in czarist Russia and elsewhere, whose empathy with the Ottoman Empire was then growing stronger.[27]

There is hardly a need to elaborate upon how much the three official ideologies, singly and jointly, worked against the Jews and even more so against Zionism. The Jews were clearly neither Muslims nor of Turkic origin; furthermore, the Zionists became suspect among C.U.P. members because of their seemingly anti-Ottomanist political claims. In this last context, the open public activity of organized Zionism provided ammunition for official suspicions of its intentions to set up a political unit that would become a separate state. At the very same time, Armenians, Arabs, and others frequently shrouded their nationalist efforts in clandestine activities, openly proclaiming only the desire for "decentralization" (in Arabic, *la-markaziyya*). This difference in approach supplied opportunities for anti-Zionist propaganda among those Arabs whose nationalist awareness was then becoming aroused. These Arabs not only concealed their own nationalist aspirations, but also cleverly employed the common bond of Islam in their propaganda. After all, the Turks and a preponderant majority of the Arabs within the Ottoman Empire belonged to the same *millet;* thus a common experience was shared not only in religion but in many other areas of thought and daily life, deeply pervaded by Islam. Recent studies, notably those of Professor Dawn,[28] indicate that the Arab national movement, innovative as it was, comprised only very limited circles, while most Arabs living in the Ottoman Empire remained essentially loyal to the sultan and his regime. In a study on the Hejaz Railway, I too independently reached the same conclusions about Arab loyalty to the Ottoman Empire.[29] In regard to this situation, there were Turks within the ruling elite who approved of far-reaching cooperation with the Arabs as a means for strengthening the Ottoman Empire, and perhaps also for maintaining it.[30] One striking example was Ömer Seyfeddin's 1914 Turkish book, whose title translates as *Tomorrow's Turan State.* The author (1884–1920), a renowned Turkish writer and poet, was closely involved in Pan-Turkish circles[31] and his works still serve as inspiration for them to this day. His utopia[32] is descriped enthusiastically as a state governed jointly by Turkish and Arab elites.

Within such a political and social framework, Jewish power was too insignificant to have any meaningful impact upon public affairs. Moreover, organized Zionism was hardly able to withstand attacks, suffering further from the lukewarm or even hostile attitudes of Jews close to the C.U.P.'s inner circle. This situation contrasted with that of the Arabs, Greeks, Armenians, Albanians, and other groups whose members, when in positions of influence, assisted their co-nationals in their nationalist aspirations, to some extent. Jews in similar positions, however, refrained from lobbying for Zionism; if they were not inactive, they worked against rather than for it. In the cases known to us, instead of moderating the C.U.P.'s anti-Zionist moves, they even encouraged them. I shall refer to three such personalities, each of whom enjoyed some standing with the C.U.P.: Emanuel Carasso, Moïse Cohen, and Haim Nahoum.

Emanuel Carasso (d. 1934), whom the Turks called Kara Su ("Black Water"), was a lawyer and head of the "Macedonia Risorta" Freemasonic Lodge in Salonica. Thanks to his influence, the Young Turks were able to use the Freemasons' lodge for their conspirational meetings; as a reward, he maintained a position of influence in the C.U.P. after the success of its revolution. He subsequently became a Member of the Ottoman Parliament, first from Salonica and then from Istanbul.[33] Close to Talat, he was active in economic matters and maintained ties with Jews, including those of Berlin, during World War I.[34] As a Turkish nationalist and a Freemason, Carasso had little to no interest in Zionism, although he was not active against it, as far as we know. However, assumedly commencing from the premise that Zionism was not sufficiently adapting itself to Ottoman interests,[35] Carasso did not promote the Zionist cause within those Ottoman ruling circles to which he was close.

Moïse Cohen (1883–1961) was born in Seres, lived in Salonica at the time of the Young Turk revolution, and then (after Salonica was conquered by the Greeks in 1912) moved to Istanbul, where he resided and worked actively for many years. His is a very interesting personality, about which very little has been written to date.[36] From his unpublished diaries (in my possession) and other evidence, one learns that he was in touch with C.U.P. members in Salonica—which served as this organization's headquarters for some time—and particularly with Adil-Bey, then its secretary-general. Cohen maintained his contacts with them in Istanbul after he and the C.U.P. central bodies moved there in 1912. His important writings (under his own name or under the pseudonym Tekin Alp), which comprised several books and numerous articles on Ottomanism and even more on Pan-Turkism, in Turkish and in various European languages, gave him unofficial but influential standing as one of the major ideologues of the C.U.P.'s new Turkish nationalism. Cohen was an intellectual who was rather typical of the minority groups, an alert and open-minded Ottoman. In his youth he had studied for the rabbinate and law, but his interests were considerably more varied: he read a great deal about socialism (and even began writing a book about it), joined a Freemasonic lodge in Salonica, and continued this activity in Istanbul as well and, while increasingly leaning toward Ottomanist—and then Pan-Turkist—nationalism, he also displayed some interest in

Zionism. He participated in the Ninth Zionist Congress at Hamburg as a delegate from Salonica and even delivered a lengthy lecture there,[37] which was essentially more an endorsement of Ottomanism than of Zionism. Upon his return to Salonica, Cohen's reservations about Zionism increased progressively, as attested to in his diaries (since 1910) and his correspondence with Israel Zangwill regarding JTO affairs (during 1910–11).[38] The main reasons for this retreat lay in his fears, as an Ottoman nationalist, that Zionism, which he perceived as a separatist political movement, might prejudice the unity of the Ottoman Empire and bring about an increase in anti-Semitism. The essential similarity of his views in this respect with those of several C.U.P. leaders can hardly have been coincidental; it is an open question whether he actually had a share in the formulation of the C.U.P. position or whether he merely identified with it and adopted it as his own.

Haim Nahoum (1872–1960) was born in Manisa and studied in Tiberias, Izmir, Istanbul, and Paris—where he was ordained for the rabbinate. In Paris he entered into a fairly close relationship with several C.U.P. leaders who, after the success of their revolution, effected his appointment as Haham-Bashi, or chief rabbi, of the Ottoman Empire. He held this post until 1920, when he emigrated from Turkey; from 1925 until his death he served as chief rabbi of Egypt.[39] The office of Haham-Bashi was an institutionalized one and carried high prestige; Rabbi Nahoum's personal connections with the empire's political leadership further increased his power. As early as 1908 Nahoum was well aware that the C.U.P. would never agree to the establishment of a Jewish autonomous political unit in Palestine.[40] Hence his reservations about Zionism which, in the best Ottoman tradition, were generally phrased ambiguously and equivocally in his public pronouncements. In light of Nahoum's eminent position, various attempts were made by representatives of the Zionist Organization to persuade him to use his good offices with the C.U.P. leaders to moderate their antagonism toward Zionism and Zionist activity within the Ottoman Empire. The Central Zionist Archives in Jerusalem contain several documents concerning these attempts. For example, in September 1910, Victor Jacobson tried—albeit unsuccessfully—to persuade Nahoum to declare publicly that Zionism had no separatist objections.[41] Furthermore, at the end of that same year Nahoum apparently sent a special emissary to Salonica to incite the Jews there against Zionism.[42] It was also rumored then that he had been working assiduously to persuade the C.U.P. to oppose Zionism.[43] In subsequent years, chiefly between 1911 and 1917, he repeatedly took a clear and often firm stand against Zionism and the dangers it allegedly harbored for the Otoman Empire.[44] While Nahoum assisted Ottoman Empire Jews who needed his help and even interceded on behalf of the Jews in Palestine,[45] his struggle against Zionism was uncompromising. Only in 1920 did he grudgingly acknowledge the significance of the Balfour Declaration, in a chapter that he wrote in English about Turkey's Jews.[46] By then, however, the Young Turks ruled no longer.

In summary: there were three Ottoman Jews who could have exerted considerable influence upon attitudes toward Zionism held by decision-makers within the Ottoman political leadership during the decade of Young Turk rule: Emanuel Carasso, the politician; Moïse Cohen, the ideologue; and Haim Nahoum, the Haham-Bashi. The first, as far as we know, displayed no involvement regarding Zionism; the second expressed reservations about it; and the third fought it. It is very likely that their positions explain, to some extent, the increased suspicion of Zionism by several Young Turk leaders and their adoption of a firmer stand against it as activities among Arab opponents of Zionism were stepped up. Moreover, anti-Zionist activities fit rather well into each of the three ideologies: Pan-Islam, Ottomanism, and Pan-Turkism.

NOTES

1. Of the numerous publications on the Committee of Union and Progress, two books should be mentioned in particular: Feroz Ahmad, *The Young Turks: The Committee of Union and Progress in Turkish Politics 1908–1914* (Oxford; Clarendon Press, 1969; Turkish translation, 1971); and G. Z. Aliyev, *Turtsiya v pyeriod pravliyeniya Mladoturok (1908–1918 gg.)*(Moscow: Nauka, 1972). Neither of them refers to Zionism. I have been unable to consult a recent book, in Russian, about the Young Turks, V. I. Shpil'kova's *Mladoturyetskaya ryevolutsiya 1908–1909 gg.* (Moscow, 1977).

2. David Farḥi, "Y'hude Saloniqi b'-Mahpekhat haTurkim haTzᶜirim," *Sefunot* (Jerusalem) 15 (1981): 137–38.

3. Bernard Lewis, *The Emergence of Modern Turkey* (London: Oxford University Press, 1961), pp. 208–9.

4. Elie Kedourie, "Young Turks, Freemasons and Jews," *Middle Eastern Studies* (London) 7, no. 1 (January 1971): 89–104.

5. Neville J. Mandel, *The Arabs and Zionism Before World War I* (Berkeley: University of California Press, 1976).

6. Isaiah Friedman, *The Question of Palestine, 1914–1918: British-Jewish Arab Relations* (London: Routledge & Kegan Paul, 1973), esp. pp. 54–55. See also Friedman's *Germany, Turkey and Zionism, 1897–1918* (Oxford: Clarendon Press, 1977).

7. C. R. Atilhan, *31 Mart faciasi*, (Aykurt Nesriyati, 1956). Idem, *Ittihad ve terakki'nin suikastleri* (Istanbul: Özaydin Matbaasi, 1971).

8. See about him in my *Radical Politics in Modern Turkey* (Leiden: Brill, 1974), pp. 185–86.

9. E.g., Hikmet Tanyu, *Tarih boyunca Yahudiler ve Türkler* (Istanbul: Yagmur Yayinevi, 1976) 1:615. Cemal Anadol, *Siyonizmin oyunlari* (Istanbul: Millî Kültür Yayinlari, 1978), pp. 88–93.

10. Several reports by Jacobsohn are mentioned in the above works by Mandel and Friedman. To these one may add A. Ruppin's report to the Central Office of the Zionist Organization, dated September 1917, kept in the Central Zionist Archives (CZA), Jerusalem, Z 3/66.

11. Cf. CZA files Z 2/427, Z 3/43–44, Z 3/796, Z 3/826–28. For additional details, see Mandel, chap. 5.

12. Cf. CZA, Z 3/48, Lichtheim's telegram, dated Pera, April 11, 1914.

13. Mandel, passim.

14. Rashid Khalidi, "Arab Nationalism in Syria: The Formative Years, 1908–1914," in W. W. Haddad and W. Ochsenwald, eds., *Nationalism in a Non-National State: The Dissolution of the Ottoman Empire* (Columbus: Ohio State University Press, 1977), pp. 207–37; Ann Lesch, "The Origins of Palestine Arab Nationalism," in ibid., pp. 265–90.

15. See Mandel, *Arabs and Zionism*, pp. 163ff.

16. I. Friedman, "The Austro-Hungarian Government and Zionism," *Jewish Social Studies* (London) 17, no. 4 (October, 1965): 241–42.

17. Ibid., pp. 236–39. CZA, 3/1486, Julius Becker's report to the Central Office of the Zionist Organization in Berlin, dated December 24, 1917. For Becker and his interview with Talat, see Friedman, *The Question of Palestine*, p. 296.

18. "Exploiting the Crescent: Pan-Islamic Aims," *The Times* (London), April 17, 1915.

19. See, e.g., Muçafir, *Notes sur la Jeune Turquie*, pp. 81–88. René Pinon, *L'Europe et la Jeune Turquie: Les aspects nouveaux de la question d'Orient* (Paris: Perrin, 1911), pp. 134–36.

20. See Muçafir, *Notes*, pp. 36–55. Pinon, *L'Europe et la Jeune Turquie*, pp. 122 ff.

21. Joseph Pomianowski, *Der Zusammenbruch des Ottomanischen Reiches: Erinnerungen an die Türkei aus der Zeit des Weltkrieges* (Zürich: Amalthea Verlag, 1928), pp. 28–30. Elie Kedouri, *England and the Middle East: The Destruction of the Ottoman Empire 1914–1921* (London: Bowes and Bowes, 1956), pp. 59 ff.

22. Cf. Ahmad, *The Young Turks*, pp. 154ff.

23. For Pan-Turkism see, e.g., Yusuf Akçura, *Türk yili* (Istanbul, 1928). Gotthard Jäschke, "Der Turanismus der Jungtürken: zur osmanische Aussenpolitik im Weltkriege," *Die Welt des Islams* (Berlin), 13 (1941):1–53. Hüseyin Namik Orkun, *Türkçülügün tarihi* (Istanbul: Berkalp Kitabevi, 1944). C. W. Hostler, *Turkism and the Soviets: The Turks of the World and Their Political Objectives* (London: Allen and Unwin, 1957). For a more recent study, see my "Some Considerations on Panturkist Ideology," *Atti della Settimana Internazionale di Studi Mediterranei Medioevali e Moderni*, Istituto di Studi Africani e Orientali, Università di Cagliari-(Milan: A. Giuffrè, 1980), pp. 113–22.

24. Edwin Pears, "Turkey, Islam and Turanianism," *The Contemporary Review* (London), 114 (Ocotber 1918):374 ff.

25. "Turkey, Russia and Islam," *The Round Table* (London), (December 1917), pp. 110 ff.

26. M. Larcher, *La Guerre turque dans la guerre mondiale* (Paris: Chiron & Berger-Levrault, 1925).

27. Hary Luke, *The Making of Modern Turkey: From Byzantium to Angora* (London: Macmillan, 1936), p. 157.

28. C. E. Dawn, *From Ottomanism to Arabism: Essays on the Origins of Arab Nationalism* (Urbana: University of Illinois Press, 1973), chaps. 5–6.

29. See my *The Hejaz Railway and the Muslim Pilgrimage: A Case of Ottoman Political Propaganda* (Detroit, Mich.: Wayne State University Press, 1971), introduction.

30. See the above studies by Ahmad and Mandel.

31. Cf., *inter alia*, Ali Canip Yöntem, *Ömer Seyfeddin'in hayati ve eseri* (1935). K. H. Karpat, "Ömer Seyfeddin and the Transformation of Turkish Thought," *Revue des Études Sud-Est Européennes* (Bucharest) 10 (1972):677–91. Yalçin Toker, *Ömer Seyfeddin* (1973).

32. *Yarinki Turan devleti* first appeared in Istanbul in 1914 and has been reprinted since, several times, in Latin characters.

33. Ahmad, *The Young Turks*, p. 173. Farhi, "Y'hude Saloniqi," pp. 138, 147.

34. Cf. Friedman, *The Question of Palestine*, pp. 296 ff.

35. Idem, *Germany, Turkey and Zionism*, pp. 142–44, 148.

36. I am now working on a monograph about him, dealing at greater length with his personality, writings, and cultural and political activities.

37. *Stenographisches Protokoll der Verhandlungen des IX. Zionisten-Kongresses in Hamburg* (Köln & Leipzig: Juedischer Verlag, 1910), pp. 267–78.

38. CZA, A 36/64.

39. Short biographical notices in *Jüdisches Lexicon* 5:382, and *Encyclopaedia Judaica* (English ed.), 12:791 (which provides additional bibliography).

40. Friedman, *Germany, Turkey and Zionism*, p. 141

41. CZA, Z 2/9, Jacobson's report, dated Istanbul, December 26, 1910.

42. "Brief aus Konstantinopel," CZA, Z 2/10.

43. Ibid.

44. Ibid., report by de De Fresco (editor of *El Tiempo*) to the Zionist Organization, dated Istanbul, January 5, 1910. Ibid., Z 3/66, Ruppin's report to the Central Office of the Zionist Organization, dated September 13, 1917.

45. Cf. Mandel, *Arabs and Zionism*, esp. pp. 71–72, 144ff., 165ff., 208. See also David Farhi, "Documents on the Attitude of the Ottoman Government Towards the Jewish Settlement in Palestine After the Revolution of the Young Turks, 1908–1909," in Moshe Maʿoz, ed., *Studies on Palestine During the Ottoman Period* (Jerusalem: The Magnes Press, 1975), esp. p. 202.

46. In a book edited by E. G. Mears, quoted by Friedman.

Herzl's *Diaries:* A Case of Selectivity in Dealing with Historic Documents

JOSEPH NEDAVA

1

The problem of selectivity has plagued chroniclers and historians through-out the ages. Different criteria have been applied in different ages, de-pending greatly on the extent of "openness" in a particular society and the state of "morality" of the day. Needless to say, there has never been, and it is very doubtful that there will ever be, an absolute standard for determin-ing which documents should properly serve as a legitimate basis for the historian's work and conclusions, and which should be suppressed. Is cen-sorship, obligatory or voluntary, ever justifiable?

It is, in any case, erroneous to suggest that human relationships today are much more frank, open, and tending to self-revelation than at any time in the past, and that, owing to the spread of psychology and psychoanalysis, almost all entrenched sex taboos have been discarded. "Bashfulness" was hardly a typical trait of antiquity. On the contrary, the naturalness, almost bordering on naiveté, of man in early civilizations is striking; in many fields of his activity it seemed to him that he had nothing to conceal. On this score the Bible's veracity, for instance, is unimpeachable. The extent of biblical authenticity is shown in an illuminating Midrashic story. A Roman lady, in a disputation with a Jewish sage, cast doubts on the reliability of the chroni-cler's assertion that Joseph, at the age of seventeen, at the height of his voluptuousness, could actually resist enticement by Potiphar's wife. Where-upon the Jewish sage made haste to dispel her misgivings by quoting simi-lar instances from Genesis: the story of Reuben and Bilha, Judah and Tamar. He might just as well have cited the disreputable affair of King David and Bathsheba, to prove that no attempt to embellish an unpleasant incident, or mythologize a historic figure, was made.

Coincidentally, a story similar to that of Joseph and Potiphar's wife is frankly related in the autobiography of the famous eighteenth-century rabbi Jacob Israel Emden.[1]

By way of contrast, Victorian rules of ethics, still prevalent during the first quarter of the twentieth century, seem to have dictated "discreetness"; selectivity was rigorously applied in the use of documents, and, of course, to that extent biographies and diaries were found lacking, and more often than not as even resorting to distortions. To cite but one instance: In 1906 Winston S. Churchill published a two-volume biography of his father, Lord Randolph Churchill. While conceding that the "biography is beautifully written and detailed," one critic points out that it is a political rather than personal biography. Another claims that "Churchill made no serious effort to discover the springs of his father's character. He passes over the tragedy of Lord Randolph's life in a way which would have led no one to suspect that he died insane," and that "Churchill distorted facts for his private purposes."[2] The reason for this is readily available: the biographer "had a profound distaste for revealing the skeletons in family cupboards."[3] In recent years modern biographers no longer felt constrained by "old-fashioned" morality; one still uses euphemism in stating that Lord Randolph "could no longer claim his conjugal rights,"[4] while another puts it bluntly that he was infected with syphilis.[5]

In recent years Zionist publications of biographies, letters, and diaries have been growing by leaps and bounds. By now a voluminous literature has appeared, and numerous archives are being made available to researchers without restraint. Problems of selectivity have become a natural concomitant to this activity.

At a joint meeting of the Board of Trustees of the Weizmann Archives and the Editorial Board of the Weizmann Letters, held at Rehovot on December 25, 1969, the chairman, Meyer W. Weisgal, recalled that an Implementation Committee, consisting of Sir Isaiah Berlin, Mr. Leonard Stein, Professor Jacob Talmon, the late Sir Louis Namier, the late Sir Charles Webster, and himself, had sat in London about fifteen years earlier and discussed exhaustively the question of selectivity or nonselectivity; it was unanimously decided to publish Dr. Weizmann's letters in full, omitting only those dealing with trivial matters.[6]

At the renewed discussion in 1969, views differed somewhat. Mr. Louis A. Pincus, chairman of the Jewish Agency Executive, saw no point in including all of Dr. Weizmann's personal letters to his wife, Vera, or to the person to whom he had been engaged or quasi-engaged. Whom could this benefit? He was not suggesting that these letters be burned, but that they be made readily available to any interested scholar in manuscript. He was not for idealizing Dr. Weizmann; he merely favored publishing only that material which helped to depict Dr. Weizmann as a leader in Jewish affairs. He was not for omitting even letters involving the denigration of a living person; but the letters under discussion strictly belong to the personal area: "in the nature of things nobody was a saint. But the lack of saintliness did not come out in his heroic stand as a Jewish leader. The lack of saintliness came out basically in one's personal life and, if that were so, then almost a priori we were doing something he thought was undesirable in injecting it into quite a different sphere of activity."[7]

Dr. Nahum Goldmann, too, was of the opinion that Dr. Weizmann's importance for Jewish history was not in his living person, but in his historical image. "A man's figure in history as a guide for future generations was a different figure than he cut to those who knew him. Nobody was a hero to his valet." He admired Dr. Weizmann precisely because he was no saint. "Who wanted to live with saints? One had been charmed by his weaknesses, his inconsistencies." He wanted to prevent any downgrading of Dr. Weizmann's image and thus did not believe it was necessary to present every aspect of his character shown in his letters. Any adherence to the principle of nonselectivity would present a distorted picture.[8]

Professor Talmon suggested sticking to nonselectivity. He quoted the great historian and thinker Lord Acton, who had said: "There's never been a historical figure whose reputation will stand the scrutiny of his personal correspondence." He maintained that the purpose should be to create a true image of Dr. Weizmann, not an uplifting, inspiring image. The historian is no propagandist. He said no line of demarcation could be drawn between the ideas, actions, and public conduct, of a man, and his inner strivings and subconscious. He held that all love letters should be published, because one is interested in the totality of a personality. One should provide the reader with every scrap of evidence to make Weizmann as understandable as possible.[9]

Professor Berlin also subscribed to the principle of nonselectivity. Because there was no real objectivity in history, any selection would reflect a particular view, and would thus preempt the views of future generations. Moreover, any letter than might appear comparatively personal or trivial to the present generation, might add something not only to the totality of Weizmann's personality, but also to a real understanding of the times and the political situation.

Professor Berlin also recalled that in his biography of Karl Marx he had published all kinds of letters that could be considered libelous and denigrating, "but the personality of Marx or the Socialist Movement of the 19th century would not have been what it was, if these letters were not known." The fact that Karl Marx had an illegitimate son was not known in his lifetime because Socialists wanted to protect his reputation. But this event definitely had a bearing on his political tactics during a highly neurotic and complicated period of his life.

Professor Berlin further argued that it was certainly not the business of the editors to worry about the moral effect of letters that might cause people to have a lower opinion of Weizmann than they had had hitherto.

Also, what is and what is not trivial cannot objectively be determined, and

Professor Berlin mentioned that "the letters of Lorenzo de' Medici were about to be issued and every jot and tittle he wrote would be published."[10]

At the suggestion of Mr. Weisgal, Dr. Weizmann eliminated from *Trial and Error* the chapter about his relations with David Ben-Gurion.[11] Yet all Dr. Weizmann's love letters have been published, including those which indicate marital infidelities.[12]

David Ben-Gurion rendered the biographer's task an easy one, for he was a keen collector of all his writings, including letters. He had an intuitive sense of his historic mission, a premonition if you wish, from his early youth. On October 14, 1906, about a month after his immigration to Palestine, he wrote a letter to his father requesting him to preserve all his letters: "It is important for me to know in the years to come what I thought of Eretz Israel at all times and periods."[13] As of the end of World War I, Ben-Gurion never wrote a letter without a copy for himself, and he never dictated a letter to a secretary. Imbued with a sense of destiny, he felt an urge to leave even his trivial jottings to posterity, and he did not even shrink from tampering with his own writings with a view to "correcting" the text.

Moshe Sharett, too, wrote extensive diaries, clearly having in mind their posthumous publication. His personal reactions to people and events are acerbic, having for the most part been recorded in a disgruntled mood. They reflect his bitter confrontation with Ben-Gurion. Some members of the Committee for the Publication of Sharett's Writings, appointed by Israel's Prime Minister Levi Eshkol following Sharett's death, expressed their view "that the diary distorts Moshe Sharett's image, does him injustice by 'laying him bare,' in times of weakness and bitterness,"[14] but Sharett's immediate family rejected this argument, refused to apply any rule of selectivity, and the diary was published in full.

Vladimir Jabotinsky's autobiography is "bare," for he refrained from describing other personalities with whom his career threw him into contact, and limited himself to dealing with "my life as a writer and activist, not my life as a man."[15] And Jabotinsky's biographer seems to have been in favor of selectivity.[16]

2

Recent years have seen a new approach toward the analysis of Dr. Theodor Herzl's personality, and an attempt has been made to establish a new setting for his life story. Psychoanalysis has come to dominate the field. Freudian theories have come to explain "everything," and therefore these theorists are never ready to accept a straight political biography at its face value. Writers-researchers are seeking to reach a deeper insight into the affairs of their "hero." Simplicity does not seem to be rewarding enough. "Data of the type available in Who's Who are inadequate to supply the investigator with enough material to answer several important questions," writes Harold D. Lasswell.[17] He claims that the usual autobiographies and biographies omit or distort much of the intimate history of the individual, and ascribes vital importance to "the sociological, psychological, and somatic influences" that contribute to the molding of the individual's personality. The modern biographer should lay particular stress on the illnesses and mental disorders of the individual, his night dreams, and day dreams, his ambitions, enthusiasms, grievances, and loyalties.[18]

Peter Loewenberg has put Herzl's life to a painstaking scrutiny in the same vein.[19] He points to the unconscious imperative in all human thoughts and actions, emphasizing in particular "the patient's neurotic system." "A psychoanalytic history gives due place to the sexuality, passions, and emotional states of the inner world of its subjects."[20]

Whatever purely scientific aim Loewenberg might have had, his "daring" exposition of the Zionist leader's "inner life" had a negative effect on the dispassionately objective reader interested in the character of the Jewish national movement. To be considered an original researcher meant plunging into an abyss of human filth in order to come up with rewarding results. Exaggerating ostensibly innocent deeds and expressions became unavoidable. But artificially complicating the patient's mental make-up does not necessarily make him more decipherable and fathomable to an outsider.

To Loewenberg's mind Herzl presents "an excellent case of the charismatic personality, whose psychopolitical fantasies influenced history."[21] He traces in him the painful regression to narcissism, suggesting that "Herzl's Zionist calling was determined by a personal need to be a messiah— saviour—political leader."[22]

He proceeds to analyze Herzl's sexuality, defining his sensual feelings as "aroused by a 'lower' type of sexual object, the woman of the street."[23] He then digs up from the Central Zionist Archives in Jerusalem a letter Herzl wrote at the age of twenty to his intimate friend Heinrich Kana, to the effect that he had contracted venereal disease (possibly gonorrhea) following his relations with a seventeen-year-old seamstress. Loewenberg builds his entire psychological edifice upon this youthful incident.

Besides narcissism, "oedipal struggle with his father," "latent homosexuality," and "sexual ambivalences," Loewenberg discovers megalomania in Herzl, an overweening self-esteem.[24]

The results of Loewenberg's research and suppositions were food for such a dire enemy of Zionism as Desmond Stewart. He made good use of Loewenberg's founts of "scientific" assertions to describe the founder of modern Zionism as a "self-doubting pessimist with underworld desires."[25] Stewart then embarks on an attempt to destroy the worship of Herzl as a saint. He naturally quotes in full Herzl's "self-incriminating" letter to Kana in his effort to explode "the pious myths in which idolaters have attempted to bury Herzl."[26]

3

All relevant material bearing on Herzl's life and activity, literary and political, is now available to the scholar. All the files, documents, letters, diaries, correspondence, personal or otherwise, gathered over the years and stored in the Jerusalem Central Zionist Archives, are now open to inspection without any restriction. Some material has unfortunately been lost. It is an open secret by now that Herzl's marriage was a wreck almost from the very beginning. The question of divorce came up time and again, but failed to materialize on account of the children. There were also periods of separation, and there was no reconciliation till his death. In the thousands of pages of his diary there is not a single direct reference to his wife. At face value his will treats his wife most harshly; he did not consider her stable enough to entrust their children to her care. However, the real extent of their mutual antagonism will never be known.

As far back as 1956 the Central Zionist Archives would not permit the free use of all available Herzl material; Dr. A. Bein, for instance, conditioned his permission to me to use "the Herzl family material" on first inspecting my then forthcoming book *Negohot min He-ᶜAvar* (Hebrew, 1961). Later, however, the curators relented on the strictness of the rules. By a special decision of Mr. Louis Pincus, chairman of the Jewish Agency Executive, the Herzl Archives, which were to have been opened in 1987, were actually opened in 1964. There are in the Central Zionist Archives 165 envelopes addressed to Herzl's wife in his handwriting, but the letters themselves are missing. Dr. Bein, the biographer and former director of the Archives, had seen the letters in the possession of Mr. Nulo Nussenblatt in Vienna, but was not permitted to copy them. They were later returned to Herzl's youngest daughter, Trude, who may have taken them with her during her deportation to Theresienstadt, and there lost them.

An abridged and censored version of Herzl's diaries (under the editorship of Leon Kellner) was first issued in 1922, and only in 1960 was it published in full (in an English translation in New York, under the editorship of Professor Raphael Patai, and in Hebrew in Jerusalem).

Herzl wrote his diaries with a view to publication. In his "My Literary Testament," he called for their immediate publication; he was convinced that after his death their value would increase, and he hoped that thanks to the royalties his wife's dowry, which he had almost recklessly spent on the Zionist cause, would be fully replenished, and his children's financial well-being assured.

Early preparations for publishing the diaries were already undertaken in 1919. A preliminary committee, proposed to handle the matter, was to consist of Dr. Max Nordau, Leon Kellner, Felix Salten, Arthur Schnitzler, Richard Beer-Hofmann, Raoul Auernheimer, Joseph Cowen, Dr. Edouard Leszynski, Moritz Reichenfeld, and Johann Kremenezky. It was further proposed that Hans Herzl should translate the diaries into English (with the cooperation of Israel Zangwill), and Dr. Jacob Klatzkin translate them into Hebrew and Yiddish.[27]

Yet, when the practical question of their publication came up, various difficulties had to be overcome. Naturally, after the publication of an abridged edition, rumors were soon circulated that abounded with sinister allusions and innuendoes. One, for instance, ascribed, totally erroneously, the censorship to deliberate excision of Herzl's anti-religious sentiments and expressions.[28]

In fact, no one, not even Herzl's sensitive son, Hans, who had undertaken the translation of the diaries into English, opposed the deletion of allusions that might have proved embarrassing to individuals or officials still alive in 1922. Thus it was suggested that certain offensive references to Leopold Greenberg, editor of the *Jewish Chronicle* in years to come, be excised.[29]

An editorial board was named, including Leon Kellner, Martin Buber, Hans Herzl, and Sigmund Kaznelson (proprietor of the Jüdischer Verlag, Berlin, which undertook to publish the diaries).[30] Nevertheless, soon after the publication of the first volume, differences of opinion regarding the deletions arose, and its was proposed to set up a small committee to review the omissions.[31] On the occasion of the meeting of the Actions Committee (Zionist General Council) in Prague in 1921, a consultation was held among several Zionist leading members, including Joseph Cowen (of Herzl's friends) and Dr. Victor Jacobson, and it was decided to see to it that no damage was caused to the Organization through the publication of the diaries. The Actions Committee itself went on record against the publication of the diaries in full, and insisted on deleting all damning passages.

Matters, however, were not easily straightened out. Dr. Jacobson was interested only in the business aspect of the project. Mr. Cowen and Dr. Weizmann were of the opinion that no harm would be caused by the publication of the diaries in full. On the other hand, Dr. Max Nordau, whose opinion carried much weight although he no longer occupied any official position in the Zionist Organization, was very reserved about publishing an uncensored edition of the diaries.[32]

4

Several hundred passages or phrases, not amounting to more than three percent, were deleted from the original German manuscript. Several distinct criteria were applied in the suppression of embarrassing views and expressions, most of which are not of consequence, but, on the contrary, tend to more clearly delineate Herzl's character and indicate natural changes in his mood. His candor and self-revelation are enticing, and add a rare quality to his diaries. He writes without constraint, being absolutely unaware and totally forgetful of the would-be publisher who, deep in the background, looks over his shoulder on what is being recorded. Herzl never poses, never attempts an affected stance, and never polishes his phrases with the view of improving his presentation. He is even unabashed in revealing that he shed tears while writing various entries. He seemed to have been ready to confide to his unknown future reader whatever he was ready to confide to himself.

Despite the attempt to draw a clear line of demarcation between the passable and the censorable, in some places the editor is inconsistent, as will be shown presently.

The following are some of the rules applied to deletions.

(a) Passages where the reader can encounter a Herzl imbued with haughtiness and feelings of grandeur, royal ambitions for his son, and self-adulation:

June 7, 1895: "If the Rothschilds join with us, the first *Doge* is to be a Rothschild. I will not and never shall be a *Doge*, for I wish to secure the state beyond the term of my own life."[33]

He further notes on June 9: "When I thought that someday I might crown Hans as *Doge* and address him in the Temple in front of the country's great men as 'Your Highness! My beloved son!' I had tears in my eyes."[34]

"In the Tuileries, before Gambetta's statue," Herzl writes "I hope the Jews will put up a more artistic one of me."[35]

Elsewhere the editor deleted this remark: "I shall leave behind a spiritual legacy. To whom? To all men," but left untouched the blatant self-praise: "I believe I shall be named among the greatest benefactors of mankind. Or is this belief already megalomania?"[36]

(b) Another set of passages was omitted from the desire to preserve Herzl's moral integrity. It was not deemed appropriate for a Zionist leader to conspire against a foreign government in South America that had granted the Jews asylum; nor should one aim at "exploiting the enmities of the republics and preserving their friendship through presents, bribes, loans, etc."[37] Nor was it considered respectable for a Zionist leader to entertain dreams of conducting duels with the Austrian anti-Semites Schönerer or Lueger in order to stage a public demonstration, or of appearing in court "making a powerful, Lassalle-like speech which would have shaken and moved the jury and inspired respect from the court, leading to my acquittal."[38]

Nor was it in good taste for a Zionist leader, in describing the hectic way he was jotting down the notes for his *Jewish State* to admit: "My God, after this confession Lombroso might consider me mad. And my friend Nordau will conceal from me the apprehension I cause him."[39]

(c) A few passages were deleted to protect Herzl's wife from an accusation, on the part of an inquisitive outsider, not of a Xantippe-like nature (such aspersions, as noted above, had been avoided by the reticent Herzl himself from the very beginning), but of a nagging materialism. This concerns a suggestion made to Herzl by his intimate friend Alexander Marmorek, the bacteriologist, to take one-tenth of the amount that the Jewish financier Benno Reitlinger was to have given for the TB serum. Herzl immediately declined; but wrote: "Now my wife reproaches me with it; perhaps my children, too, whom I have also deprived of so much earning power, would some day reproach me if Alex's remedy yields the participants a big profit."[40]

A further uncomplimentary remark was omitted; following his experience of another attack of brain anemia (in 1902), he was sure that his parents, when they found out, would be upset, and "it wouldn't make my wife any more loving either."[41]

A striking but inexplicable deletion involved his statement that, with all the evacuated European Jews who would emigrate to Palestine, "the ship on which my parents, wife, and children make the crossing will also bring over all our relations, near and distant."[42]

This surely indicates the editor's own ambivalence about the real aim of Zionism; he, too, is still haunted by the "dual loyalty" obsession. This accounts for another deletion with respect to German Jewry. Herzl wrote: "Let the German Kaiser say to me: I shall be grateful to you if you lead these unassimilable people out."[43]

The editor was also determined to conceal the all-too apparent manifestations of anti-Semitism in Germany: "Paul Lindau [a German journalist] visited me at the office and, among other things, told me the following. The Duke of Meiningen had shown him a map of Berlin on which Jewish-owned land was marked in red, Christian-owned land in blue, and doubtful property in white. The entire Tiergarten district, said Lindau, 'was as though dipped in blood.' Curiously enough, a similar propaganda map is to be produced by the People's Party in Hungary, as I heard recently."[44]

(d) Some other inexplicable suppressions apparently aim at protecting the leader against what the editor considered "over-sentimentality," such as the following line, which Herzl wrote after his father's death: "During these 29 hours I have been licking my paws like a runover dog."[45]

(e) The editor is also on guard to protect Herzl from "anti-Semitic" expressions, such as: "Finally, a certain Herman Landau, an ugly *Mauschel* [a term for "Jew" with derogatory connotations] came forward. . . ."[46] Elsewhere the remark "The Jews are difficult material" is omitted, as well as the description of "this Dirsztay [Baron Ladislaus, Hungarian Jewish merchant] seems to be a Jew as dirty as he is rich, of the *apikorsim* [free-thinking] kind."[47]

(f) Most deleted passages concern private individuals and public officials still alive when the first German edition was published in 1922. Some allusions can be considered personal slights, although, seemingly, none, or at most very few, could have given cause for civil action in the courts. Others concern financial transactions involving payments, mostly from Herzl's own pocket, to agents serving the cause.

Herzl's remarks allude to some fifty public figures referred to in over a hundred distinct passages. A few omissions concerning the most conspicuous personalities will serve as representative samples.

It is appropriate to start with the Rothschilds, the most typical of all Jewish potentates, who in Herzl's time not only still exerted tremendous influence on Jewish life and were looked up to by the Jewish masses everywhere as an awe-inspiring authority, but were also held in high esteem by the powers that be in Europe and elsewhere. Herzl's relations with the Rothschilds did not work out well; he failed to establish rapport with them. He denounced them for being blind to realities: "The Rothschilds have no idea of how endangered their property is. They live in a phony circle of courtiers, servants, employees, paupers, and aristocratic spongers."[48]

Out of anger Herzl expressed himself sharply against them: "Sooner or later I shall have to start a campaign against the Rothschilds. *Titre tout indiqué* [the definitely indicated title]: 'The House of Rothschild'—objective presentation of the world menace that this octopus constitutes."[49] He fears their conspiracy: "If Edmund Rothschild is in Constantinople, I suspect some typically Rothschildian villainy."[50] The English Rothschild fares even worse than the French. He considers the chat of His Lordship as a bag of nonsense: "It would be dancing on a tight-rope if I were to record all the silly stuff that he rattled off with great assurance," and refers to both the Lord and his brother Leopold as a "pack of idiots."[51]

Most of the suppressed passages deal with the four most conspicuous of Herzl's agents or aides: The British protestant minister, the Rev. William H. Hechler; the Austrian political agent Philip Michael Newlinski; the English journalist Sidney Whitman; and the Hungarian ex-Jewish Orientalist Arminius Vámbéry.

Here, too, the editor has proved his inconsistency in applying the rules of deletion. It seems that to his mind moral turpitude is less damning than a touch of material corruption, for otherwise how can he account for leaving such a passage in the diaries: "From the woman who gives me English lessons I had heard that Hechler was a hypocrite [Herzl makes a pun here; the German word for hypocrite is *Heuchler*]. But I take him for a naive visionary with a collector's quirks."[52] Then follows the expurgated passage:

if Hechler would declare himself ready to go to Berlin and win the German Kaiser over to the Zionist cause "would I be willing to give him the travel expenses? Of course I promised them to him at once. They will come to a few hundred guilders, certainly a considerable sacrifice in my circumstances. . . . He is an improbable figure when looked at through the quizzical eyes of a Viennese Jewish journalist. But . . . I am sending him to Berlin with the mental reservation that I am not his dupe if he merely wants to take a trip at my expense."[53] As of then Hechler was a perennial burden on Herzl's finances: "Hechler groaned softly but audibly about the discomfort of his third-class trip. I shall wire him 25 guilders from Bucks, with which he can convert his ticket into second class."[54] In 1898 "Hechler gets his traveling expenses to Palestine—1000 guilders, to start with."[55] But the reader of the abridged diaries gets no notion of these "financial transactions" in order not to mar the Reverend's "pure" idealism.

Newlinski's finances were much more extensive and became a serious drain on Herzl's resources; he was obliged to fall back on the official Zionist funds. Newlinski's trips between Constantinople, Rome, and Vienna were seemingly endless, each trip involving thousands of guilders. "Either he does not have the connections in Rome which he pretended to have, or he quite simply wants to pocket the two thousand guilders which I had paid out to him."[56]

On engaging Newlinski to the service of Zionism, Herzl did not know what he was letting himself in for; it was a kind of nightmare that lay heavy on his mind for quite a long time. And it seemed that with the sudden death of the agent, who had contributed nothing to paving Herzl's way to the sultan, the Zionist leader's responsibilities did not come to an end, what with the transportation of the dead agent back to Vienna ("He sold us his corpse, as it were"[57]), his funeral, and Herzl's having placed himself under perpetual obligation to his survivors. "Actually," writes Herzl, "the only dupe in this sad affair is myself, who failed to see through this scheme." Yet even in distress Herzl is chivalrous enough to pay the unrequited player on the diplomatic stage his due: "Newlinski himself showed courage and a father's tenderness. In my eyes, after his death, he looms head and shoulders above the whole riff-raff; to get mixed up with this rotten bunch was the tragic blunder of his life."[58]

All this exquisite characterization of a romantic figure in a shadowy behind-the-scenes world, even though he was a scoundrel—an artistic description that helps convey a real insight into the delicate soul of the writer himself—is withheld from the reader because of the old-fashioned "sensitivity" of the editor.

On the other hand, the suppression of the inner life of Sidney Whitman seems to be no loss to anyone. He received but little money, and served as no more than a appendage-entrepreneur in a will-o'-the-wisp enterprise.

Vámbéry's case is much more interesting. He was a challenging personal-

ity, a unique adventurer. Herzl had to exert all his wisdom, tact, and in-
genuity to tame Vámbéry's ferocious nature and harness his service to the
Zionist cause. Had the circumstances been different, Vámbéry, of all agents
and sympathetic statesmen, visionaries, Jew-and-Zion-lovers and well-
wishers, could, indeed, have brought Herzl's dream of obtaining Palestine
from the sultan nearer to materialization. Behind the façade of double
dealings and polar aspirations, there seems to have developed between the
two personalities an emphatic sentiment bordering on mutual fondness.
The idealist and the practical adventurer found common ground. Yet, the
reader of the abridged diaries is able to see Vámbéry only as a fragmented
image. He senses the gap; some central links are missing in order to construct the wholeness of the strange, complicated human being. The reader
is left in the dark, being unable to guess the underlying vital factor in the
whole partnership of the two: Vámbéry's zeal for money.

"Vámbéry wrote yesterday that if it turned out to be a deal, he wanted a
commission of £5000 out of the 700,000. To this I answered V. only briefly
that he was very sensible and that I had never had anything else in mind
but to let him have an adequate share."[59]

In view of the expanding prospects, Herzl learned to make use of
"Oriental" flattery; the mood was somewhat reminiscent of the
Sheherezade style: "From the very first you have behaved so cordially and
correctly toward me. . . . I regard you and your connections as a historic
opportunity of the Jewish people. Your whole fine, active, and courageous
life reaches full stature at this peak. . . . Your true mission is to help your
old people with its self-redemption."[60]

But meanwhile the "concrete" matters were all-determining: "V. is leaving next week. As traveling expenses he asked for 600 guilders, but I
offered him a thousand guilders—more correctly, 2000 francs which he
accepted, remarking: 'I shall return to you any part I don't use.' I am also
prepared for his returning without any result—but this expenditure must
be risked. Now the treasury of the A.C. [Actions Committee] is so empty
that we have to raise these 2000 francs in the form of a forced loan from
the Viennese members of the A.C. . . ."[61]

Vámbéry could, of course, lose his temper, and he was most aggravated
when financial affairs were not going his way. He refused to share payments with other co-workers: "He screamed, cursing and swearing, that I
was being cheated; he had done everything, and those people didn't deserve a thing. . . . He was furious. For three weeks he had toiled and slaved,
and now others were to reap the fruits."[62]

Vámbéry finally agreed to accept a third of the total sum. He felt it was
an ongoing business: "He said," records Herzl, 'You won't get the Charter
now. That will take a few years and will cost up to a hundred thousand
guilders.' 'Done!' I replied: 'It's all right if it costs even more.' "[63] Indeed,
Herzl was ready to pay 300 thousand for it, "and in addition to my grati-

tude you will have the everlasting gratitude of *Kol Israel* [the entire Jewish people]."[64]

A considerable number of other derogatory remarks and descriptions were excised by the editor. Here are a few samples:

Dr. Nathan Birnbaum, originator of the term *Zionism* who at first was an adherent of Herzl but later turned against him, aroused in Herzl a deeply felt animosity and bitter resentment: "Birnbaum is unmistakably jealous of me. What the baser sort of Jews express in vulgar or sneering language, namely, that I am out for personal gain, is what I catch in the intimations of this cultured, refined person. . . . I regard Birnbaum as envious, vain, and dogmatic."[65] He further accuses him of writing brazen *shnorring* letters, requesting to be elected to a post carrying with it a stipend, and inciting behind his [Herzl's] back.[66]

Another target of Herzl's bitter attack was the first socialist Zionist, Saul Rafael Landau, in whom Herzl scented "disloyalty and ingratitude."[67] He counted him among the "Galician bastards" who successfully practiced "dirty tricks."[68]

The editor deleted a frank entry of Herzl, which through a somewhat belabored praise of Nordau's stature and power as an orator, reflected, contrariwise, his subdued jealousy of his closest friend: "It was my constant concern during those three days to make Nordau forget that he was playing second fiddle at the Congress, something from which his self-esteem visibly suffered. On every occasion I emphasized that I was in the chair purely for technical reasons . . . fortunately, too, his speech was more successful than my purely political one, and I went about everywhere acclaiming his address as the best at the Congress."[69]

Herzl unhesitatingly bandied about such epithets as "bastard"[70] (to denigrate the Jewish communal leader Willy Bambus), "rascal" (Baron Rothschild's administrator of Palestinian colonies, Elie Scheid),[71] "scoundrels *à la* Herman Landau";[72] "charlatan and phrase-maker without distinction, a faithless radical with unctuous manners, a freethinker's popishness"—the French statesman, Leon Bourgeois;[73] "[Dutch-Jewish banker Jacobus H.] Kann has resigned and wants to run the Bank down publicly. They are all making in their pants, especially [David] Wolffsohn";[74] "[French-Jewish publicist and socialist] Bernard Lazare has published a mean, malicious article against me."[75] Colonel Albert Goldsmid, son of a converted Jew, who returned to Judaism and became a leader of the British *Hovevei Zion,* also lost in Herzl's diaries some of his romantic splendor; it transpired that his (Goldsmid's) enthusiasm for Zion was also tainted with uninspiring materialism. "Colonel Goldsmid was here. He wants to be in on the [El Arish] expedition. I accepted him. He will get £100 for his trip, plus expenses."[76] Later Col. Goldsmid asked "for another £150 'to send to my wife' as well as a letter of credit for expenses."[77]

The editor was careful to conceal Herzl's disappointment with the English Zionist Leopold J. Greenberg, who served as Herzl's negotiator in both England and Egypt from 1902 to 1903. Again matters of money were involved: "Greenberg asked for 'no payment,' but a £500 loan for his firm without a repayment limit. I granted everything. Greenberg is the most expensive man, but also the most important one, for he is to secure the Charter. So far he has done very excellent work and is worth any amount of money."[78]

He then suspected Greenberg's loyalty; he "didn't behave like an authorized agent at all, but like the boss and on his own authority."[79] Because of this Herzl had to make haste and go to Cairo, and then he made up his mind: "I certainly don't want to have him in Cairo now, and if it can at all be avoided, I shall see to it that he doesn't go there by himself either."[80] And the denouement is even harsher: "When I arrived Wolffsohn told me he had found out that Greenberg had taken about £1000 from the Colonial Trust in uncovered checks. This explains everything. . . . The wrong-doing of this man is counterbalanced only by his splendid achievements. . . . When the project is a success, he will be paid off and removed."[81]

Finally, Herzl has in stock a very uncomplimentary remark about Lord Cromer, British agent in Egypt; he "is the most disagreeable Englishman I have ever faced."[82]

The last entry in the diaries is of May 16, 1904. Before publication of the complete work it was rumored that numerous acid remarks about Dr. Weizmann, Menachem Ussishkin, and other Russian Zionist leaders had been suppressed. However, these rumors have proved to be groundless, and nothing sensational was uncovered.

In sum: no rule of selectivity was to have been applied in the first place. The rigors of censorship were unjustifiable even in those post-World War I moralistic years. No damage would have been done either to Herzl or to the Zionist cause had these passages been included. On the contrary, the deleted passages tend to illuminate Herzl's humanity, disarming candor, and the sterling qualities of an idealistic leader.

NOTES

1. David Kahane, *Megilat Sefer* (Hebrew), rev. ed. (New York, 5715 [1956], pp. 82–83.
2. Robert Payne, *The Great Man* (New York, 1974), pp. 112–13.
3. Maurice Ashley, *Churchill as Historian* (New York, 1968), p. 67.
4. Henry Pelling, *Winston Churchill* (New York, 1974), p. 28.
5. Ralph G. Martin, *Lady Randolph Churchill* (London, 1969), pp. 51–52.
6. *The Weizmann Letters and Papers*, Proceedings etc. (Yad Chaim Weizmann, 1969), p. 7.
7. Ibid., pp. 9–10.
8. Ibid., pp. 11–13.
9. Ibid., pp. 14–16.
10. Ibid., pp. 16–18.
11. Meyer Weisgal, . . . *So Far* (London and Jerusalem, 1971), p. 249

12. See, for instance letter to *Habimah* actress, Hanna Rovina, New York, entry of February 23, 1927, in *The Letters and Papers of Chaim Weizmann* (Jerusalem, 1978), 13:220–21.

13. See introduction to *Igrot David Ben-Gurion* (Hebrew), (Tel-Aviv, 1971, 1978), pp. 8–10.

14. Moshe Sharett, *Yoman Ishi* (Hebrew), (Tel Aviv, 1978), pp. 8–10.

15. *Ketavim, Sippur Yamai* (Hebrew), (Jerusalem, 5707–1947), p. 11

16. Joseph B. Schechtman refrains from quoting from Jabotinsky's farewell letter to his (Jabotinsky's) wife prior to his departure for the front in 1918. "It is too deeply intimate a human document to be made public." *Rebel and Statesman* (New York 1956), 1:270–71.

17. "The Study of the Ill as a Method of Research into Political Personalities," *The American Political Science Review* 23 (1929):996.

18. Ibid., pp. 997–98.

19. "Theodor Herzl: A Psychoanalytic Study in Charismatic Political Leadership," in *The Psychoanalytic Interpretation of History*, ed. Benjamin B. Wolman (New York and London, 1971), pp. 150–191. Arthur Stern meted out similar treatment to Herzl's descendants in his "The Genetic Tragedy of the Family of Theodor Herzl, "in *Israel Annals of Psychiatry and Related Disciplines* 3, no. 1 (April 1965):99–116.

20. "Psychohistorical Perspectives on Modern German History", *Journal of Modern History* 47 no. 2 (June 1975):232.

21. "Theodor Herzl: A Psychoanalytic Study," p. 150.

22. Ibid., pp. 150–51.

23. Ibid., p. 152.

24. Ibid., p. 163.

25. *Theodor Herzl* (New York, 1974), p. 70.

26. Ibid., p. 71.

27. CZA (Central Zionist Archives), HN xiii 3, HE viii 4, exchange of letters concerning the publication of Herzl's diaries, Johann Kremenezky Files.

28. Eri Jabotinsky, *My Father Ze'ev Jabotinsky* (Jerusalem, T. A. Haifa, 1980), p. 95.

29. CZA, HN xiii 3.

30. *The Diaries of Theodor Herzl*, ed. and trans. Marvin Lowenthal (New York 1956), p. v.

31. Kremenezky's letter to Dr. E. Leszynski, October 23, 1922, CZA, Hn xiii 3.

32. Nordau held this view consistently all along. As far back as April 25, 1905, answering David Wolffsohn's question as to the advisability of publishing Herzl's diaries, Nordau reluctantly agreed to an expurgated edition; then, a few months later, he expressed even greater skepticism: "I am sure that their publication would destroy Herzl's memory. Even about their partial publication I have grave doubts." Shalom Schwartz, *Max Nordau Be-Igrotav* (Hebrew), (Jerusalem, 1944), pp. 124–25.

33. *The Complete Diaries of Theodor Herzl*, ed. Raphael Patai, trans. Harry Zohn (New York, London, 1960, 1:39. All the references below are to these volumes. Herzl was an admirer of the Republican Constitution of Venice; *Doge* is the title of its elected head.

34. 1:57.

35. 1:40.

36. 1:104.

37. 1:70.

38. 1:83.

39. 1:93.

40. 3:1080.

41. 3:1206.

42. 1:68.

43. 1:42.

44. 2:530.

45. 4:1286.

46. 2:679.

47. 3:1141.

48. 1:44.

49. 2:592.

50. 3:876.

51. 4:1291, 1293.

52. 1:312.

53. 1:312–13.
54. 2:577.
55. 2:665.
56. 2:768.
57. 2:823.
58. 2:823–24.
59. 3:1009.
60. 3:1011.
61. 3:1079.
62. 3:1102.
63. 3:1103.
64. 3:1104, 1144.
65. 1:307–8.
66. 2:584–85, 623.
67. 2:578.
68. 2:653.
69. 2:582–83.
70. 2:585.
71. Ibid.
72. 2:685.
73. 3:843.
74. 3:948–49.
75. 3:1201.
76. 4:1389.
77. 4:1457.
78. 4:1397.
79. 4:1428.
80. 4:1444.
81. 4:1471.
82. 4:1446.

Israel: A View from Lebanon

MEIR BEN-HORIN

A remarkable essay, entitled "The Near East: The Search for Truth" by Charles Malik, appeared almost thirty years ago in *Foreign Affairs*.[1] A decade later Sylvia G. Haim included it in her *Arab Nationalism* (1962), published by the University of California Press.

Today the essay is of both historical and topical interest. It sheds light on conditions, whether political-historical or psychological-intellectual, that have buffeted the Jewish State since its creation and, in fact, since the time of the BILU newcomers in 1882[2] and the Balfour Declaration of November 1917.

Against its background, the psychological breakthrough intended and to some extent achieved by President Anwar el-Sadat of Egypt when he addressed the Knesset in Jerusalem on November 20, 1977, stands out in higher relief. By the same token, Arab adamant persistence in demanding Israeli self-contraction in favor of further enlargement—despite the Begin-Sadat peace agreement of 1978—of the number of Arab states, may well derive substantial and vigorous support from this essay, regardless of whether or not its author has changed his position in recent years.

Charles Habib Malik, distinguished professor of philosophy at the American University of Beirut, has served as foreign minister in the government of Camile Chamoun, at whose request President Eisenhower ordered U.S. Marines to Lebanon in 1958. Among the many positions of distinction that Malik (Ph.D., Harvard, 1937) has held are those of chairman, U.N. Human Rights Commission (1951–52), president of the World Council of Christian Education (1967–71), and president of the Thirteenth Session of the U.N. General Assembly (1958–59). A native of Bitirram, Al-Koura, Lebanon (1906), he now lives on a high hill overlooking his country's capital. In his *Zionism at the UN* (1976), Eliahu Elath, former ambassador of Israel to the U.S. and to Britain, and Hebrew University president, called Malik an "Arab friend" who "always impresses me with his

223

tolerant opinions on religion and society. He is a gallant opponent, and his attitude to those with whom he has ideological differences is one of moderation and respect." However, it is not Malik but Chamoun whom James M. Markham named in his "The War That Won't Go Away," *New York Times Magazine* of October 9, 1977, as "the most active proponent of the Israeli alliance," an action that, to Markham, was "one of the boldest overtures in the recent history of the Middle East."

The essay here being reconsidered reflects a rather different frame of mind, one compounded of psychological, philosophical, and religious elements.

By his own testimony, Malik was guided by two lights: the light of truth and the light of love. Perhaps the second light's omission from the essay's title was inadvertent. But those who hold the two interdependent in human affairs will wonder, right at the outset, whether dimming one light does not at the same time dim the other. Malik himself confesses that if there is straying from the right path, "it can only be because we have not loved enough to observe a fairer measure of the truth."

Nonetheless, one approaches this essay with high hopes. No tool of greater reliability is available to man's quest for certainty than the method of intelligence, which aims at warranted assertibility or truth,[3] combined with the method of love, which aims at the application of truth to human fulfillment. Training one's searchlight of truth-love on the Arab and Jewish Near East should, hopefully, yield results signifying more than mere tactical flexibility and temporary relaxation of on-the-brink animosity. It should unlock as well unprecedented generosity of spirit and genuine accommodation for the common good.

But read from the perspective of succeeding decades, the essay turns, as it were, the searchlight on the author himself and makes visible the learned writer's perception of truth and love as it pertains to the Near East. The latter-day reader will reach the conclusion that far from illuminating the area with the light of truth-love, the philosopher-statesman's study rather discloses the distortion that the "Near East" produces in the very meaning of truth and love.

I

Malik opens his discussion with a clarification of the words *Near East:*

> If a circle is drawn on the map with Beirut or Damascus or Jerusalem at its center and with a radius of about nine hundred miles, this circle will pretty nearly comprise the whole of the Near East. It will include the following ten cities: Athens, Istanbul, Antioch, Beirut, Damascus, Baghdad, Jerusalem, Alexandria, Cairo and Mecca. Western civilization is an offshoot, in diverse modes of relevance, of what was revealed, ap-

prehended, loved, suffered and enacted in these ten cities or in their hinterland. (P. 189)

Twenty states and principalities constitute the "Near East"—from Iraq to the Sudan and from Oman to Syria and Lebanon. All are Arab entities except Greece, Turkey, and Israel. Iran, a non-Arab state, does not properly fall within the Near East: it is "distinctly a border-line case," because it "presents a transition from the Near East to the Asiatic realm beyond" (p. 190).

It is worth noting that in Malik's view Israel is not the only "foreign" state in the Near East. A Zionist may even derive satisfaction from the company of states in which he places Israel; surely no doubt assails any sane person's mind about the legitimacy of Greece and Turkey *qua* states. Although it is a portion of the much larger "Arab World," which includes the countries clear across North Africa all the way to the North Atlantic Ocean, this "world" is not what in the greater German "world" was called "one *Reich,* one *Volk,* one *Führer.*"

Yet one must beware of reading too much into a mere recording of what any honest political map shows. If there is a place for political pluralism in Malik's view, it can only be a pluralism with "restricted circulation." A peculiar restraint is imposed upon his conception of truth and love when Jews and their State come into focus: they stand outside the parameter of both *veritas* and *caritas.*

This becomes increasingly clear as Malik proceeds. But even the opening paragraphs of the essay betray the existence of this "fence" around *ḥesed weemet.* The first paragraphs declare Malik's conviction about—to coin a phrase—the geo-civilization role of the area: "By the Near East I mean the cradle of Western civilization. Take the fundamental generic components of that civilization and trace them back across the ages to their lands of origin, and there you have the Near East" (p. 189). Spiritual Near Easterners ourselves to an extent, we may join Malik in his obvious pride. However, on second reading his formulation does not appear to extend to us an invitation to rejoice with him. He does not, of course, claim that this civilization was born and raised in Mecca or in Baghdad, Cairo, or Antioch. In fact, among the ten cities (or their hinterland) wherein "was revealed, apprehended, loved, suffered and enacted" that of which "Western civilization is an offshoot," he lists Jerusalem. Willy-nilly, the attentive ear distinguishes among the sounds of this city's name overtones of Jewish speech, echoes of Jewish religious, moral, civilizational critique and creativity. Yet we need to remark the absence of explicit acknowledgment, not to say recognition and appreciation. Also, is it quite right to suggest—by means of the ten-cities list—that Jerusalem holds no more than one tenth of the total "cradle"-space? No more than Istanbul, Antioch, Beirut, Damascus, Baghdad? It is evident that in these passages Malik is psychologically, if not philosophically, unprepared to hold the canopy of truth and love over Jewish Jerusalem. Only with difficulty, if at all, could he affirm a passage such as Cyrus H. Gordon's in *Ugarit and Minoan Crete* on Lower Egypt:

> The Delta . . . was rather a part of the Mediterranean world. . . . In a sense, the Delta can be called the cradle of Western civilization because from it emerged the Minoans who founded the first high culture of Europe, and later the Hebrews of the Exodus, who migrated to their Promised Land. Thus the forerunners of classical Greek and Hebrew cultures were kindred Delta folk.[4]

Malik rejoices in the West's rootedness in the Near East and in the awareness of it that is echoed by Greek mythology:

> This cultural-genetic relatedness between the Near East and the West has been the theme of wonder and reflection literally for thousands of years. Nobody forgets his origins, and so the Western World has never tired of brooding upon the great mystery of the eastern shores of the Mediterranean where it was born. Is it a pure myth entirely devoid of any significance that Europa was a lovely Phoenician princess who was carried off by no less a god than mighty Zeus himself? (Pp. 189 f.)

Yet here, too, he is less than generous—or truthful and loving—when he leaves Europa in her exclusively Phoenician environs. Gordon in *The Common Background of Greek and Hebrew Civilizations* explains that both in the Iliad and the Odyssey the realm of darkness, located in the *west,* is named *Erebos,* a term borrowed from Hebrew (*erev*—evening; *ma^{c}arav*—west), Ugaritic (m^{c}rb—sunset), Akkadian (*erêb šamši*—setting of the sun or west). This is much more specific than Malik's "Phoenician," and much more "truthfully and lovingly" informative about the cradle of the radiant beauty whom Zeus chose to be his queen on Crete and the mother of King Minos and sister of Cadmus (from the Hebrew *qedem*—east), founder of Thebes and inventor of writing.[5]

II

As Malik continues his "search for truth," he summarizes the story of the Hashemite Kingdom of Jordan. We are told that Transjordan was "originally a part of a vilayet of Syria." *Vilayet* is Turkish for a chief administrative province or state (in the U.S. sense) of Turkey, and Malik refers to the fact that for four centuries Syria was a part of the Ottoman Empire. This period, I interject, has been described by Philip K. Hitti as one of "oppressive rule, high taxation, economic and social decline" as well as one of intellectual sterility.[6] The problem with Malik's account is that he so condenses the Jordan story as to make its beginnings entirely unintelligible. He simply reports that "Transjordan was established as an Amirate and placed under the Mandate in 1922 and then recognized as an independent government under British tutelage in the following year." During the next twenty-five years of "growth in self-government," Abdullah was its central figure. Its development included "the transformation of the Amirate into a monarchy, and *the annexation of parts of Arab Palestine west of the river Jordan*" (p. 195; emphasis added).

There should be no doubt about the threat embedded in the last line to the existence of the State of Israel, which occupies the remaining territories of "Arab Palestine west of the river Jordan." By implication, Malik here simply strikes down the very notion of Jewish Palestine—any part of it. In Jewish hands, everything is what some still call today "occupied territories." For Malik, a Jewish Palestine is just not conceivable. The dry-as-desert-sand line, appended to a passage that purports to do nothing more about the annexation than telescope some historical events and stress the importance of Abdullah the Hashemite—this line actually makes the annexation of all of "Arab Palestine" by any Arab a matter of historically (and morally) self-evident propriety. When Transjordanian Arabs occupy and annex large parts of Jewish Palestine, they perform legal liberation. When Jews do the same, it is *occupation,* an illegal act.

As for Abdullah and his kingdom, it is worth enlarging a bit on Malik's abridgment of history.

Joseph B. Schechtman has repeatedly shown[7] that the existence of the body politic called today the Hashemite Kingdom of Jordan goes back to March 29, 1921, the day Winston Churchill, then Secretary for the Colonies, briefly met in Jerusalem with Emir Abdullah, son of Sherif Husayn of Mecca and brother of Faysal, at first king of Syria, later king of Iraq. Transjordan, it should be recalled, was part of Syria over which the Versailles Peace Conference of 1919 allowed France a free hand. But France had not actually occupied Transjordan at the time. Shortly after the French ousted Faysal in July 1920 from his Damascus throne, which had been offered him by the General Syrian Congress in defiance of the Versailles decision, Abdullah led a military force into Transjordan, in effect occupied it, and threatened to invade Syria. For her part, Britain did not wish France to deal with Abdullah and take actual control of Transjordan. Little wonder, then, that London was unwilling to drive Abdullah back to the Arabian peninsula where he had come from. Churchill, therefore, conferred with Abdullah, in the presence of Britain's high commissioner for Palestine, Herbert Samuel, and of legendary T. E. Lawrence.[8] The parties agreed that Abdullah would forgo fighting the French, would administer Transjordan in the name of the Mandatory, and would receive for six months a monthly subsidy of five thousand pounds. It was also agreed that a representative of the high commissioner for Palestine would be stationed in Amman in the capacity of adviser to Emir Abdullah's administration. No one doubted for a moment that Transjordan was a part of Palestine, that it was, simply—East Palestine.

As might have been expected, the temporary arrangement became permanent. The League of Nations Mandate for Palestine, dated July 24, 1922, includes Article 25, which entitled the Mandatory "to postpone or withhold application of such provisions of this mandate as he may consider inapplicable to the existing local conditions . . . in the territories lying between the Jordan and the eastern boundary of Palestine as ultimately determined." Britain inserted this article in the text of the mandate after Abdullah was installed as provisional ruler of Transjordan. On September 16, 1922, the League of Nations Council approved a British memorandum that actually determined the eastern boundaries and that, in fact, withheld application to Transjordan of the mandate's provisions that refer to "the establishment in Palestine of a national home for the Jewish people" and that give recognition "to the historical connection of the Jewish people with Palestine and to the grounds for reconstituting their national home in that country" (Preamble). On April 23, 1923, Herbert Samuel stated in Amman that the British government "would recognize the existence of an independent government in Transjordan by means of an agreement to be concluded." Such an agreement was signed on February 20, 1928. As for its geography, Transjordan covered an area of about 35,000 square miles. (After the Israeli War of Independence in 1948, Abdullah acquired an additional 2,200 square miles.) Its population was estimated to be 300,000. Only as late as March 22, 1946, did Britain terminate the mandate and recognize Transjordan as a sovereign state.

It is important to keep in mind that the mandatory's territory of Palestine on both sides of the Jordan covered some 44,000 square miles. The first partition of 1922 left to the development of the Jewish National Home only some 10,000 square miles or less than one quarter of the League of Nations's Palestine.

It is no less important to recall that the mandate's text is unequivocal on the meaning of "Palestine": it speaks of "the territories lying between the Jordan and the eastern boundary of Palestine, as ultimately determined"— in addition, of course, to the territories west of the Jordan. It follows that Transjordan, or now the Hashemite Kingdom of Jordan, *"is the Arab state in Palestine, the Palestinian state in the Arab world."*[9]

It is equally clear that for the authors of the mandate's text the river Jordan flowed through Palestine, not just through a part of it. Hence, Hussein's realm is the Hashemite Kingdom of East Palestine. Its citizens are East Palestinians. There is as much cultural, religious, and social difference between Palestinian Arabs living east and west of the Jordan as there is between Palestinian Jews living north and south of the Tel-Aviv—Jerusalem line. The claim, therefore, that "the Palestinians" are a homeless people desperately and legitimately in need of a second homeland, in addition to the one allegedly outside of Palestine in territories east of the Jordan River, reflects Arab territorial insatiability, Arab nationalist exclusivism, Arab recycled Judaeophobia.

One of the major Zionist bodies did not make peace with the separation of east-Jordan Palestine from the west-Jordan territory of the Jewish National Home. Zionists-Revisionists, led by Zeev Jabotinsky, condemned such a concession as conducive neither to the development of Jewish statehood through swift mass-*aliyah* nor to the achievement of an enduring peace between Jews and Arabs. It was one of their fundamental beliefs that such a peace was not a function of Palestinian geography or of Jewish concession-after-concession politics. Rather, they held that such a peace was the result of Arab acceptance of Jewish political independence and fraternal interdependence on the soil which, in the Jewish people's consciousness, never ceased to be the Jewish people's own. Such a peace, according to this party of political Zionists, could only be the consequence of Arab recognition that Zionism was not to be wished away, that the Zionists were not to be driven into the Mediterranean, that they were in Palestine to stay. From its inception in 1925, the Revisionist movement insisted that for the Zionist enterprise "the incomparably fertile lands of Transjordan are a natural and rich land reservoir. . . . It will be the task of Zionist policy to deepen this recognition and to bring about the closest possible unification of Palestine east and west of the Jordan."[10] Such a recognition that Zionism cannot be "wished away" seemed to have ripened in Sadat of Egypt.

III

In Malik's continuing summary, the circumstances of European power politics receive a rather different tinge. Syria, he asserts, suffered many frustrations at the hands of the allied French and British. They dismembered Greater Syria, placing the northern and southern parts under different administrations. Hence, "the nationalist situation in Syria was from the beginning intense": the West came to be seen not as a liberator but as a schemer "bent upon division, domination and the settlement, against the will of the native population, of countless Jews on Syrian soil." In time, Malik predicts, "Syria, by reason of her economic, human and spiritual possibilities, may play a fundamental role in Near Eastern and Arab affairs" (p. 197). Since in his view new youthful leadership is being impelled in part by "the Arab disaster in Palestine" (p. 196), I feel safe in inferring that Syria's "fundamental role" should be to turn the "Arab disaster" into an Arab triumph in Palestine, which is to say, into a Jewish disaster.

On Lebanon, whose independence from France dates from 1943, Malik comments that it "has a positive vocation in the international field. It is not political. It is spiritual and intellectual. It consists in being true to the best and truest in East and West alike. This burden of mediation and under-standing she is uniquely called to bear" (p. 197).

Sadly, the events of 1976/77/78 and 1981 show that Malik overstated the case for growing Arab spirituality and intellectuality in this century. It appeared that Syria, along with other Arab states, aimed at creating a Jewish and a Christian disaster, in fact, a Western disaster, and that it sought to restore a new Greater Syria. More than 60,000 dead—some murdered with unbelievable brutality—and perhaps 400,000 wounded—testify to the decline rather than the rise of Arab humanitarianism and peace-mindedness.[11]

Basically, the West denotes Christianity, and the East is unthinkable with-out Islam, but Israel—in Malik's discussion of Lebanon—is grounded in neither. He therefore takes issue with "some writers" who feel that Israel may function as a bridge between the two. "But how," he asks, "can one reconcile two things by being outside them?" (p. 198). Lebanon "is the only country, not only in existence today but perhaps throughout history, where East and West meet and mingle with each other on a footing of equality." Here, as he sees it, "is a wonderful possibility of creative confrontation" (p. 198).

Today one returns to Malik's analysis and prognosis only with deep sadness and regret:

> The Lebanon could not be true to East and West alike unless she stood for existential freedom. In the end, this is alone her justification. This means freedom of thought, freedom of choice, freedom of being, free-dom of becoming. Whoever is about to suffocate must be able to breathe freely in the Lebanon. Here the possibility of access to the truth, the whole truth, must be absolutely real. (p. 198)

Moreover, "the principle of international politics is power; but Lebanon's power is reason, truth, love, suffering, being."

But Markham, in the report on the Lebanese civil war already men-tioned, quoted Malik as telling him that "if the Christian community can get away with it, it would prefer to live in peace by itself." However,

> the real problem is whether the Moslem world community in general—and the Moslem Arab community in particular—can tolerate the exis-tence of a free, open and secure Christian community in the Middle East. This is the ultimate question.[12] The fight may be desperate. We may be doomed. This may be the last stand of a free society in Asia or Africa. But it is an heroic fight.

Neither in 1952 nor in 1977 did Malik show any inclination to acknowledge the existence to the south of his borders of another free society. But in 1952 he remarked that, in general, "two things dominate the Arab mind . . . : independence and unity" and that, regardless of modalities, "every Arab feels an immediate mystical unity with every other Arab" (p. 199).

Returning at this point to his essay, we find Malik aiming the truth-love method at Israel: "The fate of the Near East is now intertwined with that of Israel" (p. 200). Its existence

> presents a real and serious challenge to Arab existence. It is a test of Arab patriotism, dynamism, wisdom and statesmanship. It constitutes a virtual touchstone of Arab capacities of self-preservation and self-deter-mination. . . . There is abroad a grim sense of destiny. (P. 200)

We need to pause here. Is Malik referring to the concrete reality called Israel? Is this view of the Jewish state the reflection of Lebanese "reason, truth, love, suffering, being"? Is not the functional meaning of the Arabs' "mystical unity" that "grim sense of destiny" which implies that the Jewish state must suffer politicide no matter how grim the count of Arab casualties on the battlefield?

The answer need not be in the affirmative. Truth and love may still reassert themselves in regard to Israel and the Jewish people. Human intelligence and compassion may yet break out among the Arab peoples. "Arab patriotism, dynamism, wisdom and statemanship" may, in time and, indeed, before long, show themselves capable of transcending hatred, of achieving reconciliation, of accepting the Jewish State as the creation of man's will to justice. Islam has not necessarily exhausted its reservoir of active compassion, any more than has Near Eastern Christianity.

Such regeneration may, in fact, be Israel's true challenge to "the Arab world." But Malik did not see this at all.

IV

Instead, Malik identifies four challenges or fundamental issues that Is-rael evokes and that no other state evokes.

The first is *the political challenge*. The issue is the survival of "a completely alien state" that is "suddenly thrust upon" its immediate environment (p. 203). How alien Israel is Malik spells out rather dramatically:

> there is a profound intellectual and spiritual chasm between Israel and the rest of the Near East. Two entirely different economies, two entirely different religions, two entirely different languages, . . . two entirely different mentalities, two entirely different cultures, two entirely differ-ent civilizations, face each other across this chasm. I do not know of a single other instance in the world where there is such radical existential discontinuity across national fronties. (P. 201) [13]

In 1964 James Parkes, the noted British clergyman and historian, took up this challenge. In the concluding chapter of his insightful *Five Roots of Israel* he demonstrated "how false every one of Dr. Malik's arguments is" (p. 60). In the seven Arab countries to which Israel, according to Malik, is completely alien, Jews, "apart from Neolithic survivals and the Copts in Egypt," are "the longest settled of the identifiable inhabitants in some, and have lived longer in all the others, than Arabs have in Palestine or Egypt" (pp. 64 f.). From the Bible itself comes evidence that in Syria and Lebanon Jews lived scattered before the Babylonian exile. In Iraq, Jewish communities have existed since the exile of the northern kingdom of Israel, and from the fourth to the tenth centuries the Babylonian community provided the intellectually and religiously creative center for all of Jewry. In Egypt, Saudi Arabia, Yemen, as well as in Muslim countries in North Africa, Jewish settlements date back to deep antiquity. In the Middle East as a whole, then, "Jews, though numerically fewer, share with Arabs the claim to be a millennial element in the population of every Middle-eastern country" (p. 67). What of Palestine itself? First historical record shows that the Jewish presence is continuous throughout the millennia after the Roman conquest in 135 C.E.[14] It shows also that in major crises in Jewish communities elsewhere, "it was always from the Jewry of Palestine that the new impetus came, that Judaism was cast into the new form, which enabled Jewish history to continue its millennial development" (p. 69). Third, more than half of Israel's Jewish population hails from Islamic countries. How "completely alien" can these Iraqi or Egyptian or Moroccan or Yemenite Jews be to "the Moslem-Arab world" in which their communities lived from the beginnings of Islam and for ten centuries before its founder was born? Finally, "Israel today is a Middle-eastern country both in history and in population" (p. 60), but it is also Middle-eastern in regard to Western science, industry, and economic influences. Both Israel and Egypt, for example, face the same "problem of creating and maintaining the standards of an affluent society while still at the beginning of creating that affluence" —with the help of the West (pp. 72 f.). This parallel, Parkes concluded, "highlights the miserable tragedy of regarding Israel as alien to the area and an inevitable enemy" (p. 74).

In Malik's view, the question for the next crucial phase is whether Israel will be resourceful, "resilient and humble enough to create genuine, internal relations of confidence and cooperation between itself and the Moslem-Arab world" (p. 202). But here Malik reveals to full view what he really means by "the political challenge." One might have read Malik to say the Arabs ought to find ways of opening their "world" to intellectual, lingual, religious, cultural pluralism. But his language makes it clear that he has in mind a challenge by Israel to Israel: how best to placate the Arabs by being not *in* their world but *of* it, by blending into it with a minimum residue of "alien" otherness. The challenge is not at all how the Arabs might accept Israel in peace, in joyful embrace of collective human variety, in fraternal acceptance of cultural otherness that has often been a part of their own existence.

In the second place, Malik raises *the philosophical challenge*. His question, is "whether the concentration in one state of the factors at once of language, race and religion is not a challenge to the modern conception of the state, which is free of all the necessary determination of any of these factors, and certainly of the three of them taken together" (p. 203). Malik makes the point emphatic by following through with this amplification:

> There is no other state in the world today—nor has there been for centuries—which is nationally characterized by a race, a language and a religion none of which nationally characterizes any other state. . . . Israel as a state alone is Hebrew, Israel alone is Jewish, Israel alone is Judaic. No state is alone Moslem or Christian or Protestant or Catholic. No state is alone Aryan or Mongolian or Negro. And no state, except Israel and perhaps Ethiopia, has a national language of its own unconnected (in the sense of interaction) with any living language. This unique concentration of the three factors of race, language and religion . . . is bound to generate a tremendous exclusiveness and intensity of feeling (issuing in the most radical form of nationalism) that must find an outlet in some dynamism with incalculable consequences. (Pp. 203 f.)

Here the essay descends to its lowest polemical level. The search for truth and the profession of love fade away. It is as if classical anti-Semitism surfaced in all its xenophobic verve: "Israel alone" is this and that. "There is no other state in the world today" exhibiting these and those traits. Malik stands before this phenomenon in deep shock. He feels challenged to the very core of his philosophical conception of the state, which suggests that his philosophy is not of the open variety. Assuming the Jews are a race— actually, this is a preposterous falsehood whose anti-Semitic purpose became operational in the nazi world's extermination centers—are they, therefore, not entitled to their state in which *their* religion predominates and in which *their* language is the national tongue? One should think that a human group unified by race, language, and religion is eminently entitled to political independence. Must racial, lingual, and religious minorities be minorities everywhere and always? Far from challenging, as Malik avers, "the modern conception of the state," Israel's existence confirms its intellectual foundations, particularly in view of the fact that Israeli society is multilingual, multireligious, and multiracial within the context of the Jewish people's evolving civilization. Unless race, language, and religion severally carry unethical implications, it is hard to see why they should carry such implications when functioning in internally and externally interactive unison. Their harmonious orchestration is, in fact, the meaning of international peace which is at the heart of Jewish religio-national self-awareness. Were Malik serious about his search for truth and love with regard to Judaism and Zionism, he should have reached this conclusion. His failure to do so reflects on the quality of his search and on the interpretation he places on truth and love.

Do Saudi Arabia or Spain or Nigeria or Japan or Norway raise doubts about their entitlement to statehood? Are they not prime examples of overwhelming concentration of race (or peoplehood), religion, and language? Granting for argument's sake Israel's utter uniqueness—within the human species and within the wide range of humanly acceptable conduct—does its statehood challenge the very notion of the modern state? Let us consider the United States. In *A Grammar of Politics* (1925) Harold J. Laski of Oxford wrote that in a theoretical sense the U.S. has no sovereign organ: the Congress has limited powers, the Supreme Court can be overridden by Constitutional amendment, the Executive's veto may be set aside. "A peculiar historical experience has . . . devised the means of building a State from which the conception of sovereignty is absent" (p. 49). Is the U.S. therefore no State at all? "But a political philosophy which rejects the title of the United States to Statehood is unlikely to apply to the world of realities" (p. 50).

John Dewey's judgment of Zionism, written during World War I, offers an entirely different perspective. It was clear to him that "the rightful demand for full civil, political, linguistic and religious freedom" is at present "extremely difficult to secure and maintain . . . without some measure of definite political status." Hence "the course of Zionism has great claims upon those who are interested in the future organization of the peaceful intercourse of nations because it not only guarantees freedom of cultural development in that particular spot in which the new nation is formed, but because it gives a leverage for procuring and developing nationality in all the other countries which harbor within themselves large numbers of the Jewish folk." Moreover, Dewey was persuaded that "the Zionistic state would stand forth to the world as an inspiring symbol of victory against great odds, against seemingly insuperable odds, of the rights of nationality to be itself." He therefore felt "that the Zionistic movement has a right to appeal to the interest and sympathy of statesmen and of all who care for the future of the world's peaceful organization."[15]

Historic uniqueness is no argument against America's statehood or anybody else's. Malik has stepped beyond the boundaries of political philosophy, beyond the boundaries of truth and love. What he offers is rather an activity that may be designated philosophical warfare, a close ally of psychological warfare.

Malik's insinuation that the unity of Jewish peoplehood—this, not *race* is the proper term—the Hebrew language, and Jewish religion raises philosophical doubts about Israel's admission to statehood is as absurd as is Article 20 of the PLO's "National Covenant" of 1968, which denies the Jewish state the right to exist because Jews do not constitute a people. The article reads, in part:

The claim of an historical or spiritual tie between Jews and Palestine does not tally with historical realities nor with constituents of statehood in their true sense. Judaism, in its character as a religion of revelation, is not a nationality with an independent existence. Likewise, the Jews are not one people with an independent personality. They are rather citizens of the states to which they belong.

PLO "philosophers"—or philosophical warfarers—deny Jewish political existence because Jews are not a nation, that is, are devoid of peoplehood or "race," and have no "independent personality," which would surely include language and religion in recognizable unity. Judaism, to them, is too loose an entity to deserve statehood, while Malik questions the Jewish right to statehood because Israel is too unified in basic components. The object of their political-philosophical warfare is the same: shattering Israel's ethical, intellectual, and political foundations prior to its military destruction.[16]

On rethinking Malik's perception of a "philosophical challenge" that Israel presents not only to the Arab world but to the whole community of states on earth, the suspicion arises that Malik's purpose is to add to Israel's political isolation an enormously dangerous philosophical isolation. The philosopher Malik mobilizes political science and philosophy to surround Jewry and the Jewish State with a wall of intellectual hostility. Their uniqueness is paraded as a threat to the world's peace and security because, first, it "is bound to generate exclusiveness and intensity of feeling," which, in turn, "must find an outlet in some dynamism," and so forth. *Must* they? Here philosophical determinism is enlisted to power the charge of inevitable wrong that flows from Israel's existence. Second, vague, "incalculable consequences" are invoked to strike irrational fear in human hearts. Jewish religion brought to bear on Jewish nationalism spells dynamic fanaticism. Mankind, beware!

Supported by such philosophical underpinnings, could Arabs and their satellite states have failed to win a U.N. General Assembly vote on November 10, 1975, proclaiming that Zionism is "a form of racism and racial discrimination"? Did not Malik classify Jews as a race that must produce human evil when linked to Jewish religion and the Hebrew language under conditions of statehood in Palestine? Are not his affirmations in this section of his essay among the intellectual sources of the infamous U.N. resolution of 1975?

V

The third and fourth challenges are theological. The former relates to the "Old Testament," the latter to the New Testament. The "OT" reference documents "the great mystery of Ishmael and Isaac" (p. 204).

Malik experiences "a profound emotion of wonder" and beholds "a significance splashing irresistibly and mysteriously upon us from beyond." Something here goes beyond the immanent, the "just human or historical or economic or political." Malik vaguely suggests that the current conflict of Ishmaelis and Israelis, both children of Abraham, is no "ordinary politico-economic struggle" but something that has to do with "the awful and holy and ultimate in history." The very deepest secret of history is involved. "The rise of Israel therefore presents a great challenge: that of the mystery of the two children of Abraham after the flesh." Malik cites Genesis 21:11, where Abraham is reported to have viewed as "very grievous" Sarah's counsel to cast out Ishmael and Hagar.

The implication, undoubtedly, is that the State of Israel challenges the divine order. It violates the very memory of the man who founded the Jewish people and who only with the greatest reluctance acceded to the violation of Ishmael's legitimate rights in favor of Isaac. Malik's "secret" of history seems to be that Jewish tradition is a stupendous and tragic mis-reading of the divine will and that *ultimately* Ishmael will be restored to the position that that tradition assigned to Isaac and Jacob and their Jewish progeny. On that day, presumably, the Jews will have neither their land nor their God.[17]

The second part of Malik's "theological challenge" lifts the veil of mystery a bit more. Now he opposes the State of Israel to the New Testament. The "old Israel," according to Christian theology, "was once and for all dissolved by Christ," and the "new Israel" is the Church.[18] "Israel" appears seventy-four times in the NT, a fact that cannot be "entirely unrelated to what exists in Palestine today" (p. 205).

Two verses in particular recommend themselves to our author, Acts 13:23[19] and 1 Cor. 10:18. The first reads: "Of this man's [David's] seed hath God, according to his promise, raised unto Israel a Saviour, Jesus." The second is more difficult: "Behold Israel after the flesh: are not they which eat of the sacrifices partakers of the altar?" The implication seems to be that the Jewish people in their common fellowship will eventually come to be the Israel for which the Savior raised unto them by God is the Savior acknowledged by them.[20] Then, of course, the State of Israel will no longer be of the "old" but of the "new" Israel, and the theological challenge will be no more.

It comes as no surprise that at the Second Assembly of the World Council of Churches, held at Evanston, Ill., in 1954, Malik objected to a resolution making direct reference to Christian obligations to the Jewish people in the post-Holocaust era. In his capacity as member of the WCC's Advisory Commission, he sent a telegram to Dr. Farid Audeh of Beirut, president of the Supreme Council of the Evangelical Churches in Syria and Lebanon, who read it before the assembly. In his wire Malik disclaimed "any suggestion that political events at present involving the Jews are connected with the fulfillment of Christian hope."[21] Dr. Aziz Suryal Atiya of Egypt was sure that "the mention of Israel would be a 'disservice to the WCC' in the Near East."[22] The Assembly voted "further study" of the matter, but twenty-four delegates signed a statement entitled "The Hope of Israel."

In such a frame of mind, Malik in 1952 did not fail to follow through with the half-theological half-truth that today "Jerusalem is made a political center. But can the world ever forget the salvation wrought in Jerusalem?" (p. 205). Neither in 1952 nor in 1967 nor in 1977 did Israel convert the Holy City into anything but a secular, merely political, place. Malik himself has insisted that in Israel, Jewish nationalism and religion interpenetrate so as to endanger world peace. Hence Jerusalem could not possibly be a political center only, even to mere Jewish nationalists. Nor is it entirely correct to imply that Israel, unlike the rest of the world, forgets "the salvation wrought in Jerusalem." Since David and Solomon, the city has been in the very heart of its hope for salvation.

Nor—one may be quite dogmatic about this—does a truthful survey of the Jewish career in history give the slightest support to anticipations of Jewish mass conversion to Christianity (or any other religion) and to the fading away of Judaism as a theological challenge.[23]

VI

In sum, the fundamental challenge of Malik comes from his own terms. What he regards as truth and love appears in his treatment of Israel and the Jewish people to be their mobilization for Arab political goals and their conversion to Christianity. He takes their names in vain. Israel, it is true enough, embodies a historic challenge—to bibliolatrous religion, to demonic nationalism, to genocidal racism, to monolithic totalitarianism,[24] to the fear of democracy and science. Moreover, it stands as living evidence to the fact that Jews are a people, that Jewish religion is not *prelude* to salvation but *its ever valid source*, notably when united with the land of its fathers.

This reality can and should be explored in its full historical range and philosophical-theological depth. But *qua* reality it is not subject to doubt in the name of truth and love. Indeed, truth and love are measured by the extent to which they are open to this reality. So are monotheistic religions, the this-worldly faiths of Russia and China, the political formations of the Arab "world," measured by what they know, think, feel, and do to Jews and the Jewish land.

Nolens volens, the Jewish people came to represent the human spirit. It did so in antiquity and the Middle Ages. It did so in nazi Germany. It does so in the Soviet Union. And it does so before the Near Eastern *world of human silence* in which chiefly the voices of tyrants and dictators were heard over the Arab airwaves and from the rostrum of the U.N.

When he breaks away from the subject of Israel, Malik is able to say of the Near East that "there is lack of unity, lack of responsibility, lack of sincerity, lack of understanding and lack of love," a "disturbing rise of fanaticism," and loss of its own "transcendent vision" (pp. 22–24). It does not change this situation appreciably that in part it is the fault of the West that needs to achieve its own spiritual recovery.[25]

One may be tempted to associate oneself with Malik when he calls on both East and West to return to their original insight of a transcendent "order creating, judging, disturbing, healing, forgiving" (p. 224). But the temptation subsides when what is intended by these words is understood. Three passages found in Malik's Introductions to *God and Man in Contemporary Christian Thought* and *God and Man in Contemporary Islamic Thought* explain our text beyond a shadow of doubt. In the latter he states his belief that "the Graeco-Roman-Judaeo-Christian tradition . . . is the greatest and deepest and truest living historical fact in existence." This tradition "is a synthesis that judges everything else, whereas nothing, neither the Chinese, nor the Indians, nor the Marxists, nor the Muslims, in so far as they lie outside it, are capable of judging it." On the same page he affirms his faith in Jesus as "the supreme man and the supreme reality, the freest man who is wholly 'above.' " In the former introduction he reaches the conclusion that "Jesus Christ of Nazareth is the meaning and summing up of all history" and that we all stand judged by Him and thus "we may repent in love and gratitude." It is clear, therefore, that if Jesus is "the supreme reality," he must be "the greatest . . . historical fact in existence" and the all-judging transcendent "order" of our passage.

Jews will agree with Malik that East and West require "creating, judging, disturbing, healing, forgiving." However, orthodox-revelationist Jews will, against Malik's, set their faith that this is the work of God, the God of Israel's patriarchs, prophets, and pharisaic teachers from the Tannaim of the Mishnah and the Amoraim of the Gemara through the Geonim and the medieval rabbinic authorities to the spiritual leaders of the Jewish people in our time. The non-Orthodox and nonrevelationist religious and secular Jews will, against Malik's, set their faith in the liberated mind-love power of human beings and in the Jewish people's tragic and majestic history as capable, in the political and social order, to set criteria for judging the genuineness with which the mind-love power is applied. Together, all Jews will uphold Rabbi Yehudah ha-Levy's famed line in his *Kozari* (ca. 1135): "Israel amidst the nations is like the heart amidst the organs."[26] Although the most susceptible to ailments, the heart is the most vigorous in health. So does Israel register the quakes of social, religious, and philosophical evils and the recovery of the human mind.

As Jews, we are united in claiming the right to national self-determination. Neither Malik nor the "National Covenant" nor the U.N. General Assembly will determine our identity for us, whether in terms of a biological entity, or a conspiracy of religio-national fanatics, an ethnic question mark, or a divine or demonic mystery, or an intransigent adherent to an old and obsolete "Testament."

Instead of a question—"the Jewish Question"—we regard ourselves as the People of the Answer, an answer that grows in validity and universality.[27] Part of the Answer, toward whose fullness we sense ourselves to be moving with the core of our essential being, is the return to us and for us of the Land through which the Jordan flows—the return whereby we and the human kind can achieve a new birth of genuine truth and love.

The human kind? We?

Saul Bellow addresses all of us in words that at the same time are corrosive of confidence too easily developed and that summon Israel to a new state of preparedness, mankind to a new state of ethical humanhood:

> at this uneasy hour the civilized world seems tired of its civilization, and tired also of the Jews. It wants to hear no more about survival. But there are the Jews, again at the edge of annihilation and as insistent as ever, demanding to know what the conscience of the world intends to do.[28]

NOTES

1. Vol. 30, no. 2 (January 1952).

2. *See* Chaim Chissin, *A Palestine Diary: Memoirs of a Bilu Pioneer, 1882–1887* (New York: Herzl Press, 1976).

3. John Dewey, *Logic, the Theory of Inquiry* (New York: Henry Holt and Co., 1938), p. 7 and passim.

4. Cyrus H. Gordon, *Ugarit and Minoan Crete—The Bearing of Their Texts on the Origins of Western Culture* (New York: W. W. Norton & Co., 1966), p. 30.

5. Idem, *The Common Background of Greek and Hebrew Civilizations* (New York: W. W. Norton & Co., 1965), p. 269.

6. Philip K. Hitti, *Syria, A Short History* (New York: Macmillan, 1959), p. 219.

7. Joseph B. Schechtman, *Jordan—A State that Never Was* (New York: Cultural Publishing Co., 1968).

8. Suleiman Mousa, *T. E. Lawrence: An Arab View* (London: Oxford University Press, 1966), pp. 236–41.

9. Cf. also Mordechai Nisan, "Jordan is the Palestinian Arab State," *The American Zionist* 67, no. 6 (February 1977): 15–17.

10. Wladimir Jabotinsky, "Die Geschicke Transjordaniens" (The Fortunes of Transjordan), *Rasswjet* (Berlin), (1925), p. 55. See also idem, *Medinah Ivrit—Pitron Sheelat ha-Yehudim* (A Hebrew State—Solution to the Question of the Jews) (Tel-Aviv: T. Kopp, 1937). Cf. Joseph B. Schechtman, *Rebel and Statesman—The Vladimir Jabotinsky Story*, vol. 1 (New York: T. Yoseloff, 1956), chap. 20.

11. Charles Helou, a former President of Lebanon, in *The New York Times*, 15 June 1976: "Meanwhile, the tragedy continues with over 100 killed every day (the equivalent of 10,000 in the United States) and countless wounded and maimed. Human beings fall like beasts in a slaughter condemned by the United Nations. What solution can there be to this bloody nightmare?" Professor Fouad Ajami of Johns Hopkins University refers to the current violence in "Lebanon: Myth and Reality," *The New York Times*, 20 April 1981. Sadly he notes the distance between the myths and the images about Lebanon's natural beauty and religious tolerance. But "deep down we must have known that it was all a show, that the forced and excessive love for the country was motivated by our subliminal fear of the country's capacity

for self-destruction." Today "no one bothers to count the cease-fires anymore," and the Lebanese "continue to die for wretched plots of land that no longer matter." Today Lebanon holds up a mirror in which "we can see the follies of outsiders, and the impotence of us all."

12. Professor Franklin H. Littell, chairman, Department of Religion, Temple University, cites this line in his *CCI* [Christians Concerned for Israel] *Notebook*, n.s., no. 1 (November 1977), pp. 1 f. and comments: "But this is no question at all. The answer is, as it has been for generations, that a romantic pan-Arabism cannot bear any challenge to its racist ideology—Christian, Jewish, of Marxist. (Most of the 'Arab' peoples are not Arab at all: 'Arab' is an ideological reality, like 'Teuton' or 'Aryan' a few years ago.) In a world controlled by medieval despots and modern dictatorships, and dominated by a pre-scientific religious ideology comparable to that of Christendom in the 13th century (including a large measure of Antisemitism), there is no secure place for Christian and Jewish minorities with self respect."

13. It may be noted in passing that the traditionalist Seyyed Hossein Nasr, Chancellor of the Arya-Mehr University of Technology in Iran, in his *Islam and the Plight of Modern Man* (London: Longman, 1975), opposes Freud and his school (along with evolution and Western science and philosophy). "Freudianism," he writes, and one is tempted to read, in our context, Israel and Israelism, "as well as other modern Western schools of psychology and psychotherapy, are the by-products of a particular society very different from the Islamic. It needs to be recalled also that Freud was a Viennese Jew who turned away from Orthodox Judaism. Few people know that he was connected to a messianic movement which was opposed by the Orthodox Jewish community of Central Europe itself, and that therefore he was opposed to the mainstream of Jewish life, not to speak of Christianity" (pp. 140f.) This "messianic movement" can only be Zionism, and Nasr appears to be at one with Malik in charging "two entirely different mentalities, . . . cultures, . . . civilization."

14. For additional historical and other data see Solomon Zeitlin, "Jewish Rights in Eretz Israel (Palestine)," *The Jewish Quarterly Review*, n.s. 52, no. 1 (July 1961), 14–34. Zeitlin's paper is a reply to a brief essay by Arnold J. Toynbee, "Jewish Rights in Palestine," ibid., pp. 1–11. Professor Zeitlin's crucial lines are: ". . . the Jews never left Palestine which they called the Land of Israel. . . . There was never a period when there were no Jews in Palestine" (p. 23).

15. John Dewey, "The Principle of Nationality," *The Menorah Journal* 10, no. 4 (October 1917):207 f.

16. In his important article "Christians and the State of Israel" (*Christian Attitudes on Jews and Judaism*, ed. C. C. Aronsfeld and published by the Institute of Jewish Affairs, in association with the World Jewish Congress (London, no. 39, December 1974), the German Protestant theologian Rolf Rendtorff observes that "the Jews have always, unambiguously, considered themselves to be a people. . . . Religion and nationality have always been merged, and we are faced with the seemingly paradoxical phenomenon that the national identity of the people has been preserved because of their common religion, just because a national consciousness forms an integral part of this very religion." Rendtorff follows through with this comment on the current situation: "Now it is interesting to note that certasin conservative Christian ideas denying the existence of a Jewish people coincide strangely with Arab and extreme-leftist anti-Israel propaganda slogans." His major conclusion is that on the Christian side "there must be a new appreciation of this Jewish State, since recognition of the Jewish nation, both as a fact and in its self-image, involves recognition of its historical and religious ties with the country commonly referred to by Jews as the *Land of Israel*" (pp. 4–5).

17. N. Bruce McLeod, pastor of Westdale United Church, Hamilton, Ontario, Canada, is much more reasonable in his essay, entitled "Isaac and Ishmael: 1967," *The Christian Century*, 84, no. 30 (July 26, 1967). Responding to the Six-Day War, which had just come to an end, he recalled the passages in Genesis on Hagar and concluded: "Unless Ishmael really accepts, really accepts, the fact and right of Isaac's existence, there will be no peace in the Middle East, and any settlement arrived at will only be preparation for a disaster which may engulf us all." He urged all parties involved and world opinion "to help two brothers to accept each others and live together in peace" (p. 961).

18. In his introductions, in matters Christian and Islamic often brilliant but on things Jewish almost entirely silent, to the two large volumes edited by him on *God and Man in Contemporary Christian Thought* and *God and Man in Contemporary Islamic Thought*, published by American University in Beirut Centennial Publications, 1970 and 1972, respectively, Malik always links Abraham to Jesus. Thus, "It all started with Abraham. The existing beyond spoke

and the heart of faith responded. . . . The thing was not the separate act of an individual here and there—the thing at every point was part of the historical formation of a whole nation and community, first the Israel of old and then the Church of Jesus Christ" (*Christian Thought,* pp. xxxiiif.). He urges as helpful to Islam "existential scepticism," i.e., skcepticism that dares to raise fundamental questions about origins and roots . . . about the nature of the revelation of the God of Abraham, Isaac and Jacob, of the Father of Jesus Christ of Nazareth" (*Islamic Thought,* p. 19). In "The Crisis Defined," *Youth in Crisis—The Responsibility of the Schools,* ed. Peter C. Moore (New York: Seabury Press, 1966), Malik confesses, "I am a Christian. I believe in God, the Creator from nothing of heaven and earth. . . . This Creator-God is the God of Abraham, Isaac and Jacob, who is also identically the Father of our Lord Jesus Christ" (p. 6). One wonders whether for Malik, a philosophy symposium on God and man in contemporary Jewish thought, urging existential skepticism on Christianity and Islam, is possible.

19. In his Introduction to *God and Man in Contemporary Christian Thought,* Malik writes that "The Book of Acts is a necessary prerequisite for the understanding of the unspeakable tragedy of Near Eastern existence now and throughout history. . . . The parallelism is truly uncanny" (p. xxxiv).

20. In *God . . . in Islamic Thought,* Malik states that only "the fellowship of openness and love . . . can lead me to the truth" (p. 76). But on p. 29 he cites (in German) John 14:6, "I am the way, the truth, and the life." Malik's comment is that this answer and the person who gave it "will infuse us with the greatest freedom we need and the most lucid intelligibility we can support."

21. David P. Gaines, *The World Council of Churches—A Study of Its Background and History* (Peterborough, N.H.: Richard P. Smith, 1966), p. 588.

22. *Loc cit.*

23. For example, Raphael Patai, *The Jewish Mind* (New York: Charles Scribner's Sons, 1977), p. 238: ". . . Jewry managed to survive the effects of Enlightenment, just as it did the genocidal attack that was launched against it from the same country in which the Haskalah started some 150 years earlier. That it survived, and that today, after both Enlightenment and Holocaust, it is more vital and vibrant than it was for many a generation, is the most eloquent testimony to the ability of the Jewish mind to cope with and adapt to the most unforeseen exigencies."

24. Malik in *God and Man in Islamic Thought,* p. 75, praises tolerance and differences. He warns that totalitarianism "arises when the false idea of unity and oneness gets hold of people, causing them to become unwilling or afraid to face difference. . . . There is freedom only in the presence of variety . . . . There is freedom only before a stubborn other who absolutely resists being reduced to *fana'* (nothingness)." In Gaines, *World Council of Churches,* p. 744, he is quoted as telling a plenary session of the WCC that the important thing "is not uniformity of culture but the growth of an international and intercultural order wherein every people and every culture will freely develop its own genius as much as possible. . . ." Zionism, I add, is grounded in this self-same conviction.

25. Abdallah Laroui, professor of history, Muhammad V University in Rabat, Morocco, cautions his Arab readers in *The Crisis of The Arab Intellectual: Traditionalism or Historicism?* (Berkeley: University of California Press, 1970–76), pp. 171–74, against using "the Palestinian affair" as an argument to reinforce ideological and political traditionalism and "the traditionalist mentality" that compounds "retardation." "The bare fact, impossible to deny," he writes, "is that Israel by its very existence has checked the Arabs' progress and has been one of the determining causes in the process of continual traditionalization. All liberal, secularizing, and progressive thought appeared as a ruse of Zionist and imperialist (!) propaganda." He nonetheless holds that "the progressive Arab intellectual must accept the Palestinian drama as a fact and the attitudes of others (rational or irrational) as facts, and he must define his position with regard to the cardinal problem of the Arabs: their historical retardation."

26. *The Kosari of R. Yehuda Halevy,* trans. Yehuda Even Shmuel (Tel-Aviv: Dvir, 1972), p. 71 (in Hebrew).

27. Meir Ben-Horin, "The Jewish Question and the Jewish Answer," *Reconstructionist* 40, no. 9 (December 1974):15–21 and no. 10 (January 1975):15–22.

28. Saul Bellow, *To Jerusalem and Back* (New York: Viking Press, 1976), p. 57.

Haim Arlozorov

SIMHA KLING

Introduction

The name Arlozorov should be familiar to anyone who lives in or visits Israel—nearly every town and city has a street bearing that name. In addition, there are other places named for the same person: a suburb of Haifa, Kiryat Hayim; a kibbutz, Givat Hayim; a village, Kfar Hayim. People may not know much about the man so honored, but they rightfully conclude that he must have been "a great man." That conclusion is a correct one; Haim Arlozorov was indeed "a great man," one of the outstanding personages of the state-on-the-way. He was not able to serve as a leader very long—he was assassinated when only thirty-four years old. But during the years of his leadership he proved to be eminently qualified. Though his prodigious talents were only beginning to be fully manifested, he left an indelible mark on his comrades and on the cause to which he dedicated his life.

One of the foremost Labor Zionists, Berl Katznelson, observed while eulogizing Arlozorov: "He rose to the level of a leader not only in his own family, the Workers' Movement in which he had been reared, but to the level of a leader of the entire people."[1]

He excelled as a diplomat. Endowed with a brilliant mind, vast learning, and considerable charm, he was supremely well prepared to meet with the representatives of nations in behalf of Zionism. From youth on, his talents and passionate commitment to the renascence of the Jewish people moved him to direct his entire being toward advancement of the Zionist cause. When he was murdered, he was genuinely and deeply mourned. The circumstances of his death were so baffling and disturbing that they continue to be somewhat mysterious even today.

It is to pay tribute to Haim Arlozorov, one of the noblest builders of

Zion, that this essay is written. It is hoped that many will come to know him
and appreciate him.

Early Years

When Haim Arlozorov rose to prominence in Zionist circles, he was
regarded as an offshoot of German Jewry. Indeed, he had grown up in
Germany and was immersed in German culture. His roots, however, lay in
East European Jewry. Arlozorov was born February 23, 1899, in the Ukra-
nian town of Romani to a prominent family. His grandfather (who died
when Haim was only three years old) was a distinguished rabbi, highly
respected and greatly loved. His father, Shaul Arlozorov, was reared in the
rabbi's pious home and was thoroughly immersed in the Jewish tradition,
but he was more of a secularist than a pietist. When Rabbi Arlozorov died,
Shaul was invited to be his successor but he refused, preferring to earn his
livelihood by engaging in business. His wife came from a prominent
Lithuanian family and shared her husband's views although she was more
observant. Together they built a home that became a meeting-place for
intellectuals, and raised a son and two daughters in a harmonious, loving
environment.

The family calm was interrupted by the pogroms that took place in 1905.
The Arlozorovs were themselves victims. The five year-old Haim happened to be sick in bed when the rioters attacked. One of them threw a
stone through the window and it shattered the bowl from which the youngster was being fed. The family fled immediately, escaping through a small
window to a next-door Christian neighbor who hid them in her laundry-
room. When the immediate danger passed, the Arlozorovs decided to leave
Russia and made their way to Germany.

They settled in the East Prussian town of Stalupenen, where they had
relatives and adjusted easily. The children had already learned some German and quickly abandoned Russian, which they associated with the ter-
rifying pogrom. Haim became Viktor, was enrolled in school, and proved
himself an excellent student. His Jewish studies were not neglected; a tutor
was engaged to teach him Hebrew. His peers, non-Jewish as well as Jewish,
turned to him for leadership, and the youngster excelled in such physical
feats as riding and swimming.

In 1913 the Arlozorovs moved to Koenigsberg. Viktor-Haim enrolled in
a gymnasium, where he again proved himself an excellent scholar as well as
a leader among his peers. Although he read a great deal, he was outstanding in dueling and other sports. He also studied Jewish subjects privately.
Fortunately, his tutor was a good pedagogue who instilled in his charge
strong, positive feelings about Judaism. When World War I broke out, the
Arlozorovs were still Russian citizens and therefore were in danger of
incarceration.

They moved to Berlin, thinking to make a temporary home there but were able to remain in the German capital. Viktor continued to make great strides academically and to study Hebrew privately with a teacher who inspired him to ardent Zionism. He soon resumed the name of Haim, and became the head of a group of fellow Jewish students. One of his comrades of that period later recalled:

> At first, we saw Jewish nationalism only as further national boundaries in a world blighted by blind nationalism. But it wasn't long before our hearts were captured by him. His entire personality influenced us and convinced us: his clear thinking and analyses, he had personal charm, his inner modesty in the presence of an opponent, the understanding he displayed towards every honest thought—all that later made him the all-Zionist leader came to expression in those days. . . . Haim Arlazorov was a leader whose authority was not questioned. The life of the group centered in his mother's home where we would meet daily.[2]

Haim taught his friends Hebrew and organized discussion seminars. He was admired by his fellow Christian students as well, even though he was known to be a committed Zionist. When he was sixteen, he wrote to a friend: "Is your Zionism well? If not—I'm ready to renew my missionary work at once."[3] His understanding of the Jewish national undertaking was remarkably mature. It is reflected in a letter which he wrote to a friend in late 1915:

> You write that it is necessary to establish in *Eretz Yisrael* a safe refuge for the Jews of Russia and Rumania. That is not the main goal of Zionism. Its goal is the awakening of great masses of Jews to develop a national life. And, if the Zionist accomplishments in settlement are paltry, the fault lies not with the goal itself but with the indifference of Jews and their lack of understanding.[4]

In other letters he expressed his great love for Jews and for Judaism. He stated that he appreciated German culture, even loved it, but nevertheless felt that it was not really his. His own roots lay in Judaism and his own culture was the Hebraic one. The teenager was concerned about his people's loss of freedom, their inability to develop their own traditions and ideas freely. Imbued with the dream of national liberty, he decided that his life could have meaning only if it were dedicated to the service of the Jewish people.

First Steps

The precocious young man read widely and thought much about Jewish nationalism, particularly its political and economic aspects. As he did so, he became convinced that the rebuilt homeland would have to be based on self-labor and social justice. He more and more turned to socialism, but not

in its Marxian garb. The teacher whose ideas attracted him, whose philosophy he espoused, was A. D. Gordon, the spiritual father of the pioneers in
Palestine. As Arlozorov was growing up, Gordon was still preaching his
doctrine of "the conquest of labor" and was teaching what came to be called
"the religion of labor."

By the time he was twenty, Arlozorov was considered a leading theoreti-
cian of his movement. He wrote a pamphlet "Folk Socialism of the Jews," in
which are found the basic ideas that he later expounded in a more mature
fashion. He insisted that real socialism did not deny nationalism; hence it
was legitimate for Jews to follow their own socialist way. The economic laws
of normal peoples did not apply to the Jews, and therefore the concept of
"class warfare" was inapplicable. The Jewish problem was not one of the
exploited versus the exploiters but the complete economic structure of
Galut (Exile), not social in nature but national, not prolitariat versus
bourgeoisie but a return to the soil.

> The Jewish people which, in its exile, has forgotten labor must—if it
> wants to create its own future for itself—find the way to return to labor.
> To return the Jewish masses to productivity (in the real sense of the
> word)—that must be our primary goal.[5]

That goal, he insisted, could be achieved only on the soil of the homeland. Moreover, it was not based on a mechanistic "historical process" but
on human will and the human mind. Indeed, Arlozorov asserted that the
generally accepted socialism had been made into a question of the stomach
and ignored the power of the spirit. Thus the Jewish desire to return to
Eretz Yisrael was not rooted simply in economic needs but in Jewish history
and in Jewish idealism.

Arlozorov amplified these ideas further as he grew older. Thus in 1926
he again asserted that the concept of class warfare did not apply to the
Jews, that the situation in Eretz Yisrael was different from that of other
countries and therefore required a different approach. He refuted Marx's
premise that nationalism was inauthentic and maintained that national
groups were natural and desirable. He held that his party must aim for a
creative Jewish society in which there would be neither exploiters nor exploited.

The young Arlozorov set about organizing a movement that embodied
his principles. It was called Hitaḥdut (Unity), and he became one of its
leaders. It was affiliated with the Palestinian party, Hapoᶜel Hatzaᶜir, which
rejected the concept of class warfare and the idea that Zion would be
rebuilt because of "objective forces." Hapoᶜel Hatzaᶜir was based on the
teachings of Gordon; it called for personal dedication to work and for the
highest ethical standards. It was opposed to the other dominant labor
party, Poᶜale Zion (also founded in 1905), which was more Marxist in its

orientation. In contrast to Po^cale Zion, Hapo^cel Hatza^cir did not have a clearly defined doctrine and was not affiliated with the Second International.

Po^cale Zion held that the history of mankind was a series of national and class struggles. Since there was no developed capitalism in Palestine, a capitalist class would have to develop, and then a Jewish working class would come into being with events following the "normal" historic process. Hapo^cel Hatza^cir, on the other hand, was pragmatic and insisted that Jewish workers in Eretz Yisrael faced a situation that was totally different from that of any other labor movement, that they were pioneers in a Jewish national renascence, and that all efforts should be directed to effecting this renascence rather than emphasizing class distinctions. Thus it did not regard the Jewish worker as a laborer with interests rigidly opposed to other classes, but as an active force in building the national home on the basis of social justice.

First Visit

In January of 1921, Haim Arlozorov went to Palestine for the first time. He stayed nine months, during which he absorbed the mood and the feelings of Jewish Palestine. Soon after his arrival, he wrote to his mother that Eretz Yisrael was a magic land with a unique, wonderful power of its own, and that whoever came there and left was bound to return. He did not become involved in public affairs, though he was widely recognized as being wise far beyond his years. Quietly and passively, he spent his time in learning and becoming part of the labor camp.

When the riots broke out in May of 1921, Arlozorov joined the Jewish defense forces and stood guard with his comrades. Afterwards he wrote an article in *Hapo^cel Hatza^cir,* the publication of his movement, in which he reviewed British policy, Arab nationalism, and Jewish strength. Warning against excessive criticism of the British, he asserted (as he was often to do in later years) that Zionists must evaluate realities and base future policies on them rather than on exaggerated emotions, and that they must think constructively rather than hysterically. He warned against discounting Arab nationalism, even though it did appear to be an artificial creation of feudal landlords seeking to retain power. Since the only way for Jews to attain their purposes was that of peace and reconciliation, he called for developing a *modus vivendi* in which both nationalisms could live together.

After living for nine months in Eretz Yisrael, Arlozorov returned to Berlin. He had concluded that those who were urging him to complete his university studies were correct, that he had to prepare himself properly if he were to make a contribution to the cause. Earlier he had thought of medicine as a career, but now he felt that he needed thorough grounding in economics and political science. He was an outstanding student, but he did not restrict himself to academia. He continued his Zionist activities, writing and speaking and traveling to meetings. For him, Zionism was no mere extracurricular activity; it was deeply personal and had to be expressed in action.

He was one of the key people who planned and carried out the Third Conference of Hitaḥdut in 1922. His address (delivered in Hebrew) dealt with the inappropriateness of Marxist doctrines for Palestinian socialism. As earlier, he stressed the inapplicability of the concept of class warfare and called for "a mutual society" made up of social and economic cells reflecting the socialist spirit. This position was the one adopted by the Hapoᶜel Hatzaᶜir party.

On the International Scene

The World Zionist Conference held in Carlsbad soon after the Hitaḥdut meeting in 1922 was the scene of Arlozorov's debut on the international Zionist scene. When he rose to speak, a twenty-three-year-old in the midst of delegates far older and more experienced than he, he did not seem to be anything but a youngster. "Bashful, retiring, modest with not a trace of color in his cheeks, his eyes hidden behind thick glasses, he seemed removed from the world about him, absorbed in deep thought."[6] Nonetheless, he compelled the attention of the congress, not because of his impassioned oratory—in all of his addresses he refrained from rhetorical flourishes and empty clichés—but because of the content of his message, because he revealed amazing knowledge and depth.

> He had his own style and vocabulary and had no other object in view than the point under discussion. It was an extemporaneous address, for he did not have any notes. The audience was impressed and wondered who he was.[7]

From the congress, Arlozorov returned to Berlin to complete his dissertation on "Class Warfare in Marx's Teachings" and received his doctorate in economics. Dr. Haim Arlozorov was now prepared to devote himself to Zionism completely. He began work on a book dealing with the financial problems of the World Zionist Organization and proposed a solution to which he frequently returned as he rose to the upper ranks of leadership: an international loan to enable the Jewish people to build their national home.

In 1923 Arlozorov participated in the thirteenth World Zionist Congress and so impressed the delegates that, despite his youth, they elected him to the Actions Committee. Henceforth Zionism was to be his principal occupation and preoccupation. Still, he reserved occasional hours for his favorite hobbies: books and stamp collecting (he was an expert philatelist).

In the Land

In the spring of 1924, Arlozorov (with his wife and young daughter) moved to Palestine. He did not want to accept a position in either the Party or the Histadrut. Instead, he went to work at the Agricultural Station of the Jewish Agency, where he was to conduct studies in agricultural economics. He had time to work for Hapoᶜel Hatzaᶜr and became a member of its secretariat as well as of the Histadrut executive. He also wrote many articles for the party press and for journals abroad. He lectured at various branches of the movement, drawing large and enthusiastic audiences, "to the degree that the public got to know him better, he became more endeared. His appearance always attracted thousands."[8]

In 1926 Arlozorov was elected to both the governing body of Palestinian Jewry (Asefat Hanivḥarim) and its executive (Vaᶜad L'umi). Soon afterwards he and two others (Meir Diezengoff and Rabbi Uziel) were chosen as a special delegation of the Jewish community of Eretz Yisrael to the Leage of Nations in Geneva. Before leaving, Arlozorov published an article in *Hapoᶜel Hatzaᶜir* that expressed his basic ideas; it was entitled "Ḥoma Shel Z'khukhit" (A Wall of Glass). It dealt with one of his overriding political concerns: the need to clarify British-Jewish relationships. Arlozorov always supported mutual cooperation, but realized that working together meant overcoming very real hurdles. Thus he dealt with the British colonial system in this article, explaining the factors underlying reactions of the officials. Arlozorov pointed out that those in service of the Colonial Office were not trained to be sensitive to the feelings, yearnings, demands, and complaints of the governed. They were responsible to London, not to the people being ruled. They rigidly adhered to the rules and regulations by which they were to operate, not to the needs of the colonial peoples or to the exigencies of the hour.

This colonial psychology made dealings with Jews very difficult because Jews were very different from others governed by Britian. They were not primitives but educated, not subservient but insistent upon their rights, not passive but active. The Jews asked questions, criticized, protested, insisted upon their rights. They were therefore a disturbing element in official eyes. The result, Arlozorov concluded, was the erection of a high glass wall through which the sun shone but that remained impenetrable.

Yet the purpose of the delegation was not to attempt to break down that wall. Since the Jews had to deal with England not only in the present but for some time in the future, it was vital not to attack but to improve relations. The Jews should not set about proving how formidable the wall was but should instead find ways how to scale it. That did not mean ignoring offenses nor keeping silent about legitimate complaints. What it meant was a positive rather than a negative approach, securing the good will of the League's members and enlightening the British. The delegation's task, as he saw it, was to elicit financial as well as political and moral support for the Jewish national home.

In Geneva, Arlozorov was the moving force of the delegation. He was an unusual linguist; besides Hebrew and Yiddish, he was thoroughly at home in German and English, knew French and some Russian, and often quoted the Latin classics in the original. He well understood the world of diplomats and diplomacy. He was thoroughly versed in the subjects under discussion and able to answer all questions without hesitation. These qualifications plus his personal charm and mastery of political and economic issues made a tremendous impression on those with whom he met and served to create a greater sympathy for the cause he represented.

Haim Arlozorov proceeded to London from Geneva to attend a meeting of the Actions Committee before returning home to prepare for the twentieth Conference of Hapoʿel Hatzaʿir (of which he was then general secretary). His address there was a mature presentation of his views on socialism, views that he had previously offered but not in so polished a manner. With the conference behind him, Arlozorov was ready to accept Weizmann's invitation to join him on a mission to America in behalf of Keren Hayesod. Long interested in what had already become the largest Jewish community of the world, one upon whose generosity so many hopes rested, he eagerly accepted.

America

Arlozorov arrived in the United States in November of 1926 and remained until the following March. What he found was most disconcerting. The American Zionist leaders virtually ignored him and seemed hostile to the young representative of Palestinian Labor; in his diary he complained of being given "the silent treatment." Yet, when Arlozorov did appear in New York, the audience responded with enthusiastic applause and the Jewish press praised him generously. Arlozorov was able to establish close relations with labor leaders, one of the most prominent of whom (Max Fein) observed to several American Labor Zionists: "I have learned a great deal from you in recent years—but what I learned in one hour's conversation with Arlozorov I never learned from you in years."[9]

On this trip and a succeeding one (from the beginning of 1928 until May 1929) Arlozorov traveled over most of Canada and the United States, from the East to the West Coast. The pace was grueling but he did not complain. He was able to establish warm relationships with many young Jews and to influence those in Zionist youth groups. Yet he continued to meet with indifference on the part of the leadership.

Arlozorov was very disturbed by the frightening alienation of so many Jews from Judaism, by the overwhelming threat of assimilation. And yet he was not pessimistic. He saw that the American environment was different from the European and hence required a new approach. He published his impressions and opinions in a series of letters entitled *New York VIrushalayim* ("New York and Jerusalem"); they contained exhaustive sociological and economic studies of American Jewry.

Realistically, Arlozorov pointed out that the fate of Yiddish was sealed in the New World, that it was no longer part of a living culture nor could it be so in the future. He understood that new forms were emerging in a culture that was unlike any in Europe, one inhospitable to national autonomies, different languages, and political parties associated with ethnic or religious groups. Therefore American Jewry had to be accepted as a unique segment of the Jewish people, one that would live and develop in accord with its unique historical situation: " . . . we cannot measure American Jewry by any measure of accepted concepts but only by its own life, according to the economic, social and cultural phenomena."[10]

Arlozorov was very critical of the Zionist establishment in the United States. He saw the leaders embroiled in personality confrontations while neglecting to build a movement. He regarded them as men devoid of character and principles, and as sowing confusion and distrust and cynicism. He took them to task for their failure to work with the youth and imbuing them with the basic fundamentals of Zionism. He was so revolted by what he saw that he could write: "If, throughout my life, I was ever, for one moment, embarrassed at being called a Zionist, it was here in America."[11] He concluded that a thorough reorganization was necessary, and called on the World Zionist Organization to step in to bring about the required radical changes.

Mapai

Following his first American tour, Arlozorov undertook the realization of a project he had earlier opposed. A decade before, there had been an attempt to unify all Labor Zionists. The labor camp in Palestine was then divided into three camps: Po⁽ale Zion, the unaffiliated, and Hapo⁽el·Hatza⁽ir. The first two eagerly sought a merger; Hapo⁽el Hatza⁽ir, however, refused to go along. Its members feared the loss of their principles and feared the proposal as a victory for Marxism. Po⁽ale Zion and the unaffiliated proceeded alone and created a new party, Aḥdut ⁽Avoda. Refusing to become part of the new party, the leaders of Hapo⁽el Hatza⁽ir nevertheless recognized the common issues confronting all labor groups and agreed to join in establishing an umbrella organization, the Histadrut.

In the succeeding years of working together, the ideological differences increasingly faded. Many of the Hapo⁽el Hatza⁽ir apprehensions proved groundless. The leaders of Aḥdut ⁽Avoda were not doctrinaire Marxists and approached their tasks pragmatically. By the close of the twenties, the key people in both Aḥdut ⁽Avoda and Hapo⁽el Hatza⁽ir were fully aware that separateness was an anachronism. Yet all their followers were not convinced, and considerable effort had to be expended before the two could merge. The Aḥdut ᶜAvoda leaders, Ben Gurion and Berl Katznelson, together with the chief Hapoᶜel Hatzaᶜir leader, Arlozorov, agreed to persuade their constituents. Arlozorov frequently pointed to the disappearance of former distinctions: the Hapoᶜel Hatzaᶜir's championing of Hebrew rather than Yiddish had been fully accepted by Aḥdut ᶜAvoda as had its rejection of class warfare. Indeed, he contended, the party programs reflected turn-of-the-century thinking and were not applicable to the thirties.

In both parties there were small factions who refused to endorse the proposed merger and insisted on going their separate ways. But the majority of each was convinced by the persuasive and cogent arguments of their leaders. Thus in 1930, Hapoᶜel Hatzaᶜir and Aḥdut ᶜAvoda jointed together to create a new party, Mapai, one that led to the dominance of Labor not only in Palestine but also on the World Zionist scene.

Rising Star

As a Mapai leader, Arlozorov became more and more involved in party work—speaking, writing, and attending meetings, especially diplomatic efforts. He was an ardent supporter of Chaim Weizmann, with whose policies he occasionally disagreed but to whom he was always loyal. He boldly opposed Jabotinsky and his right-wing Revisionist party, which militated against socialism and insisted that the future Jewish state must include the territory on both sides of the Jordan River. Arlozorov, like his comrades, regarded the Revisionists as militant chauvinists, as Jewish fascists. Yet he recognized Jabotinsky's sincerity and brilliance and considered him as one who made premature rather than erroneous demands. When asked how he would feel if the mandatory power, which had forbidden Jabotinsky to enter Palestine, were to allow him to come to the country, he replied:

> Even though I well know that Jabotinsky will attack the Jewish Agency more than the Government, I do not for one moment hesitate to demand permission for him to enter the country. Jabotinsky was here for years and we fought him successfully. The Palestine Government has made him into the pursued; to my mind it has no right to forbid him entry.[12]

Although he was neither so acrid nor so bitter as about Revisionists as most of his colleagues, Arlozorov was not viewed more temperately than they by the Revisionist spokesmen. He did regard their philosophy and tactics as dangerous, while they classified him as one of their enemies. The differences became more acute as Arlozorov rose to his party's highest echelons.

To appreciate the pinnacle reached by Arlozorov in 1931, it is necessary to understand what took place in the preceding two years. Events in the first part of 1929 encouraged Zionists tremendously. On the one hand, a Labor government (headed by Ramsey MacDonald) came to power in England, and it promised much because the British Labor Party had long been a faithful friend of Zionism. On the other, prominent non-Zionist Jews entered into a formal agreement to help in the task of building a Jewish Palestine. They and the Zionists formed the expanded Jewish Agency and thus involved themselves financially and morally in the practical affairs of Eretz Yisrael.

Unfortunately, the high hopes were speedily frustrated. Shocking atrocities took place in Palestine in the summer of 1929. The Mufti of Jerusalem succeeded in fomenting violent attacks upon the Jewish community and found the mandatory government either too weak or too indifferent to bring them to a speedy halt. Following the 1929 riots, London sent an investigatory commission headed by Sir Walter Shaw, and it absolved the Mufti, the Arab Executive, and the administration of any guilt. The Commission contended that Palestine could not absorb many new immigrants and alleged that Jewish acquisition of land dispossessed large numbers of Arab peasants.

Haim Arlozorov wrote a blistering attack on the methods as well as the findings of the Shaw Commission. He called its members naive and pointed out that they had failed to study all the sociological and economic facts before arriving at conclusions. Moreover, no local people with firsthand knowledge of the country were drafted to the Commission. "But what the Shaw Commission derived from its cross-examinations on the land and immigration problems is an indefinable mixture of tourist trivialities, ignorance of facts and a large dose of animosity."[13] Arlozorov pointed out that land policy could not be an isolated issue, but had to be considered as part of the economic development of the country as a whole, that what was involved was not a static situation but one of social dynamics. The commission thought solely in terms of legalities rather than the social, political, and economic realities and potential. Its conclusions, Arlozorov held, constituted a superficial, mechanistic formula; they were a mixture of "economic innocence, lack of touch with the concrete Palestinian issues," and "a goodly dose of outspoken prejudice."[14]

The Shaw Commission was followed by another (in 1930) headed by Sir John Hope Simpson. Even before Sir John submitted his report, which was a general condemnation of practically everything the Jews had done in Palestine, London announced the suspension of Jewish immigration and a general acceptance of the Shaw Commission's conclusions. It issued a white paper (known as the Passfield White Paper), which held that the Jewish national home was not meant to be the principal feature of the mandate.

The new policy virtually negated the Balfour Declaration, severely curtailed Jewish immigration, and prohibited Jews from further acquisition of agricultural land.

The Passfield White Paper evoked a tremendous reaction from non-Jews as well as Jews. The government was attacked in Parliament. Weizmann resigned as president of the World Zionist Organization and of the Jewish Agency. Lord Melchett, who resigned from the chairmanship of the Jewish Agency Administrative Committee, declared: "The grotesque travesty of the purpose of the Mandate given in the Government's Paper can only be described as an insult to the intelligence of Jewry and a deliberate affront to the Mandates Commission."[15] Floods of protest came from all over the world.

The British government could not ignore such an overwhelming negative reaction. The prime minister announced that the white paper had been misunderstood and no change of policy was intended. He told Dr. Weizmann that it could not be legally retracted, but agreed to write a letter reassuring him and his fellow Zionists. The McDonald letter acknowledged that what the Jews had done had benefited the whole country and that the government would carry out its mandatory commitments. It did not repudiate the Passfield White Paper but, couched in a friendly tone, explained away its objectionable passages. The Zionists accepted the letter, albeit without enthusiasm; the Arabs fulminated against it.

At the Seventeenth Zionist Congress (July 1931), the British proposals and the McDonald letter were the focus of stormy deliberations. Arlozorov's address to the delegates was widely hailed and won him recognition as one of the key men of the movement. Weizmann, who was forced out of the presidency because of his seemingly naive and unwarranted faith in England, was so impressed that he sent him a note: ". . . my only consolation at this sad Congress is that there arose a leader of great ability and tremendous promise for the Zionist movement such as you."[16]

Head of Political Department

A new executive was elected at the end of the Seventeenth Congress. Nahum Sokolow succeeded Chaim Weizmann and the executive was opened to Labor representatives. Haim Arlozorov was given a portfolio admirably suited to his talents. He became head of the Political Department in Jerusalem, a post comparable to that of foreign minister in a politically recognized state. He was indeed eminently qualified for the position. He held a doctorate in economics from the University of Berlin: he was well versed not only in the English language but in the entire Anglo-Saxon culture; he was a suave European completely at home in Western civilization as well as one who knew his own tradition and his own people intimately. Moreover, he possessed the character and personality traits required for a diplomat: charm, tact, wit. One of the Zionist activists once commented:

He could argue his point without arousing anger or animosity. He was always in the very center of the party struggle and frequently was the prosecuting attorney, but he invariably performed this unpleasant duty without a trace of bitterness and with great tolerance and tact.[17]

Chaim Weizmann, the leading Zionist protagonist in the period between the two World Wars, called attention to Arlozorov's talents in his autobiography: "He was a man of brilliant mind and he was particularly fit to present our philosophy of Zionism to the younger generation. It was a privilege to watch him work."[18]

Arlozorov's appointment was not hailed by all Zionists. Many of the non-Laborites were not pleased with a Labor representative's holding such a position, particularly one so young. The Revisionists were vociferous in their denouncement. Indeed, when Arlozorov returned to Jerusalem in his new capacity, the first newspaper he saw was the rightist newspaper, *Doar Hayom,* bearing the headline: "Raq Lo Arlozorov" ("Only Not Arlozorov"). He was naturally offended, even though he knew that the antisocialists looked upon him as an enemy. He was momentarily tempted to reply, but he restrained himself; he would not become involved in petty defamations. He decided that his record would speak for itself and that he would devote all his energies to the tremendous tasks before him.

One of his duties was to attempt to effect a rapprochment with the Arabs. He had long felt that it was possible to work out a *modus vivendi* with moderate Arabs, and he now proceeded to meet with them, to discuss their common purposes and differences, to persuade them to accept Zionism. At a time when many Zionists argued that Arab nationalism was an artificial creation and need not be taken seriously Arlozorov contended that it was real. He warned his colleagues not to deceive themselves and told them that there was "nothing more damaging than to deceive the mind by an erroneous evaluation of the enemy's strength."[19] Arlozorov understood that Arab nationalism would grow, that it was only beginning to take shape in the twenties. He saw the changes that took place after World War I, the emergence of educated and literate young Arabs who were seeking their own national identity. In 1929 he stated:

It seems to me that so far we have not properly evaluated the level to which a large part of the young Arab generation in this country has reached, that which has gone through the schools of government, the Histadrut, the scouts and then the English university.[20]

Arlozorov perceived that Arab sensitivities called for an adequate Zionist response. He suggested various projects to influence Arab thinking, to persuade them to live amicably with the Jews, and to cooperate in building the land they both inhabited. He recommended sponsorship of an Arab newspaper that could counteract the irresponsible rantings of Arab extremists. He urged the establishment of loan societies and welfare organizations concerned with the unhappy lot of the Arab masses. He also counselled Jewish students to major in Islamic studies and thereby become qualified to serve as mediators between Arabs and their own people.

Arlozorov's earlier optimism waned as he was confronted with reality, as he faced the irrational hostility of the Arab leaders with whom he met. He did not cease to advocate cooperation and to continue to consult various Muslims personally, but his enthusiasm and faith were sorely tested. He had to deal with the forces of the Mufti of Jerusalem, who was not merely intransigent himself but who used all methods, fair and foul, to silence those more moderate than he. He found Palestinian Arabs increasingly inflexible, deaf to logic and reason. It was not long before his sense of despair intensified and he began to wonder if his fellow Zionists should not adopt a very different course.

His doubts were sharpened by his experiences with the British. Arlozorov had shared Weizmann's confidence in the philo-Semitism of the English and had advocated trust in the good-will of His Majesty's government. His position was not rooted in naiveté; he frequently stated: "We are commanded to see reality as it is."[21] He recognized the antagonism of many colonial officials, and their failure to appreciate Zionist aims and goals. Yet he knew that the future of Palestine was tied up with Great Britain and he believed that it was possible to befriend and to influence British officials. Even though the mandatory regime had displayed open and flagrant favoritism toward the Arabs, even though it had failed to carry out promises made to the Jews, Arlozorov continued to advocate slow, plodding efforts to find avenues of cooperation.

As head of the Political Department, Arlozorov attempted to educate both the British and the Arabs as to the real meaning of Zionism and to persuade them that they would benefit from its realization. He spent countless hours with their representatives as well as with many visitors and all the diplomats in Jerusalem. He became personal friends with the British high commissioner, Sir Arthur Wauchope, who came to admire and have high regard for him. Arlozorov tried to get Sir Arthur to understand the Jews and their problems. He persuaded him to read Leo Pinsker's "Autoemancipation," which presented an incisive analysis of anti-Semitism and which Arlozorov considered the basis of the Hebrew national movement. The high commissioner understood what Pinsker meant by speaking of anti-Semitism as an incurable disease, yet he did not accept that analysis as pertinent for the English. Indeed, he wrote to Arlozorov that anti-Semitism was not endemic to Great Britain nor was it likely to develop. Similarly, in matters affecting Zionism and the Jewish national home, Wauchope was sympathetic, but still attempted to follow a course that would not offend the Arabs.

As Arlozorov sought to influence the British and the Arabs and as he carried out the grueling tasks of his office, he felt an increasing sense of frustration. Each day brought new aggravations and nerve-wracking irritations. He began to lose faith in the possibility of cooperation with the mandatory power. Just two weeks before his death, he told a colleague:

> You have no idea how difficult it is to bring together such diverse elements as the British and the Jews, with their tremendous differences in character and moods and world-outlooks. Sometimes it seems to me that these two worlds will never meet. And yet the undertaking depends to a large degree on mutual understanding.[22]

Arlozorov began to question the policy heretofore followed by Weizmann and his colleagues, which he himself had espoused, that of gradualism and step-by-step development. Weizmann could not believe that the British would ever betray their commitments or renege on their promises to the Jews. He believed that Zionism would be achieved slowly, by gradual development and continued negotiations with London. Arlozorov had long agreed, and had even been attacked for excessive faith in the British, but now, after the experiences of his position, he was no longer sure. In a letter to Weizmann, he said:

> I am reaching the conclusion that, with the present procedures and the present regime, there is almost no possibility of solving the problems of immigration and mass settlement. Why? The basis of our policy is that it is necessary and possible to reach our goal step-by-step, one level after another. To be sure, that was the proper and the only way in the past; any alternative to be considered today has to reckon with the actual strength of the Jewish community in *Eretz Yisrael*.[23]

Arlozorov saw that that strength was limited by virtue of the Jews constituting a minority. He feared that the continuation of the same policy would keep them as such. Moreover, he foresaw a world war in five or ten years and was certain that Great Britain would then openly favor the Arabs for imperial reasons and renounce all obligations to the Jews. He also understood what would happen in Germany and perhaps all Europe, and that would make the need for admission of Jews into Palestine imperative.

Thus Arlozorov came to a bold conclusion. He confided it to no one but Dr. Weizmann and it was not revealed to the public until many years later. In a secret letter written in June of 1932, he suggested that the Jews take over the government of Palestine. Democracy would be suspended until there would be a Jewish majority. During the interim revolutionary period, masses of Jews would be brought into the country and development would proceed apace. The Jewish control of the military would prevent the Arabs from uprising and the "greater Zionism" would be effected.

Weizmann did not comment, and the pressure of duties prevented further discussion. Arlozorov had no time to work out a program and proceeded with his daily efforts to persuade the Administration to allow more Jews entry into Palestine and to achieve whatever was possible.

Germany

The rise of the nazis reinforced Arlozorov's sense of urgency—the need to save Jews, and to move quickly toward the fulfillment of Zionist goals. He drew up a program and personally went to examine the situation at firsthand. Before leaving for Germany on April 26, 1933, he presented his program to his Jewish Agency colleagues: negotiate with the German government about Jews' leaving and taking their money with them; negotiate with the British about admission of German Jewish immigrants; prepare for the absorption of the immigrants. There was opposition to any negotiations whatsoever with the nazis, but Arlozorov maintained that there was no alternative to rescuing everyone possible.

In Germany he met with the leaders of German Jewry, with Zionists, with many friends and acquaintances. Everything that he saw and learned convinced him of the need to proceed as rapidly as possible. He suggested the establishment of a liquidation bank, and the immediate sending of children, who would be settled in kibbutzim and youth villages. He also proposed training people in agriculture and in the Hebrew language in order to facilitate their absorption upon arrival.

At the end of May he left Berlin for London, to report to the Zionist Executive and to persuade his colleagues to effect his proposals without delay. He then returned to Europe to tour Czechoslovakia, Poland, and Austria, addressing large assemblies wherever he stopped. He returned home on June 14, physically and emotionally exhausted.

The Murder

The first day of his return was spent with the family in Tel Aviv. The second day was one of meetings in Tel Aviv and Jerusalem. On the third day, a Friday, he met with the high commissioner and, late in the day, returned to Tel Aviv for a quiet, restful Sabbath. He had agreed to schedule no appointments, no meetings. He and his wife had dinner at a hotel and then went for a stroll on the seashore. They walked for some time, beyond the city lights, alone. Mrs. Arlozorov was apprehensive about going so far, but her husband reassured her.

While returning, they became aware of two men who followed them, then passed them a few times only to fall behind and follow them again. After a short while, the pair stopped the Arlozorovs. One shone a flashlight in Arlozorov's face while the other made an obscene sexual gesture toward his wife. The first then asked the time while the second took a gun out of his pocket and shot Arlozorov. As he fell, the assailants fled. Mrs. Arlozorov called for help and people quickly appeared. They carried Arlozorov to the street, put him in a car, and took him to the Hadassah Hospital. Mrs. Arlozorov was taken to a nearby hotel for questioning by the police. By the time she was able to reach the hospital, her husband had been unsuccessfully operated on and was dead.

For years, the identity of the murderers was the source of bitter controversy. Arlozorov himself had not been able to identify them. In the hospital, while still conscious, he was asked by a police officer: "Do you know who it was?" He replied: "No." The officer went on: "Do you suspect anyone?" Arlozorov answered: "No—no one."

The murder took place at a time when relations between the Revisionist and Labor parties had become intensely hostile. In the Revisionist press such epithets as "traitor" and "despicable lacky of the British" were frequently hurled at Weizmann and Arlozorov. The Laborites, in turn, spoke of the Revisionists as fascists and destroyers of Zionism. Abba Achimeir, head of an extremist Revisionist faction, had written:

The concept of a political crime is subjective. The guilty party and his followers not only do not regard it as a crime but see it as a positive act. . . . One who kills for profit is a murderer. But the zealot who kills an administration personage is not simply a murderer. It is ethically permitted to kill for public welfare. It is not the murder itself that determines the verdict but the purpose for which the murder was undertaken.[24]

On the other hand, on March 15, 1933, Ben-Gurion sent a letter to the members of his party in which he compared the Revisionists to the nazis.

We do not have storm-troopers but those who oppose us fight exactly as Hitler fought the workers. The aims and programs are alike—but there is a difference. The German people will not be destroyed by Hitler while we can be destroyed if we do not take steps against our Hitlers . . . we are confronted by a life and death struggle.[25]

The acrimony was so bitter and the atmosphere so tense that many were convinced that the Revisionists had plotted and carried out the assassination of Haim Arlozorov. There was no clear evidence. Mrs. Arlozorov was confused and her testimony, which was definite at the trial, was actually unreliable. Much later it was brought out that at first, at the hotel, she had stated that the murderers were Arabs. Then, for reasons never explained, she identified the culprits as Jews. Because the beach was dark she could not positively identify the two men who had accosted her husband and herself, but she was able to describe one as tall and the other short. She was also able to recognize the Hebrew accent of the one who had asked the time as Near-Eastern rather than European.

Before the first week was out, three Revisionists were regarded as suspects by the police. Abba Achimeir was accused of plotting the murder; Avraham Stavsky and Zvi Rosenblatt were held as the two on the seashore. All three vehemently denied involvement. Two were acquitted for lack of evidence: Achimeir and Rosenblatt (who was at a meeting out-of-town that Friday night). Stavsky was judged guilty and held in prison for nearly a year until released for lack of positive evidence. The defense accused the police of manipulating the testimonies for political reasons and set forth the theory that the murder was committed by two Arabs who intended a sexual assault on Mrs. Arlozorov.

Indeed, there were two Arabs who fit the description of Mrs. Arlozorov. They were incarcerated in a Jaffa prison on charges of murdering an Arab. Both were known as rifraff and degenerates. Moreover, one of them had twice confessed to Arlozorov's murder but twice retracted the confessions. The British, however, declared that they were not the culprits. They ignored Stavsky's contention that he had been in Jerusalem the Friday night of the murder, that witnesses had seen him in a restaurant at 8:00 P.M. and at his hotel at 6:30 A.M. Instead, the prosecution argued that he had driven to Tel Aviv, committed the murder, and immediately returned to Jerusalem.

Many Jews refused to accept the idea that one Jew would spill the blood of another Jew for political purposes. The venerable Chief Rabbi Kook stated that he was prepared to swear before the Ark of the Torah on Yom Kippur that Stavsky was innocent. The national poet, Bialik, privately agreed with Rabbi Kook. The renowned scholar Joseph Klausner later wrote in his autobiography:

> From the first moment, it was difficult for me to believe that Jews, be they the extremists among the extremists, would kill a Zionist-Jew who was not among the extreme Socialist Zionists who opposed class warfare in *Eretz Yisrael*, who had been a member of *Hapo^cel Hatza^cir* and had opposed unification of this party with the more leftist *Ahdut ^cAvoda*, and when the merger of the two took place merely acquiesced and remained one of the most moderate in *Mapai*. Why should the Revisionists have murdered him specifically?[26]

And, to be sure, Jabotinsky strongly defended Stavsky's innocence. He wrote an article paying tribute to Arlozorov and declaring the murderer an anathema. Nevertheless, the Labor majority continued to suspect the Revisionists of having a hand in the affair. Eventually, after Stavsky was released from prison, the tensions eased. yet the case was not forgotten. In

1948 Stavsky was a member of the crew of the ill-fated ship *Altalena,* which attempted to bring arms to the Irgun during the armistice. He was killed in the battle that took place following Ben Gurion's order that the cargo was not to be landed. With his death, new articles about Arlozorov's murder appeared. Abba Achimeir addressed an open letter to the minister of police, Behor Shitrit (who had conducted the government's investigation in 1933), asking him to declare publicly that Stavsky was innocent. The letter went unanswered.

In 1955, shortly before elections to the Knesset, one of the key Labor leaders who had been the investigating officer of the police for a short while in 1933, Yehuda Arazi, called a conference of one hundred journalists to declare that he was convinced that Arabs had slain Arlozorov and that the Jews were innocent. He had reached that conclusion within forty-eight hours after he began his investigations. He submitted a report of his doubts as to the veracity of the witnesses to his superior, but the document was suppressed. Arazi was soon removed from the case and his copy of the report was kept in a secret file until 1973, when it was published in the afternoon paper, *Ma'ariv.*

It is now generally accepted that the two Arabs were indeed the murderers, but the reason for the murder has not yet been fully clarified. Perhaps Stavsky's defense was correct in alleging that Arlozorov was killed in frustrating a sexual attempt upon his wife. Or perhaps Margot Klausner, in her book on Arlozorov, was correct in suggesting that the murder was commissioned by someone who vehemently opposed Arlozorov's plans to effect the immigration of large number of European Jews. "I am not sure that Isa El-Abrash (the alleged assassin) was not sent by the Mufti or some other official, e.g. a Nazi, who had an interest in preventing the mass immigration of Jews from Europe."[27]

Conclusion

The news of Arlozorov's death spread quickly throughout the country and evoked not only deep mourning but also countless tributes. Thousands accompanied the body to its last resting place in the Tel Aviv cemetery, and memorial meetings were held in numerous places. The outstanding figures of Palestinian Jewry eulogized the fallen leader. Bialik spoke of his deeply moral character; Berl Katznelson referred to him as the "prodigy" of the Labor Movement; Moshe Sharett characterized his brief but stunning career as "a miracle."

The lavish praise of the fallen leader was not mere rhetoric nor simply exaggerated laudations prompted by the tragedy. They were accurate descriptions of Arlozorov's character, personality, and achievements. Haim Arlozorov had indeed been a rare, remarkable, and sensitive human being. His keen intellect reflected an outstanding mind, which applied all that he had thought, read, and learned to the goal of his people's redemption. He had endeared himself to many and was highly respected by friend and foe alike.

Arlozorov was a gifted orator, one who moved audiences by the clarity of his thought rather than by emotional forensics. He was also a prolific writer who wrote about political, social, and economic problems and composed moving poetry. The last of the seven volumes of his writings (published by Mapai after his death) consists of the poems, many of which were written in German and were translated into Hebrew by outstanding men of letters. The diary he kept while political head (published in 1949 and entitled *Yoman Y'rushalayim, Jerusalem Diary*) related his manifold activities in rich Hebrew. German may have been his native tongue as he matured, but he had succeeded in gaining amazing mastery of the Hebrew language.

At first glance Arlozorov may have appeared to be an intellectual unaffected by emotion. His approach to problems and his method of expression were indeed intellectual. Yet he was far from a cold rationalist. Behind the exterior lay passion, fervor, deep feelings. Arlozorov was a man of vision and great faith, a believer in ideals and the power of dreams. This union of intellect and passion was recognized by Berl Katznelson who, when eulogizing Arlozorov, observed:

> Outwardly, in practical matters, in analyzing things, in explaining issues—he appeared before us as a complete rationalist, as one who has no other path but that of logic, of *real-politik;* of mathematical calculation, and he approached every practical question, economic and political, with a sharp scalpel. He would dissect illusions and destroy them and was unafraid of the inward gulf that might loom between him and the audience he was addressing. But, inwardly, under the rationalistic mask, an irrational faith burned, a faith that defied all experience, all winds of negation and rejection.[28]

Arlozorov was only thirty-four years old when he was struck down. He was just at the beginning of a brilliant career and would undoubtedly have made prodigious contributions in the difficult years ahead. But what he did accomplish in his brief lifetime won him a never-to-to-be-forgotten place in the history of the Jewish people's national rebirth.

Those who treasure his memory should remember the last poem he wrote (in Hebrew):

> My sun has set and night descends,
> With dawn the rebel shall die.

> My flag has fallen, the banner of freedom,
> With it my hopes will not go unto death.

> . . . .
> I shall die—but generations to come
> Will fight after me the battle of God.

Rise to battle, the young generation,
Let the dead die—our day will shine.[29]

NOTES

1. B. Katznelson, *K'tavim* (Tel Aviv: Mifleget Po‘ale Eretz Yisrael, 1947), 6:120.
2. *Kitve Hayyim Arlozorov*, (Tel Aviv: A. Y. Shtibel and the Center of the Mifleget Po‘ale Eretz Yisrael, 1934), 1:*Yod Tet*. Shaul Arlozorov died in 1918, a victim of cholera.
3. Ibid., 6:137.
4. Ibid., 6:139.
5. Ibid., 2:48–49.
6. Abraham Goldberg, *Pioneers & Builders* (New York, Abraham Goldberg Publication Committee, 1943), p. 273.
7. Ibid., p. 274.
8. *Kitve*, 1:*Mem*.
9. Ibid., 1:*Mem Tet*.
10. Ibid., 5:108.
11. Ibid., 5:165.
12. Haim Arlozorov, *Yoman Y'rushalayim* (Mifleget Po‘ale Eretz Yisrael, 1949), p. 168.
13. *Documents & Essays on Jewish Labour Policy in Palestine* (Westport, Conn.: Greenwood Press, 1975), p. 175.
14. Ibid., p. 190.
15. *Palestine* (New Haven, Conn.: Yale University Press, 1947), pp. 648–49.
16. *Kitve*, 1:*nun dalet*.
17. Goldberg, *Pioneers & Builders,* p. 275.
18. Chaim Weizmann, *Trial & Error* (Philadelphia: The Jewish Publication Society, 1949), p. 300.
19. *Kitve*, 1:9.
20. Ibid., 1:128.
21. Ibid., 5:104.
22. Berl Locker, *Mikitov ‘Ad Y'rushalayim* (Jerusalem: Hasifriya Hatziyonit, 1970), p. 121.
23. Arlozorov, *Yoman Y'rushalayim*, p. 334.
24. Margot Klausner, *Sufat Sivan* (Tel Aviv: Sifre Gadish, 1956), p. 171.
25. Tamar Meroz, "Hatzel Ha'arokh," *HaAretz*, June 20, 1973.
26. Yosef Klausner, *Autobiografia* (Tel Aviv: Masada, 1955), 2:180.
27. Klausner, *Sufat Sivan*, epilogue, p. 14.
28. Katznelson, *K'tavim*, p. 147.
29. *Kitve*, 7:169–70.

Bibliography

Ahimeir, Aba. *Hamishpat*. Tel Aviv: Hava‘ad Lehotzaat Kitve Aḥimeir, 1968.
Arlozorov, Hayyim. *Yoman Y'rushalayim*. Mifleget Po‘ale Eretz Yisrael, 1949.
Arlozorov, Kitve Hayyim. 7 vols. Tel Aviv: A. Y. Shtibel and the Center of Mifleget Po‘ale Eretz Yisrael, 1934.
Hayyim Arlozorov: Leyom Hashana. Tel Aviv: Hamerkaz Lano‘ar Shel Histadrut Ha‘ovdim b'Eretz Yisrael, 1934.
Bilitzki, Eliyahu. *Ḥayyim Arlozorov*. Tel Aviv: Tarbut V'ḥinukh, 1966.
Gerter, Miryam. *Ḥayyim Arlozorov*. Tel Aviv: University of Tel Aviv - Hakkibutz Hame'uḥad, 1977.
Katznelson, Berl. *K'tavim*. vol. 6. Tel Aviv: Mifleget Po‘ale Eretz Yisrael, 1947.
Klausner, Margot. *Sufat Sivan*. Tel Aviv: Sifre Gadish, 1956.
Shapira, Yosef. *Ḥayyim Arlozorov*. Tel Aviv: ‘Am ‘Oved - Tarbut V'ḥinukh, 1975.
Encyclopedia Judaica. vol. 3. Jerusalem: Keter, 1971.
Encyclopedia of Zionism & Israel. vol. 1. New York: Herzl Press & McGraw Hill, 1971.

The Orthodox Bloc of Israel: The Early Years

JOSEPH ADLER

Religion plays virtually no role in the lives of a great part of the socially active elements in Israel. Indeed, in their thinking, religion is an anachronism, a remnant of medievalism, which is destined to disappear in this modern age of science and technology. Nevertheless, this state, so secular-minded in its background and leadership, ranks among those nations in the world in which religion is still a matter of governmental administration and coercion.

This paradox is in part the result of the special historical circumstances in which Israel came into being. Basically, some of these inconsistencies can be traced to the successful efforts of a highly organized religious political bloc in the early Israeli governments. Although always a minority, it was able to use its voting strength to wrest concessions from the socialist majority. How did this remarkable situation come about? To answer this question properly, one must first consider the multiparty system of Israel in the formative years 1948–54.

The parties represented in the First Knesset were the political products of organizations developed in the Palestine of the mandate period.[1] These parties were extremely diverse in their political beliefs. Ideologically, the principle issues dividing them were: labor versus management, collectivism versus private enterprise, separation of church and state versus theocracy, orientation toward the United States of America versus orientation toward the Union of Soviet Socialist Republics, nationalism versus internationalism, and expansionism versus territorial status quo.

The largest and most powerful political party in Israel in 1948 was Mapai (Israel Labor Party), a modern non-Marxist socialist party, the product in 1929 of a series of amalgamations of Palestinian Jewish labor parties with varying ideologies. The backbone of Mapai was the Histadrut[2] (General

Labor Federation), the largest trade union federation in the country with a membership embracing about 75 percent of all wage earners. Uniquely, Histadrut was also the country's largest single employer, with vast interests in industry, commerce, and agriculture.

In foreign policy, Mapai's orientation was toward the United States and against the Soviet Union. Domestically, it favored a gradual democratic planning of the economy with step-by-step nationalization of natural resources, public service, and public utilities.

In January 1949 Aḥdut ᶜAvoda (Unity of Labor), a group within Mapai that felt that the latter was becoming too moderate in its socialism, split away. Together with the radical agricultural-collectivist HaShomer HaT-zaʿir (The Young Watchman) and Poalei Zion S'mol (Leftist Workers of Zion) the Ahdut 'Avoda formed a new left-wing socialist Zionist Labor Party called Mapam (United Worker's Party).[3] Mapam advocated the ultimate establishment of a classless socialist society. It stressed Jewish and Arab unity, and favored the political leadership of agricultural collective labor rather than that of the industrial labor movement. Combining Zionism and Marxism, Mapam campaigned on a program that emphasized class struggle, a collectivist economy, and friendship with the Soviet Union.

At the extreme left of Israel's political party system was the Communist Party, with its program of aggressive class struggle, orientation toward the Soviet Union, opposition to the United States, and anti-Zionism.

The major party of the center was the General Zionist Party (organized in 1946). Its program advocated private enterprise based on economic laissez-faire, Zionist and national unity as opposed to ideological and class warfare, the strengthening of national institutions, and orientation toward the United States.

In August 1948 a division occurred within the ranks of the General Zionists. A faction favoring a more liberal, although nonsocialist, outlook toward labor and social welfare, withdrew and formed the Progressive Party. The latter advocated unity of all classes, a written constitution[4] with specified guarantees of individual liberties, and collective bargaining rights for labor.

To the right of the Progressive Party was the Mizrachi (Orthodox Party), composed mainly of urban middle-class Orthodox Zionist Jews. This party desired Israel to be built, and governed, according to the traditional teachings of the Orthodox rabbinate. It believed that the basis of Israel's culture was Orthodox religion, customs, and literature. In its foreign policy the party favored an alliance with the United States. Domestically, it opposed socialism, collectivism, and labor domination of social welfare, education, and the agricultural settlements. Middle class in composition, it favored private enterprise and individualized farming.

Mizrachi's conservatism alienated a group of religious Orthodox industrial workers and farmers, who broke away to form HaPoᶜel HaMizrachi

(Mizrachi Workers Party), which combined Orthodox religion, socialism, Zionism, nationalism, internationalism, and friendship with both the United States and the Soviet Union.

To the extreme right of the middle-class religious parties was the Ultra-Orthodox Agudat Israel (Association of Israel)[5], which, prior to World War II, held that cooperation with irreligious elements would bring down the wrath of God upon the Jewish national homeland, and would prevent the coming of the Messiah. Therefore it opposed affiliation, or cooperation, with the Zionist Movement. After World War II, Agudat Israel made a volte-face, and sanctioned the establishment of the Jewish state. It hoped that the new entity would be based on the precepts and teachings of Orthodox Judaism. Early in its history the party also developed a labor-orientated faction known as the Po‘ale Agudat Israel (Workers of the Association of Israel).

The four Orthodox religious parties (Mizrachi, HaPo‘el HaMizrachi, Agudat Israel, Po‘ale Agudat Israel) combined their forces politically in November 1948, to form the Religious Bloc. During the entire period under study, the Bloc never commanded more than 13 percent of the votes cast by the Israeli electorate.[6]

At the extreme right of the Israeli parliament was the Herut (Freedom) Party, a forerunner of today's Likud Party. It was supernationalist, expansionist, and advocated territorial jurisdiction over Israel's ancient biblical boundaries. Stridently anti-socialist, Herut favored private enterprise without any restrictions.

In addition to the above major political groups, there were several small community parties[7], which represented the special interests of certain sections of the population.

The first general election of Israel, held on January 25, 1949, revealed the following party strengths:[8]

Party	Votes Received	Percentage of Total	Seats Won
Mapai	155,274	35.72	46
Mapam	64,018	14.73	20
Religious Bloc	52,982	12.19	16
Herut	49,782	11.46	14
General Zionists	22,661	5.22	7
Progressives	17,786	4.09	5
Sephardim	15,287	3.52	4
Communists	15,148	3.49	3
Arab Democrat List	7,387	1.70	2
Fighters	5,363	1.24	1
Women's I.Z.O.	5,173	1.19	1
Yemenites	4,399	1.01	1
		Total Knesset Seats	120

Soon after the results of the election were officially announced, Dr. Chaim Weizmann, the newly elected president of Israel, charged David Ben-Gurion, the leader of the Mapai, with the task of forming a government. Finding his party fifteen seats short of a majority, Ben-Gurion looked around for a workable coalition. The most likely prospect, a Mapai-Mapam coalition, proved impossible to form when Mapam demanded too high a price for its cooperation.[9] Ben-Gurion then turned to the General Zionists who also demanded conditions for coalition, to which he was not willing to accede.[10] Thus the Mapai leader was forced to fall back upon the one viable alternative remaining—a coalition with the Religious Bloc. The Sephardi and Progressive groups were also approached to give the proposed coalition a broader base and nine more seats, but it was the sixteen seats of the Bloc that were essential for success. The Sephardim and Progressives accepted the offer, but the Religious Bloc proved obstinate until Ben-Gurion agreed to grant them concessions in return for their political support. The terms of the coalition agreement included a minimally controversial program of national defense and development, and a strict understanding to maintain the status quo on everything else. In particular, the fundamental relationship between the state and religion was to remain unchanged. The Religious Bloc, for entering the government coalition, also received three cabinet posts (the Ministries of Religion, Social Welfare, and Immigration).

Ben-Gurion's concessions had avoided a possible Kulturkampf at a time when Israel was facing a hostile Arab world and a severe economic crisis. Sagaciously, he was willing to modify, during this turbulent period, his personal feelings as well as the traditional socialist stand on church-state relations. On March 10, 1949, the Knesset approved Ben-Gurion's cabinet, and the new state was launched upon a course of ordered parliamentary government.

The Religious Bloc did not long remain idle in taking full advantage of the political exigencies that had made them the major partner in the coalition government. It extracted from the Prime Minister a promise that certain enactments of the old Provisional Government would remain intact on the statute books.[11] In this matter Ben-Gurion was pressured to accept a relic from the mandate period—the concept of religious rather than secular jurisdiction over certain areas of Israeli life. To further appease the Bloc, the Prime Minister did not strenuously resist its demands to issue Bibles to every man aboard naval vessels, and to ground all airplanes of the state-owned El-Al airlines from sunset Friday to sunset Saturday. He also went along with Orthodox claims for ritual rectitude in public institutions. The army and government agencies were instructed to purchase only kosher meat. Passenger trains as well as ships were scheduled to avoid running or unloading on the Sabbath.

Fearful that his compromises might alienate his socialist colleagues and the secular element of the electorate, Ben-Gurion took great care to avoid formalizing his religious concessions. His political maneuvering emphasized administrative action, rather than the writing of basic laws for religious privilege. Whenever feasible, he patterned his grants on procedure inherited from the days of the mandate. Thus buses were not to operate in Tel Aviv and Jerusalem on the Sabbath because that had been the practice under British rule, whereas in Haifa some buses could run, because that had been the usage before Israel had become a state. Stores were closed on the Sabbath by "municipal ordinance," just as they had been under the mandate, and not by government decree. Ham and pork products were restricted, not by formal prohibition, but by quiet instructions issued to the appropriate officials that foreign exchange would not be made available for its import. Throughout these early years Ben-Gurion consistently reminded his sometimes impatient colleagues that sweet reasonableness had to prevail—at least until a strong and solidified state materialized that could ignore religious questions with impunity.

Nevertheless, the Religious Bloc remained far from satisfied with the gains it had exacted from the government. It continued to press for further concessions. These soon came by virtue of the Bloc's control over the Ministry of Religious Affairs. The latter had been originally created to render financial support to Jewish religious bodies and institutions, and to maintain the religious rights of other faiths within the country.[12] Of great importance was the fact that the Jewish religious courts, known as the Rabbinical Courts, functioned under the Ministry of Religious Affairs. The courts, which had been officially recognized during the mandate era had: (1) exclusive jurisdiction over members of the Jewish community (this included all Jews whether or not, Orthodox, Reform, or Conservative) in matters of marriage, divorce, alimony, burial, as well as in cases involving inheritance and confirmation of wills when both parties to the litigation agreed to their jurisdiction; (2) concurrent jurisdiction with the civil courts in the above matters in cases involving foreigners who consented to the religious court's jurisdiction; and (3) concurrent jurisdiction with the civil courts in all other matters involving the personal status of all members of the Jewish community.[13]

Control of the religious court system and of the government purse strings in relation to general religious affairs gave the Bloc an unparalleled opportunity to fulfill their dream of turning Israel into a theocratic state. Since all the parties in the Bloc were Orthodox in religion, dominion over the Ministry of Religious Affairs virtually meant that the state had recognized Orthodoxy as the only official denomination in Judaism. Reform and Conservative congregations that had arisen during the past century and a half in Europe and America suddenly found themselves outcasts from the Jewish community. No Reform or Conservative rabbi was permitted to officiate in Israel at a Jewish marriage ceremony. Non-Orthodox rabbis were not even fully acknowledged as rabbis, although they were qualified graduates of bona fide seminaries. The entire Jewish community— Orthodox, Reform, Conservative, as well as atheist and agnostic—had become subjected to Orthodox laws of personal status interpreted by rabbinical courts, whose salaries and costs were paid by the state.[14]

Elated by its newly found power, the Religious Bloc turned its attention to other matters. In the late summer of 1949 the Mapai majority in the cabinet toyed with the idea of introducing a bill into the Knesset that would provide for compulsory education. It was hoped that such legislation would relieve the education emergency that had developed in the hundreds of temporary camps, which had been hastily erected to house the flood of newly arrived immigrants. The bill offered the immigrants a choice between secular and religious education. This initiative on the part of the Mapai cabinet members angered the Religious Bloc. It was particularly anxious to exempt Yemenite immigrants from such legislation. Plucked from the medieval isolation of South Arabia, where their faith had been the rock to which they had clung during centuries of persecution, the Yemenites were religious to the bone—and wholly innocent of such Western concepts as nationalism, citizenship, socialism, and free enterprise. The Bloc argued that the parents of a Yemenite child should not even be subjected to the bewildering problem of choosing between "educational trends,"[15] since the concepts of school and religion simply did not exist separately in their minds.

Inside the cabinet the Bloc fought this issue and won a significant victory when it secured exemption for Yemenites in immigrant camps from the general provisions of the Education Act.[16] In the immigrant camps non-Yemenites were given the right to opt for religious or secular education under special state supervision, and without "trend" control; for the Yemenites a religious schooling—again under state supervision—was to be automatic.

This political triumph was followed by still another, as the Religious Bloc persuaded the prime minister to agree to the exemption of women from service in the armed forces if they could prove it interfered with, or violated, their religious principles.[17]

Encouraged by success, the Bloc suggested that the institution of the Sanhedrin (supreme council of ancient Judaism, which had jurisdiction over religious, criminal, and civil matters) be resurrected. However, the rank and file of Mapai protested to its leadership the dangers inherent in Ben-Gurion's compromises. It pointed to the numerous signs of Orthodox intransigence, and patent thrust for power. Was it not evident that Orthodoxy's ideal had always been a theocratic community, in which all Jews would be subjected to Talmudic law? Was not the rabbinate's participation in the marketplace of politics a clear omen of their desire to reach this goal? What did the Orthodox insistence on supervision of family relationships and family life mean? These and many similar questions were openly voiced as the Mapai membership stirred itself into action.

Socialist resentment of the religious parties slowly crystallized into political action. On January 24, 1950, the Religious Bloc received its first setback when the government forced a marriage law through the Knesset.[18] This law, vehemently opposed by the Orthodox, in essence made marriage unlawful for girls who had not yet completed their seventeenth year. The Bloc was of the opinion that the law was primarily directed against the Oriental Jews, who still followed the Middle Eastern custom of marrying off their daughters at a young age. Since the Oriental Jews were extremely Orthodox in religion, and were entering Israel by the thousands, the Bloc felt that its own interests were at stake if it did not oppose the marriage law.

Undaunted by its failure to block the marriage law, the Bloc now concentrated on the Voice of Israel, the state-owned-and-operated radio network. From its very inception this radio system had been the subject of a continuous controversy between elements inside and outside the government. Since religious Jews did not turn on electricity on the Sabbath and on holidays, the question inevitably rose as to whether broadcasting should be permitted on those days. The more conservative elements of the population, as reflected by the supporters of the Religious Bloc, were of the opinion that the network should close down. Some moderates wanted the programs on Sabbath and holidays to continue, but insisted that the network broadcast only appropriate material, for example, music. The majority of the population of Israel favored broadcasts on these days, for it was only on the Sabbath and holidays that they had the leisure time to enjoy the radio. Ben-Gurion, determined to hold his coalition together by avoiding an open rift with the Bloc, favored a compromise. The prime minister, after much haggling with his own party, which was still smarting from the insults heaped upon it by the Bloc during the struggle over the marriage law, eventually won his way. The Voice of Israel was given permission to broadcast on the Sabbath and holidays, with the exception of the Day of Atonement—the holiest day of the year.[19] Special programs were to be introduced on religious holidays that would explain their significance. The radio network was also to provide listeners, who, out of religious convictions, refrained from tuning in on the Sabbath, a special news summary on Saturday evenings detailing the events of the previous twenty-four hours.[20]

Although the Bloc had fought to prevent the radio network from broadcasting on the Sabbath, it wisely accepted Ben-Gurion's compromise. It knew that a large majority of the representatives of the Knesset were adamantly opposed to its viewpoint. The Bloc's shrewd appraisal also revealed that it had correctly read the signs that had emerged from the protracted struggle over the marriage law. It had become evident to the Bloc that the prime minister would turn it out of the cabinet if his party demanded a showdown.

The inherent differences between Mapai and the Religious Bloc boiled once more to the surface in October 1950. This time the issues involved the prime minister's refusal to grant the Bloc a separate division for religious schools in the Education Ministry;[21] and a proposal to create a new Ministry of Commerce and Industry. Ben-Gurion expressed the desire to have the new ministry headed by a person who was a member neither of the Knesset nor of a political party. By picking an outsider to guide the new agency, he hoped to keep intact the status quo of the cabinet's political representation. Angered by this stratagem, the Bloc warned the prime minister that it would bolt the cabinet. Ben-Gurion countered by threatening to resign, which in turn would have forced the entire cabinet to follow suit.[22]

Two weeks after Ben-Gurion's resignation threat, and after much interparty debate, an agreement was once again hammered out. The Bloc accepted the new ministry, with a nonpartisan member at its head, and promised to fully support the government until the First Knesset terminated. In return, Mapai consented to retain the status quo on religious matters. Ben-Gurion's determination to have things done his way had carried the day.

The coalition government remained stable until February 17, 1951, when the issue of education for Yemenite children in immigrant camps erupted once more into a crisis. This time the Knesset debate centered about the residents of the *ma'abarot*. The *ma'abarot* were work camps where immigrants were accommodated in the intermediate stage between arrival and integration, and engaged in public work projects. It was in these camps that the immigrants began in earnest the process of transforming themselves from destitute refugees into self-supporting citizens. Introduced originally as a temporary measure to reduce the heavy costs of the reception camps, the *ma'abarot* soon mushroomed throughout the country.

In the eyes of the Mapai hierarchy the immigrants living in the *ma'abarot* were apprentice Israelis, well along the road toward complete absorption into the national community. Even those immigrants in the *ma'abarot,* they maintained, who had come from the most backward areas of the world, were capable of appreciating the options available to them. Hence the Mapai leadership insisted that the error made in surrendering educational training in the immigrant camps to the Religious Bloc was under no circumstances to be repeated in the *ma'abarot*. The choice among the "trends," they stressed, must be offered to the inhabitants of the work camps. Only in this way could immigrant children be afforded an opportunity to acquire a secular education. As a special inducement to the religious immigrants, the Histadrut proposed to establish in the *ma'abarot* a modification of the labor "trend" with socialist instructors teaching religion as part of the regular curriculum.

Provoked by the actions of Mapai and the Histadrut, the Religious Bloc reacted energetically. Mustering their forces in and out of government, they tried to sway the cabinet from carrying out the majority party's proposed *ma^cabarot* educational reforms.

At the height of the exigency, the General Zionists, sensing an opportunity to embarrass the government, introduced a bill of censure in the Knesset. In the ensuing vote the Religious Bloc, still incensed by its failure to forestall the educational plans of Mapai, withdrew its support from the government, and the censure motion was carried by a vote of 49 to 42. Piqued by the vote (even though the censure motion was not a vote of no confidence), the prime minister immediately resigned. His action, in turn, compelled the cabinet to follow suit and forced a general election upon the nation.[23]

Ben-Gurion had carefully weighed the reactions to his resignation. He had come to regard the religious parties as political blackmailers, and felt that the moment was propitious for a complete break with the Bloc. In addition he assumed that Mapai would again emerge victorious in the balloting, and that the election would facilitate the formation of a more suitable coalition. Ben-Gurion was convinced that he could expect no further support for his legislative program from the Bloc, and that he had gained as much as he could from their political backing.[24]

Following the coalition's collapse, Ben-Gurion took charge of the caretaker government pending national elections. In England, when a government fell a national election usually followed within a matter of weeks. In the newly created State of Israel, lacking the centuries of English parliamentary experience, it was to take five months before a general election could be held. No procedures, legislation, or precedents existed for dissolving the old Knesset, for holding a new national election, or for maintaining parliamentary continuity.[25]

Finding it no longer necessary to placate anyone, Ben-Gurion, in the interim period before the national election, pushed legislation that had previously been considered unacceptable to the religious parties. He introduced into the Knesset an amendment to the Compulsory Military Service Law of 1950,[26] which obliged women, previously exempted from the armed forces for religious reasons, to serve in military offices, farm settlements, hospitals, and social welfare agencies.

In justifying his action, the prime minister charged that many unmarried women between the ages of 18 and 26 had used "religion" as a means to escape their military obligations. He categorically dismissed all protests that the amendment violated Orthodox canons of female modesty, or that it ran counter to universal peace-time usage. Ben-Gurion's arguments prevailed, and the amendment achieved easy passage through the Knesset to become the law of the land.

Making the most of the favorable political climate in which he found himself, Ben-Gurion now guided a new labor law[27] through the Knesset, with only the Religious Bloc acting in opposition. The law established a forty-seven-hour-work week, which displeased the Bloc on two counts: it failed to make Wednesday a half-holiday, which would have given workers an opportunity for sports, travel, and recreation in mid-week, thereby reducing the temptation for violating the Sabbath; and it authorized the minister of labor to permit individuals to work on the Sabbath if such work was considered essential to the security or economy of the state.

The Bloc suffered an additional setback in the Knesset with the passage of an Equal Rights for Women Law.[28] Questions of marriage and divorce were to remain under religious jurisdiction, but agreement of both parties to a divorce was made mandatory. Bigamy was outlawed, and husbands who abandoned their wives without mutual or court agreement were made liable to imprisonment up to five years. This legislation also gave married women the right to hold property, and overruled many other disciminatory religious statutes.[29] Inheritance laws, for example, were radically changed, as male and female heirs were now considered equal when no will existed. To a large extent, the Equal Rights for Women Law took away from the Bloc many of the advantages that had accrued to them from their control of the religious courts.

Ben Gurion, enjoying the full support of his own party as well as that of other non-religious elements in the Knesset, seemed now willing to risk the very Kulturkampf that he had once dreaded. The Religious Bloc, totally surprised by the prime minister's turnabout, hoped that he would yield enough for mutual face saving. However, once the gauntlet had been hurled down, the Bloc had no choice but to pick it up. Demonstrations against military service for religious women were staged throughout the country. From America came unexpected support for the Bloc, as the Union of Orthodox Rabbis ominously reminded the Mapai leadership that it had, in the past, always supported Israel's "legitimate interests." Anti-religious secular education, and insistence on mobilization for women, the union of rabbis stressed, could only lead to the destruction of the family— the very foundation of Jewish society.[30]

In Jerusalem the rabbinate warned that a worldwide day of fasting would be proclaimed to protest the legislative enactments of the Ben-Gurion government. Orthodox Jewry, they stated, would "fill the prisons in Israel with their daughters rather than comply with the law. . . ."[31]

Encouraged by the general tumult, the ultra-Orthodox joined the fray. Extremists in Jerusalem burned cars that had been driven in violation of the Sabbath; and the country was startled by the news that a plot had been foiled to prevent debate on the mobilization bill by exploding a homemade bomb in the Knesset.[32]

Although Ben-Gurion had brought about the cabinet's fall because of the Bloc, he was anxious to play down religious issues in the national election campaign. This strategy was dictated by a desire to win over the Oriental Jews who were, by and large, religious and Orthodox. The prime minister therefore decided to concentrate on the serious economic problems confronting the country. No one, he believed, could be neutral about food shortages, high prices, inadequate wages, rationing and price controls—no matter what their faith, origin, or ideology.

Seven parties participated in Israel's second national election, which was held on July 30, 1951. The results were as follows:[33]

Party	Votes Received	Percentage of Total	Seats Won
Mapai	256,456	37.3	45
General Zionists	111,394	16.1	20
Mapam	86,095	12.5	15
Religious Bloc	81,623	11.8	15
Herut	45,651	6.6	8
Communists	27,334	4.0	5
Progressives	22,171	3.2	4
Arab Democrats	16,370	2.4	3
Sephardim	12,002	1.8	2
Yemenites	7,965	1.2	1
Arab Progress Party	8,067	1.2	1
Arab Farmers Party	7,851	1.15	1
		Total Knesset Seats	120

On August 15, 1951, Israel's president, Chaim Weizmann, formally requested David Ben-Gurion, the leader of the victorious Mapai, to form a new government. The latter's initial gambit was to call for a government of national union, which would include all of the parties that had won seats in the Knesset, with the exception of the Communists and Herut. To accomplish this alliance, Ben-Gurion was willing to modify collective cabinet responsibility by permitting individual cabinet members to vote their conscience against the government on issues involving foreign policy. Unable to form a national union, Ben-Gurion turned elsewhere. From August 15 to October 4 he concentrated on the Mapam and the General Zionists. Mapam, always doctrinaire, demanded as its price for entering into a coalition, the enactment of a "soak the rich" legislation and the expropriation of foreign concessions. Ben-Gurion rejected these proposals, and Mapam immediately broke off negotiations. The General Zionists, in turn, desired control of the Ministry of Commerce and Industry, with some authority over rationing and price controls. They also insisted on the easing of restrictions on private enterprise, and on the encouragement of private investment. Ben-Gurion and Mapai's central committee feared that such economic power in the hands of the General Zionists would undermine the

Histadrut, the backbone of Israel's labor movement. The Prime Minister, therefore, with great reluctance, rejected the demands of the General Zionists.

Caught on the horns of a dilemna, Ben-Gurion once again reversed directions and turned to the Religious Bloc in his attempts to form a government. An agreement was soon reached, and the Bloc received, as its reward for entering the coalition, four new ministries (interior, health, social welfare, and communications) in addition to the Ministries of Religious Affairs and Immigration, which they had held in the former government. Mapai's concessions to the Bloc also included a one-year moratorium on the recruitment of women for military service; continuation of the ban on the importation of nonkosher food; state support of, but not control over, religious schools; and the naming of an Orthodox rabbi as deputy minister of education.[34]

The new cabinet was confirmed by the Knesset on October 8, 1951, and survived until November 3, 1952. During this period the Bloc developed new tactics in dealing with the socialist majority. Instead of openly antagonizing the Mapai cabinet members, the Bloc compromised wherever possible, and consolidated the gains that it had already achieved. Typical of this new approach was the manner in which the Bloc settled a problem involving the importation of meat from Argentina. In April 1952 the Council of the Chief Rabbinate had declared three thousand tons of beef from Argentina nonkosher, despite Argentinian rabbinical supervision of the slaughtering. After a long debate, involving the rabbinate, the Bloc, and the cabinet, a Solomonic decision was reached. The disputed cargo of meat was to be admitted into the country, but it could only be distributed to persons who did not adhere to the laws of *kashrut*. Although superficially a compromise, the decision in reality was a considerable gain for the Religious Bloc. Henceforth meat was not to be admitted into the Jewish state unless it was butchered by Israeli slaughterers. To facilitate the entire process, slaughterers were to be sent to all countries exporting meat to Israel.[35]

On rare occasions, when nothing further could be gained from opposition, the Bloc yielded to socialist pleas for flexibility. Thus, after much coaxing, it agreed to support a bill that allowed medical courses to include dissection of the human body. The Orthodox group had originally strenuously opposed such a measure because of the belief that such medical practices violated the doctrine of the resurrection of the body after death.

In June 1952 the government, in order to conserve fuel supplies, imposed temporary restrictions on transportation. These controls provided for the immobilzation of private cars, taxis, and trucks for two days of every week. To assuage the Orthodox, it was decided that the Sabbath would be one of the two days in which transport would remain idle. The cabinet, in its deliberations, had failed to take into consideration the many occupations that would be adversely affected by the transportation restrictions. Typical was the reaction of the Taxi Drivers Association. Registering their disapproval of a law that limited their means of earning a livelihood, the association purposely chose Friday and Saturday as the two days in which they would not operate. Left with little transportation on heavily traveled Fridays, and without any transportation on the Sabbath, many segments of the general public began to voice their protests. With the realization that the position that it had taken was neither timely and popular, nor feasible, the Religious Bloc did not object too vociferously when the cabinet relaxed the original restrictions on taxis running on the Sabbath.[36]

It was during this interval of tactical adjustments that the Bloc made its boldest move toward achieving its ultimate goal—the theocratic state. Keenly aware that all of the major parties favored a policy of encouraging Jews who wished to immigrate to Israel, the Bloc, through its control of the Ministry of Immigration, facilitated the admittance of a large number of Oriental Jews into the country. It hoped, by this move, to swell the ranks of the Orthodox parties, since most Oriental Jews were pious and Orthodox.[37] Although cognizant of the Bloc's designs, the socialist majority was willing to risk the implied threat to their political supremacy. The Oriental Jews, they believed, would in time acculturate, and support the socialist party, which had played such an important role in the creation of the state and in their lives.

The hopes of the Bloc to achieve a theocracy were once again dashed by the mercurial Ben-Gurion. At the opening of the Second Knesset (November 5, 1952), the prime minister announced his intentions of pursuing his original plans in regard to military service for religious women, and for the unification of the four-trend system of education. The Bloc, unprepared for this new challenge, found itself unable to marshal its forces effectively. With tensions steadily mounting, the Bloc split asunder as the Agudat Israel, and the Po'ale Agudat Israel, without waiting to consult the other two religious parties, withdrew from the government coalition. At this juncture, Ben-Gurion's political opposition forced through the Knesset a motion for a vote of no-confidence. However, the motion failed to carry.[38]

Ben-Gurion, realizing that his government was now in jeopardy (the withdrawal of the two religious parties meant the loss of five seats), immediately entered into negotiations with various factions in the Knesset, with a view to broadening the parliamentary basis of the coalition. Confident of achieving a more practical government without the parties that had defected, the prime minister tendered his resignation, and that of his cabinet, to the president of the state on December 9, 1952. After consultations with other members of the Knesset, the president once again entrusted Ben-Gurion with the task of forming a new government. With his usual skill, the prime minister quickly forged a new coalition, consisting of the following parties:[39]

Israel Labor Party	45 seats in the Knesset
General Zionists	20 seats in the Knesset
Progressive Party	4 seats in the Knesset
HaPoᶜel HaMizrachi	8 seats in the Knesset
Mizrachi	2 seats in the Knesset
Arab Faction	5 seats in the Knesset
Sephardim	2 seats in the Knesset
Yemenites	1 seat in the Knesset
Total seats	87

The new government consisted of a sixteen-man cabinet in which the General Zionists and the Progressives replaced the two Orthodox parties (Agudat Israel and Poᶜale Agudat Israel) that had precipitated the electoral crisis. HaPoᶜel HaMizrachi and the Mizrachi, the two remaining parties of the old Bloc, were allowed to retain control of the Ministries of Religious Affairs and Social Welfare. Ben-Gurion also promised them that in the proposed unified educational system for primary schools provision would be made for religious instruction for those children who desired such training.

The government remained fairly stable until November 1953, when Ben-Gurion announced to a startled nation his intention of retiring from public affairs and the cares of the state.[40] The prime minister's resignation was reluctantly accepted by the president of Israel, Itzhak Ben Zvi, on December 7, 1953, and the country once again was confronted by a political crisis.

Moshe Sharett, the former minister of foreign affairs, was asked by the president to head the interim caretaker government, and later on was designated by Ben Zvi to form a cabinet. Sharett's position was much weaker than that of his predecessor. In order to form a viable coalition he was compelled to make more concessions than he had originally anticipated. The beneficiaries of this largesse were the General Zionists and the two religious parties that had remained in the last Ben-Gurion government—the Mizrachi and the HaPoᶜel HaMizrachi. On January 25, 1954, the Knesset approved the coalition, and Sharett officially became the new prime minister of Israel.[41]

The strategy of appeasing the religious parties in exchange for their political support, which had marked the state's formative years under Ben-Gurion's leadership, continued undiminished under Sharett. A precedent had been established that would influence every Israeli government down to the present day. The first prime minister of Israel, a skillful and wily politician, and hypersensitive to the theocratic tendencies of the Religious Bloc, had cleverly evolved a policy to divert the zeal of the latter whenever possible into programs that benefited the state. Like a man on a tightrope, carefully balancing himself before taking each step, Ben-Gurion, when conditions allowed, pushed through the Knesset legislation favoring separation of church and state. However, when his government depended for its very survival on the support of the Religious Bloc, he unhesitatingly granted the latter concessions to keep them in line. Always, he sought to bestow his concessions administratively rather than by formal legislation.

*   *   *

David Ben-Gurion's successors, by and large, adopted the same tactics when dealing with the religious parties—some with more success than others. In recent years, notably with the election of Menachem Begin (1977) of the Likud party as prime minister, the powers of the heirs of the old Religious Bloc (currently the National Religious Party, Agudat Israel, and Tami) have increased, as has their influence over social and foreign policy.

Indeed, the religious parties had become adept in what some commentators have described as the art of political compromise, while others considered it the art of political blackmail. A case in point is the recent national election of June 30, 1981—a political drama that at this writing (July 20, 1981) has not yet been completely played out. After an acrimonious campaign, the two major parties of Israel emerged from the election fray almost dead even (forty-eight seats for Likud, and forty-seven seats for Labor), leaving the balance of power once again in the hands of the religious parties.

Although they had been aligned with the previous Begin administration, the religious parties saw an unparalleled opportunity to further increase their power by sounding out what the Labor party would offer them for their support. Labor, recalling that the religious parties had in the past cooperated with them, offered concessions and informed their rank and file that they would ". . . not give them everything, but will try to establish the old understanding we [previously] enjoyed with them."[42] The talks led nowhere.

Begin and his colleagues also courted the religious parties. If successful, a government formed from such a union would give the Likud leader a bare-bones majority of sixty-one seats (the minimum required) in the hundred-twenty-member Knesset. However, the price for such a coalition will, without a doubt, be high.[43] Josef Burg, the leader of the National Religious Party, had publicly stated that his party would demand three or four cabinet posts for its six Knesset members. Agudat Israel, not to be outdone with four seats to offer Likud, was calling for increased government funds for religious institutions; a strict ban of Sabbath work, except for security and medical personnel; a change in the legal definition of a Jew to exclude those converted by non-Orthodox rabbis, or born of mothers so converted; a ban on the sale of pork throughout the country; a modest dress code for women in government offices, and similar restrictive legislation. Tami, a splinter group that had broken off from the National Religious Party, was demanding that Begin offer the Religious Affairs portfolio to its leader Aharon Abuhatzira (who had previously held this post, and had been accused of accepting bribes but found not guilty).

In retrospect, it is difficult to foresee what the future holds in store for Israel in regard to this basic struggle between parties who view the world from a religious angle, and parties who conceive their objectives in secular and materialistic terms. However, if one was to hazard a guess, it would be that in the short run the status quo will prevail, and the religious parties will continue to enjoy power greatly in excess of their actual numbers. As for the long run, the political trends that emerged in the June 1981 elections seemed to suggest that the electorate is gradually gravitating toward a two-party system. A continuation of this process may eventually produce a party with an absolute majority, eliminating the need for coalition governments. This objective can also be achieved by reforming the current electoral system, which encourages the growth of numerous minority parties. As for the institutions of Israel, such as the army and the universities, by their very existence they promote secularism. Religious youth, upon whom the future political power of the religious parties rests, cannot ignore the influence of these institutions upon their way of life.

Thus it can be said that Israel stands at the crossroads. One of the roads leads to a truly democratic secular state with political maturity and stability. Future generations, looking back, may see that this road was only a mirage. In that event, it will be clear that the second road, leading to a theocratic state, was actually enetered upon—a road fraught with dangers and threatened by the spector of a self-destructive Kulturkampf.

NOTES

1. On the origins of these parties see Harry L. Kessler, *Jews and World Affairs: A Study in Current Jewish Events* (New York: Block Publishing Co., 1939), pp. 99–100; Arthur Koestler, *Promise and Fulfillment:Palestine 1917–1949* (New York:The MacMillan Co., 1949), pp. 289–310; and Joseph Dunner, *The Republic of Israel:Its History and Its Promise* (New York:Whittlesey House, 1950), pp. 126–39.

2. See Koestler, *Promise and Fulfillment*, pp. 291–94.

3. Ahdut ʿAvoda was a revolutionary, but non-Marxist, socialist party. HaShomer HaTzaʿir was Marxist and pro-Soviet, and Left Poʿale Zion somewhere between the other two in its political philosophy. Left Poʿale Zion had been formed in the period following the Russian Revolution during World War I.

4. Israel still has no written permanent constitution. The state's fundamental political structure, including the powers and functions of the Knesset, government, and president, rests on a number of laws, most important of which is the Transition Law of February 16, 1949, better

known as the "Small Constitution." See State of Israel, *Government Yearbook 5711 (1950)* (Jerusalem: The Government Printer, 1950), pp. 259–60.

5. Another group not represented in the First Knesset, but closely akin to Agudat Israel in their thinking was the Nature Qarta (Guardians of the City), a small but extremely militant group of zealots based in Jerusalem. They opposed Zionism, and to this day have not yet become reconciled to the existence of the Jewish state.

6. Raphael Patai, *Israel Between East and West* (Philadelphia: The Jewish Publication Society of America, 1953), p. 269.

7. For example, the Sephardi Party, composed of Jewish immigrants of Spanish and Portuguese ancestry; the Yemenite Party, consisting of immigrants from Yemen; and several Arab parties that campaigned vigorously in the Arab communities.

8. Moshe Rosetti, *The Knesset: Its Structure and Development* (New York: Israel Office of Information, I.M.83, 25 October 1949), p. 1. There were other parties that participated in the election, but only the ones listed above obtained seats in the Knesset.

9. Mapam insisted on the immediate nationalization of industry and agriculture. Ben-Gurion was also reluctant to collaborate with the pro-Soviet Mapam.

10. The General Zionists demanded legal protection for private industry, and assurances that some nonsocialist programs would be considered.

11. The Provisional Government served from May 14, 1948, to March 10, 1949. It enacted the Days of Rest Ordinance that made Saturdays, and other Jewish holidays, official days of rest throughout Israel. However, what constituted rest, and how it should be observed, had been deliberately omitted from the law. Ben-Gurion knew this and was willing to retain the law, since it really did not restrict the average Israeli citizen. He was not so anxious to extend the Kosher Food for Soldiers Ordinance also enacted by the Provisional Government, but was forced to do so by the Bloc. The prime minister believed that the latter decision would eliminate the possibility of a native hog industry developing, and that the law would inflate meat prices. See State of Israel *Government Yearbook 5711 (1950)*, pp. 261–62 for detailed descriptions of the "Days of Rest Ordinance of 1948," and the "Kosher Food for Soldiers Ordinance of 1948."

12. See "Religious Services Budget Law of 1949," *The Official Gazette of the Government of Israel*, June 1949. This law provided for partial state subvention of the activities of the various religious communities in Israel, and authorized the Ministry of Religious Affairs to pay the expenses and salaries of the religious courts.

13. On the powers of the religious courts see Geroge Horowitz, *The Spirit of Jewish Law* (New York: Central Book Co., 1953) pp. 719–27, also R. Gottschalk, "Personal Status and Religious Law in Israel," *The International Law Quarterly* 4 (December 1951): 454–61.

14. Gottschalk, "Personal Status," p. 458.

15. Until August 1953 there were four basic school systems, called "trends": (1) the General Zionists-nonsectarian and nonideological schools attended by about 33 percent of the nation's children; (2) the Histadrut schools, which provided general and craft training for about 37 percent and taught subjects with a socialist labor viewpoint; and (3&4), the religious schools, operated by Mizrachi and Agudat Israel, and attended by about 26 percent of the total school population. See Norman Bentwich, *Israel* (London: Ernest Benn Ltd., 1952), chap. 9.

16. See "Compulsory Education Law of 1949" *The Official Gazette of the Government of Israel*, September 1949.

17. See "Compulsory Military Service law of 1950," *The Official Gazette of the Government of Israel*, January 1950.

18. See "Marriage Law of 1950," *The Official Gazette of the Government of Israel*, January 1950.

19. Although it opposed the law, the Bloc did not feel it was important enough to leave the cabinet when it was enacted over their protests.

20. See Elizer Whartman, "Israel Calling," *Hadassah Newsletter*, no. 14 (November 1952), pp. 33–35. For a history of the development of the broadcasting system see Daniel Sher, "Our Broadcasting System," *Zionist Newsletter*, no. 121 (9 November 1949), pp. 17–22.

21. The Religious Bloc had complained of socialist dominance in the Education Ministry, which was charged with carrying out the Compulsory Education Law of 1949 in the immigrant camps. They feared that the socialists exerted a godless influence on the children in the camps.

22. Ben-Gurion's move outwitted the Bloc, for he never made any formal move to resign.

23. Bentwich, *Israel,* chap. 6.

24. From March 1949 to February 1951, the period of the coalition, Ben-Gurion had achieved the following: Israel's admittance into the United Nations; the implementation of an unrestricted immigration policy; armistice agreements with most of the Arab nations; stabilization of the Israeli pound; the right to float bonds in the United States; economic aid from the United States, and recognition from the Great Powers. The government had also enacted legislation covering conscription, compulsory education, child marriage, capital investment, and land transfers. It had launched programs in pure and applied science, inaugurated an air lift to remove Jews from Yemen, and had made Jerusalem the capital of the country. See State of Israel, *Government Yearbook 5713* (1952) (Jerusalem; The Government Printing Press, 1952), pp. 100–220.

25. Gerald de Gaury, *The New State of Israel* (New York; Frederick A. Praeger, 1952), pp. 80–84.

26. Ibid., pp. 84–91.

27. See "Labor Law of 1951," *The Official Gazette of the Government of Israel,* June 1951.

28. See "Equal Rights for Women Law," *The Official Gazette of the Government of Israel,* June 1951.

29. Traditionally, a Jewish wife could not divorce her husband, or make a will, without his consent. A childless widow could not marry anyone except her deceased husband's oldest unmarried brother, unless the latter was willing to go through a special ceremony absolving her from this obligation. If a wife could not prove that her missing husband was dead, she could not remarry. Under Orthodox doctrine, a woman's testimony in court need not be accepted as valid, and women did not possess the right to inherit property.

30. See *Israel Speaks* (June 18, 19, 20, 1951), p. 1.

31. Ibid., June 19, p. 1.

32. Gaury, *New State,* pp. 89–90.

33. Rosetti, *The Knesset,* p. 5 Five parties failed to obtain seats in the Knesset and therefore do not appear in the above list.

34. Rosetti, *The Knesset,* p. 3.

35. *Israel Digest,* April 26, 1952, p. 3.

36. *Zionist Newsletter* 4, no. 21 (5 August 1952):10.

37. It is estimated that the Oriental Jewish population in Israel in this manner increased from 42,000 to 197,000 in less than two years. *See Story of Immigration* (New York: Israel Office of Information, R.P. 17A, April, 1952), pp. 1–58.

38. State of Israel, *Government Yearbook 5715* (1954) (Jerusalem:The Government Printer, 1954), p. 55.

39. Rosetti, *The Knesset,* p. 4. All parties marked with an asterisk supported the coalition in the Knesset but had no representation in the cabinet.

40. *Israel Speaks,* 12 June 1953, p. 1.

41. *New York Times,* 26 January 1954, p. 3.

42. *Time* 118, no. 2 (13 July 1981):26–28.

43. *New York Times,* 15 July 1981, p. A8.

A Jewish Childhood in Cairo

VICTOR D. SANUA

What Am I?

More than thirty years ago, I left Egypt to study psychology in the United States. I had been accepted for graduate work at Michigan State University. While I could speak English correctly, being a graduate of the American University at Cairo, I had a foreign accent. Most of the time people I met would ask me about my background. This put me somewhat in a dilemma, since a simple answer would not provide the required information. I would counter by asking what they meant by my background. If they referred to my place of birth, it was Egypt, but in the same breath I would add that I was not an Egyptian. The next question, which was often raised, was the kind of passport I had, and the answer was that I had an Italian passport. But again I had to add that I had never lived for any length of time in Italy. I had simply inherited Italian citizenship from my father. The next inquiry would then be about my family origin. My reply would be that my family had originally lived in Spain, and had left the country in 1492 when the Jews were expelled. Subsequently, my ancestors settled in Leghorn, Italy. While at home we spoke Ladino, a kind of archaic Spanish that served as our mother tongue, technically we could not consider ourselves Spaniards, despite the fact that my parents used to tell me "mosotros somos Espagnolis" ("we are Spaniards"). Another question raised was where did I live during my formative years. My reply was that I had spent eight years as a youngster in Belgium, but my parents never acquired Belgian citizenship. The next question might possibly be about the kind of education I had received. Here there was no doubt that my early education was purely French, and that at times we felt more French than the French themselves. But certainly we could not claim any official affiliation with France. The last question may have been, where was my mother born? To this my answer was that she was born in Istanbul, Turkey. But my mother was not Turkish.

283

By that time my interlocutors would give up, and, as a final remark of my own, I would add that the only thing I was sure of was that I was Jewish. After I obtained my American citizenship, if the question was raised, I would add that I was an American citizen. Because of my particular background and problems of identity it may not be strange that my areas of research has been cross-cultural, with special emphasis on the Jews, the Arabs, and schizophrenia.

In this paper I wish to present some memories of a young Jew growing up in Cairo, Egypt. Many individuals have expressed interest in how a Jewish family would fare in Egypt between the two World Wars in view of the hostility it would encounter in a Muslim environment, and in the kind of life Jews led in a country that at the time was regarded as underdeveloped. To illustrate how little was known about Egypt, I recall showing an early picture of mine to a well-educated acquaintance. In the picture I was surrounded by trees. My friend expressed surprise at seeing trees, since he had visualized Egypt as being a land of deserts. When I showed him another picture in which I was roller-skating, his puzzlement increased: such modern amenities in a backward country! In fact, Cairo had practically everything a major European capital would offer: an opera, symphony concerts, horse racing, sports, fabulous nightclubs with elaborate shows. The most recent movies from France, Italy, and the United States were shown on Egyptian screens, the latter two with French subtitles. The latest fashions were displayed in Cairo stores.

I was born in a middle-class family which, as indicated above, was shaped by various cultural currents. Both my father and mother spoke Ladino, a medieval Spanish with many Hebrew words as well as French words with Spanish endings. There were no schools in this language for the young generation; it was learned at home. My parents corresponded in Ladino, written in Hebrew characters. Besides Ladino, the other language of communication was French, at home as well as outside the home. In most businesses French was the dominant language. While the French spoken by Jews in Egypt did not sound precisely like that spoken in Paris, it was nevertheless quite correct, and there were numerous newspapers and periodicals published in this language.

Historical Background of Jews in Egypt

The Jews had a long history in Egypt. Alexander the Great built the city of Alexandria with the assistance of the Jews. Philo, the great Jewish philosopher, was one of its distinguished inhabitants. Under Roman rule, tensions and struggles between the Greeks and the Jews increased, much of Alexandria was destroyed, and the Jewish community was virtually annihilated. In the year 638 Egypt was occupied by a Muslim army led by

Amr ibn al-As, who proceeded to conquer the rest of North Africa. Very little is known about the Jews until the tenth century, when they figured in the historical annals. S. D. Goitein pointed out that a converted Jew, Yaᶜqub ibn Killis, was instrumental in the founding of el-Azhar, the great Muslim center of learning that still exists today. Toward the close of the tenth century, during the reign of the Fatimid caliph al-Hakim, there was a departure from the policy of tolerance toward non-Muslims. Al-Hakim forced Jews to wear a distinctive garb; they were not allowed to ride horses; synagogues were destroyed. A number of Jews either emigrated or converted to Islam. However, periods of persecution and degradation alternated with periods of relative calm. The great Maimonides (1135–1204), escaping persecution in Spain, found refuge in Egypt.

In 1517 Egypt was conquered by the Turks. Initially, the Jews were well treated. Because of the arrival of Jews from Spain, the standard of Jewish learning in Egypt improved. As a result of the subsequent political and economic decline of the Ottoman Empire and the widespread corruption, the Jews sustained great losses. In many instances Jews who had become ministers, particularly in finance, were summarily executed by despotic rulers. Early in the eighteenth century, Mohammed Ali, an Albanian officer in the Turkish army, slowly developed Egypt into an independent country and founded a dynasty. King Farouk, the last king of Egypt, was his descendant. The number of Jews living in Egypt at the beginning of the eighteenth century is estimated to have been approximately 5,000. During the 1870s, Yaᶜqub James Sanua, one of my relatives, was associated with the Egyptian nationalistic movement in spite of his foreign Italian lineage. He was subsequently exiled to France because of his excessive criticism of the Khedive Ismail, a despot who caused great harm to the country with his excesses in modernization. After World War I, many Spanish-speaking Jews from Salonika and Turkish towns settled in Egypt. William Edward Lane, the famous English Orientalist, reporting of his travels in Egypt in the early nineteenth century, gives an eyewitness account on the status of the Jews in Cairo.

The Jews are detested by the Muslims far more than are the Christians. Not long ago, they used often to be jostled in the streets of Cairo, and sometimes beaten merely for passing on the right hand of a Muslim. At present, they are less oppressed; but still they scarcely ever dare to utter a word of abuse when reviled or beaten unjustly by the meanest Arab or Turk; for many a Jew has been put to death upon a false and malicious accusation for uttering disrespectful words against the Kur'an or the Prophet.

During the latter part of the nineteenth century the conditions of the Jews improved. Several of them, such as the Cattaoui family, became financiers, ministers, and members of the Parliament. During that period of prosperity many Jews from France, Italy, and the Balkans immigrated to Egypt, and their descendants retained their parents' citizenship, in spite of the fact that many of them had never seen the. country whose passports they carried. There was an advantage in maintaining foreign citizenship; in case of litigation with an Egyptian, the case had to be dealt with by the Mixed Courts, since it was problematic that a European would receive adequate justice in an Egyptian court. Such arrangements, which came to be known as Capitulations, were granted to the Europeans in order to attract them to settle in the country. The Mixed Courts were abolished in 1949.

Early Experiences and Education

Because of business reverses that Egypt suffered due to the world economic crisis, my father decided to join his brothers in Belgium prior to World War II. He even worked for a short time in the Belgian Congo, where many Jews from Egypt had gone. The family, however, stayed in Belgium. There I attended schools in which French was the language of instruction. We also learned Flemish as a second language. I recall that my parents suggested that if anyone, particularly other children, inquired as to my religion, I should answer "libre-penseur" (free-thinker). Neither I nor my classmates knew what I was talking about, but apparently, it spared me the agony of abuse. A few years later a combination of increased anti-Semitism in Europe fostered by Hitler, and a kind of nostalgia for Egypt, made my father decide to return to Cairo. This move was certainly a fortunate one in view of the decimation of the Belgian Jews after the German occupation of the country. My immediate relatives were able to leave before the arrival of the Germans. Years later I returned to Belgium and tried to locate some of my friends and the rabbi who had taught me Hebrew. Very few had survived the Holocaust. I also learned that the synagogue where my father used to take me had been used as a stable by the Germans.

My first reaction when, as a young adolescent, I landed in Alexandria with my family was one of disappointment bordering on revulsion. The sight of people walking barefoot, the beggars in tatters, and the miserable conditions of life for the Egyptians was totally strange and unpleasant to me. Egypt presented a stark contrast to the neatness of the cities and the excellent social conditions of Belgium. Our first home in Cairo was near Abdin Palace, residence of the Egyptian kings. Every day I saw the palace guard parade in the large square. On special occasions, when the king had to leave the palace for an official function, the main street would be covered by sand. It looked as if it were carpeted.

Since my father was an Italian citizen, the Italian Consulate suggested to him that I be sent to an Italian school. However, since my father was not sympathetic to the Fascist regime, he declined, and instead enrolled me in a Catholic school.

In 1937, a year after we returned to Egypt, my father died of a stroke, leaving me, an adolescent, the only man of a family consisting of my three sisters and my mother. I was the third of four children. The death of my father was a great blow to all of us. For me, in addition, it meant a new status of responsibility according to the traditional values of the Jewish family, in which the male is supposed to play the role of head and protector.

There were only a few Jewish schools in Cairo, primarily on the elementary level. They were in general attended by children of Jewish families with modest means. The insufficiency of Jewish educational institutions in Egypt may be attributed to two major causes. First, Jews preferred to keep a low profile in a Muslim country; and second, in view of the fact that many Jewish students went abroad for their professional studies, it was more advantageous for them to receive their high school credentials from an institution that was recognized in the mother country.

A good example of our Francophile tendencies was the celebration by the Jews of Egypt of the 14th of July (Bastille Day) with as much enthusiasm as by the French themselves. We all learned to sing the Marseillaise with great gusto. However, the Jews did not limit themselves to French; many learned to speak Arabic, and, depending on the origin of their families, they also spoke Greek, Italian, Yiddish, English, and so on. Because of the cosmopolitan character of the city, an educated person spoke, on the average, four or five languages.

Beyond the elementary level of education, practically all young Jews attended either the Lycée Français, which represented the French educational system in Egypt, or the College des Frères, a Catholic school. It is interesting to note that because of the common French language and culture that most Jews had adopted, one's background was of no consequence. This is why I was somewhat puzzled when I came to the United States and found that here the question of background was of considerable importance. I was often asked whether I was a Litvak or a Galicianer. Obviously, my reponse was, Neither. People were somewhat surprised that, in spite of my Jewishness, I could not speak a single word of Yiddish. It was only when I came to New York that I first heard of the word *bagel*.

My first school in Egypt was the College des Frères at Bab el-Louk. Because of the excellence and strictness of the educational system of the Frères, many Jewish parents preferred this Catholic school to the Lycée Français. My estimate is that more than half of the students in the Catholic schools were Jewish. Fear of conversion did not seem to be a problem, despite the fact that the study of the Catechism and the New Testament was compulsory. About once every hour the bell range, whereupon there was a short prayer recited by one student while the other Christian students would follow responsively.

During that period I was introduced to the Arabic language, which was studied two hours a week. This was hardly adequate for a language as difficult and intricate as Arabic. In addition, whatever literary Arabic was taught had little relation to the Arabic spoken in the street. Thus many European Jews, because of the limited time devoted to Arabic, never achieved a proficiency in the language of the country, since what they learned in school could not be applied in their daily activities. The literary Arabic taught in the school was even foreign to lower-class native-born Egyptians. Only students who had gone through several years of instruction in it were able to handle its complexities. The little spoken colloquial Arabic I learned was a kind of kitchen Arabic spoken by maids, porters, and day laborers. In all major stores and large businesses, French was the dominant language.

There were six junior high schools of the Catholic Brothers in the city, and their graduates, who expected to continue, had to go to the high school located in the Khoronfish district. Every two months we had to take stiff examinations at Khoronfish so as to be admitted to the high school at the end of our junior high school studies. The results of the examinations were published in the school bulletin. The names of the students were arranged in the order of the points they had achieved. I can recall the names of at least seven Jewish students among the 140 participants who had achieved the highest number of points at one of the examinations. There certainly was a predominance of Jewish boys in academic achievement. Report cards showing our ranking had to be signed by the parents every week. Medals were given weekly to those who were first in French, English, and Arabic. Just before World War II, France and the French language were beginning to lose some of their importance. There was a decided trend toward learning English. At that time it was decided that I should attend the high school attached to the American University at Cairo which, incidentally, was close to my home, while Khoronfish was far away. Because of my limited knowledge of English, I was put in a lower class. But with intensive work I managed to shorten the five years of study to three years, so that I received my high school diploma at the right age (18). By that time going to Europe for further education was out of question since World War II had broken out. It was impossible for me to consider going to an Egyptian university, since I had gone to a French school and later attended an American school, and therefore my Arabic was quite inadequate. The American University in Cairo provided only a liberal arts degree, while I was aiming for a professional degree. This situation prompted many young Jews to start working in business or to take their chances with the Egyptian universities, in which medicine and the physical sciences were taught in English, and law in French. However, before receiving any diploma the candidates had to prove their proficiency in Arabic.

After the fall of France, English became of paramount importance. My knowledge of English had become a source of income since there was a great need for instructors of the English language. I taught English in a school by day and gave private lessons at night. I hoped that the war would soon end and I would be able to study abroad.

Religious Education and Practices

Religious education and religious practices tended to be limited in the acculturated Jewish circles in Cairo. Very few Jews maintained kosher homes. There were too few kosher butchers. One of my greatest surprises when I came to the United States was to see the inscription *Kosher* in many store windows. Such a sign would have been offensive to the Muslims, and therefore did not exist in Egypt. Religious education for the Bar Mitzvah consisted in general in having a teacher come to the home of the boy for a few months and teach him the rudimentary knowledge required for the ceremony. It is to be noted that all Jews in Egypt belonged to the Orthodox branch of Judaism. There were no other Jewish trends. While religious practices were in general minimal, during the High Holidays synagogues, clubs, and even private homes had services that were well attended. During the Passover the eating of unleavened bread was strictly observed, and the two nights of the Seder were generally celebrated with relatives. There was some irony in the Seder, since God was repeatedly thanked for having delivered us from the hands of the Egyptians and having taken us out of Egypt, while the fact was that we were still in Egypt. It is interesting to note that we learned to sing the Hatikva in Ladino.

Many times during the year the ritual of what was called "meldados" (reading in Ladino, or "Jahrzeit") was observed. The custom was to celebrate it at home. There were several religious men who kept the dates and made a living by conducting such services in the homes. Usually, a few of these men came, just in case there were not enough men to have a "minyan" (a quorum of ten). The men sat around in the house, and between prayers discussed in Ladino passages of the Bible. For the "meldados" some food was prepared and nuts and raisins were distributed. It was customary for the women to cry when the name of the departed was mentioned in the course of the prayers.

There were no funeral homes. If a person died at home, he was prepared for burial right there. If he died at a hospital, the body was brought home for a service. Funerals tended to be elaborate. The coffin was placed in a flower-decked horse-drawn hearse, and men with large wreaths of flowers walked in front and behind it. Members of the family walked be-

hind the hearse for a few blocks, and later went to the cemetery. The body
was interred in a shroud. No coffins were used for that purpose, but it was
surrounded by brick walls over which a stone slab was fitted.

Social Activities

Immediately after graduating from junior high school a few of us
banded together to start a camping club. We rented a run-down basement
close to King Farouk's palace, and renovated it. Besides storing our camping gear we used the premises for games and social purposes, such as ping-
pong and dances. We called it the Jewish Camping Club. With the outbreak
of World War II, and particularly when Italy entered the War and the
enemy threatened to conquer Egypt, it was decided to close the club. When
conditions bcame more normal I joined a social club that was originally
called Judeo-Espagnol Club, because it was founded by Ladino-speaking
Sephardi Jews. In the postwar years, because of the intense xenophobia
that swept the country, the name was changed to Judeo-Egyptian Club.
Again, dances, ping-pong tournaments, lectures, dramatic productions,
and planned excursions dominated the activities of the club. Because of the
deteriorating conditions of Jewish life in Cairo, it was not considered appropriate to carry on any discussion of Judaism and Israel. In another
section of this paper, we shall see how justified this fear was. During the
High Holidays the premises were used for services, but even then there was
always some fear regarding our security.

War Years in Cairo

There were three distinct classes of Jews in Egypt. There was a small
wealthy upper class whose members had amassed fortunes in industry,
banking, and agriculture, particularly cotton. A number of them obtained
high positions in the government. For example, Joseph Cattaoui Pasha
(pasha was an honorary title bestowed by the king) was finance minister
and was in the delegation of Egyptians that had gone to London in 1922 to
discuss the details of independence from Great Britain. Then there was a
large middle class, which included businessmen and professionals, bank
and company employees. A third group of relatively poor, tradition-bound
Jews lived in the Harat el-Yahud, the Jewish quarter. Their language was
primarily Arabic. They were the descendants of Egypt's original native
Jews, whose families had lived in the country for centuries. It was estimated
that the total Jewish population, which was highly urbanized, amounted to
80,000 individuals. Today, approximately 100 Jews, all old people, still
reside in Egypt. Thus an indigenous Jewish community that had been in
Egypt for more than 2,000 years is practically extinct.

Because of my Italian citizenship I was considered an enemy alien. Many of the Italians were put in concentration camps. However, Jews with Italian citizenship were spared, since it was felt that they had no sympathy for the Axis powers. My Italian citizenship prevented me from working for the British army. However, I was able to get a position with the British Red Cross, which provided amenities to the troops. The Red Cross was independent of the Army and was able to employ me despite my Italian citizenship. It was during that period that Rommel had reached El-Alamein and was poised to conquer Egypt. The British forces were ready to pull out and evacuate the country in that event. In the eleventh hour, British forces, reinforced by troops from the Commonwealth—Australia, New Zealand, India, Canada—and by forces of occupied countries of Europe, such as the Free French and Poles, and by Jewish units from Palestine, counterattacked. The British offensive, under the leadership of General Montgomery, succeeded in throwing the German forces back. During that period I was scheduled to take my vacation. I went to Alexandria, and daily saw the units going to the front, which was about sixty miles to the west. There were a few air raids at night, but they did little damage. As an enemy alien, I had to get special permission from the Egyptian authorities to travel from Cairo to Alexandria.

In those days working hours in Egypt usually started anywhere between 8:30 and 9:00 in the morning and lasted until 1 P.M. Then people went home to have lunch—the homes were never too far away—and returned to work from 4 to 7 P.M. Saturday was also a working day. However, a few firms observed what was called "semaine Anglaise" (English week), letting the employees off after half a day on Saturday. After lunch it was the general custom to take a siesta, but the more hardy souls preferred swimming in the sporting clubs. During that period I was a member of a sporting club situated on a beautiful island in the Nile called Rhoda. By that time many of my friends had married, and I was able to establish new friendships at the sporting club. There were two reasons why marriage was not possible for me. First, I was determined to go abroad to study as soon as the war was over. Second, I had three unmarried sisters, and at that time it was not considered proper for a man to marry before his sisters.

Since the man was considered to be the mainstay and support of the family, and by that time the funds left by my father were running short, I decided to start a dressmaking business. My oldest sister had learned the trade and has had some experience as well. Though it was difficult, we managed somehow to obtain material for dresses despite the general shortage of supplies in the postwar years. Within a short time we were quite successful. Once my family was financially secure, I could think in terms of continuing my studies abroad. Since the war lasted longer than expected, I decided to return to the American University in Cairo, and was able to get my B.A. in the social sciences within two years. During the latter part of the war I obtained employment with the United States Office of War Information in its radio division. At the close of the war I was working for the United States Information Service. Since there was no assurance that the position would be permanent, I switched to a business firm, where I was in charge of English and French correspondence.

Because of the large number of soldiers returning from the war and going to school, it was very difficult for foreigners to get admitted to a university anywhere in the Western world. I therefore resigned myself to having to wait for some time before applying for admittance at a university in the United States or England. It was only in 1950 that I took serious steps to come to the United States. When I did, I was fortunate to obtain offers of full scholarship and room and board from no less than three universities.

Postwar Years

During the war, Egypt was a hub of the Allied war effort, and economic conditions in the country were excellent. Fortunes were made by providing supplies to the British army. However, it could be foreseen that after the war and the actual signing of the peace treaty, life for Europeans, and Jews in particular, would not be ideal. The struggle for Egyptian independence had gone on for years and it was felt that foreigners, generally would not be welcome. Because of these misgivings about the future, I registered my family with the American consulate for immigration to the United States. However, the quota for Egypt was very small in 1945, and the waiting time was approximately fifteen years. Since the listing depended upon one's country of birth, my mother had to go on the Turkish quota, which had been a waiting time even longer than the Egyptian. Nevertheless, this move on my part proved to be of extreme and fortuitous importance.

About two years after World War II a new law was introduced in Egypt called Company Law, which provided that firms owned by either Egyptians or foreigners had to have at least 75 percent Egyptians among their office personnel, with at least 65 percent of the salaries going to Egyptians. In factories, 90 percent of the salaries had to be drawn by Egyptians. Egyptians meant persons having Egyptian citizenship. The term *native-born* would not be appropriate, since the majority of foreign subjects were native-born. At the time almost half of the Jewish population had foreign citizenship, and most of the others were considered "*apatride*" (stateless), even if they had been in the country for generations. Not more than 10 percent of the Jews had Egyptian citizenship. Thus employers faced a dilemma: they either had to employ Egyptian personnel, who in most cases would prove unqualified to function in a business enterprise and cause the business financial losses, or had to fire their non-Egyptian personnel so as to achieve the balance required by law. The latter course was generally adopted. Within a short time thousands of Jews found themselves jobless.

Many departed to their country of citizenship and a large number managed to go to Palestine illegally.

Some Jews tried to obtain Egyptian citizenship, but this required a good working knowledge of the Arabic language. Since very few Jews had attended Egyptian schools, it was almost impossible for them to obtain what, in the end, became a highly valued status—Egyptian citizenship. It was a period when it was very difficult for a Jewish firm to obtain export and import licences. Thus many of the Jewish businessmen took Egyptians as partners. In the firm where I was working the newly appointed director was an employee who had worked as the man Friday of the business. For one reason or another he developed an antipathy toward me, and saw to it that I was discharged in 1948 while the war against Israel was in progress. I was fortunate to find employment in an Egyptian firm as office manager, where I was given a great deal of responsibility. On one occasion I felt compelled to make some remarks to the owner's brother-in-law to which the Egyptian took exception. He asked me to pay a fine of three days' work as a penalty. I refused, and he reduced the fine to two days, then he even went farther and reduced it to one days' pay. But I remained adamant. The next day I received a letter of discharge. Immediately I dashed to his office, stating that I would prefer to submit my resignation. I felt, I said, justified in making the remarks, since I was working for the benefit of the firm. He accepted my argument, and thus I have a letter of discharge, and at the same time another letter from the same firm accepting my resignation.

In November 1945 the first anti-Jewish action was initiated by the Misr al-Fatat (Young Egypt), a chauvinistic youth group. Its members wore green shirts patterned after the brown shirts of Hitler's youth groups. Gamal Abdel-Nasser, later President of Egypt, was a member of this organization. The group was under the leadership of Ahmad Husayn. Synagogues, Jewish hospitals, and numerous Jewish institutions and shops were damaged or destroyed. In the process many foreign, non-Jewish institutions were also attacked. These riots, burnings, and occasional killings continued intermittently. During that period Jews had to disassociate themselves from Zionism or bear the consequences. During the 1948 war against Israel, Jewish firms were obliged to donate money to the Palestine Fund, which supported the anti-Jewish Palestinian Arabs. In this period of great anxiety many Jews tried to leave Egypt, but were unable to, since they were required to obtain exit visas. At times a high price had to be paid for such an exit permit. The slightest excuse sufficed to arrest a Jew. Many Jews were accused of being Zionist spies. The situation was especially perilous during the war against Israel, when there were numerous bombings, riots, arrests, and sometimes killings. Carrying a camera in the vicinity of what was considered a military site, or being caught in possession of some Hebrew text was enough to be thrown into jail. I remember vividly that in one of those riots I sat in a cafe where Europeans were set upon and beaten. I escaped such mishandling by hiding under a table covered by a long tablecloth.

During these riots a French boxer by the name of Gaillard, who had been invited to train the Egyptian team, was killed with an ice pick by the mob. The number of Jews and foreigners who were killed was never revealed.

We had blackouts during the war against Israel, and there were a number of alerts in which we had to be extremely careful not to show lights from the buildings, on pain of being arrested and accused of providing guidance to Israeli planes. One Friday evening there was an alert and, being close to my home, I rushed back to find a group of very anxious neighbors pointing with fear to the light flickering through the blinds of a window. They begged me to turn off the light, which came from the Sabbath candles we usually lighted Friday nights. To my dismay, I discovered that I had not taken the house key with me. Since it would have been foolhardy to take chances, I decided to break in the heavy door. My great fear seemed to provide me with the necessary strength to break the lock with a few well-placed kicks. It was known that most of these alerts were sham alerts, since Israel had practically no air force during that period. However, these blackouts were used for taking the wounded returning from the front to the hospitals. The authorities did not want the people to witness these convoys, particularly since the media reported easy victories.

After the armistice there were parades of the "victorious" troops in Cairo. At the time, a law was introduced dispossessing Jews of their apartments, which happened to be close to military objectives. The vacated apartments were immediately given to Egyptians. The interpretation of what constituted a military object was left very loose, so that even a gasoline station was considered a military objective. An uncle of mine, who lived near the Arab League headquarters, was among those who lost their homes. He moved to our apartment for a short time, and later was able to go to the Belgian Congo. Our apartment was close to a gasoline station and even closer to the Marconi Telegraph Company. We were afraid that we, too, would be dispossessed, but the intervention of foreign consulates terminated the practice just in time. However, meanwhile a lot of damage had been done.

During that period Jewish businesses were sequestered and expropriated. Unscrupulous government officials were given the responsibility of running these businesses, and caused ruin to many of the owners. The compensation a few received never amounted to more than a fraction of the lost assets.

Because of my Italian nationality it was very difficult for me to find employment. For a time I was able to work in a one-man office, run by a representative of the Hungarian government who was trying to reestablish business with Egypt after the war. He was trying to sell heavy machinery. In 1949 I left this job, which was all but promising, to work for the American

Friends Service Committee. The Friends were assigned by the United Nations to care for Arab refugees in the aftermath of the Arab-Israeli War of 1948. Apparently, the conditions of the Company Law were not applicable to international agencies. From today's perspective, it is somewhat ironic to see a Jew working in an agency helping Arab refugees. In those days the problem had not yet become politicized, and the work had philanthropic overtones. However, one of the problems in my position was that, as a Jew, I could not go to the Gaza strip, which contained a large concentration of Arab refugees. My function was to work on the finances in Cairo. During my regular academic high school work at the American University in Cairo, I had carried a dual load with accounting and business courses, which now served me in good stead. Indeed, I was very fortunate to be able to make a living at that time, handicapped as I was by being an Italian citizen and a Jew. A short time afterward the United Nations took over the function, and the United Nations Works and Relief Agency (UNWRA) was established. As a result, I became a United Nations worker. It was from this last position that I left Egypt to come to the United States in 1950.

Part V

THE ANCIENT NEAR EAST

War and Peace
The Theoretical Structure of Israelite Society

CYRUS H. GORDON

"War and peace" is a merism signifying the totality of life. War may be hellish and peace heavenly, but the human condition is heir to both. This merism has been expressed in art pictorially since remote antiquity—for example, the Sumerian Standard from Ur.[1] One major panel depicts battle, with ass-drawn chariots carrying victorious warriors, while slain foemen are trampled beneath the hooves of the beasts. The other major panel, on the opposite side of the standard, portrays a banquet scene, with seated victors quaffing liquor from cups served by attentive domestics. Such are the brutality of war and the joy of peace.

A more familiar embodiment of the same merism is described by Homer.[2] The Shield of Achilles portrays a city at war, and a city at peace. The one shows troops engaged in their baleful acts of war. The other reflects social institutions ranging from happy marriage to strife and litigation that mar the bliss of peace. Actually "peace" means "the interludes between wars." As a whole, the Shield of Achilles represents the totality of life in terms of the merism "war and peace."

Homeric epic is itself in the form of a merism. The *Iliad* depicts the Heroic Age at war, while the *Odyssey* portrays the same Heroic Age between wars. The *Odyssey* deals with homecoming, marital life, relations between the young and the old, kinship, and economic productivity on the plantations of the warrior class.

Few scholars of our time can match Raphael Patai's record of erudition, originality, and productivity. I have enjoyed the privilege of being his academic colleague and getting to know him personally. This brief contribution to his Festschrift is a small token of my great admiration for him.

The Bible includes a parallel pair of books: Judges, reflecting the Heroic Age of Israel during the military campaigns, and Ruth, reflecting the peaceful interludes between wars.[3] Like the *Odyssey,* Ruth tells of a homecoming: from Moab to Judah; of marriage (Ruth and Boaz); of relations between the young and the old (notably Ruth and her mother-in-law, Naomi); of kinship (for the child that Ruth bears to Boaz is the ancestor of King David); and, in general, of life on the plantation of a warlord.

Ruth 2:1 calls Boaz a *gibbor ḥayil,* identifying him as a member of the warrior and land-owning aristocracy during the Heroic Age of the Judges (Ruth 1:1). Ruth (3:11) is identified as an *eshet ḥayil,* which means a woman of the same aristocracy. Classes, then as always, cut across national or ethnic lines. Though not a Judean but a Moabitess, Ruth belonged to the same class as Boaz. Their union was appropriate in the same sense as it is proper for royal couples to come from different countries, provided that both husband and wife hail from kingly stock.

A heroic age is evoked by dislocation, often resulting from the vicissitudes of war and migration. Such times call for rough-and-ready types like Samson (or, more recently, the bad men of our Wild West). Shamgar mowed down Philistines by the hundreds (Judges 3:31). Samson (like Achilles) goes into a rage because a woman is taken away from him, so that many an innocent bystander perishes.[4] Jephthah (like Agamemnon) sacrifices his own daughter to secure military success.[5]

Sparta provides a parallel to the emergence of Israel in a heroic age. The Israelite (like the Spartan) conquistadores won a land by force of arms. The victors thus became the élite officer class: warriors, administrators, and priests. The menial work was to be performed by the vanquished (the Canaanites in Israel; the Helots in Sparta). The land won was parceled out as grants in perpetuity to the warlords and their descendants in exchange for national defense in time of war. Between wars, the aristocracy manage the plantations on their land-grants. The Book of Judges (corresponding to the *Iliad*) depicts that society during military campaigns; whereas Ruth (corresponding to the *Odyssey)* depicts the same society on the plantations between wars.

The *eshet ḥayil* is nowadays mistaken to mean "a model housewife" along middle-class lines. That this is not the case is made clear by the tribute to the *eshet ḥayil* in Proverbs 31:10–31. There she is the able manager of a well-to-do household. Her husband is an Elder *(zaqen)* who is known publicly. He sits in the gate *cum senatoribus terrae* (as the Vulgate aptly puts it). If we may Latinize, the *eshet ḥayil* is the wife of a *senator.*[6]

Israel's theory of its own society, down to and including the return from the Exile in the sixth and fifth centuries B.C., required that a true Israelite be a member of the landed, warrior aristocracy. To be a full-fledged Israelite, one had to be accepted as a descendant of some warrior in Joshua's

Conquest. The Book of Joshua tells how the land was won and parceled out to the victorious clansmen in the name of God, by lot under the joint supervision of a priest, of Joshua, and of the tribal chiefs.[7]

The theory is already anticipated in Leviticus 25, which states that the land belongs to God and the Israelites are simply His tenants.[8]

Though the menial work of gathering wood and drawing water[9] was to be done by the vanquished Canaanites, things did not turn out quite that way. Solomon's great building projects required more labor than the dwindling supply of Canaanite manpower could provide. As a result, the noble Israelite tribesmen became subject to corvée.[10] This loss of status was largely responsible for the secession under Jeroboam of northern Israel from southern Judah in the reign of Solomon's son Rehoboam.

Solomon had taken various measures to break down the old system of the tribal warrior class and to strengthen his centralized government. He reorganized his realm into new districts that deviated from the old tribal borders. The number of the regions remained, but they were not the same tribal twelve.[11] Instead of local calendars,[12] there was now a national calendar with the colorless names "First Month," "Second Month," and on to "Twelfth Month." This certainly facilitated a unified, federal system of taxation, cultic practice, and the like. But whatever lasting changes Solomon effected, he did not succeed in obliterating Israel's old theory of society. When the exiles returned to establish the Second Commonwealth and rebuild the Temple, they were obliged (if they wished to rank as first-class citizens) to provide written genealogies to prove that they were *bona fide* members of the priesthood as well as of the landed aristocracy.[13] They did not merely return (like modern Zionists) to the Holy Land, but the landed aristocracy went back specifically to their ancestral estates in specific areas. In theory, they were not "Jews in general" but rather the heirs of the tribal *conquistadores*, who had been allotted land in perpetuity after Joshua's Conquest. Returnees who did not come forward with acceptable "papers" might become members of the Commonwealth, but only as second-class citizens.[14]

I have stressed that this was the "theory," however much the actual situation had changed. We may even speculate that since written genealogies were indispensable for first-class Israelite status, there must have been a lively traffic in forged documents. What I have been describing is the idealized pattern of society, and not all of the prosaic facts.

The Scroll of Ruth reflects many aspects of the theory of Hebrew society. Boaz and Ruth, both members of the *gibbor ḥayil* aristocracy, have the proper credentials to be the ancestors of King David (Ruth 4:18–22). Any other origin would have made him a usurper.

The scroll also reflects the need to return to one's specific tribal land-grant. Naomi's deceased husband's land had to be redeemed for his descendants. Since the death of Elimelech and of all his children made this biologically impossible, levirate marriage[15] took care of matters. Ruth was the *y'vama,* and her deceased husband's kinsman was her *yavam.*[16]

There is no question that Ruth 1:1 attributes the story to the age when "the Judges were ruling" (the Heroic Age),[17] even though the scroll as we have it is post-Davidic, perhaps by centuries.[18] The scroll consciously refers to ancient customs that had already fallen in disuse.[19] But the theory of Hebrew society required that they be remembered, and hopefully revived.

Just as the transcriber(s) of Homer lived well after the Mycenaean Age, the authors of Judges and Ruth lived well after the Heroic Age "when the Judges were ruling" (twelfth and eleventh centuries B.C.). But both Greece and Israel cherished distant memories of their Heroic Age, though some of the facts and institutions were imperfectly transmitted and sometimes forgotten.

By the Christian Era, great changes had taken place. As far back as the Achaemenian Age, the returnees began to realize that independence under the Davidic Line was an impractical and dangerous illusion.[20] It was safest to defer the Messianic Age to a distant End of Days. By the time of Roman domination, the level-headed mainstream of Judaism had substituted the aristocracy of learning for the aristocracy of the *gibbore ha-ḥayil.* The Written and Oral Law took the place of prowess on the battlefield. Messianic warlords like Bar Kokhba were tragic liabilities to Jewry. But the aristocracy of scholarship could flourish and preserve a Judaism that had no secular power in a Gentile World. It was only in the lunatic fringes of Judaism, like Qumran,[21] that Jews refused to give up a military program of redemption.

Jewish and Christian concepts of Old Testament society have been molded by theologians rather than sociologists.[22] Consequently, Israel's theory of its own society as spelled out in the Bible is not even recognized in the Anchor Bible commentaries on Judges[23] and Ruth,[24] where it is essential for us to understand the crystal-clear evidence of the Hebrew text. Obviously this article aims not at propounding a new theory but rather at recognizing the theory held by the ancient Israelites themselves.

NOTES

1. Reproduced (in color) in C. L. Woolley, *Ur Excavations,* vol. 2 (London: Oxford University Press, 1934).
2. Homer, *Iliad* 18:483–608. The city of peace is described in lines 490–508; the city of war, in lines 509–40.
3. Detailed discussions of the Heroic Age portrayed in Judges/Ruth and *Iliad/Odyssey* are in my *Common Background of Greek and Hebrew Civilizations* (New York: Norton, 1965), pp. 241–42 and passim.
4. Judges 15:1–18; *Iliad* 1:1–4.
5. Judges 11:30–40.

6. Proverbs 31:23.
7. Joshua 19:51.
8. Leviticus 25:23.
9. Joshua 9:21, 27.
10. 1 Kings 5:27–28.
11. 1 Kings 4; see my *Ancient Near East* (New York: Norton, 1965), pp. 182–83.
12. Cf. my *Ancient Near East,* p. 186, n. 17.
13. Ezra 8:1 ff.
14. Ezra 2:62–63; Nehemiah 7:64–65.
15. There are different kinds of marriages, and even of levirate marriages. Thus levirate marriage is not exactly the same in Deuteronomy 25:5–10, in Genesis 38, and in Ruth. Legally, levirate marriage is not a new marriage but merely the continuation of the widow's previous marriage.
16. The terminology is taken from Deuteronomy 25:7, 9. In Ruth (1:15) the root YBM is used rather differently, designating the relationship of dead brothers' widows to each other.
17. ŠPṬ is regularly translated "judge" (verb as well as noun), though it also means "rule." In Ugaritic it is a synonym of MLK "king" or "to rule" (*Ugaritic Textbook* §19.2727).
18. Possibly even Josianic (late seventh century, B.C.), when attempts to restore ancient glory were the order of the day. Nebuchadnezzar was trying to restore the empire of Hammurabi; Necho II, the realm of Thutmose III (to the Euphrates River!); and Josiah, the United Kingdom of David.
19. Ruth 4:7.
20. Note the War Scroll; Eduard Lohse, *Die Texte aus Qumran* (Munich: Kösel Verlag, 1964), pp. 177–225.
21. It is interesting to note that the Qumran community required both intensive study (N.B. the Manual of Discipline) and preparation for the military victory of the Sons of Light over the Sons of Darkness (N.B. the War Scroll).
22. This holds even for Father Roland de Vaux's commendable *Ancient Israel: Its Life and Institutions* (New York: McGraw-Hill, 1961).
23. Robert G. Boling, *Judges* (Garden City, N.Y.: Doubleday, 1969).
24. Edward F. Campbell, Jr., *Ruth* (Garden City, N.Y.: Doubleday, 1975).

Women, the Law, and the Ancient Near East

SAVINA J. TEUBAL

Civilization means an advanced state in social development. Implicit in this statement is a progression from one stage to another, improved, stage. It can be argued, however, that the status of women, in the Old or the New World, has not kept pace with the progression of social development considered characteristic of civilization. In fact, certain aspects of the women's position evinced a regression in the ancient Near East from the earliest times to the period in which the Assyrian laws were promulgated. Repressive attitudes toward women emerged about the time of the Eshnunna laws (twentieth century B.C.E.), became harsher during the time of Hammurabi (eighteenth century, B.C.E.), and reached their zenith with the Assyrian laws about four centuries later.

The most obvious deterioration of women's status took place within the milieu of religious officiants. A representation of a female officiate attests the existence of that office as early as the Jemdet Nasr period (2900 B.C.E.).[1] Subsequently, for several centuries, females occupied at least the same positions in the clergy as males.

The most elevated post, that of the *en(tu)*, (comparable to that of high priestess), is perhaps best represented by En-hedu-anna, who held priestly offices at Ur as well as Uruk. She was also a poet of renown during her lifetime.[2]

The office of the *en(tu)* ceased to exist by the end of the Old Babylonian empire (16th century B.C.E.). It was restored for a brief period in the sixth century B.C.E. when Nabu-na'id (Nabonidus) attempted to revive the office by installing his own daughter in Ur as *en(tu)* of Sin. Apart from the position of the *en(tu)*, ancient Mesopotamian religions offered women a variety of positions within the structure of the clergy. Subsequently, all of these were gradually phased out.

Officiants of similar religious ritual were still present in Israel during the lifetimes of the prophets Samuel (11th century B.C.E.), Hosea (eighth century B.C.E.), and Amos (775–750 B.C.E.). When Samuel was still a child, the sons of Eli, the priest, were "lying with the women who served at the entrance to the Tent of Meeting" (1 Sam. 2:22). Hosea (4:14) and Amos (2:8) also make reference to religious practices of women, which they denounce as abhorrent; but it is significant that *kohenet,* the feminine form of *kohen* (priest), does not even exist in biblical Hebrew.

In Mesopotamia at least three classes of women who were in the service of a deity, the *en(tu),* the *naditu,* and the *ugbabtu,* were restricted from having children during their term of office,[3] though the *ugbabtu* were often married.[4] It is not clear how these women avoided pregnancy. The oldest extant medical prescriptions for the prevention of conception are found in the Petri Papyrus, which dates from the Twelfth Dynasty of Egypt, ca. 1850 B.C.E.[5] Hence it is possible that Sumerian and Akkadian priestesses were also familiar with some form of contraception, which would have allowed them sexual activity without fear of pregnancy.

Abortion, as a means for remaining childless was, and is, the most universal recourse.[6] Why women such as the *entu, naditu,* and *ugbabtu* chose (or were forced) to remain childless is not of particular concern to this paper. But whatever form of contraception was practiced by the female functionaries, there is a definite possibility that it was a general practice among other women as well; in addition to using certain herbs, roots, or bark, women resorted to abortion or even infanticide. Priestesses often reflected in their way of life the behavior that was believed to characterize the goddesses, and the latter were models for their human counterparts. As an example one can mention that the prestigious and beloved Inanna had no child[7] (nor a husband until she was associated with Dumuzi).

Women continued to officiate in a religious capacity after Old Babylonian times, but their functions became increasingly restricted. They were still included in the clergy, used some form of contraception, and, depending on the era, wielded political powers inherent in their religious office or relationship to the ruling class.

The early favorable conditions for women were not restricted to those of the upper classes. The legal provisions to protect women of all classes compare favorably to legal practices of today.[8] Rape, under certain conditions, and incest, were punishable by banishment or death. The Eshnunna Laws (section 26) provide that if a betrothed girl is forcibly seized by another man who deflowers her, the attacker shall die. The Code of Hammurabi (CH #130) echoes the earlier law: if he is caught, the rapist "shall be put to death, while that woman shall go free." Later Assyrian law (AL #55), however, stipulates that if a man rapes a girl, "the father of the virgin shall take the wife of the rapist. . . . and deliver her to be prostituted; he shall not return her to her husband, he shall take her. The father shall give his deflowered daughter to the rapist as consort." In other words, the Assyrians allow the rapist to go free while punishment for his offense is meted out to the rapist's wife and the raped girl. In our society women fare scarcely any better. The rapist still generally gets off free, and the raped woman or girl is often made to suffer humiliation by her husband, her family, or the authorities. Data show that the violation of women in America is on the increase.[9]

Biblical lore regarding rape mirrors a more favorable attitude toward women than Deuteronomic law. In the story of the rape of Leah's daughter Dinah (Gen. 34:2), the rapist, Shechem, offered to make retribution for his wrongdoing by marrying the raped girl. To Dinah's brothers, however, such outrage was a capital offense. Simeon and Levi, sons of Leah, devised a way to put Shechem, his father Hamor, and all the town's able-bodied men to the sword, in order to avenge the violence done their sister. Later biblical law, as Raphael Patai points out,[10] is less severe in its attitude toward the rapist. A man is only put to death if he rapes a betrothed girl; if she is not betrothed, the rapist must marry the girl and may not divorce her (Exod. 22:15–16; Deut. 22:25–29).

Incest is also penalized by Hammurabi: "If a man has intercourse with his daughter, they shall banish that man from the city" (CH 154). Biblical attitudes toward incest changed in the course of centuries in the direction of severity. Early Hebrew custom was more lax in permitting marriages between paternal half-siblings. Abraham married his half-sister Sarah, and even in King David's days such marriages were still legal. However, they are later condemned in Leviticus: "Cursed be he who lies with his sister, whether the daughter of his father or his mother."[11]

The Assyrians also regulated women's dress in public (AL #40). An Assyrian was permitted to divorce a woman with the stipulation that "if it is his will, he may give her something: if it is not his will he shall not give her anything and she shall go forth in her emptiness" (AL #37).

In the second millennium B.C.E., then, "appropriate to the more savage condition of Assyrian society,"[12] women's *rights* become curtailed in a manner reminiscent of the legal inadequacy suffered by women of today. Most characteristically that "savage condition" was reflected in the rules on abortion: "If a woman by her own deed has cast that which is within her own womb, and a charge has been brought and proven against her, they shall impale her and not bury her" (AL #53).

It would seem from the available documents containing rules and regulations, that the intent of early rulers of Mesopotamia such as Ur-Nammu (2112–2095 B.C.E.) and Lipit-Ishtar (1934–24 B.C.E.) was to regulate a changing economy. Everywhere in the ancient Near East the soil was originally regarded as belonging to the community and its deity, and as owned by the "houses" (i.e., lineage) constituting the community.[13] The advent of centralized government brought with it a hierarchical system based increasingly on private (immovable) property with political power concentrated in the hands of military leaders. The earlier corporate kinship groups could not be accommodated within the emerging polity of private ownership, and laws were passed primarily to protect the wealth and power of the elite groups that supplanted them.[14]

Ancient Sumerian law (YBC 2177) and the laws of Eshnunna (#22–23) punished a man if he either purposely or accidently "buffeted" another man's slave girl. And if, without cause, he battered another man's wife or child to death, this was a capital offense. "The batterer who battered shall die" (#24). Later, Hammurabi's "reform" provided punishment only to offenders of pregnant women (other than a man's own wife), and then only if the battery caused a miscarriage. In other words, under Semitic influence, the welfare of the fetus was placed above the well-being of the woman. Battery of a man's own wife was condoned also by the Assyrians. It was perfectly legitimate for a man to flog his wife, pluck her hair, or strike her and damage her ears. Assyrian law (#59) assures us that there is no guilt involved in this. It is estimated that today over two hundred thousand American husbands a year consistently batter their wives.[15]

The Hammurabi amendments are dedicated in considerable part to the regulation of women's lives. They deal at great length with women in religious service. Presumably these women still had a voice in political decision-making. A considerable portion of the Assyrian laws direct their policy on women to the female population in general. Hammurabi must have achieved his intent of wresting from women the only power left to them at the time, that within the clergy—a necessary step toward control of all women.

To sum up, women in ancient Mesopotamia enjoyed considerable prestige within the extended family or kinship group. Together with men, they formed part of religious institutions. After being segregated in the patriarchal family they were made totally dependent on male heads of the patrilineal system. In earlier times women had also been in control of their own bodies, as expressed in the right and practice of contraception.[16] As respected members of society women did not have to fear sexual assault or battery, which subsequently became a serious threat in the "savage condition of Assyrian society."

That the condition of the female population is still universally regulated on principles basically in accord with those espoused by Assyrian lawmakers over three thousand years ago is a sad comment on societies that pride themselves on their civilization and morality. Indeed, from the female perspective civilization has been neither progressive nor moral, nor has it reached the moral goal of the equality of all members of its society.

NOTES

1. Uruk alabaster vase. For description, cf. Eva Strommenger, *The Art of Mesopotamia* (London: Thames and Hudson, 1964), plates 19–22 and p. 384.

2. W. W. Hallo and J. J. A. van Dijk, "Enheduanna: Her Life and Works," in *The Exaltation of Inanna* (New Haven, Conn.: Yale University Press, 1968), p. 1.

3. Tablet III of the Atra-hâsîs epic, vii:6–9, enumerates the categories of women who remain childless.

4. J. J. Finkelstein, *Late Old Babylonian Documents and Letters,* Yale Oriental Series: *Babylonian Texts* (New Haven and London: Yale University Press, 1972), 13:15.

5. N. E. Himes, *Medical History of Contraception* (Baltimore, Md.: The Williams and Wilkins Co., 1936), p. 59.

6. Ibid., p. 4.

7. Although the gods Shara and Lulal (Latarak) are counted as her sons, cf. Th. Jacobsen, *Towards an Image of Tammuz* (Cambridge, Mass.: Harvard University Press, 1970), p. 27.

8. *The Ancient Near East*, ed. W. H. McNeill and J. W. Sedlar (New York: Oxford University Press, 1968), pp. 138–39.

9. Del Martin, *Battered Wives* (New York: Simon and Schuster, Pocket Books, 1976), p. 11. The Federal Bureau of Investigation, *Uniform Crime Reports for the United States* (1973), p. 14, states that a woman is raped every eight minutes.

10. Raphael Patai, *Sex and Family in the Bible and the Middle East*, (Garden City, N.Y.: Doubleday & Company, Inc., 1959), p. 107.

11. Cf. Gen. 20:12; 2 Sam. 13:12–13; Lev. 20:17. Cf. also Patai, *Sex and Family*, pp. 24–25.

12. H. W. F. Saggs: *The Greatness That Was Babylon* (New York: The New American Library, Inc., Mentor Books, 1962), p. 211.

13. Igor M. Diakonoff, "On the Structure of Old Babylonian Society" in *Ancient Mesopotamia* (Moscow: Nauka Publishing House, 1969), p. 18.

14. Ruby Rohrlich-Leavitt, "Women in Transition: Crete and Sumer," in *Becoming Visible*, ed. Renate Bridenthal and Claudia Koonz (New Jersey: Houghton Mifflin, 1977), p. 57.

15. M. F. Hirsch, "To Love, Cherish and Batter," in *Women and Violence* (New York: Van Nostrand Reinhold Company, 1981), p. 174. Also, A. A. Zullo and R. Fulman, "Wife Beating in Nice Homes," *New Woman*, March 1976, pp. 68–69.

16. J. J. Finkelstein, "Late Old Babylonian Documents and Letters," p. 10, suggests that these women remained childless as a means of population control.

Why Did Moses Strike the Rock?
A Psychoanalitic Study

DOROTHY F. ZELIGS

Why was Moses not permitted to enter the Promised Land? Surely it seems that he, of all people, most deserved this fulfillment. As with other problems that evoke deep human feelings relating to questions of justice, of reward and punishment, the Bible frequently gives no clear-cut answer in regard to specific situations. The general principles of morality are laid down with great definiteness, as in the Ten Commandments. But the behavior of the Deity himself is often a source of bewilderment and frustration to even his most faithful followers.

Martin Buber epitomizes this enigma by saying, ". . . man must not subject God to the rules of logic.[1] *Man's behavior*, however, must be subjected to the rules of the *psychologic*, that is, a study of the underlying motivations of his conduct.

A dramatic episode in the latter days of the life of Moses leads to the sad consequence referred to above. He was not to have the privilege of entering the Promised Land. Although he would bring his people to its borders, he himself was to die in the wilderness. This situation developed out of one of the hardships of desert life, a scarcity of water. It was reminiscent of what had happened at Rephidim many years before, according to biblical chronology (Exod. 17:1–7).

It will be helpful to recapitulate here some aspects of that previous experience as interpreted in another study.[2] The text concerning it is as follows: "And all the congregation of the children of Israel . . . encamped at Rephidim; and there was no water for the people to drink. Wherefore the people strove with Moses, and said: 'Give us water that we may drink.' And Moses said unto them: 'Why strive ye with me? Wherefore do ye try the Lord?' And the people thirsted there for water; and the people murmured against Moses, and said: 'Wherefore has thou brought us up out of Egypt, to kill us and our children and our cattle with thirst?' And Moses cried unto the Lord, saying: 'What shall I do unto this people? they are almost ready to stone me.' And the Lord said unto Moses: 'Pass on before the people, and take with thee of the elders of Israel; and thy rod, wherewith thou smotest the river, take in thy hand, and go. Behold, I will stand before thee there upon the rock in Horeb; and thou shalt smite the rock, and there shall come water out of it, that the people may drink.' And Moses did so in the sight of the elders of Israel. And the name of the place was called Massah (Trying) and Meribah (Strife), because of the striving of the children of Israel, and because they tried the Lord, saying: 'Is the Lord among us, or not? (Exod. 17:1–7)' "

Two aspects in the above passage are especially relevant to the present study. One is the reaction of Moses to the aggressive demands of the people. He clearly feels frightened, powerless, and dependent on God for leadership. The other element is the instruction that God gives Moses, telling him to strike the rock, a command directly opposite to the one now given at Kadesh, where he is told to *speak* to the rock and it would give forth its water.

It can be assumed that Moses had some understanding of the natural process that causes stratified porous limestone rock based upon an underlying spring to give forth its water when struck a heavy blow.[3] This knowledge could have been gained earlier during the time spent in crossing the wilderness after his flight from Egypt, and while among the nomadic Midianites, when he was a member of the household of Jethro. What, however, might have stood in the way of his immediately attempting this solution?

Striking the rock must have had an unconscious, symbolic meaning for Moses that made it difficult for him to perform this act. The concept of God as a rock, strong and steadfast, is a figure of speech frequently found in biblical literature. Its popularity in the later writings of the Prophets and in the Psalms stems from the time of Moses. One biblical scholar comments upon its use in Deuteronomy 32 known as the *Song of Moses*. He says, "Nine times in the course of this single hymn is repeated this most expressive figure taken from the granite crags of Sinai and carried hence through psalms and hymns of all nations. . . ."[4] The origin of this symbol is thus related to Mount Sinai, itself a massive rock. Indeed, the closest Moses came to experiencing the Presence of God had been from a cleft in that sacred mountain (Exod. 33:18–23).

In the realm of unconscious fantasy, the symbol can assume a reality of its own. The rock, especially in the area of the holy mountain, could have represented the Deity himself. As Ernest Jones points out, the definitive characteristic of a symbol is its connection with unconscious representations. As he puts it, "The process of symbolization is carried out unconsciously, and so the individual is quite unaware of the fact that he has employed one at all, since he takes the symbol for the reality."[5]

Awe and wonder at the grandeur of nature are often associated with deep religious feelings in biblical literature.[6] In the impressive environs of the Sinai wilderness, to the responsive heart of Moses, the concept of the rock as Deity may have taken on a mystical significance, of whose full extent he was not aware. Striking the rock could thus have become a form of aggression against God himself.

But if this method was the only way of getting water for the people, Moses would be in a state of conflict, torn between a sense of reality and his own resistance to an act that unconsciously had a special meaning for him. In that earlier experience at Rephidim, specific directions from God had been necessary, not only for the purpose of defining the task in a time of confusion, but also as indicating permission to perform the deed. God says," 'Behold, I will stand before thee, there upon the rock in Horeb.' " This was an odd form of reassurance. Moses' concept of God did not generally require this kind of physical proximity. But if we assume that the act of striking the rock was unconsciously associated with anxiety, then the closeness of God's Presence would help to alleviate this feeling. As suggested in connection with that episode, if God was felt as an Actual Presence, the rock would lose its symbolic significance, for the Deity would then be experienced on a level of consciousness that would make the symbolism of the rock unnecessary for that specific occasion. The puzzling biblical verse, " 'Behold, I will stand before thee, there upon the rock in Horeb," would be understandable within this context.

Some scholars believe that the later incident at Kadesh, with which we are now primarily concerned, is just another version of the previous happening at Rephidim and Mount Horeb.[7] There are, however, significant differences between the two. Moreover, the people must have suffered from a lack of water on more than one occasion.

The time of this second episode is many years later. Yet the earlier experience may have left its mark upon Moses. There must also have taken place a deepening and mellowing of his religious spirit. The thought of striking the rock would thus have been even more abhorrent to him.

The biblical narrative regarding this event begins as follows: "And the children of Israel, even the whole congregation, came into the wilderness of Zin in the first month [of the fortieth year of wandering]; and the people abode in Kadesh; and Miriam died there. And there was no water for the congregation; and they assembled themselves together against Moses and against Aaron. And the people strove with Moses, and spoke, saying: 'Would that we had perished when our brethren perished before the Lord! And why have ye brought the assembly of the Lord into this wilderness, to die there, we and our cattle? And wherefore have ye made us to come up out of Egypt, to bring us into this evil place? This is no place of seed, or of figs, or of vines, or of pomegranates; neither is there any water to drink.'" (20:1–5).*

These reproaches of the people against their leaders expressed not only need but considerable anger. Masochistically they declare that it would have been better for them to have perished with their brethren *before the Lord,* indirectly implying that the God of Moses, Who had not spared their relatives on a number of other occasions, could hardly be expected to save those who had thus far survived. At the same time, they proudly present themselves as *the assembly of the Lord,* who were thus worthy of better treatment. It was Moses and Aaron who had brought them into this *evil place,* which was such a contrast to the delights of the land that had been promised them.

As had happened before in such situations, Moses was unable to respond to this diatribe (14:5; Exod. 15:24). He tended to become speechless, overwhelmed with emotion, when strongly berated by the people. He and Aaron retreat to the Tent of Meeting, where God now gives them specific instructions about how to deal with the crisis. "And Moses and Aaron went from the presence of the assembly unto the door of the Tent of Meeting, and fell upon their faces; and the glory of the Lord appeared unto them. And the Lord spoke unto Moses, saying: Take the rod, and assemble the congregation, thou, and Aaron thy brother, and speak ye unto the rock before their eyes, that it give forth its water; and thou shalt bring forth to them water out of the rock; so thou shalt give the congregation and their cattle drink.' And Moses took the rod from before the Lord, as He commanded him. And Moses and Aaron gathered the assembly together before the rock, and he said unto them: 'Hear now, ye rebels; are we to bring you forth water out of this rock?' And Moses lifted up his hand, and smote the rock with his rod twice; and water came forth abundantly, and the congregation drank, and their cattle. And the Lord said unto Moses and Aaron: 'Because ye believed not in Me, to sanctify Me in the eyes of the Children of Israel, therefore ye shall not bring this assembly into the land which I have given them.' These are the waters of Meribah, where the children of Israel strove with the Lord, and He was sanctified in them" (29:6–13).

There is no consensus among scholars about the real nature of the sin Moses committed. The impression conveyed by the narrative and accepted by the casual reader is that Moses did wrong both in addressing the people so angrily and in striking the rock instead of speaking to it as commanded by God. The fact that he struck the rock twice also suggests a loss of control. Talmudic opinion, in the main, tends to agree with this commonsense interpretation.[8]

*All biblical references, unless otherwise noted, are to the book of Numbers.

The text itself, however, seems to avoid a direct statement about the specific nature of the wrongdoing of Moses. Other instances of this avoidance are even more apparent when the unhappy incident is mentioned again. On three separate occasions in his later discourses to the people (Deut. 1:37; 3:26, 4:21), Moses refers sadly to his not being permitted to enter the Promised Land, and each time he gives the same reason in almost identical words: "'the Lord was angry with me for your sakes . . .,'" that is, because of how the people had behaved. He thus blames them for his responses. The great leader here reveals a common human weakness that makes him all the more believable as a genuine human being.

We return to the intriguing question: In what did his wrongdoing consist? For indeed, the act of striking the rock and speaking angrily to the people do not in themselves seem sufficiently serious to merit the severe rebuke and punishment that followed.

The nearest the text comes to a definitive answer to this question is in the words, "Because ye believed not in Me, to sanctify Me in the eyes of the children of Israel, therefore ye shall not bring this assembly into the land which I have given them'" (20:12). Clearly, in some way, the offense involved the Deity himself.

Reference to the nature of the guilt is brought up again a little later in the same chapter, at the time of the approaching death of Aaron. God says, "'Aaron shall be gathered unto his people; for he shall not enter the land which I have given unto the children of Israel, because ye rebelled against My word at the waters of Meribah'" (20:24). And in regard to Moses himself, when he is allowed to view the Promised Land from a distant mountain top in Moab, God explains once more why the two leaders were excluded from entering Canaan: "'. . . because ye rebelled against My commandment in the wilderness of Zin, in the strife of the congregation, to sanctify Me at the waters before their eyes.'" (27:14).

Both these times the *disobedience* is equated with *rebellion*. This rebellion stemmed from a lack of faith in God—*ye believed not in Me*. This disbelief must have consisted of a doubt on the part of Moses that water could be brought forth from the rock by the power of the word alone even though that word had the authority of the Deity behind it. The dimly felt apprehension within him of the fear of failure was, of course, known to God, the Superego.

This was not the first time that Moses had faltered in his belief that God could meet the needs of the people in ways that clearly went beyond the bounds of natural forces. The earlier situation had occurred at the time when God declared to Moses that He would provide meat for the entire host of the Children of Israel (Num. 11). On that occasion, however, although Moses was rebuked by the Deity with the words, *Is the Lord's hand waxed short?*, he was not punished. Significantly, that breach of faith had not affected the leader's behavior *in the eyes of the people,* as had occurred at

Kadesh. Moreover, the feeling had been expressed openly and thus was not repressed, as on this second occasion.

This lurking doubt in the power of God, deep within the heart of Moses, must have been generated in part by an unconscious *wish to rebel*, a reactivation of competitive feelings against the oedipal father of his childhood. *To rebel* is to defy authority. *It is an act of will.* Thus it suggests more than an expression of anger and a loss of self-control. What could have been involved was the emergence of a *counter-will*, an unconscious, unverbalized intent to defy the father. Freud explains the counter-will as stemming from an *antithetic idea.* He says that it is dissociated from the conscious intention. When it comes to carrying out the conscious intention, the counter-will takes over, often to the surprise of the individual himself.[9] Elsewhere, he comments, ". . . antithetic ideas arise in us in a marked manner when we feel uncertain about whether we can carry out some important intention."[10]

In regard to Moses, the counter-will was set up against the superego command *to speak* to the rock and must indeed have been influenced by doubt about the outcome, the lack of faith for which God reproached him.

The conditions denoting indecision about what he would actually do were inherent in the very wording of the command as received by Moses. "And the Lord spoke unto Moses, saying: " 'Take the rod, and assemble the congregation, thou and Aaron thy brother, and speak ye unto the rock before their eyes, that it give forth its water' " (20:7–8). If Moses was to speak to the rock, why did he need to take the rod with him? Perhaps having the rod in his hand may have been intended to serve as a source of strength and reassurance, a symbol both to himself and to the people that he was endowed with the authority to act as the representative of the Deity. Did it become, instead, a stimulus for rebellion, the rod of God being used for the leader's own unconscious purpose?

The situation at Kadesh was a particularly complex one. The intrapsychic conflict with which Moses was struggling stemmed from several sources impinging upon each other. It was for the very purpose of avoiding an aggressive act toward the Deity that Moses was reluctant to strike the rock, although that method had proved successful on an earlier occasion. A logical alternative, it then seemed, was to speak to the rock instead. Such an approach would represent a desired sublimation of forbidden aggressive impulses. Certainly this resolve, coming in the form of a command from the Deity, was also an expression of the will of Moses, a conscious intention of what he planned to do.

But the hoped-for solution had the characteristics of a *compromise formation*, unconsciously containing within itself another form of aggression, even more serious in nature than that which it sought to avoid—competitiveness with the Deity.[11]

In the biblical tradition, God had created the whole world through the power of *the word* (Gen. 11). Would not a command issued to the rock, such as, "Pour forth your water!" be frighteningly similar to those fateful words, *Let there be light!* To the unconscious of Moses, such words addressed to the rock could have had a magical connotation related to feelings of God-like omnipotence. Significantly, God's command to speak to the rock gives no instructions about the exact words to be uttered. And Moses suffered from a certain inhibition of speech, especially in times of anxiety. He was *of slow tongue.* As suggested in another study, this disturbance of function may have had its beginnings in early childhood, growing out of a defeated sense of sibling rivalry with Aaron, who was three years older. When Moses was just learning to talk, Aaron could already *speak well.* This conflict must have affected the later oedipal striving with the father also. Thus for Moses the fantasy of the magical power of words, common to childhood, may have retained its significance in the unconscious to an undue degree. The intensity of his wish to be powerful would thus have taken on forbidden aspects of competitiveness, leading to his *slowness of tongue.*[12] It was both a defense against aggression and a wish for omnipotence. Perhaps it was because of this disability that he could not respond to the verbal attacks of the people when these were especially violent. It was this sense of weakness, as will be recalled, that had led to his pleading many years before, at the theophany of the burning bush, to be excused from the mission ordained for him, saying, " 'Oh Lord, I am not a man of words, neither heretofore, nor since Thou has spoken unto Thy servant; for I am slow of speech and of a slow tongue' " (Exod. 4 : 10).

How God had dealt with this plea of His chosen prophet is enlightening. Like a good therapist, the Deity gave him Aaron, a supportive *alter ego,* to act as his voice. The acceptance of the older brother in this role suggests a reaction-formation to the childhood hostility, an act of reparation. The underlying wish for omnipotence against which Moses was so strongly defending himself is also partially satisfied. God said, " '. . . and he shall be to thee a mouth, and thou shalt be to him in God's stead' " (Exod. 4 : 16).[13] At a later time, when Moses was commanded to appear again before the Egyptian ruler after the first rebuff, he said to God, " 'Behold, I am of uncircumcised lips, and how shall Pharaoh hearken unto me?' And the Lord said unto Moses, 'See, I have set thee in God's stead to Pharaoh; . . . and Aaron, thy brother, shall speak unto Pharaoh, that he let the children of Israel go out of his land' " (Exod. 6 : 30–7 : 2).[14]

In both these situations the complaint of weakness in speech was met with permission for Moses to play a God-like role, first to Aaron and then to Pharaoh. The tendency to verbal inhibition is thus clearly related to a wish for omnipotence. Only with God's express permission could he be powerful in the use of words.

It might be noted that during all the periods of crisis through which the Children of Israel passed, from the time of the plagues in Egypt to the exigencies in the wilderness, when saving acts were performed for the people, these miracles were never brought about by direct verbal command on the part of Moses over the forces of nature. They occurred following his prophetic words expressing the will of God.[15] Thus his speaking directly to the rock would have been a significantly new element in the situation. Even though he would be acting as the agent of God's will, the underlying wish for omnipotence could have changed the meaning of the situation for him. The leader was faced with an insoluble dilemma. In terms of his unconscious conflict, he either had to commit an act of aggression by striking the rock, unconsciously symbolic of the Deity, or be competitive with Him in the wish for omnipotence through the power of speech.

The situation at Kadesh differed from the earlier experience in another important respect. At that time only the elders had been present (Exod. 17:6). Now, the whole congregation was to witness this happening, significant of the power of God. Moses and Aaron are clearly instructed to assemble *all* the people and are told, "'. . . speak ye to the rock *before their eyes,* that it give forth its water'" (20:8; italics added).

If viewed as emanating from the unconscious of Moses himself, this directive may give further evidence of the personal element involved. Moses *wanted* all the people to witness this manifestation of power, perhaps as a compensation for the sense of inadequacy he had experienced when exposed to their humiliating accusations. The derogatory terms in which they had made their demands must have touched to the quick this area of vulnerability—his tendency to feel verbally powerless.

A further aspect must have influenced the final outcome, this time one that stemmed from a sense of reality. Suppose he failed before that entire assembly because he had used the untried method of speaking to the rock! He would have to face the scorn and derision of the people, perhaps even the danger of personal violence. And beyond that there was the possibility that his leadership would be undermined and that the whole purpose of the larger undertaking would come to naught.

When the actual moment came, when Moses found himself standing beside the rock, facing the taunting multitude, his conflicting feelings must have reached a state of unbearable tension. No doubt he felt that it was they, the people, who had placed him in this untenable situation. The release of his pent-up feelings came in an outburst of anger. ". . . and he said unto them: 'Hear now, ye rebels; are we to bring you forth water out of this rock?' And Moses lifted up his hand, and smote the rock with his rod twice; and water came forth abundantly, and the congregation drank, and their cattle" (20:10–11).

Several meanings seem to be concentrated in the one explosive sentence uttered by Moses. Hertz interprets it as, "*Can* we bring you forth water from this rock?" and says concerning it, "In that moment of irritation and gloom, Moses gives expression to doubt in front of the masses as to the fulfillment of God's power.[16]" Martin Noth describes the verse as ". . . an expression of embarrassment and doubt with a reproachful address to *the rebels* whose behavior has caused that embarrassment and that doubt."[17]

Clearly Moses feels that *he* was being tested as well as God, which was undoubtedly true. The implication of his reproach seems to be that an impossible task was being asked of him. The leader's own faith to achieve such a miracle must have faltered at that point. Since he felt unable to obey God's commandment, he may have *anticipated the possibility of failure* in getting water for the people. Therefore, as a protective measure but without awareness of what he was doing, he was preparing them in advance for an unfavorable outcome. The words "'Ye rebels, are we to bring *you* forth water out of this rock?'" (italics added) suggest that they were unworthy of such a miracle because they were rebellious, that is, lacking in faith. He was, in effect, accusing the people of the very sin with which God subsequently confronted the leader himself.

The text specifically states that Moses struck the rock twice. Perhaps the real need to draw forth the water made this repetition necessary. It seems more likely, however, since he evidently struck the rock in rapid succession, half expecting that nothing would happen, that Moses needed a further outlet for his feelings of frustration and rage. After the second blow, ". . . water came forth abundantly, and the congregation drank, and their cattle." Now come the significant words: "And the Lord said unto Moses and Aaron: 'Because ye believed not in Me, to sanctify Me in the eyes of the children of Israel, therefore ye shall not bring this assembly into the land which I have given them.' These are the waters of Meribah (Strife), where the children of Israel strove with the Lord, and He was sanctified in them" (20:11–12).

There is a striking contradiction in these verses. First we are told that God reproached Moses and Aaron for having failed to sanctify Him in the eyes of the people, and immediately after that come the words *and He was sanctified in them.*

Something of significance seems to have been omitted here. What has been left out can be understood as representing a repression on the part of Moses, the substance of which would explain the contradiction referred to. In the words, "These are the waters of Meribah, where the children of Israel strove with the Lord," Moses himself is directly identified with God since it was actually the *man* with whom the people were striving. Therefore the pronoun in the second part of the verse, *and He was sanctified in them,* may also refer to Moses.

The sudden gushing forth of the waters must have been unexpected for Moses himself. He had been in a mood of defeatism and anger, feeling that *he* did not deserve a miracle, especially through an act of disobedience. The words he had addressed to the people must unconsciously have been experienced as being directed to him by the Deity: "You rebel, am I to bring *you* forth water from this rock!" And the appropriate response, according to the conscience of Moses, should have been, "No, Lord God, I do not deserve it." But nevertheless, *the water came forth abundantly.*

The leader must have experienced a sudden change of mood, a deep sense of relief. He was still powerful with the rod of God! The responsive shouts of joy and appreciation from the multitude that must have followed would indeed have been like the proverbial balm to his troubled spirit. The disbelief and anger in the sea of faces surrounding him had suddenly changed. Now there must have been awe and reverence instead. *He was sanctified in their eyes,* as if he were, indeed, the very embodiment of the Lord!

But other feelings quickly take over. In the words of reproach that follow immediately, God confronts Moses not only with a lack of faith but with its consequences: " 'Because ye believed not in Me, *to sanctify Me in the eyes of the children of Israel.* . . .' " And that, indeed, must have been the crux of the matter. Moses had failed to give due honor to God *in the eyes of the people.* As the rabbis point out, if the leader had produced water from the rock by the power of the word alone, the accomplishment would have redounded to the greater glory of the Deity Himself through the man who spoke in His Name.[18]

The ego can be caught off-guard by persistent wishes of unconscious fantasies that seek realization. In the very moment when Moses should have been exalting God in his heart, he may have felt instead a narcissistic gratification, an all-too-human emotion. This brief self-indulgence is quickly repressed. The only indication in the narrative of its existence is the contradiction that states first that Moses failed to sanctify God in the eyes of the people and follows it with the words, ". . . and He *(he)* was sanctified in them." After that passing moment of self-exaltation, Moses must have been assailed by feelings of guilt. He had fallen short of his own ego ideal in several respects. First, the leader had acted out his aggression and struck the rock after having resolved to speak to it instead. Also, by his angry words of reproach he must have evoked feelings of guilt in the people, together with doubt about whether the miracle would actually take place. Then, against this background of uncertainty, came the gushing forth of the waters, making Moses appear especially great *in their eyes* as well as in his own. It may have been in response to this sense of awe in the people that *Moses felt himself sanctified in them.*

Nachmanides, the noted medieval commentator, touches upon this point. He thinks that the wrongdoing of Moses lay in the words he used, for these implied that Moses and Aaron rather than God were to perform the miracle.[19] For the grave sin of usurping the place of God in the eyes of the people, for even momentarily being competitive with God Himself, the punishment of not being allowed to enter the *Motherland* was meted out.

Indeed, the original rivalry between son and father is in relation to the mother.

Striking the rock served a further unconscious purpose. The conflict was terminated in an outburst of anger against the people, as noted above. This reaction not only helped to alleviate his tension but also changed the focus of his thoughts and feelings. Instead of speaking to the rock as intended, Moses turned his attention to the multitude before him. Since his verbal anger was directed against them, it can be assumed that the blows he struck the rock also served as an expression of his rage toward them. Thus, instead of being the filial son, relating to the Father-God and obeying His commandment, Moses became the father himself, chastising his rebellious children. In this situation, the rock would have lost its symbolic significance as the Deity, becoming instead an object for the displacement of his anger against the people. The originally feared impulse, aggression against God, was thus, in a sense, avoided. But, as is generally true in a compromise-formation, the warded-off impulse finds another pathway for gratification.[20] Not only was the aggression satisfied but the narcissistic wish also finds an outlet. In the relief and exultation at the success that followed upon striking the rock, the fantasy of feeling God-like found expression. This forbidden wish-fulfillment had to be repressed and denied. But the immediate announcement of the punishment that would follow indicates an awareness of guilt and the return to a sense of reality in terms of his own identity. The omission in the text referred to above could be replaced by an expanded version of God's reproach to Moses, as follows: "You failed to sanctify Me in the eyes of the people because you yourself wished to be sanctified in them, in My stead."

The role of Aaron in this situation is a characteristic one. He too suffered the penalty of dying in the wilderness. Commentators have wondered about the nature of *his* guilt. Perhaps Aaron's sin was one of omission. *He did nothing.* Probably, under the circumstances, that was all he could do. God's commandment concerning Aaron came through Moses. "And the Lord spoke unto Moses, saying: 'Take the rod, and assemble the congregation, thou, and Aaron thy brother, and speak *ye* unto the rock before their eyes that it give forth its water; and *thou* shalt bring forth to them water out of the rock; so *thou* shalt give the congregation and their cattle drink'" (20:7–8, italics added). It cannot be accidental that the commandment to assemble the people and speak to the rock uses the plural form of the pronoun, *ye,* thus including Aaron, while in the positive results that are to follow, providing water for the people, the singular form, *thou,* used twice, is found, thus disregarding Aaron. He is allowed to share in the responsibilities but not in the reward. Again, the tendencies in Moses that make him so understandably human unconsciously manifest themselves. He could not permit the brother to share his own special relationship with the

Father. Aaron, however, had to be involved in this event. It would have been unthinkable to have allowed him the privilege, denied to Moses, of entering the Promised Land.

And now we come to another aspect of this psychologically important event in the personal life of Moses. It is significant that the situation about the scarcity of water follows immediately upon the statement that Miriam had died at Kadesh. The text says, "And the children of Israel, even the whole congregation, came into the wilderness of Zin in the first month; and the people abode in Kadesh; and Miriam died there, and was buried there. And there was no water for the congregation" (20:1–2).

The relationship between cause and effect is frequently established in biblical literature through the use of sequence.[21] Thus the implication is that *because* of the death of Miriam there was no water for the congregation. There is indeed a psychological connection between the two happenings. Symbolically, the loss of Miriam was experienced as that of a mother figure and her nurturing breast. Water is as basic to life in the desert as milk is for the infant. Yet the Bible does not even record that the people mourned for her. In contrast, when Aaron died shortly thereafter, the event is treated in a much more expansive fashion, occupying eight verses (20:22–29). Moreover, we are clearly told, "And when all the congregation saw that Aaron was dead, they wept for Aaron thirty days, even all the house of Israel" (20:29).

This contrast may reflect the attitude of a patriarchal society in which the importance of women, both in their nurturing and sexual roles, is repressed, thus minimizing on a conscious level the emotions relating to *mother* and *wife*. Unconsciously, this repression increases the affects associated with these relationships.

How does Moses himself react to the death of Miriam? No mention is made of a sense of grief on his part either. Characteristically, he did not allow himself to experience feelings of this kind on a personal basis, especially in family relationships. That aspect of his life tended to be ignored even beyond cultural conditioning. Psychologically, this renunciation favored a deeper relationship to God and a strengthening of his role as leader of *all* the people.[22]

We shall assume, however, that the death of Miriam was not an unimportant event for her brother Moses. She had been a mothering figure to him in his infancy. She had endured with him the perils of the escape from Egypt, had led in the rejoicing at the crossing of the Sea of Reeds, had participated in the hardships of the wilderness, and gloried in the Covenant at Mount Sinai.

Losing the mother may reactivate the oedipal hostility toward the father by evoking a repressed childhood image of him as a rival for her love and attention. This psychic process of loss and resentment may have taken place within the people as a whole. The fact that no public mourning for her is recorded and may indeed have been kept to a minimum, suggests that there was little opportunity for catharsis. Feelings of grief and anger would then remain unabated, with increased ambivalence toward the father figure. Unconsciously the people may have blamed Moses for this loss. Their complaint about the lack of water may have taken on a greater degree of animosity under these circumstances. Moreover, Moses himself may have had similar feelings toward the Father-God, Who had done this to him.

A rabbinic legend intuitively picks up the underlying theme of Miriam as the group mother and a source of nurturance. It says that after Rephidim, for as long as Miriam lived, the Children of Israel never lacked water. A well magically accompanied them. "This well," says Ginzberg, " was in the shape of a sieve-like rock, out of which water gushed forth as from a spout. It followed them on all their wanderings, up hill and down dale. Wherever they halted, it halted too, finally settling opposite the Tabernacle. Thereupon the leaders of the twelve tribes would appear, each with his staff, and chant these words, " 'Spring up, O well, sing ye unto it; nobles of the people digged it by direction of the lawgiver with their staves.' Then the water would gush forth from the depths of the well." When Miriam died, so says the legend, the well dried up.[23]

Interestingly, in this postbiblical fantasy, the leaders of the tribes are able to accomplish what Moses could not. Although carrying their staves, they *spoke* to the *sievelike rock* and the water came forth. Here, the rock can be understood as symbolic of a combined parental figure, both father and mother. This image is conceptualized even more clearly in the *Song of Moses,* referred to earlier (Deut. 32:18). The leader, in his final words, warns the people Israel about their conduct in the future and predicts their unfaithfulness, saying, " 'Of the Rock that begot thee thou wast unmindful./ And didst forget God that bore thee.' "[24] Hertz comments concerning these lines, "A figure as bold as it is beautiful. God is represented as a Father, to whom Israel owed its existence as a people; and, at the same time, as a Mother, travailing with her infant, and forever watching over it with tender affection."[25] As has been suggested, Moses too must have identified with both these roles, and some of his character traits can best be understood in that context.[26]

The legend about Miriam's well may also have served the purpose of subtly indicating the positive approach that Moses should have used in his own experience with the rock, thus gently reproving him for his aggressive act. That he learned the lesson is indicated by a later happening. The people were then on the eastern border of Moab, in the wilderness of the Arnon River gorge. Evidently they were in need of water but this time we hear no complaints. They moved on to a place called *Beer* (well). The text says, " . . . that is the well whereof the Lord said unto Moses: 'Gather the people together, and I will give them water.' Then sang Israel this song,

'Spring up, O well, sing ye unto it' " (21 : 16–18). This verse is the source of the later legend quoted above. Here the water is supplied in a seemingly natural way, by the supplication of the people themselves, under the immediate direction of God, with Moses serving only to *gather the people together.*

The symbolism of the rock as the mother's breast comes through in another legend, which states that blood flowed from the rock instead of water. Moses complains to God but is rebuked for striking the rock instead of speaking to it as commanded. Moses is reminded by the Deity that during the period in Egypt when Pharaoh ordered all male children to be destroyed, many women hid their newborn infants. An angel was sent to care for them and gave each child two smooth pebbles, one of which provided milk, the other honey.[27] Thus, through the good offices of an angel, God plays the role of the nurturing mother, offering her breasts to the abandoned children. The clear inference of the legend is that in striking the rock, Moses was symbolically drawing blood from the maternal bosom, showing anger and a lack of faith in God, here the maternal provider. The primitive aspect of the fantasy points to its preoedipal source in the unconscious of the people from whom it stemmed. It seems that the people intuitively understood a deeper source of man's common anger, which may go back to the time of the frustrated nursling who bites the mother's breast. They were identifying with the Children of Israel at this point and blaming the leader even as he was blaming God.

The profound influence of the mother image in psychic development is subtly merged into the figure of the Hebrew and later Jewish Father-God.[28] In the above legends the rock symbolizes the combined parental figure, while Moses is given the role of the rebellious child, who thus deserves punishment. The opportunity to make the most of a revered leader's moment of weakness is here fully utilized by his followers. Actually, the fantasies present in reverse the role generally played by Moses. His tendency was to take on the responsibilities of both father and mother to the Children of Israel, here also modeling himself upon his concept of God.

Frequently, a series of events occurring simultaneously play a part in bringing about psychic conflict. Thus a further element may have been involved in the situation at Kadesh. The people were now fairly close to the Promised Land, whose conquest they were about to begin. Even before the episode relating to the rock, Moses must have felt, somewhere deep within him, that for reasons he could not comprehend he would not have the privilege of entering that land. Psychoanalytically, the implication is that Moses was forbidden by his own superego to do so, a taboo that may have been rendered more threatening by the imminent approach of the tribes to Canaan. The conflict about striking the rock, against the background of the latter situation, could have reactivated an oedipal rebellion stemming from the past, now directed against the Father-God, Who had also deprived him of Miriam, a mother figure. Since this area of conflict belonged to the unconscious, Moses could not have had any awareness of the real reason behind the prohibition, which was projected to God.

The Talmudic rabbis, in their own need for explanations, suggested that the theme of a heroic leader and a favored son of God who was himself subject to a punishment so severe, pointed to a lesson in Divine justice for the benefit of the people.[29] However, a feeling must have persisted that an element of mystery surrounding the situation remained. Something about the disparity between the punishment and the *crime* was puzzling on a rational level.

Legend tries to deal with this elusive factor. It portrays God as having decreed long before that Moses was to die in the wilderness, and then used the offense at Kadesh as a rationalization to justify the penalty. But, so the story goes, God was more explicit with Moses himself. The leader is told that his glory would hardly be enhanced if he were the one to bring a new generation into the Promised Land while those of his own age group, whom he had led out of Egypt, were buried in the desert. As a consolation, Moses was told that after the Resurrection, he himself would bring those disinherited ones into the Motherland.[30]

While obviously intended to be comforting, this myth suggests that Moses may have been suffering from a sense of guilt, familiarly known as the guilt of the survivor, because he had outlived so many of his peers. Besides himself, only Caleb and Joshua were left of that earlier generation (14:38).

Rabbinic legend also says that Moses pleaded with God to ascribe a definite reason that would explain why he was being punished. Otherwise posterity would associate him with those others whose sins of disobedience and rebelliousness had brought about their deaths in the wilderness.[31] What is suggested here is a wish on the part of the rabbis to deny that the sin of Moses was indeed also one of rebelliousness against God and thus subject to the same punishment that the others had received. By the specific nature of the request attributed to Moses, that a reason for his punishent be stated, the rabbis were intuitively indicating an awareness that the leader, in his protest and denial, suffering from an unconscious sense of guilt, was in need of a more satisfactory rationalization than he himself could find.

Some commentators observe that the Bible purposely withheld the exact nature of the sin for which Moses was not permitted to enter the Promised Land. The real reason was to remain unknown, they maintain, as part of the mystery surrounding this great figure, even as the exact site of his grave is unknown.

The vagueness underlying these speculations suggests that the deeper psychological truth could not be fully grasped because its nature was hidden in the unconscious.[32] Moses, struggling with competitive feelings toward the Father-God, could not take possession of the Mother-land.[33]

The act of striking the rock was an expression of inner conflict, a loss of control compounded not only by oedipal competitiveness and disobedience, but also motivated by an unconscious need for punishment by the Father, a punishment that would fit the *crime*.

NOTES

1. Martin Buber, *Job. On the Bible:Eighteen Studies.* (Ed. Nahum M. Glatzer) (New York: Schocken Books, 1968), pp. 196–97.

2. Dorothy F. Zeligs, *Moses, A Psychodynamic Study* (forthcoming).

3. Werner Keller, *The Bible as History* (New York: William Morrow & Co., 1969), p. 126.

4. Joseph Hertz, *The Pentateuch and Haftorahs (Hebrew Text, English Translation, and Commentary)* (London: The Soncino Press, 1973) (2d ed.) pp. 896–97)

5. Ernest Jones, The Theory of Symbolism: *Papers on Psychoanalysis* (Baltimore: William & Wilkins Co., 1950), p. 97.

6. Rudolf Otto, *The Idea of the Holy* (London: Oxford Univ. Press, 1923), pp. 81–84.

7. S. R. Driver, *The Cambridge Bible: Exodus* (London: Cambridge Univ. Press, Revised ed., 1953), p. 158.

8. Louis Ginzberg, *The Legends of the Jews* (Philadelphia: Jewish Publication Society of America, 1909–1938), vol. 6, p. 108, n. 610.

9. Sigmund Freud, "A Case of Successful Treatment by Hypnosis." In *Collected Papers* (London: Hogarth Press, 1950), vol. V., pp. 38–40.

10. Josef Breuer & Sigmund Freud, *Studies on Hysteria* (New York: Basic Books, 1957), pp. 92–95.

11. Sigmund Freud, "Obsessive Acts and Religious Practices" In *Collected Papers* (London: Hogarth Press, 1950), pp. 32–33.

12. Sigmund Freud, *The Problem of Anxiety.* (Trans. by H. Bunker) (New York: The Pschoanalytic Quarterly & W. W. Norton, 1936), pp. 14–15.

13. Dorothy F. Zeligs, "Moses in Midian: The Burning Bush." *American Imago*, vol. 26, 1969, pp. 398–99.

14. Dorothy F. Zeligs, "Moses and Pharaoh: A Psychoanalytic Study of Their Encounter." *American Imago*, vol. 30, 1973, p. 199.

15. Yehezkel Kaufmann, *The Religion of Israel* (Translated and Abridged by Moshe Greenberg) (Chicago: University of Chicago, 1960), pp. 82f.

16. Hertz, p. 656.

17. Martin North, *Numbers, A Commentary* (Great Britain: SCM Press, 1968), p. 146.

18. Ginzberg, Vol. 3, p. 312.

19. Abraham Cohen, (ed.) *The Soncino Chumash (With an Exposition based on the Classical Jewish Commentaries)* (Great Britain: The Soncino Press, 1947), pp. 902–3.

20. Sigmund Freud, *"The Problem of Anxiety,"* p. 44.

21. Joh. Pedersen, *Israel: Its Life and Culture* (London: Oxford University Press, 1926), vol. 1–2, p. 115.

22. Sigmund Freud, *Group Psychology and the Analysis of the Ego* (New York: Liveright Publishing Co., 1949), pp. 122–23.

23. Ginzberg, vol. 3, p. 53.

24. Raphael Patai, *The Hebrew Goddess* (New York: Avon Books). Revised Ed., 1978. (For general background on the anthropological and psychological aspects of the role of the mother figure in the development of religion.)

In a personal communication, Dr. Patai gave me his own translation of the Hebrew verse, Deut. 32: 18, "Thou didst forget the Rock that bore thee/ and didst not remember God Who brought thee forth." His comment: "Both Hebrew verbs used clearly mean *to bear*, the female function."

25. Hertz, p. 899.

26. Dorothy F. Zeligs, "Maternal Aspects in the Personality of Moses." In *Moses, A Psychodynamic Study* (forthcoming).

27. Ginzberg, vol. 2, p. 257.

28. G. G. Barag, "The Mother in the Religious Concepts of Judaism." *American Imago,* vol. 4, 1946, pp. 32–33; Dorothy F. Zeligs, "The Role of the Mother in the Development of Hebraic Monotheism." *The Psychoanalytic Study of Society* (eds. Muensterberger & Axelrad) (New York: International Universities Press) vol. 1 (1960), pp. 287–310.

29. Ginsburg, vol. 3, pp. 313–14.

30. Ibid., pp. 312–13.

31. Ibid.,

32. Bronson A. Feldman, "Mother-Country and Fatherland." *Psychoanalysis: Journal of Psychoanalytic Psychology.* vol. 3, 1955, pp. 27–45.

33. Dorothy F. Zeligs, *Psychoanalysis and the Bible: A Study in Depth of Seven Leaders* (New York: Bloch Publishing Co., 1974), chapter 1.

Part VI

HEBREW SECTION

אוכלי השולחן כדי שיתמהו על הדבר וישאלו וכל מה שיכולין לעשות שנוי כדי
להתמיה עושין".

בקטע הראשון המתחיל **ומצאתי** מוזכרֶת הגבהת הקערה, שהיא סילוק הקערה
מן השולחן.[8] בקטע המתחיל **עוד מצאתי** נמסרת תוספת למנהג ההגבהה: עם
ההגבהה, או ההסרה, של הקערה מן השולחן מעבירים אותה על ראשי המסובים.
ואם אמנם הסרת הקערה לבד יש בה כבר לעורר סקרנות, העבירו את הקערה
על ראשי המסובים כדי להגביר את הסקרנות.

הננו למדים כי העברת הקערה על ראשי המסובים לא היתה אלא **תוספת**
למנהג סילוק הקערה, מנהג המובא בפוסקים והנפוץ בקהילות ישראל.

במהלך הדורות שכחו משמעותו של המנהג וסברו שיש בהעברת הקערה על
ראשי המסובים משום סגולה או מתן ברכה, והיו שהתחילו לעשות זאת שלוש
פעמים, כדרך השימוש הנפוץ בסגולות.

הערות

1.   ר' חיים יוסף דוד אזולאי, **מעגל טוב השלם**, ברלין, תרפ"ח, ע' 62.

2.   בנימין השני, **ספר מסעי ישראל**, מתורגם ע"י דוד גורדון, ליק, תרי"ט, ע' 126.

3.   אלכסנדר לוינסון, **ספר המועדים**, כרך ב' תש"ח, ע' 398.

4.   יעקב משה טולידאנו, **נר המערב**, ירושלים, תרע"א, ע' 215.

5.   Ida Cowen, *Jews in Remote Corners of the World*, Englewood Cliffs, N.J.: Prentice Hall, 1971,
   p. 303, 309.

6.   שם טוב גאגין, **כתר שם טוב**, ח"ג, לונדון, תש"ח ע' 129.

7.   מנהג סילוק הקערה היה נהוג בספרד. הוא נזכר בספרי הפוסקים של ארץ זו. בהגדה כ"י מן המאות
   הי"ג-הי"ד מארץ ספרד (ברשות הספריה של הסמינר התיאולוגי היהודי בניו-יורק) כתוב לפני הא
   לחמא עניא: "ועוקר הסל... (מלה קטנה שאיננה ניתנת לקריאה ההגדה כדי שיראו התינוקות
   וישאלו".

8.   כי ההגבהה הנזכרת כאן היא סילוק הקערה מן השולחן רואים גם מן הלשון: "ושלא יחזירנה
   למקומה עד שיאמר מה נשתנה וכו'". ועיין הדברים המובאים בס' **חקת פסח**, באותו עמוד, בשם
   "הר' יונה ז"ל בפי' ההגדה שלו': "ומה שמגביהין הקערה כדי שיראו התינוקות את השנוי
   וישאלו... לפיכך יצוה להסיר הקערה מעל השולחן ולהניחה בסוף השולחן כאילו כבר אכלו כדי
   שיראו התינוקות וישאלו..." (ועי' שולחן ערוך, אורח חיים, סימן תע"ג, סעיף ו'). לפי הר' יונה
   הנ"ל מחזירים הקערה למקומה כשמתחילים "עבדים היינו".

מיטלמאן 2 מוגה

לחמא עניא": "ונושאין הקערה על ראשי התינוקות...".

דומה שהמדובר כאן בסילוק הקערה מן השולחן, שהוא במקום עקירת השולחן שהיה נהוג בימי התלמוד.

בימי התלמוד כאשר היה שולחן קטן לפני קורא ההגדה ושולחן קטן לפני כל אחד ואחד מן המסובין, היו נוהגים לעקור את השולחן בתחילת הסדר, כדי שיתעוררו הילדים לשאול.

מובא בבבלי במסכת פסחים קטו, ב: "למה עוקרין את השולחן? אמרו דבי ר' ינאי כדי שיכירו תינוקות וישאלו".

עוד שם: "אביי הוה יתיב קמיה דרבה. חזא דקא מדלי תכא מקמיה. אמר להו: עדיין לא קא אכילנן, אתו קא מעקרי תכא מקמן. אמרו ליה רבה: פטרתן מלומר מה נשתנה" (אביי היה יושב [בסדר] לפני רבה. ראה שמגביהים השולחן מלפניו. אמר להם: עדיין לא אכלנו ובאים ועוקרים את השולחן מלפנינו? אמר לו רבה: פטרת אותנו מלומר: מה נשתנה [כלומר: כבר שאלת אותנו על השינוי ואין צורך עוד לשאול: מה נשתנה]).

הרשב"ם בפירושו לתלמוד שם, מפרש שכזה היה המנהג בימי התלמוד, אך בימינו כשכל המסובים אוכלים על שולחן אחד, מסלקים הקערה מן השולחן.

מנהג סילוק "הקערה" בתחילת הסדר, שבא במקום עקירת השולחן, כדי שיתעוררו הילדים לשאול, היה נפוץ בקהילות ישראל.[7] אמנם היו חלוקים המנהגים כיצד לסלק את הקערה היו שסילקו אותה לשעה קלה לקרן זווית והיו שעשו את הסילוק באופן אחר (כמו הגבהה מן השולחן).

במלים "נושאין הקערה על ראשי התינוקות" בהגדה הנ"ל הכוונה בודאי לסילוק הקערה מן השולחן, אלא בכמה אזורים בספרד היה כנראה המנהג בשעה שסילקו הקערה מן השולחן העבירו אותה מעל ראשי הילדים. היה בכך משום עשיית יתר לעורר סקרנותם של הילדים — הרי עיקר סילוק הקערה היה בשבילם.

ד.

בהגדת ואדי אלחגארה לא נמצא מפורש כי העברת הקערה על הראשים היא תוספת לסילוק הקערה מן השולחן וכי היא נעשית כדי להגביר הסקרנות, אבל הדברים מפורשים בספר **חקת פסח**, פירוש להגדה מאת הרב משה ב"ר חיים פיזאנתי שנדפס בסלוניקי בשנת שכ"ט (1569).

מובא שם, דף ח, א: "ומצאתי כתוב שקודם שיתחיל ההגדה שהצריכוהו להגביה הקערה ולומר הא לחמא עניא ושלא יחזירנה למקומה עד שיאמר מה נשתנה וכו'. עוד מצאתי כתוב שכשמגביהין הקערה שמעבירין אותה על ראשי כל

בכוונה להזכיר להם את קריעת ים סוף. נימוק זה מצא חן בעיניהם וכולם יחד
התחילו לשיר את הפסוק ושאבתם מים בששון ממעיני הישועה ושוב מילאו את
הכוסות.[3]

גם הרב יעקב משה טולידאנו מזכיר מנהג זה בספרו **נר המערב** והוא קורא
לו משונה: "בחג הפסח נמצא בין יהודי מארוקו איזה מנהגים משונים... את קערת
הסדר יקח בעל הבית ויסבב על ראשי המסובים כולם ויאמר בקול רם: 'בבהילו
יצאנו ממצרים'".[4]

המנהג היה קיים גם במדינות אחרות. מרת איידה קואן מספרת בספרה האנגלי
יהודים בפינות נידחות של העולם כי בהיותה באיזמיר בתורכיה עשתה את הסדר
הראשון בביתו של רב העיר. בתחילת הסדר, לפני אמירת "מה נשתנה", הגביהו
לרגע את קערת הסדר מעל ראשו של כל אחד מן המסובים. לסדר השני היתה
אורחת במשפחה אחרת באיזמיר — וגם שם נהגו מנהג זה.[5]

ב.

הרב שם טוב גאגין ביקש לעמוד על טעמו של מנהג זה. בספרו **כתר שם
טוב** הוא מציין את המנהג: "מנהג הספרדים במארוקו לסבב הקערה עם מיניה על
ראשי המסובין".[6]

בהערה הוא כותב: "שאלתי לרבני מארוקו בהיותי שם עובר אורח בשנת
התרצ"ב בטעם מנהג זה, ואמרו לי כי הם מאמינים שאם יסבבו הקערה עם כל
המינים שבה על ראשי המסובין, יכולה היא שתגן אלף המגן להצילם מכל פגע
וצרה וטומוס של ברכות יחולו עליהם, ונוהגין עוד שבעת הסיבוב אומר המסבב
'היום אנחנו עבדים, לשנה הבאה בירושלים בני חורין' ואומרים כן שלושה
פעמים".

הרב גאגין מוסיף כי לדעתו הונהג מנהג זה בשביל הילדים "למען יתעוררו
לשאול ולחקור בדבר, ואז האב מספר להם הנסים והנפלאות שנעשו לאבותינו".

ג.

להלן נראה כי בהשערתו קלע הרב גאגין אל האמת. אך יש לתמוה שהרי יש
מנהגים עתיקים, מובאים בספרי הראשונים, שמגמתם לעורר את הילדים לשאול.
מה ראו יהודי צפון-אפריקה לזנוח מנהגים אלה ולנהוג במקומם מנהג אחר?

נציין כי מנהג העברת הקערה על ראשי המסובים נזכר כבר בספרים מלפני
חמש מאות וארבע מאות שנה. מתוך דבריהם יתברר לנו כיצד התפתח המנהג
המיוחד הנ"ל מתוך מנהג נפוץ שהיה קיים מכבר.

בהגדה הנדפסת הראשונה הידועה לנו, היא ההגדה שנדפסה בואדי
אלחאגארה, (Guadalajara) בספרד, בשנת רמ"ב (1482) בערך, נמצא כתוב לפני "הא

מנהג סדר מוזר ומקורו

מאת: טובי' פרשל

א.

מנהג סדר מוזר נהוג אצל יהודי צפון־אפריקה: מגביהים את קערת הסדר מעל ראשי המסובים.

מוסר על מנהג זה רבי חיים יוסף אזולאי בספר מסעיו. בחג הפסח של שנת תקל״ד היה החיד״א בתוניס. בספרו על ליל הסדר הוא כותב כי רחמים, משרתו של הגביר המארח, היה לוקח את "כלי המצות וירקות חובה" והעבירו שלוש פעמים על ראשו של כל אחד מן המסובים. לאחר מכן ניגש אל הנשים שהיו יושבות מן הצד ושאל אם גם להן צריך לעשות ההעברה על הראש שלוש פעמים. החיד״א ענה לו בשעשוע לשון. כתוב: "רחם רחמתים לראש גבר" (שופטים ה, ל). צריכים שלוש פעמים רחמים — שיבוא המשרת רחמים — לראש גבר, אך לא לראש אשה.[1]

גם בנימין השני מזכיר מנהג זה בספר מסעיו. בדברו על יהודי צפון־אפריקה הוא כותב: "סדר הפסח אצלם כאשר הוא אצלנו. מלבד כבואם באמירת ההגדה אל החלק הראשון מסיפור יציאת מצרים, לוקח אחד מבני המשפחה את הקערה ומגביה אותה מעל לראש כל אחד מן המסובים על רגעים אחדים, וזה האיש אשר לא ייעשה לו כזאת מאמין להיות גבר לא יצלח בימיו. ביחוד נמצא מנהג זה אצל בני ישראל אשר בטוניס, בעוד אשר המשכילים בעם באלגיריען אינם משמים לב על המנהג הזה.[2]

מעניינים הם הדברים שהרב אלכסנדר לוינסון מספר על ביקורו בפסח במדבר סהרה. הוא כותב בין היתר: "זקן בני הבית תפס את המגש [עליו היו שלוש המצות, מרור וחרוסת, וכוסות מלאים יין] והתחיל להקיף את השולחן, בהפליטו את המלים כהא כהא לחמא..." במגש זה היה עליו לגעת בראשו של כל אחד מן המסובים. מכיון שגם אני "חכם" — ביקש לכבדני במנהג זה. כמובן, לא ידעתי מזה כלום ובהרגישי על ראשי משא כבד, קמתי במהירות ממושבי ולצערי הרב הפכתי את כל המגש עם כוסות היין על בגדי... והיה להם הדבר לסימן רע. קמה מהומה ובהלה וכל המסובים התחילו לצעוק ולהתרגש. מבטים פראיים נעוצו בי מכל צד. עשיתי עצמי כאילו איני מרגיש כלל. ואמרתי להם שעשיתי מה שעשיתי

40. מעלת.

41. כבוד מורנו הרב רבי.

42. נטריה רחמנא ופרקיה (שמרהו אל והצילהו). על ר׳ שבתי אהרן מריני (נפטר בתקס״ט) ראה בספרם של גירונדי־ניפי, **תולדות גדולי ישראל וגאוני איטלייא**. טריאסטי, 1853, עמ׳ 353, 355.

43. על אמירה זו ברבים המזכה לחוטא בגיהנום, ראה Revue des Etudes Juives 35 (1879) p. 80.

44. ישעיה נח, ח.

45. אמן כן יהי רצון.

46. במהדורת ירושלים תשכ״ב הסיפור נמצא בעמ׳ רג-רד. הסיפור הועתק בידי ר׳ מנשה בן ישראל לספרו נשמת חיים, אמשטרדם תי״ב, קח ע״א-קט ע״א. ועיין: ר׳ אליעזר אשכנזי, גדולים מעשי ה׳, ויניציאה שמ״ג, חלק מעשה בראשית, פרק ב, ה ע״א.

שלאחריו, מתוך הנחה שהרוח שוטט באוויר, ושמע משדים ורוחות דברים
הנעלמים מבני־תמותה. מובן מאליו, כי הרוח — דהיינו החולה — מספר את
אותן האמונות הנפוצות בסביבתו והקהל שומע את מה שרצה לשמוע. בכלל אין
חידושים רבים ממקרה למקרה, והן השאלות שהרוח נשאל והן התשובות שהוא
משיב הן סטיריוטיפיות. כזה הוא גם המשא־ומתן המתנהל במרבית הסיפורים
במהלך הגירוש וכזה הוא גם הגירוש עצמו.

בהיות הכל מאמינים שלרוח מימדים גופניים, אין הוא יכול לצאת מגוף
החולה מבלי לגרום לנזק לאחד מאיבריו. הרוח עצמו מעוניין לעתים, כך הוא
אומר, להזיק; ומכל מקום הוא מעמיד פנים שרצונו להזיק לחולה. המגרש, לעומת
זאת, דורש ממנו במפגיע לצאת דרך בוהן היד או הרגל, מקום בו אין הנזק ניכר.

ב״שד יהיר״, שהוא קרוב לסטיריוטיפ, יוצא הרוח והנער החולה מבריא. לא
כן ב״רוח עועים״, שהוא סיפור יוצא־דופן בין סיפורי הרוח היהודיים, הן בגין
הימצאותם של שלושה רוחות בחולה, הן משום שמדובר בחולה נוצרית. אף
״השתכנותם״ של שני רוחות יהודים עם רוחו של נוכרי באותו גוף היא מן
המוזרויות שרק אדמת איטליה יכלה להצמיח. בדומה לסיפור הרוח שבשלשלת
הקבלה הנ״ל, אף כאן אין כל מידע על הוצאת הרוחות.

בעוד שבדברי אבן יחיא אולי חסר הסיום משום שלא מצא בו ענין, הרי כאן
מתערבים השלטונות, אוסרים על ההתקהלות של יהודים ונוכרים, וספק רב אם
ניתן למישהו לטפל בהוצאת הרוחות.

מעלי־סיפורי־הרוחות על הכתב בכל הדורות התייחסו לסיפוריהם ברצינות
והאמינו בגילגול־נשמות, שלא כמעתיקים של שני הסיפורים דנן, שבהקדמותיהם,
ובעצם השמות שנתנו לסיפוריהם, מביעים יותר מקורטוב של ספקנות באמונת
הדיבוק. הרקע התרבותי־חברתי של כל המשתתפים בדרמה האנושית הזאת מועיד
לכל משתתף (חולה, מגרש וקהל) תפקיד מוגדר למדי. תוצאה כמעט־כללית של
החוויה העוברת על כל משתתפיה היתה פישפוש במעשיהם וחזרה בתשובה. זאת
היתה אף הסיבה שרבים ממקרי־הדיבוק תועדו והועלו על הכתב.

הערות

1. שימוש היתולי של פסוקי איוב ה, כא־כב.

2. עד כאן לשון השער של ר׳ יוסף אלמנצי, העושה שימוש היתולי בתהלים יט, יד. מסיכום
האותיות המודגשות יוצא ששנת ההעתקה היתה תקצ״ב (1832).

3. עד כאן לשון הקדמתו המליצית של ר׳ אליעזר חפץ.

א3. השוה לפירוש רד״ק ליש׳ נב, טו (״כן יזה גויים רבים עליו...״) ...שיתמהו על שפלותו... וידברו
עליו תמיד״.

4. עיר איטלקית על הגבול היוגוסלבי, לא רחוק מטריאסט.

הרחמן יתן בלבנו להבין, ויסלק יצר הרע מקרבנו, ויתן מנוחה לנפשותינו ונפשות הרוחות האלה יתקן ברחמיו ותנוח נפש ונפש כל שכני ישראל בגן עדן, אכי״ר[45]

שני סיפורי הרוח המובאים כאן שייכים לתחום התרבות של יהודי איטליה. תיאור ראשון בדפוס על כניסת רוח ביהודי בארץ זאת נמצא בספר שלשלת הקבלה לר׳ גדליה אבן יחיא, שנדפס לראשונה בוניציאה שמ״ו (1586).[46] אבן יחיא, שהתענין בתופעה וביקר את חולת-הדיבוק, מתאר מקרה שאירע בפררה בשנת של״ה (1575). החולה היתה יהודיה צעירה נשואה, ואילו הרוח היה זה של רועה בהמות איטלקי פשוט. אבן יחיא מוסר את הדעה הנפוצה בסביבה האיטלקית, שסברה שרוחות הנכנסים בבני אדם חיים: "...הם בני אדם אשר מתו במיתות משונות". רועה הבהמות אכן מספר, כי נתלה כעונש על גנבותיו.

מהשוואתם של למעלה מחמישים סיפורים על דיבוקים יהודיים שאספתי ניתן לעמוד על הצדדים המשותפים של מחלת-הנפש, שנתפסה בתודעת הציבור ככניסת רוחו של מת לגופו של אדם חי. הנחתם היתה, כי הרוח הוא זה של חוטא, אשר לא הורשה להיכנס לגיהנום, וגילגולו ודיבוקו בבני אדם עשוי להביא למרוק עוונותיו. הרוח שב״שד יהיר״ חטא בהמרת דת, והחולה בביזוי מצות ציצית. חטאיהם של שני הרוחות היהודיים ב״רוח עועים״ מפורטים יותר: רוח לוריה חטא בחילול שבת, בזילזול במצוות, אך במיוחד בזנות. רוח דינא חטא בזנות, אך גם באיבוד עצמו לדעת.

אין ספק שחטאים חמורים אלה הצדיקו בעיני הסביבה היהודית את העונשת הרוחות, ואנו יכולים ללמוד מהם על נורמות ומוסכמות חברתיות ודתיות של אותה סביבה.

הנחת יסוד של תיאורי דיבוק יהודיים, הבולטת גם כאן, היא האומרת שהחיים יכולים לעזור למתים. לימוד משניות ואמירת תפילות מזכות למת, ומעלות אותו למדרגה בה הוא יכול להתחיל בריצוי עונשו בגיהנום.

לסובבים את החולה "נודעת" כניסת הרוח על ידי סימני המחלה: רעד וכפיון (אפילפסיה), אלם או היסטריה והוצאת קולות לא-אנושיים מפי החולה. לפעמים מופיע סימן בודד ולפעמים סימנים אחרים ביחד. ממילא מובן שהתופעה מעוררת ענין רב בציבור, וקטנים וגדולים (וכמובן גם נוכרים) באים לראות לשמוע.

להוצאת הרוח וגירושו מתוך החולה דרוש מומחה, לרוב איש הקבלה המעשית. בדרך-כלל נאמרות תפילות (כגון: "שיר של פגעים" — ראה שבועות טו ע״ב) והשבעות. על ידי החדרת אדי גופרית לנחירי החולה מכריחים את הרוח (הנתפס כבעל מימדים גופניים זעירים) לדבר, שכן המגרשים אינם יכולים לפעול ללא ידיעת שם הרוח. לא-אחת מבקשים מפי הרוח אף מידע על המות ומה

חייהם? ובצעקה גדולה ומרה ומר וקול בכיה השיבוהו: 'ולו הואלנו בימי חיותנו חיים
על האדמה ונשמע בקול מוכיח, ונלך בדרך אמת לשמור ולקיים לעשות את כל
המצווה עלינו, הן מדאורייתא הן מדברי סופרים, כי לא היינו סובלים עכשיו כמה
יסורים קשים כגידים וחלאים רעים, שבכל יום ויום הולכים ומתגברים וניתוספים
עלינו. ומי יודע אם תהיה תקומה עוד למפלתנו, יען כי בימי חיינו עברנו על דברי
תורה והלכנו אחרי שרירות לבנו'. וישאל מהם ג״כ החכם הנ״ל על רוח של כל
אחד מהם כמה גדול ושיעורו? ויענו, כי הוא כשיעור זבוב גדול. וישאל מהם
ויאמר אליהם: 'חפצים אתם שאנחנו בני ישראל נבקש מן הבורא ב״ה בכח התורה
שנלמוד [!] בעדכם ונאמר קדיש על נחת רוחכם?' ויענו: 'והלואי! וגם תאמרו
"ברכו את ה' המבורך".[43]

ומיד הלכו משם כל הבאים. וישובו אליהם יום יום. ויבואו רבים, זה הולך
וזה בא. גם מן החכמים עברים ונכרים הלכו שם לשמוע באזניהם את הדברים
הנוראים האלה. ונכרי אחד ביניהם [!], שהיה אוהבו של דינא בחייו, קרא אותו
בשמו, וישאלהו אם מכיר אותו, מי הוא? ויענהו דינא, כי הוא מכיר אותו ויודע
שמו ומעשיו, כי הוא רופא פלוני נוצרי אוהבו. והזכיר לו דינא הימים אשר היו
הולכים יחד לזנות את הנוכריות, אחת הנה ואחת הנה, ולשמוח עמהן. והזכיר לו
הרבה דברים אחרים, עד שנשאר הנוצרי הנ״ל בלא כח לדבר על כל הדברים
האמתיים שאמר לו, ויצא משם בפחד ואימה עצומה.

וישובו שם מבני עמנו, מן הלומדים שלמדו תורה על קבריהם במנין עשרה
והתפללו ואמרו קדיש וברכו, והגידו לרוחות את אשר בקשו על נחת רוחם.
ויאמרו הרוחות: 'גם אנחנו יודעים כל אשר עשיתם, אבל כתוב: "והלך לפניך
צדקך",[44] ומי יודע אם לעת כזאת נשאר לנו תקות תקון. אוי נא לנו כי חטאנו!'

ויבא שמה בין הבאים הרופא המובהק איש ירא אלהים מע' החבר ר' רפאל
קונסילילי נר״ו, ושאל מן הרוחות על ענין חבוט הקבר. ויאמרו לו, כי ארבעה
חדשים אחר מיתתן נדונו בו, וכי אין הפה יכולה [!] לספר הצרות הגדולות
שעברו עליהם בו. וישאלם אם לעת עתה הם מאמינים באמונה שלימה במציאות
ה' ובתורתו הקדושה, וכי העולם נברא ממנו ב״ה מאין הגמור? והם באימה ויראה
ענו כי מאמינים המה בכל מכל כל. וישאל עוד מהם אם יודעים בנשמות שאר
אנשים שהכירו בחייהם שחטאו כמותם ומתו ונענשו ללכת באויר העולם
ולהתגלגל הנה והנה כמותם? ויאמרו לו, כי הנה רוח איש פלוני אלמוני, שהכיר
אותו גם החכם הנ״ל בחיים, שראו אותו הרוחות האמורים מתגלגל באויר. והחכם
הנ״ל לא רצה לפרסמו ולהגיד שמו משום כבוד הבריות.

אחר הדברים האלה, מושל העיר גזר לאנשי הבית, אשר שם הרוחות
המגולגלים, שלא יניחו ליכנס שם שום אדם, לא עברי ולא נצרי, בגזירת קנס גדול
על המכניס והנכנס. וכן היה, כי מן היום ההוא והלאה לא נודע דבר מכל אלה.

לאסוף ימיו[34] בזולת וידוי וחרטה, בלי חולי ארוך ויסורין קשים, כי כפי מחשבתו אין מיתה טובה ממנה, ואחריה אין דין וחשבון ולא כלום, ובאשר נפל שם טבע ותצא נשמתו ומת ר״ל.[35]

ששה ימים אחר שטבע מצאו אותו עכו״ם[36] צף על פני המים פגר מובס, ויוציאוהו משם ויתנוהו ביד היהודים, אשר קברו אותו חוץ מבית הקברות[37] זה ששה [!] שנים בקירוב.

רוח השני רוח לוריה נקרא שמו בחיים חייתו רפאל חי, גם הוא מתושבי עיר פאדובה, לא סר גם הוא מעשות הרע בעיני ה׳ כל ימיו. ויזן עם נשים נכריות, ויטמא עצמו במשכב זכור ובמאכל ובמשתה אסור. והיה מחלל שבת בפהרסייא [!] עם הפי״פא בלע״ז,[38] ולא שמע לקול מוכיח. וכל אשר שאלו עיניו מתאוות אסורות לא אצל מהם, לא מנע עצמו מכל שחוק וקלות ראש. ויתהל ברז״ל וידבר נגד כבודם ונגד תורתנו הקדושה עד יום מותו בתוך ביתו יחידי, במיתה פתאומית בזולת וידוי ועזיבת חטא. וימצאו אותו מת מוטל על גבי קרקע כנבלה סרוחה. ויקברוהו במקום אשר שם רוח דינא האמור, רחוק מקברות ישראל. וימי שני חייו קרובים לשבעים שנה, זה ארבעה [!] שנים בקרוב עד היום.

המקום ישים בלבנו לשמור לעשות ולקיים כל דברי תורתו הקדושה, למען הראותנו בנעם ה׳ אשר יכנס נדחי ישראל אלה וכאלה, אכי״ר.[39]

ויהי כראות היהודים האמורים את המעשה הגדול ונורא הזה וכשמעם דברי הרוחות האלה, יצאו משם בפחד גדול ובחרדה עצומה. ויספרו הדברים אשר שמעו מקול הרוחות האלה בחצר היודים [!]. ועברה השמועה מפה אל פה והכל [!] נשמע ונתפשט בכל העיר, עד כי ביום המחרת, בין בני ברית ובין שאינם בני ברית, הלכו לשמוע באזנהם [!] אמתת הדברים [קסז ע״ב] למען יתאמת אצלם איך המתים יהללו יה ויודיעו אחרי מותם אמתות הבורא ואמתות תורתו הקדושה שבכתב ושבעל פה ואמתות דברי רז״ל. ותהום כל העיר עליהם. ורבים בין הבאים קראו את הרוחות האלה בשמם ושאלו מהם דברים רבים. ויענו הרוחות לכולם כראוי, על הן הן ועל לאו לאו. ובפרט מע[40] החכם כמהר״ר[41] שבתי מארינו נר״ו[42] שאל אותם שאלות חכם כערכו בדברים רבים. הוא שאל אותם כענין והם השיבוהו כהלכה, עד שהגידו לו עונש הרע ומר אשר נגזר עליהם בגיהנם, וכי כמה וכמה כתות של מלאכי חבלה היו מצערין אותם בכל מיני צרות ויסורין קשים שבעולם, יותר מכל מה שהפה יכולה [!] לדבר והאוזן לשמוע אחד מני אלף. ואחר הגהינם נענשו להיות נעים ונדים באויר העולם ורוח דינא הנ״ל נענש להתגלגל בגוף חתול. ובצאתו ממנו נכנס בתאנה אחת וימצא בה רוח לוריה ורוח מומולו, אשר עתה הם עמו בקרב הנוצרית הזאת, אשר אכלה התאנה הזאת, כי אשה מכשפה נתנתה [!] לה לאכול, עד שנתגלגלו בה בדרך זה שלשת הרוחות האלה כאחד, ואינם יודעים מה אחריתם ולא מתי ינתק החוט המשולש הזה. וישאלם החכם הזה בין שאלותיו אם עתה הם מתחרטים על מה שהרשיעו בימי

רוח עועים

[קס"ז ע"א] אספר לכם אחי מעשה שקרה בעיר פדובה[27] בימי היותי שמה,[28]
לעיני כל בית ישראל ובני הארצות, אשר כל שומעו תצילנה שתי אזניו, ויתן לב
לשוב לעבודת הבורא ולהאמין באמונה שלמה בדברי תורתו ובדברי חכמים
זלה"ה.[29] ובפרט אלו המינים והאפיקורסים הכופרים בעיקר ואומרים 'אכול ושתו
כי מחר נמות',[30] ובמיתת הגוף מתה עמו גם הנפש, כמו זה כן מות זה, אין שכר
ואין עונש, אין דין ואין חשבון אחר המות ח"ו. ישמעו יקחו מוסר וידעו כי יש
אלהים שופטים בארץ, והוא נותן שכר טוב לצדיקים ועונש רע ומר לרשעים. אוי
לנו מיום הדין, אוי לנו מיום תוכחה, רחמנא ליצלן. וזה לנו האות:

ויהי ביום ט' לחדש אדר שנת **התלקח**[31] ויצאו שלשה גבירים מתושבי עיר זו
פאדובה, הן המה היו אליה לוי ושני אחים רוקא, יהודה הגדול ומשנהו יצחק
שבתי, וישימו פניהם לחקור ולדרוש מנכרי אחד הידוע להם רפואה על בת
ישראל חולה מחולי הכישוף, ולא מצאהו. ויהי בשובם איש איש לדרכו, אמרו
איש אל אחיו: לכו ונלכה (טרם שנפרד איש מאחיו)[32] אל בית הנצרי הסמוך לבית
הקברות שלנו, אשר שם גויה אחת זה ג' שנים חולה ג"כ מחולי הכשוף עצמו
כישראלית, ובני ביתה יגידו לנו מה עשו להצלתה, ונעשה כן גם אנחנו. ויעשו כן
וילכו שלשתם שם. וישאלו על דבר החולה ומה עשו לה. ויענו בני ביתה, כי לא
מצאו לה רפואה, ולא הועילו לה כמה וכמה פעולות שעשה כומר אחד על זה.
ונתנו להם רשות ליכנס החדרה לראותה. ונכנסו שלשתם וראו אותה מוטלת על
ערשה כמו מת, בלתי תנועה והרגשה אפילו בא' מאבריה.

עודם רואים ותמהים לראותה והנה קול צועק וקורא בקול גדול וחזק: 'אחינו
אתם! אחינו אתם!' עד שלוש פעמים, עד כי היודים [!] האלה, כשומעם את הקול
הקורא אותם בשם אחים, חרדו איש אל אחיו, לאמר: 'מי הוא זה פה הקורא
אותנו אחים? ואנחנו מזרע ישראל ואת האלהים אנחנו יראים?!' ויען הקול ויאמר:
'וגם אנחנו פה שנים מזרע ישראל, אבל אשמים אנחנו, ממשפחות דינה ולוריא
מתושבי העיר הזאת שנינו אנחנו, ורוח נוצרי אחד עמנו בתוך גוף זה, מומולו
שמו. ועל רוב עונותינו ופשעינו נתחייבנו ללכת נעים ונדים עד היום, כמה צרות
עברו עלינו, אין לנו מרגוע רגע. אוי נא לנו כי חטאנו!' עד כאן דברה [!] הקול.

ואולם רוחות אלה,[33] רוחות שני עברים עוברים על דת, המה אנשים רקים
ופוחזים, רקים מכל מצוה, מלאי עברות כרמון, כל ימיהם הלכו בשרירות לבם
הרע, עוברים ואת עברים [?] בדרכי ה' ובתקנות רבותינו זלה"ה, לא עשו רק רע
כל ימיהם, ואומרים: אין טוב לאדם כי אם למלאות תאוותיו ולעשות כל מה שלבו
חפץ בעולם הזה. אוי להם, אוי לנפשם! רוח דינא נקרא בחייו בשם יצחק דוד,
איש בריא וחזק, בן ארבעים שנה היה היה עשיר ובעל אשה ושתי בנות טובות עם
אלהים ואנשים, כן יגזור ה' עליהם חיים טובים, אמן. ויהי היום וישכם בבקר, כי
פחז עליו יצרו, וילך אל הנוצרית אשר היה זונה עמה יום יום, ויאכל וישת
מאכלות אסורות ויין נסכם וישכב עמה. וילך אח"כ אל הנהר ויגמור בדעתו

הלא תצא דרך בית הרעי?!   אצא דרך אצבע קטנה של יד אחת.

והכיש אחר זה מיד אצבע קטנה של יד אחת ביד אחרת והיה סומך בתוך זה ובתוך זה. וצוהו ר׳ אברהם כי ביציאתו יכבה לסימן נר שהיה דלוק שם. והשיב כי אין זה יכולתי ומיד יצא באמת דרך החלון.

מה אות תתן ליציאתך?   הנער ילך על רגליו וידבר כבראשונה.

סימן זה לבדו אינו מספיק!   הנער יאמר דברי תורה וילך תיכף לבית
                                        הכנסת שהיה שם ממאן עוד הרוח בו.

אנה היית קודם שנכנסת בנער?   מתגלגל באשפת החצר בבית זה.

ואנה תלך ביציאתך מזה?   בטבור הארץ (...)[25]

מפני מה היית נובח ככלב?   זה היה ענשי.

השבעה לי בשם ה׳ שלא תזיק לכל
בר ישראל מעתה ועד עולם!   אנכי אשבע!

[97a] ויחל ר׳ אברהם לקרות לו לשון השבועה. והיה הרוח אומר אחריו מלה במלה בלשון עצמו של ר׳ אברהם. דרך משל: ׳שלא תקים לי׳, היה אומר המקרא והקורא שניהם למדובר בעדו. וגער בו ר׳ אברהם הרבה עד כי בפעם השלישית התחיל הרוח לקנתר, וירם הנער אגרופו נגד העומדים שם באף ובחמה ובקצף גדול. לולא נייר הדלוק עמד במרץ על אפיו והכניעה. וישא הנער את קולו ויבך וישבע כדאתי, וכן אמר: ׳בשם ה׳ צבאות אלהי מערכות ישראל אני נשבע כי לא אזיק לר׳ אברהם ולכל בר ישראל, לא אשקר ולא אכזב מכל מה שהבטחתי׳. וכאשר גמר שבועתו אמר: ׳עתה אני יוצא׳!

והרים בידו אחת אצבע קטנה של ידו האחרת ויהפוך אותה, גלגלה ועוה פניה, והראה כתמים כתמים דקים דקים כמו כתמי דם לקוי וצרור. ותכף ומיד באותו רגע ממש ניעור הנער משנתו ונהפך לאיש אחר ולבריה חדשה בצלמנו וכדמותנו. וישב קלסתר פניו כבימי בריאותו. ותחלת דבריו היתה לתת שלום לר׳ מנשה הנצב על ימינו בסבר פנים. וירחץ פניו וידיו ויתנו לו טלית קטן ויברך עליו, וירץ לבית הכנסת ויקרב אל הארון הקדש וינשק את הפרוכת וילך למקומו. ויקח סידור תפלות וינגן את הזמירות וכל התפלה. ויען קדיש וברכו מרצון עצמו בחפץ ותשוקה רבה, וחזר לביתו לשלום. ורוב הקהל עמו מורידים דמעות מרוב שמחה בראותם פלא פלאים. ונשאר אחר זה הנער בריא וחזק, לא נודע מהכרת פניו כי רוח בא אל קרבו, כי מראהו טוב כאשר בתחלה טרם חלותו.

המקום יפדנו מכל החולאים ויראנו נפלאות ונוראות, ויקים סוכתנו הנופלת וישלח מושיע לפדותנו מבין שני אריות ב״ב אכי״ר.[26] כה דבר הצעיר נבהל ומשתומם.

אליעזר חפץ

לעשות ככל אשר יצוה — יגידו לו בעברי, כי הוא יודע את אשר יעשה לו. וכן עשו.

אלה הדברים אשר דברו אל הנער ותשובותיו אליהם.

שאלות	תשובות
מי אתה? יהודי או גוי?	השיב ברוגז גדול: גוי.
מאיזה מקום אתה?	מעיר רומי.
מה שמך? מה שמך? (פעמים רבות, כי לא היה משיב כי אם בגמגום ובלעגי שפה).	(השיב מגומגם ולא הבנתי אם אמר אבטל או עלטל. ונודע אחר כך כי קרטר היתה משפחתו).
אמור שם העצם שלך מהו?	(לא השיב כלום עד שהכהו ר׳ אברהם בנר הדלוק ונשאר מבוהל ומשומם).
אמור האמת, יהודי אתה או לא?	יהודי הייתי.
מה שמך?	יהודה.
כהן, לוי או ישראל?	לוי אנכי.
שמא מומר אתה?	כן הוא.
באיזה מחוז המרת?	(לא אבה להשיב עד שהכהו בנייר) בעיר נאפולי.
אמור איפוא [!] המרת?	בעיר נאפולי.
איך נכנסת בנער שאינו בר מצוה?	מפני בזוי מצות ציצית (ולא גלה יותר מזה בכל השאלות ששאלו ממנו הרבה פעמים).
כמה שנים שאתה פה?	עשרה [!] שנים.
אימתי נכנסת בנער הזה?	זה לי שנה אחת.
ואיך לא נודע לנו חליו כי אם זה ו׳ חדשים?	ו׳ חדשים ראשונים לא נתחזקתי בו כמו באחרונים.

צוו אותו בשם ר׳ אברהם שלא יעכב אל הנער מלכת על שתי רגליו כאחד האדם, וכי יתהלך הנער מיד לארכה ולרחבה כא׳ מן הנצבים. וכן עשה. אך התחיל אז לצעוק כי רוצה ומסכים לצאת מיד מתוך הנער, ולא ישוב בו עוד.

מאיזה אבר אתה אומר לצאת?   מן הצואר.

והתחיל סמוך לתשובתו לגרגר בגרונו וצוהו ר׳ אברהם לעמוד, כי אינו רוצה שיצא דרך הצואר ועמד.

הלא תצא דרך בית הרעי?!   לא אצא כי אם מן הצואר ולא אזיק לנער.

שמנו ממנו ויניחוהו ערום ועריה בחוסר כל שבוי בידם, עד הביאם אותו לעיר
ליורנו[19] ויעזבוהו שם נודד ללחם אין, עובר ממקום למקום למצוא כדי פרנסתו
וחיים [?]. ויהיה מדי עברו הנה נכמרו רחמי עליו ואדבר לו טובות, ואומר לו, כי
לא יחוש על הצרות שעברו עליו ויקבלם באהבה וכפרת פשע. ונשב בחדוה ימים
שלשה כיד ה׳ הטובה עלי, והענק העניקתיהו לחמי ומימי שמני ושקויי. באמת לא
במקרה קרה לנו, כי האלהים אנה דרך גמר נס שילך העני זה ביום א׳ לחולו של
מועד של פסח לאכול בבית אבי הנער. ובכן באזניו שמע וראה בעיניו את
המעשים אשר היה עושה הנער החולה מדי יום ביומו. לערב חזר האורח לביתי
ללון כמנהגו, וסיפר לי כי ראה נער אשר, כמדומה לו, תפסו שד או רוח רעה,
וכי רצונו לנסות, אם יעזרהו הבורא, מזה המאורע. ואמנם, אתודה ולא אבוש, כי
היה כמצחק בעיני והתלתי בו, כי לא האמנתי לדבריו.

ביום ג׳ לחש״מ[20] הלך לבקר את הנער, ועשה מה שעשה, וכתב על מצח
הנער מה [96a] שכתב. ויפתח הנער את פיו וכה דבר: ׳תכלית מה שתוכל לחייבני
הוא שאדבר, אך אין בידך כח, ולא זכות, להוציאני מזה, ופה אשב!׳ שם נמצא
ושם היה זקן ונשוא פנים בקהילתנו, בן ביתו ודודו של הנער, וגם גיסי החבר
הנזכר למעלה. כשמעם את הקול מדבר, והנה איננו קולו של הנער, הבינו כי רוח
אחרת היתה אתו. ויענו בקול ויאמרו אל הרוח המדברת: ׳צא, צא איש הדמים
ואיש הבליעל! ואם לא תצא ברצון — תצא באונס, כי נשבע אותך בשבועת
האלה בכל חוקת התורה׳. ויען הרוח פעמים בקול גדול: ׳ לא אצא! אין אתם
נחשבים בעיני כל מאומה ׳! סוף סוף כתב האורח ר׳ אברהם מה שכתב, וישם
אחר אזנו של הנער. ומיד נראה לעין כל הנצבים כאילו אחזתהו פתאום לנער כל
חולי וכל מכה, כפשע בינו ובין המות. וצעק בקול מר כדברים האלה לאמר: ׳אם
לא תניחוני אחנק אותי [!] בפניכם!׳ והיה הנער צועק בקול בכיה: ׳אבי! אבי!׳, עד
שנכמרו רחמי אביו וכל הנצבים עליו, ונמנו וגמרו שלא לצער אותו עוד עד
לאחר הפסח, יען ראו כבר ממעלות העני הזה, מה שאם יסופר להם לא היו
מאמינים בו. גם הוא אמר, כי צריך להכונות רבות לא יסכנו לו עד אחרי הפסח.

ויעבור הפסח, גם כל החדש הראשון,[21] עד יום השלישי לחדש זיו,[22] הוא יום
ב׳ בשבת, שנת התקכ״ב, ויכנסו את הנער בחדר אחד. גם הוא נחפז ללכת, כי
בטח בה׳ ובאיש הזה אשר שיפדהו מחוליו. וכבר הכין ר׳ אברהם הקטרות רבות,
וכבדים על נייר אשר גלל תוך בגד פשתן עם גפרית, והדליק וחמם בידו הבגד
וישם קמיע א׳ על הנער. והתחיל הנער לברוח. ויעש ר׳ אברהם הקטרה והעמיד
בה את הנער מוטל בארץ, מבלי שיברח הנה והנה. וילחוש עליו שם ג׳ פעמים
במהירות ובהבל פיו לחש א׳. ואז התחיל הרוח לדבר: ׳נכבדי ר׳ אברהם, צוה
לעומדים שיאמרו שיר של פגעים ומזמור לדוד הבו לה׳ בני אלים׳.[23] ויתן הנייר
דלוק אשר בידו תחת נחירי הנער ונצטער הנער מאד, וצעק בשברון מתניים. והיה
שם לימין הנער ר׳ מנשה חפץ ויעש מיד כאשר צוהו ר׳ אברהם לשאול מן הנער
בלע״ז[24] כל מה שירצה ולתרגם לנו בלשון איטלייאנו. כי אם מאן יימאן הרוח

ויהי היום ויבא שמה גיסי כמהר״ר[8] ישעיה סיניגאליה בתוך הבאים לבקרו, ואמר בלחישה שיר של פגעים,[9] ושנה ושלש פסוק ״כי מלאכיו יצוה לך״,[10] רק שפתיו נעות וקולו לא ישמע. וירגז הנער ויתחלחל מאד וינהום כארי. ויהי אחרי ראותם זה ונסו מאת הנער שקצה בו נפשם.[11] וכן יעשה יום ביומו מדי עלותו אצלו איש או אשה וסדור תפילות, או חומש, עמו, אפילו טמון בחיקו ובלתי נראה ושם בסתר בכיס, הנער רעדה אחזתהו חיל כיולדה, ולא יניח ולא ישקוט, עד אשר יעבירו הספר מעליו ושקט ושאנן.[12]

אחר הדברים האלה נתגלה לשומרי אורחותיו ונודע, כי יש לו לנער סדר מבחן לשנה זו לעשות דבר יום ביומו לא יסור ממנו. והוא, כי ב׳ פעמים בכל יום, לפי שעות ידועות ומוכרות לו, היה נותן הנער ראשו בין ברכיו ומתהפך כמו גלגל, נלחם עם קרובי נפשו כמו חצי שעה. וככלותו נשאר מושלך כאבן, נרדם חסר התנועה, כגוף בלי נשמה זמן מה ועומד אח״כ על ברכיו ומכסה ראשו [95b] והיה נובח ככלב ממש וזועק כשה, תוקע ומריע ומרים קול ומנגן, וישב לסורו הולך על ארבע ולא ידבר. ככה יעשה כל ימי היותו נמשל כבהמה נדמה.

וינסו כמה פעמים, בשעת היותו מוטל כמת, לתת עליו קמיע, או תפילין, והיה מתעורר בבהלה ומקפץ ומגביה את עצמו מהארץ באויר עד אמה ויותר, ונוהם נהימות וזועק זעקות גדולות, עד הסירם מעליו הקמיע ושכב וינמנם. כאלה וכאלה ברוב ימים נעשו לנסות מאת רוב מבקריו הרבה מאד מאד, ועוד אחרת שמענה ואתה דע לך, כי אחר גמר המעשים מסודרים אשר אמרנו היה נח ושקט בכל פעם מהמעשה. פעמים אשר היה מתנודד כאמור, רק בערב שבת בהכנס כל העם, כי היתה אז שעתו לפוש ולנוח כבכל שאר ימי השבוע, היתה נכנסת בו חלחלה, ומן הרגע ההוא עד הרגע ממש שאומרים ברכו בבה״כ[13] במוצאי שבת היה נוהם נהום. ימים נושך ממקומו ונביחותיו ברעש וברוגז. וכוונו פעמים לא מעט הרבה מבני קהלתנו וידעו אל נכון, כי תכף אחרי עניית ברכו בק״ש[14] של ערבית במו״ש[15] היה מוציא מפיו כמו אנחה ושוקט וישב לסדרו כאשר בתחלה קודם השבת.

סוף דבר, רבו המעשים הנוראים כלם בשעור והגבלה, מעשים ראויים להכניס יראת ה׳ אמיתית ואמונת תורתו ואמונת חכמים בלבות הרואים ובלבות המאמינים בכתב הרואים אשר עין ראתה כל אלה, כי קצר מצע שכלי מהשתרע לכתוב במראות רב משפטי הנער ומעשהו, אשר הראונו משך ששה חדשים אשר זכרנו.

ויהי ביום כאשר ישר בעיני האלהים להמציא פדיום לנפש מבוהלה, לתת תחת יגון גילה, בא אלינו, בין העניים מבקשים לחם וחוזרים על הפתחים, איש עני ומדולדל, בארבעה לחדש הראשון, לא תאר לו ולא הדר, מראהו ומלבושו כאחד המלחים תופשי משוט. ואקחהו על שלחני ואעמידהו לימיני ואשאלהו על שמו ועל אודותיו. ויענני ויאמר לי, כי שמו אברהם בלייליוס אשר בא מן המערב, כי נשבה נמל סמברדי[16] בשנה שעברה. מהם ברח וישב אל טטואן[17] עירו ומשם נסע במעט סחורה ושמן זית ופגע באני[18] אינגליזי אויבי הצרפתים, ויקחו את

בגופה של נוצריה, הוא יוצא־דופן למדי בין סיפורי הרוח היהודיים. בניגוד לרוב סיפורי הרוח לא הוצאו הללו מגוף החולה ואין אנו יודעים את סוף המעשה.

שד יהיר

[94a] לץ שמו עושה בעברת זדון בקרב איש גוריציאה, זה שמו מנשה בן כמ״ר יצחק רפאל חפץ. ויהי בשנת התקכ״א בא שמה מארץ המערב כמ״ר אברהם בליליוס ויוצא אותו החוצה ככל הכתוב בספר הזה. קחנו, קורא נעים, ועינך שים עליו, כי אז לשד ולכפן תשחק ולא תירא משד כי יבוא.[1]

נעתק מהצעיר יוסף אלמנצי בשנת גם משדים חשוך עבדך אל ימשלו בי אז איתל לפ״ק.[2]

[95a] אל אצילי בני ישראל, הקוראים בשם אל:

התמהו ותמהו על אשר אספר לפניכם. הן לא אביעה חידות מני קדם. אותותינו ראינו, פי המדבר אליכם. שמעה אזני ותבן לה ואשר שמענו ונדעם מפי עדה שלימה, נקובים בשמות, שם נמצאו ושם היו בשעת מעשה, וגם מחוץ המון רב. אחלי יכונו דברי לפניכם ויהי ה׳ עמכם.[3]

מילדי העברים זה וגוים רבים יזה,[3א] מנשה בן כמ״ר יצחק רפאל חפץ תושב גוריציאה,[4] והוא בן י״ב שנה[5] נער זיו אורו פנה. ויהיה היום מימי שנה שעברה, שנת התקכ״א לבריאה, בחדש תמוז, ותחל רוח ה׳ הרעה להבעיתו לעוות אורחותיו, כי נשתנו פניו כהגלות נגלות אחד החולים. ונפשו נבהלה מאד, יבא רעד בעצמו וגופו ירעש כדמות פאראלי״טיקו.[6] חשדו אנשי ביתו לעושה מעשה נערות, או בחסרון רצון ללמוד, כתינוק הבורח מבית הספר ערום יערים, ולא השגיחו בו יותר מזה.

בחודש אלול חלה את מעיו הרבה מאד, עד אשר כמעט לא נותרה בו נשמה. סמוך לראש השנה התקכ״ב הבריא ונשאר כחוש ודל, עד אשר לא הספיק ללכת ברגליו כי אם על ידי סומך עד חדש ימים. וירבו הימים ויתמו הלימודים, וגם אל בית הספר בזולת לימוד כלל שלחו האב ולא אבה, כי מאוס מאס ממש בכל דברי ישרים השם. ויודינהו אביו לכף זכות כמשפט הילדים לברוח מבית הספר, מי מעט ומי הרבה. ויגער בו אביו פעם אחר פעם, ויקללהו כדי להממה. ויפול הנער מלא קומתו ארצה על פניו לפני אביו, ולא עמד עוד על רגליו, ולא התהלך כשאר אדם, כי אם על פניו ועל ברכיו ככל ההולך עלי ארבע. אף בזאת נמשל כבהמה נדמה, כי באותו רגע ממש נפסק דבר פיו, מלתא אזלא מינה,[7] פי בלתי מדבר מתגולל באפר מחבק אשפה, מסיר אזניו משמוע תורה משך ו׳ חדשים, עושה מעשים מבהילים, אשר הלכו אצלו לבקרו זקנים עם נערים.

סיפורי רוחות באיטליה במאה הי"ח

(לפרופ׳ רפאל פטאי בידידות ובהוקרה)

מאת: גדליה נגאל

מאז שפירסמתי את מאמרי המקיף ׳ה"דיבוק״ במיסטיקה היהודית׳ ברבעון
דעת, חוברת 4, רמת גן תש"ם, הגיעו לידי כמה טכסטים אודות רוחות-דיבוק.
שניים מהם, הנמצאים בכתבי-יד נדירים, הנני מפרסם בזה ותודתי ל British
Library ולד"ר דוד גולדשטיין, ולסמינר התאולוגי היהודי בני-יורק ולפרופ׳ מנחם
שמלצר, על הרשות לפרסם כתבי-יד אלה.

שד יהיר הוא השם שניתן לסיפור שבכתב יד מס. 27088 שבבריטיש מיוזיאון
(ראה קטלוג מרגליות ג, עמ׳ 459, סי׳ 1075. במכון לכתבי יד ומיקרופילמים שליד
האוניברסיטה העברית סימנו הוא 5733) על ידי מעתיקו ר׳ יוסף אלמנצי. ההעתקה
שלפנינו נעשתה — כפי שמעידים דברי ההקדמה של המעתיק — בשנת תקצ"ב
(1832). אלמנצי (1801 — 1860) היה סופר ומשורר יהודי ידוע באיטליה, ובעל
ספריה גדולה שהצטיינה בדפוסים יקרי ערך ובכתבי-יד רבים. הכותב הראשון, ר׳
אליעזר חפץ, מוסר בסיפורו על מנשה בן יצחק רפאל חפץ בגוריציאה, בו נכנס
רוחו של מומר בשנת תקכ"א (1761). ר׳ אברהם בלילוס, עני נודד ׳מארץ המערב׳
שנזדמן לגוריציאה ונתארח בביתו של ר׳ אליעזר חפץ, הצליח להוציא את הרוח
והנער בן השתים עשרה חזר לאיתנו.

רוח עועים הוא השם שניתן לסיפור שהתרחש אף הוא באיטליה שנים לא
רבות אחרי המאורע המסופר בסיפור הקודם. אף שם זה ניתן על ידי ר׳ יוסף
אלמנצי שהעתיקו לכתב-יד הנ"ל שבבריטיש מיוזיאון בשנת תר"ד (1844), כפי
שמתברר מלשון השער: ״רוח עועים ה"ה סיפור מעשה א׳ קשה להולמו אשר
נארע בפאדובה בשנת התקל"ח נעתק מהצעיר יוסף אלמנצי בש׳ התר"ד". למזלנו
נמצא בידינו כתב יד נוסף של סיפור זה, שהועלה לראשונה על הכתב בידי ר׳
מרדכי (מרקו) בן נתן לוצאטו מטריאסטי (1720 — 1799) ויתכן שלפנינו המקור
הראשון ממש. כוונתי לכתב יד מס. 22964 Mic 7392 Acc 153 D של הסמינר
התאולוגי היהודי בני יורק, הכולל גם את תרגומו של ר׳ מרדכי לוצאטו (משנת
1774) לחיבורו של אברהם גר מקורדובה ״צריח בית אל״ (ויכוח עם הנצרות).

סיפור רוח עועים, המספר על שלושה רוחות (שניים יהודים ואחד נכרי)